Warplanes
of the Fleet

Warplanes of the Fleet

General Editor
David Donald

AIRtime Publishing Inc.

United States of America

Published by AIRtime Publishing Inc.
120 East Avenue, Norwalk, CT 06851
Tel (203) 838-7979 • Fax (203) 838-7344
email: airpower@airtimepublishing.com
www.airtimepublishing.com

ISBN 1-880588-81-1

Editors
  David Donald and Robert Hewson

Authors
  David Donald, Robert F. Dorr, Brad Elward, Tom Kaminski,
  Jon Lake, Bill Sweetman

Artists
  Mike Badrocke, Chris Davey, Zaur Eylanbekov, Mark Styling

Jacket Design
  Zaur Eylanbekov

Controller
  Linda DeAngelis

Operations Director
  E. Rex Anku

Retail Sales Director
  Jill Brooks

Sales Manager
  Joy Roberts

Publisher
  Mel Williams

PRINTED IN SINGAPORE

To order more copies of this book or any of our other titles call toll free within the United States 1 800 359-3003, or visit our website at: *www.airtimepublishing.com*

Other books by AIRtime Publishing include:
  United States Military Aviation Directory
  Carrier Aviation Air Power Directory
  Superfighters The Next Generation of Combat Aircraft
  Phantom: Spirit in the Skies Updated and Expanded Edition
  Tupolev Bombers
  Black Jets
  Century Jets
  Air Combat Legends Vol. 1
  Modern Battlefield Warplanes

New books to be published during 2004 include:
  Russian Military Aviation Directory Vols 1 and 2,
  Air Combat Legends Vol. 2

Retail distribution via:

Direct from Publisher
AIRtime Publishing Inc.
120 East Ave., Norwalk, CT 06851, USA
Tel (203) 838-7979 • Fax (203) 838-7344
Toll-free 1 800 359-3003

USA & Canada
Specialty Press Inc.
39966 Grand Avenue, North Branch
MN 55056
Tel (651) 277-1400 • Fax (651) 277-1203
Toll-free 1 800 895-4585

UK & Europe
Midland Counties Publications
4 Watling Drive
Hinckley LE10 3EY
Tel 01455 233 747 • Fax 01455 233 737

INTRODUCTION

This unique book is based on highly detailed reports first published in *World Air Power Journal* and *International Air Power Review*. They have been thoroughly updated and expanded to cover recent events, and augmented with new sections. Together they provide a comprehensive review of the aircraft that are part of today's sea-going US Navy.

Warplanes of the Fleet

CONTENTS

Today, when the Tomcat grabs the headlines, it does so principally as a bomber, yet it should not be forgotten that the F-14 remains the world's most 'complete' fighter in terms of its range of air-to-air weaponry. It is a testament to the aircraft's existing weapon capabilities that it was felt unnecessary to equip it with the AMRAAM – the 'death ray' missile of the 1990s and 2000s. And it should not be forgotten that the F-14 also ranks among the world's most capable tactical reconnaissance aircraft. In an illustrious career spanning nearly 30 years, Grumman's last and finest 'Cat' has become a true icon of American military might, and joined the handful of aircraft that have transcended their world to enter the imagination of the public at large. When captured in a classic pose such as that demonstrated by this VF-103 F-14B, no aircraft symbolises the terrible power and beauty of the jet fighter better than the Tomcat.

With its replacement, the F/A-18E/F Super Hornet, entering Fleet service, the F-14 Tomcat is in its twilight years. In the 1990s the career of the fleet defender *par excellence* saw a dramatic resurgence with the adoption of the bombing role, and the F-14 soon established itself as the carrier air wing's prime long-range attack platform. The integration of LANTIRN allowed the Tomcat to deliver weapons with great precision, and to designate targets for other aircraft in the 'fast-FAC' role. In these duties the F-14 has seen considerable action over Iraq, Yugoslavia and now Afghanistan. Scheduled to be out of service before the end of the decade, the Tomcat will not disappear without a fight. In the 1990s the F-14 community claimed that 'The Cat is Back' – 10 years on and it has not gone away.

Northrop Grumman
F-14 Tomcat
US Navy today

With around two years remaining until the last front-line Tomcat is withdrawn, and with the rundown of the remaining fleet already well underway, one would expect the F-14 to be kept operational with a minimum of expenditure, and with no real expansion of the type's role and responsibilities. In fact, the F-14 force has undergone major changes, introducing dramatic improvements in capability, and is embracing more fully the air-to-ground rôle which it first picked up only as it entered the second half of its career.

For the first 15 years of its service life, the F-14 was very much a single-role aircraft – a dedicated fleet air defence interceptor – and underwent the minimum of changes and upgrades. Known weaknesses and problems were addressed, with the AIM-54C model of the Phoenix being rushed into service after the original model was compromised following the fall of the Shah in Iran, and with new variants being developed with new, more powerful and more reliable engines. Otherwise, remarkably little happened until the Cold War began to draw to a close.

Although the aircraft-carrier was essentially an offensive 'Power Projection' weapon, the defensive F-14 was regarded by many as being the most important element within every Carrier Air Wing (CVW), and the F-14 force became an élite. During the Cold War, US aircraft-carriers represented the most tempting targets possible for Soviet long-range bombers, which could often attack using very-long range stand-off weapons, including cruise missiles. Only the F-14, with its AWG-9 weapons system and AIM-54 Phoenix AAMs, could hope to intercept such attackers before they could launch their missiles, 400-500 miles out from the carrier, or to successfully intercept incoming cruise missiles.

Aircrew flying other types pointed out that 'Fighters are fun, but bombers are important', but they were seldom heard. The F-14 was good-looking (except in the circuit, when its ungainly appearance led to the aircraft's unflattering 'turkey' soubriquet), and was a technological triumph. The Navy itself promoted the Tomcat above all other aircraft types in its PR and recruiting effort. The first Tomcats in service also wore extremely colourful unit markings, and the aircraft was glamorised by Hollywood, lionised by the press, and adored by aviation enthusiasts.

Cold War air wings

At the height of the Cold War virtually every Air Wing (11 in total, plus two Reserve Air Wings) included two Tomcat squadrons, and the F-14 equipped 22 front-line squadrons, four Reserve fighter squadrons and two training units (one for each Fleet). A 12th Air Wing (CVW-10) even began to form with two more Tomcat squadrons, but this was disestablished during 1988 as part of a package of defence cuts.

Most carriers embarked a standard Air Wing (known as the Conventional CVW), with two 12-aircraft F-14 squadrons, two light attack squadrons with 24 F/A-18s, one medium attack squadron with 10 A-6E bombers and four KA-6D tankers, and single ECM/EW, ASW, AEW and SAR/ASW squadrons equipped with a total of 24 EA-6Bs, S-3s, E-2Cs and SH-3s or SH-60s. The USS *Midway* never

embarked any F-14s, instead having three F/A-18 units, while *Ranger*'s Air Wing embarked two F-14 squadrons and two A-6 units, but never embarked any F/A-18s.

At one time, it seemed likely that the Conventional CVW would be replaced by the so called '*Roosevelt* Air Wing', with each Tomcat and F/A-18 unit reduced by two aircraft, with no dedicated KA-6D tankers, and with a second A-6 squadron and with single extra EA-6B and E-2C aircraft being carried. It was then expected that the '*Roosevelt*' and 'Conventional' Air Wings would give way to a 'Power Projection Air Wing', with two 12-aircraft F/A-18 squadrons, 16 A-6Es or AXs, and only 20 F-14s in two 'light' ten-aircraft squadrons. In fact, there were insufficient A-6s to allow two Intruder units (or even a single 16-Intruder squadron) to become 'standard' and, in the event, the A-6E was retired without being directly replaced.

The subsonic Intruder's integrated track and search radar, and target recognition/attack multi-sensor (TRAM) system, with its chin-mounted forward-looking infra-red (FLIR) and laser designator and receiver gave the aircraft an unparalleled all-weather low-level attack capability. The aircraft also had an impressive payload and long range. Unfortunately, however, the A-6E's slow speed, lack of agility and acceleration made it rather vulnerable, and its age made it maintenance-intensive and difficult to support. While the F/A-18A achieved 17 maintenance man hours per flying hour (MMH/FH), the A-6E fleet averaged 44 MMH/FH, making it one of the Navy's most expensive front-line aircraft to operate. Moreover, individual examples of the Intruder were also running out of fatigue life, and large numbers were grounded or subjected to severe g-limit restrictions.

The US Navy initially planned to replace the A-6E with a new Intruder variant, newly-built, with new smokeless General Electric F404-GE-400D engines, a new AN/APQ-173 Norden Synthetic Aperture Radar and new digital avionics. This was cancelled in 1988, shortly after the prototype's first flight. Attention then turned to the advanced, stealthy A-12 Avenger, though this programme soon became mired in technical difficulties, mismanagement and cost escalation, and it was then cancelled in January 1991. This led to a requirement for an alternative long-range strike aircraft for the US Navy's carrier air wings. The proposed A-X and later A/F-X were cancelled in September 1993.

By this time the Navy had already decided to acquire an advanced derivative of the Hornet as an interim type, pending the A/F-X, and when the latter was cancelled, the new Super Hornet was left as the Navy's only new fixed-wing combat aircraft. Moreover, after the debacle of the A-12, it was decided that development and production could not

be concurrent, making it impossible for the new aircraft to be ready in time to replace the A-6. To make things worse, plans to re-wing the remaining A-6Es were dramatically cut back, and the type was instead simply retired. The last Intruder unit, VA-75 'Sunday Punchers', finally decommissioned in early 1997, but the bulk of the fleet had gone several years earlier.

The retirement of the A-6 left the Carrier Air Wing without a sophisticated, long-range all-weather strike attack aircraft, and in the absence of any alternative, the Navy began to look at air-to-ground modifications and derivatives of the F-14 and F/A-18.

Super F-14s

It was always apparent that the F-14 had a number of attributes which offered great potential in the air-to-ground role, including its relatively long range, impressive payload and two-man cockpit. But it was a question of potential, since although the aircraft had always had a secondary, reversionary air-to-ground capability, it had never been exploited by the US Navy. When the original VFX specification was first released in June 1968 it included an important secondary close air support role, with a payload of up to 14,500 lb (6577 kg). Early Grumman publicity material for the winning design (303E) included illustrations of the 'Tomcat-to-be' toting heavy loads of air-to-ground ordnance, and even during the F-14 flight test programme at least one pre-production Tomcat was photographed

Not a 1973-vintage aircraft, 'Bullet 101' was the last F-14D(R) to be redelivered to the US Navy, and was painted in late 1995 in an almost exact replica of VF-2's first scheme to commemorate the 25th anniversary of the Tomcat's first flight. The markings inside the fin proudly proclaimed that 'The Cat is Back'.

Grumman products have dominated US Navy carrier decks for decades, but in the 2000s their days appear to be numbered. The Tomcat is due to disappear by 2008, while the EA-6B Prowler is scheduled for replacement soon after. The nature of its successor has yet to be determined, although EW versions of the F/A-18F and F-35 (JSF) have been proposed. This 'Cat' is a VF-2 F-14D.

A scene once unthinkable in the Tomcat community: inert Mk 83 1,000-lb (454-kg) bombs and LGTRs (on the trolley at left) wait to be loaded on to the VF-2 and VF-213 Tomcats in the background, in preparation for air-to-ground training work at NAS Oceana, Virginia.

Below right: In the 2000s the Tomcat's main Achilles heel is its time-consuming maintenance requirements and unreliability of what is now a true veteran. It has become commonplace to launch air spares on operational missions as an insurance against inflight technical faults. Suffering no such problems is this VF-31 F-14D, cruising with wings fully spread.

Below: Low, slow manoeuvring, as demonstrated by this LANTIRN-carrying VF-143 F-14B, has been made much safer by the incorporation of the DFCS (Digital Flight Control System), which inhibits the Tomcat's propensity to depart.

carrying 14 500-lb (227-kg) Mk 82 bombs attached to modified Phoenix pallets. Much later, when the one-off F-14B Super Tomcat prototype was being used for F-14D development work, the Tomcat was again extensively photographed with air-to-ground weapon loads (usually four Mk 83 1,000-lb/454-kg bombs) and these photos were used for marketing purposes. When the F-14D entered service it incorporated the necessary software and hardware to enable it to carry iron bombs, and the incorporation of more advanced weapons would have been relatively simple.

But this capability remained latent. For as long as A-6 Intruders were deployed aboard US Navy carriers, there was simply no incentive to add the air-to-ground role to the Tomcat squadrons' repertoire. But once the Intruder needed replacing, Grumman turned its attention to unlocking the air-to-ground potential of the Tomcat.

The first Tomcat derivative proposed as an A-6 replacement was the so-called Quickstrike, a minimum-change

version of the F-14D with navigation and targeting FLIR and FLIR/designator pods, and with additional modes for the APG-71 radar, including Doppler Beam Sharpening and synthetic aperture. This would have brought the radar up to the same standard as the APG-70 used by the F-15E Strike Eagle. The cockpit was to have been fully NVG-compatible, with new colour displays, including a digital moving map. Quickstrike was also to have featured four underfuselage hardpoints, each with five sub-stations, and two underwing hardpoints, each with two sub-stations. The Quickstrike's warload was to have included LGBs, Harpoon, SLAM, Maverick and HARM. Despite its long range and two-man crew, the proposed Tomcat Quickstrike was judged by the US Congress as being inferior to even the basic F/A-18C in the air-to-ground role, because it lacked the Hornet's synthetic aperture ground mapping radar capabilities, and was not compatible with the full range of smart air-to-ground ordnance, but only with LGBs.

Super Tomcat 21

The relatively modest Quickstrike therefore soon gave way to the Super Tomcat 21, which was developed as both an Intruder replacement, and as a lower cost, multi-role alternative to the proposed NATF, claiming to offer 90 percent of ATF's capability at 60 percent of the cost. Incorporating all of the improvements offered by Quickstrike, with a new ISAR version of the APG-71 radar and helmet-mounted sights, the Super Tomcat 21 was to have had improved F110-GE-129 engines offering 'supercruise' capability, and thrust-vectoring. Supercruise is defined as the ability to attain and then sustain supersonic cruising flight without recourse to reheat, and the Super Tomcat 21 promised to do so at speeds of up to Mach 1.3. The aircraft also featured a new, single-piece wraparound windscreen, giving a much improved view for the pilot.

Fuel capacity was increased through the addition of reshaped wing gloves (which broadly matched the planview outline of a standard Tomcat's wing glove with the original vanes extended). These new LERXes added around 2,500 lb (1134 kg) of fuel.

To compensate for the increased weight of fuel and weapons, Super Tomcat 21 also featured modified, increased lift single-slotted Fowler-type flaps, increased chord slats and revised all-moving tailplanes, which were enlarged by extending the trailing edge aft. These improvements were intended to allow heavyweight take-offs (or take-offs in zero-wind conditions) and reduced landing speeds.

Grumman hoped for a programme go-ahead in 1990, leading to a 1993 first flight date, and production deliveries from 1996. The company's anticipated development costs

were a relatively modest $989 million, and the 233 planned new-production Super Tomcat 21's were expected to have a unit cost of $39 million, with another 257 being remanu-factured from F-14Bs and F-14Ds at a unit cost of only $21 million.

Grumman's final 'Super Tomcat' proposal was the Attack Super Tomcat 21, which was based on the Super Tomcat 21, with further improvements and refinements. Structurally, the so-called AST-21 introduced thicker outer wing panels, containing increased capacity fuel tanks, while the aircraft also featured increased capacity external fuel tanks. The flaps and slats were redesigned and refined, further reducing approach speeds by an estimated 18 mph (29 km/h).

Some sources suggest that the new supercruise engine was a feature of the Attack Super Tomcat, rather than the original Super Tomcat 21, but this cannot be confirmed.

Attack Super Tomcat was designed to carrying the same navigation and targeting FLIRs as the other 'Super Tomcats', but also replaced the AN/APG-71 radar with a new elec-tronically scanned phased array radar, perhaps the Norden set originally developed for the A-12. Defensive aids would also have been improved, with new jammers and 135 chaff/flare cartridges in launchers built into the LAU-7 missile rails. However, the Attack Super Tomcat was judged to be unaffordable, and the Navy finalised its plans to develop the F/A-18E/F Super Hornet instead.

Super Hornet v. Tomcat

The F/A-18E/F development contract was signed in June 1992, launching an aircraft that was advertised as being larger and more capable than the baseline F/A-18, offering a substantial increase in payload, range, bringback and internal volume (for fuel and avionics).

It is true that the Super Hornet cannot carry an A-6 payload over A-6 distances, but it can fly about 35-50 percent further than the F/A-18C, and can land back with 9,000 lb (4082 kg) of fuel and weapons instead of only 5,500 lb (2495 kg). Moreover, the aircraft is designed to operate in today's post Cold War world, in which the nature of the threat has changed. The disappearance of mass fleets of 'Backfires', each armed with armfuls of AS-6 cruise missiles, has allowed the US Navy to conduct littoral operations, in which the primary threat comes from fighter-type aircraft carrying Exocet-type missiles.

In 1994, accepting and recognising that littoral warfare marked a shift away from open-ocean warfighting and toward joint-service operations conducted from the sea, the Secretary of the Navy said that 85 percent of the Navy's potential targets were within 200 miles (320 km) of the coast, and thus within the F/A-18C's range, even with an aircraft-carrier operating 100 miles or more offshore. F/A-18Cs carrying four 1,000-lb (454-kg) bombs and exter-nal fuel tanks have an unrefuelled mission radius of about 340 miles (547 km), while the F/A-18E/F is projected to carry the same weapon load up to 520 miles (837 km), even without inflight refuelling.

With comparable warloads, and under the same condi-tions, it has been suggested that the F-14 has a radius of action of about 750 miles (1200 km). This is an impressive difference, but one which the Navy's experts believe to be irrelevant. If greater range is needed, the Navy's Tomahawk cruise missile has a range of about 805 miles (1300 km), and Air Force bombers have even greater range.

The question of whether the Super Hornet is a much better bet for the US Navy than any Tomcat derivative could ever be remains a controversial and much argued point of view. Super Hornet supporters maintain that the reduced long-range stand-off threat allows an F/A-18E/F with AMRAAM to represent a viable replacement for the Tomcat/Phoenix combination in the Fleet Air Defence role.

However, while the Super Hornet (as a derivative of the 'Legacy' Hornet) promised to be fairly quick and simple to develop (in the event this proved not to be quite the case), it was clear that something would have to be done if the

Despite attempts to tone down the fleet, colour has always been a feature of the Tomcat community, although now it is restricted to CAG and CO's aircraft. This was VF-31's 'CAG-bird' F-14D while assigned to Abraham Lincoln in late 1997.

Known as Operation Southern Watch, or OSW, the policing of Iraqi airspace south of the 32nd Parallel has occupied the US Navy since the end of the Gulf War in 1991. After a flourish of activity in late 1992/early 1993, the OSW mission became rather tedious, but in more recent times Iraq has increased its challenges to UN fighters overflying its territory, leading in turn to numerous strikes being mounted against Iraqi air defences. With full air-to-air armament, this VF-2 F-14D returns to 'Connie' after a 1995 OSW patrol.

With Desert Fox bomb drop markings on its nose, VF-32's 'CAG-bird' F-14B refuels from a Marine Corps KC-130. Carried on underfuselage TERs (Triple Ejector Racks) are two LGTRs (Laser-Guided Training Rounds), used to mimic the behaviour of full-size Paveway weapons. The F/A-18D from the USMC's VMFA(AW)-224 in the background also carries LGTRs.

Right: As well as three Sparrows, a single Sidewinder and an instrumentation pod, this VX-9 F-14B is carrying a live AIM-54C Phoenix. The underfuselage Sparrow is carried in a recess: three similar recesses are located further forward, under where the Phoenix pallets are mounted on this aircraft. Combined with the lower wing pylon stations, the recesses allow up to six AIM-7s to be carried.

F-14As surplus to Fleet requirements have found a useful role with NSAWC (Naval Strike and Air Warfare Center) at NAS Fallon, Nevada. NSAWC was created by the amalgamation of 'Top Gun' (NFWS), 'Top Dome' (CAEWS) and 'Strike U' (NSWC) and provides an air combat training centre for all Navy pilots. Tomcats are allocated to provide fighter adversaries.

placed on multi-role versatility, there was an attitude that "if the FAGs (Fighter/Attack Guys) could do it, then so should the Tomcat community!"

F-14 air-to-ground capabilities were quietly explored by Naval Systems Command, culminating in the dropping of two inert 2,000-lb (907-kg) Mk 84 iron bombs by a VX-4 F-14A on 10 November 1987. OTEF tests followed in 1988, and front-line trials began during 1990. The first 'Bombcats' were the F-14A+s of VF-24 'Fighting Renegades' and VF-211 'Checkmates', which began developing air-to-ground tactics and techniques. VF-24 won the honour of becoming the first fleet F-14 squadron to drop air-to-ground ordnance, (four Mk 84 bombs), inaugurating a new role for the F-14. VF-211 participated in Desert Storm, but only in the interceptor and TARPS roles, since weapons clearance trials continued at such a slow pace that it was not until July 1992 that Fleet Tomcat squadrons actually received a full clearance to use even GP bombs.

In the interim, VF-101 took a lead role in training the F-14 fleet in strike warfare from late 1990, one of the squadron's instructors dropping two inert Mk 84s on 12 September 1990. VF-211 was the first Pacific Fleet unit to complete the Tomcat Advanced Strike Syllabus (TASS) in June 1992. This course is now known as AARP (Advanced Attack Readiness Program). Clearances for CBUs (cluster bomb units) and LGBs followed soon after, however, expanding the 'Bombcat's arsenal.

In May 1991, VF-143 claimed to have become the first fleet Tomcat squadron to drop live air-to-ground ordnance, during a detachment to NAS Fallon, though VF-24 had already achieved this distinction a year earlier. Adoption of the 'Bombcat' role was somewhat patchy and uneven, some Air Wings becoming entirely 'Bombcat'-qualified

withdrawal of the A-6 were not going to leave an unacceptably large hole in the Carrier Air Wing's capability mix, with a particular long-range gap. One obvious solution was to activate the F-14's long dormant air-to-ground capability.

'Bombcat' – modest but useful

Much has been made of the Tomcat's increasing adoption of an air-to-ground role as the so-called 'Bombcat', though this was initially, in truth, extremely limited.

Small sections of the Tomcat community had pressed to be allowed to reclaim an air-to-ground role, ever since the introduction of the Hornet had shown that one aircraft could perform both roles with aplomb. With the Cold War drawing to a close, and with increasing emphasis being

almost immediately, with others remaining unqualified, and some converting only one of their two squadrons (usually the non-TARPS unit) to the bombing role. When the USS *Constellation* deployed in late 1994, without A-6Es, its F-14Ds still could not drop bombs because they lacked the necessary computer software.

'Bombcats' entered combat on 5 September 1995, when two F-14As from VF-41 participating in Operation Deliberate Force over Bosnia-Herzegovina dropped LGBs (designated by F/A-18 Hornets) on an ammunition dump in eastern Bosnia. The squadron also dropped dumb bombs on Serb targets during the same cruise, but whenever it used PGMs, it required targeting support from Hornets.

Expanding the 'Bombcat's 'bite'

With work proceeding on the F/A-18E/F, and with the 'Bombcat' in service in a limited air-to-ground role, attention was turned to giving the existing F-14 force a limited all-weather/precision attack air-to-ground capability to help replace the A-6 Intruder in the interim.

In the absence of the A-6, the Joint Conference Committee on the FY 1994 Defense Authorization Act directed the Navy to add an 'F-15E equivalent' capability to its F-14D aircraft, including the capability to employ modern air-to-ground stand-off weapons. This went beyond the Navy's intention, which was merely to add a 'more robust' ground attack capability.

A COEA (Cost and Operational Effectiveness Analysis) completed in December of 1994 examined different proposals for turning the in-service F-14 into a precision strike platform. The US Navy had already outlined a $2.5 billion two-stage upgrade for the F-14A and F-14B. The initial phase of the planned upgrade, known as the 'A/B Upgrade', consisted of structural modifications to extend the Tomcat's fatigue life to 7,500 hours, improved cockpit displays, improved defensive systems, and the provision of digital avionics architecture and new mission computers to speed data-processing time and improve software capacity. This A/B upgrade was to be incorporated into 76 F-14As and 81 F-14Bs, conferring a degree of commonality with the F-14D before the second phase would be added to all surviving Tomcats.

This second stage, confusingly known as 'Block I', was to have added a built-in FLIR, an NVG-compatible night-attack cockpit and enhanced defensive countermeasures. Overall, this was not felt to offer anything that was not already offered by the F/A-18C, and the 'Block I' Tomcat even lacked some important Hornet capabilities, including compatibility with vital weapons such as HARM, Harpoon, SLAM, Maverick and Walleye. In the event, funds for the A/B structural and survivability modifications were authorised, but funding for the F-14 Block I ground attack upgrade was eliminated.

Ambitious upgrades

One alternative studied was an F-14D-based upgrade known as the F/A-14D, a rolling four-phase upgrade which was not intended to alter planned F/A-18E/F procurement, but which would improve the F-14's capabilities as an interim A-6 replacement.

Proposed by Grumman as an alternative to the planned 'Block I' upgrade to the F-14A and F-14B, and sometimes referred to as 'Phase II', the $9.2 billion programme would have seen some 210 Tomcats (198 F-14As and F-14Bs and 53 F-14Ds) brought to a common (digital) standard, all with F110 engines, AYK-14 computer (with XN8 memory upgrade), an attack FLIR, MIL STD 1760 weapons capability (for JSOW), new displays, a one-piece windscreen, frontal RCS reduction measures and dry foam fuel tank protection. The second phase would add a navigation FLIR, an NVG-compatible cockpit, the F/A-18C(N)'s digital moving map, a Raster HUD and an inert gas fuel tank protection system, together with an AN/ALE-50 towed radar decoy. The proposed third phase added software modes from the F-15E's radar, and the fourth and final phase added JSOW and JDAM. Grumman also proposed a more limited programme, applying the same upgrade only to the 53 remaining F-14Ds, at a cost of $1.5 billion, to begin in 1995, and with Opeval in 1997. The Navy judged this proposal to be unaffordable.

In October 1994, Robert C. Byrd, and David R. Obey, respective Chairmen of the Senate and House of Representatives and Committees on Appropriations, and Sam Nunn, and Ronald V. Dellums, respective Chairmen of

Top: In the line of their adversary duties NSAWC F-14s are called upon to mimic a variety of foreign fighter systems. Naturally the Su-27 'Flanker' figures prominently, for which a number of the unit's aircraft received this 'Flanker'-style camouflage. F-14s are also used to mimic MiG-31s, occasionally working with E-2s which can imitate the A-50 'Mainstay'.

Above: Among the NSAWC fleet are aircraft wearing Iranian-style camouflage (not to be confused with the last F-14 from Iran's 80-aircraft order which was embargoed and delivered to the US Navy). It has been reported in late 2001 that all NSAWC aircraft will adopt this colour scheme. This machine has its modified Phoenix pallets/bomb racks lowered down from the underside of the 'tunnel' between the engine trunks.

Naval Air Warfare Center – testing the F-14

Subordinate to Naval Air Systems Command (NAVAIR), the NAWC has three principal divisions: Aircraft, Weapons and Training. Two of these operate Tomcats on a permanent basis.

Above: The NAWC-AD's Strike Test Squadron operates this F-14B modified with a Digital Flight Control System, which improves high-g manoeuvring and low-speed handling. DFCS underwent its first sea trials in November 1996 aboard USS John C. Stennis.

Naval Air Warfare Center Aircraft Division

NAWC-AD at NAS Patuxent River, Maryland, reports to Commander Naval Air Systems Command, and is responsible for the development of air vehicles, propulsion systems, avionics, and items like catapults and arrester systems. The unit parents the USNTPS and has three Aircraft Test Squadrons. One of these deals only with rotorcraft, and of the other two, the **Naval Strike Aircraft Test Squadron** flies most (if not all) of the Tomcats based at Patuxent River.

Although the Tomcat is nearing the end of its career, modifications to the type have continued to provide a great deal of work for the Naval Strike Aircraft Test Squadron's F-14s. During 2000-2001, the squadron were heavily committed to testing (and expansion) of the F-14's new DFCS, integration of JDAM, improvements to the VDIG and retrofit of the AN/ALE-47 chaff dispenser.

During 2001-2002, the DFCS is being further expanded, and the F-14D is gaining a new back-up Navigation Guidance System (NGS) and an upgrade to the current mission computer. The Tomcats are also to gain LANTIRN pods with higher altitude capability.

Finally, the ageing F-14s may gain structural improvements, and the Naval Strike Aircraft Test Squadron is to examine loads on the wing (to determine its service life), and on the Nose Landing Gear Steering Collar (NLGSC), and to evaluate new stronger engine mounts for the F110 engine.

Above and right: The Naval Weapons Test Squadron – Point Mugu is part of the NAWC-WD, and was formerly the Pacific Missile Test Center (and Naval Missile Center before that). As its earlier names suggest, it is devoted to missile trials over the Pacific Missile Range, and has operated various Tomcats since the early days of the programme, firing its first Phoenix in 1972. This is one of the unit's NF-14Ds.

Naval Air Warfare Center Weapons Division

NAWC-WD at China Lake was formed by merging the Naval Weapons Centre at China Lake and the Pacific Missile Test Center at Point Mugu in January 1992. Today, the NAWC-WD is tasked with the development and testing of air-launched weapons and associated tactics, and can call upon a highly favourable climate, a large fleet of aircraft types and massive ranges to fulfil its duties. The NAWC-WD is estimated to have $3 billion of infrastructure.

The division now parents two flying Naval Weapons Test Squadrons, the Naval Weapons Test Squadron (NWTSCL) 'Dust Devils' flying Hornets, Harriers and Cobras from China Lake, while the Naval Weapons Test Squadron (**NWTSPM**) **'Bloodhounds'** at NAS Point Mugu, operates a mix of aircraft, including the YF-4J, QF-4N/S, NP-3D and NF-14A/D. In recent years, the latter unit's achievements have included the early completion of Operational Testing of the Operational Flight Program (the radar tape load) for the F-14B. While VX-9 at Point Mugu conducted Operational Test (OT) of the aircraft, the maintenance departments of NWTSPM and VX-9 combined into one unit to complete the work two months early, allowing VF-102 to deploy months ahead of schedule, thereby participating in operations over the Balkans.

Point Mugu is also home to the **F-14 WSSA** (Weapons System Support Activity). This is part of the Naval Air Systems Command (NAVAIR) Tomcat Integrated Product Team (IPT), which reports to the F-14 Program Office, known as PMA-241. This provides cradle-to-grave F-14 weapon system support, including reliability and readiness improvements, the correction of latent defects, the replacement of obsolete parts and periodic functional upgrades in response to changing threats, and to enable the aircraft to meet new requirements. PMA-241 has also strived to establish a common baseline avionics standard for the three in-service F-14 variants.

The WSSA can call upon a unique range of F-14 system rigs and other facilities, which allow software development and synthetic 'airborne' testing at a fraction of the cost of relying on airborne platforms alone. These rigs have proved their worth in integrating JTIDS on the F-14, and in issuing revised Operational Flight Program Software loads. The rigs consist of the forward fuselages of F-14A, F-14B (Upgrade), and F-14D aircraft, each fitted with appropriate and representative avionics. Real and simulated weapons can be connected to the rigs, allowing ground-based compatibility testing and missile-on-board aircraft RF testing.

the Senate and House of Representatives Committees on the Armed Services, released a damning report about the various Tomcat upgrade proposals.

These distinguished politicians carefully evaluated the implications of the Navy's decision to spend an estimated $2.5 billion between fiscal years 1994 and 2003 for what was described as "a limited ground attack upgrade and other modifications to 210 F-14 Tomcat fighters", consisting of 76 F-14As, 81 F-14Bs and 53 F-14Ds and found that the Navy had "not made a compelling case to proceed with its $2.5 billion plan", for a number of reasons, which it carefully outlined.

Although the Navy had justified its proposed F-14 attack upgrades as being necessary to replace some capability that would be lost with the retirement of the A-6E, it was clear that upgraded Tomcats actually would not be available to fill the gap between the retirement of the A-6E and the introduction of the F/A-18E/F. Delivery of the first upgraded F-14s was not scheduled to begin until some time after the A-6Es were retired, and it looked as though they might not even be available before the F/A-18E/F. No F-14s were scheduled to begin receiving upgrades until fiscal year 1998, a year after the last A-6s were retired, and none

was to be delivered until 1999. Two CVWs would by then have been without A-6Es for at least five years. With the F/A-18 E/F aircraft entering service during 2000 the gap which could have been filled by the upgraded F-14 would have been very short.

Attack gap

By default, carriers would have been deploying for several years without either A-6Es or upgraded F-14s, instead relying on extra F/A-18Cs for all attack missions. This was said to demonstrate the Navy's willingness to rely on the Hornet for its strike capability, although senior officers disputed this, claiming that the arrangement was a considered risk, and reflected temporary affordability constraints, and not a willingness to permanently forgo capability.

As well as failing to 'plug the gap', the proposed Tomcat did not offer the capability which the politicians expected from its $2.5 billion price tag. They noted with concern that current Navy plans would not provide F-14s with F-15E-equivalent capabilities, and that if Congress wished to provide these, the Navy's own estimates show that it would cost very much more.

A desert-camouflaged NSAWC F/A-18 peels away from VX-9's latest black-painted Tomcat, an NF-14D. Traditionally using the callsign 'Vandy One', the succession of black test aircraft (F-4s and F-14s) at Point Mugu also used to wear the Playboy bunny insignia on the tail, but that was deleted in the interests of political correctness.

VX-9 is the Navy's operational test and evaluation unit for fighter/attack aircraft. The detachment at Point Mugu, California was formerly designated VX-4, and has operated Tomcats since their entry into service, being the first Navy squadron to get the F-14.

Inside the F-14 Tomcat

Left: The aft cockpit of an F-14B shows the large central square PTID (Programmable Tactical Information Display) which replaced the circular AWG-9 radar display. The PTID can present LANTIRN and Digital TARPS imagery, as well as its normal nav/radar functions. Above it is the 5-in (12.7-cm) DDD (Detail Data Display).

Right: The radome of an F-14D is raised to reveal the scanner of the APG-71 radar. This has far fewer raised dipole aerials than are found on the AWG-9.

F-14D Tomcat cutaway

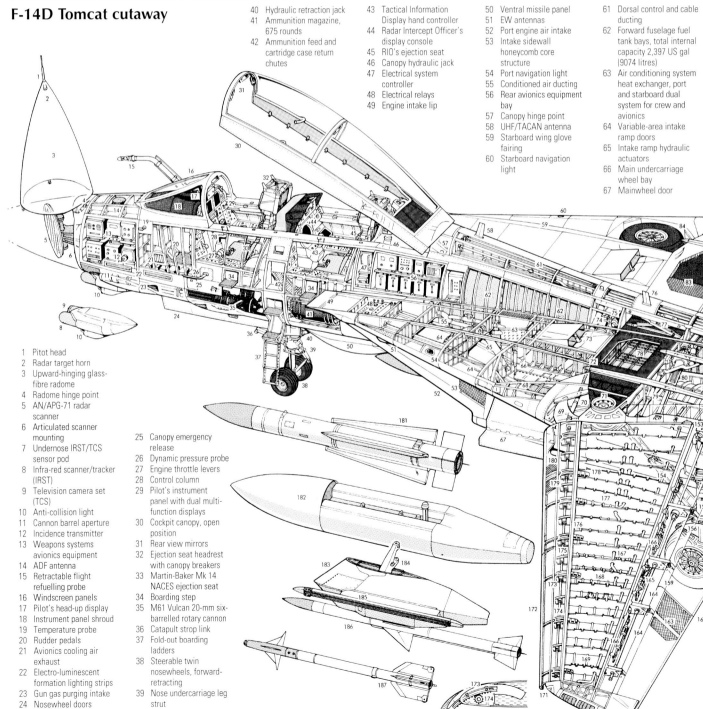

1. Pitot head
2. Radar target horn
3. Upward-hinging glass-fibre radome
4. Radome hinge point
5. AN/APG-71 radar scanner
6. Articulated scanner mounting
7. Undernose IRST/TCS sensor pod
8. Infra-red scanner/tracker (IRST)
9. Television camera set (TCS)
10. Anti-collision light
11. Cannon barrel aperture
12. Incidence transmitter
13. Weapons systems avionics equipment
14. ADF antenna
15. Retractable flight refuelling probe
16. Windscreen panels
17. Pilot's head-up display
18. Instrument panel shroud
19. Temperature probe
20. Rudder pedals
21. Avionics cooling air exhaust
22. Electro-luminescent formation lighting strips
23. Gun gas purging intake
24. Nosewheel doors
25. Canopy emergency release
26. Dynamic pressure probe
27. Engine throttle levers
28. Control column
29. Pilot's instrument panel with dual multi-function displays
30. Cockpit canopy, open position
31. Rear view mirrors
32. Ejection seat headrest with canopy breakers
33. Martin-Baker Mk 14 NACES ejection seat
34. Boarding step
35. M61 Vulcan 20-mm six-barrelled rotary cannon
36. Catapult strop link
37. Fold-out boarding ladders
38. Steerable twin nosewheels, forward-retracting
39. Nose undercarriage leg strut
40. Hydraulic retraction jack
41. Ammunition magazine, 675 rounds
42. Ammunition feed and cartridge case return chutes
43. Tactical Information Display hand controller
44. Radar Intercept Officer's display console
45. RIO's ejection seat
46. Canopy hydraulic jack
47. Electrical system controller
48. Electrical relays
49. Engine intake lip
50. Ventral missile panel
51. EW antennas
52. Port engine air intake
53. Intake sidewall honeycomb core structure
54. Port navigation light
55. Conditioned air ducting
56. Rear avionics equipment bay
57. Canopy hinge point
58. UHF/TACAN antenna
59. Starboard wing glove fairing
60. Starboard navigation light
61. Dorsal control and cable ducting
62. Forward fuselage fuel tank bays, total internal capacity 2,397 US gal (9074 litres)
63. Air conditioning system heat exchanger, port and starboard dual system for crew and avionics
64. Variable-area intake ramp doors
65. Intake ramp hydraulic actuators
66. Main undercarriage wheel bay
67. Mainwheel door

Access to many of the F-14's components is achievable through hinged or easily removed panels, including many of the engine accessories (left). The engine drops down and slides out easily for deeper maintenance requirements (below).

Left: The General Electric M61A1 Vulcan cannon is installed in the lower port fuselage, with a drum for 675 20-mm rounds mounted behind. Ammunition is loaded from a dedicated cart. The weapon is driven by a 20-hp (15-kW) electric motor at either 4,000 or 6,000 rounds per minute. Muzzle velocity is 3,380 ft (1030 m) per second.

68 Rear intake ramp
69 Wing glove sealing horn fairing
70 Telescopic flap/slat drive shaft
71 Port wing pivot bearing
72 Electron beam-welded titanium wing pivot box
73 Intake bypass air spill duct
74 Emergency hydraulic generator
75 Central flap/slat drive motor
76 UHF datalink/IFF antenna
77 Fuselage upper longeron/pivot box attachment links
78 Wing pivot box integral fuel tank
79 Telescopic fuel feed pipes
80 Variable wing sweep control screw jacks

81 Centre-section fuel tankage
82 Intake ducting
83 Honeycomb skin panels
84 Starboard mainwheel, stowed position
85 Starboard wing pivot bearing

86 Flap/slat interconnecting drive shaft
87 Starboard wing integral fuel tank
88 Starboard two-segment leading-edge slats
89 Wing forward position (20° sweep)
90 Starboard navigation/strobe light
91 Wingtip formation lighting panels
92 Two-segment slotted flaps, down position
93 Starboard spoiler panels
94 Inboard auxiliary flap
95 Wing glove flexible sealing plates

96 External glove stiffeners/dorsal fences
97 Forward/rear fuselage longeron joint
98 Flight control system artificial feel units
99 Control rods and linkages
100 Rear fuselage fuel tank bays
101 Starboard engine bay
102 Fin root fairing
103 Pneumatic wing root glove seal

104 Starboard wing, fully swept position (69° wing sweep).
105 Starboard fin
106 Fin honeycomb core skin panels
107 Fin tip antenna fairing
108 Tail navigation light
109 Starboard rudder, honeycomb core structure
110 Port fin tip antenna fairing
111 Anti-collision light
112 Formation lighting strip
113 ECM antenna
114 Starboard all-moving tailplane
115 Variable-area afterburner nozzle
116 Carbon-fibre composite nozzle shroud
117 Flexible sealing plates
118 Flight control system back-up hydraulic module
119 Dorsal airbrake panel, split lower surfaces
120 Airbrake hydraulic jacks
121 Airbrake housing
122 Ventral AN/ALE-39 chaff/flare dispensers
123 Fuel jettison
124 ECM antenna
125 Deck arrester hooks stowed
126 Port engine exhaust nozzle
127 Afterburner duct outer sealing plate
128 Variable-area nozzle actuator
129 Afterburner duct
130 Rudder hydraulic actuator
131 Fin/tailplane main mounting frame
132 Tailplane pivot bearing
133 Multi-spar tailplane structure
134 Arrester hook, down position
135 Honeycomb trailing-edge panel
136 AN/ALR-45(V) radar warning antenna
137 Boron-fibre tailplane skin panels
138 Wing rib (typical), machined on inner face
139 Port wing, fully swept position
140 Ventral fin
141 Afterburner duct cooling air intake
142 Tailplane hydraulic actuator
143 Rear fuselage sponson fairing structure
144 Port General Electric F110-GE-400 afterburning turbofan

145 Hydraulic system filters
146 Formation lighting strip
147 Hydraulic reservoir, port and starboard
148 Engine bay access panel
149 Engine accessory equipment bay
150 Port auxiliary flap
151 Main undercarriage hydraulic retraction jack
152 Auxiliary flap hydraulic jack
153 Main undercarriage leg pivot mounting
154 Retraction breaker/drag strut
155 Shock absorber leg strut
156 Torque scissor links
157 Port mainwheel
158 Trailing-edge flap section, cruise condition
159 Flap eyebrow fairing
160 Flap 10° down, manoeuvre position
161 Slotted flap, 35° down landing position
162 Port outboard flap segments
163 Flap honeycomb core structure
164 Port spoiler panels
165 Flap drive torque shaft
166 Spoiler hydraulic actuators
167 Fuel system piping
168 Machined wing ribs
169 Bottom wing skin/stringer panel
170 Wingtip formation light
171 Port navigation/strobe light
172 Two-segment leading-edge slat, extended
173 Slat guide rails
174 Slat drive torque shaft
175 Leading-edge ribs
176 Two-spar wing torsion box structure
177 Port wing integral fuel tank
178 Slat guide rail fuel sealing cans
179 Leading-edge slat honeycomb core construction
180 Tank pylon beneath intake trunk
181 AIM-54C Phoenix long-range air-to-air missile
182 267-US gal (1011-litre) external fuel tank
183 Glove pylon
184 Pylon attachment link
185 Shoulder-mounted Sidewinder launch rail
186 AIM-120 AMRAAM medium-range air-to-air missile
187 AIM-9L Sidewinder short-range air-to-air missile

Mike Badrocke

In March 1999 F-14Bs from VF-32 engaged in air combat exercises with F-16A/B Netz fighters of the IDF/AF over Israeli ranges. According to the hosts, the results were heavily in favour of the F-16s, but the nature of the engagements was not released and any assessment would be highly speculative.

Not only did the upgraded F-14 fail to measure up to the F-15E, the politicians also judged that it would not offer "any capability not available or planned for the F/A-18C," while most upgraded F-14s would actually be considerably less capable than the F/A-18s then in service. They were particularly scathing of the fact that the planned upgrades would not include the kind of air-to-ground synthetic aperture radar required for precision ground-mapping, or which would permit crews to locate, identify and attack targets in adverse weather and poor visibility.

The bulk of the Tomcat force was thus effectively limited to clear-weather ground-attack missions. Only the 53 F-14Ds, with their APG-71 synthetic aperture ground-mapping radar, would have capabilities approaching those

of the F/A-18C. By contrast, even early F/A-18Cs, with APG-65 radar, enjoyed synthetic aperture ground-mapping with Doppler beam sharpening, and their capability was only improved by the addition of APG-73 radar from 1994.

They were also disappointed that no F-14s would be able to launch "current or planned precision munitions or stand-off weapons, except for LGBs". It was acknowledged that LGBs are a useful (and sometimes war-winning) weapon, but expressed concerns that the usefulness of laser targeting would be severely limited when targets were obscured by clouds, smoke, haze, dust or moisture – all of which could potentially prevent laser beams from illuminating and marking a target.

There were important weapons routinely carried by both the A-6E and the F/A-18 which could not be used by the upgraded Tomcat, including the AGM-88 High-speed Anti-Radiation Missile (HARM), the AGM-84 Harpoon anti-ship missile, the AGM-65 Maverick anti-armour missile, Walleye guided bomb and the Stand-off Land Attack Missile (SLAM), while other newer weapons were compatible with the F/A-18C but not with the planned F-14 upgrade. These included the Joint Direct Attack Munition (JDAM) and the Joint Stand Off Weapon (JSOW).

With tight budgets and numerous other priorities, the politicians judged that the planned F-14 upgrades "did not appear to be cost-effective", offering little or no improvement over current capabilities and probably being unavailable until after the F/A-18E/F began to enter service. They noted that the Navy itself, "In setting its priorities" had already eliminated the F-14 upgrade from its Program Objectives Memorandum, which they took to be a clear admission that the Navy had weighed its needs and found that it had more important priorities.

'Cheap and cheerful' precision attack

In the end, the COEA report recommended the cheaper and quicker option of simply integrating a stand-alone laser designator and FLIR on all Fleet F-14s, to give rudimentary night capability and compatibility with the basic range of laser-guided bombs. Such weapons could already be carried by the 'Bombcat', but the F-14 relied on third-party targeting and designation. Giving the Tomcat a basic self-designation capability was therefore felt to represent a useful baseline capability.

As a result, the Navy applied the first stage of its planned upgrade to 76 surviving F-14As and to 81 F-14Bs, incorporating structural improvements to give a 7,500-hour fatigue life, together with a new dual MIL STD 1553B digital avionics architecture, with new mission computers, improved cockpit displays (with a new HUD for the F-14B), and

Above: This immaculate four-ship of F-14As is from VF-154, the Tomcat squadron forward-deployed in Japan at Atsugi and assigned to Air Wing Five aboard USS Kitty Hawk (CV 63). Unlike US-based units, Air Wing Five is 'always on deployment', and does not follow the standard 2-year work-up/deployment cycle.

Right: 'Blacklion 111', an F-14D(R) of VF-213, is carefully lined up for launch from Carl Vinson during a Southern Watch cruise. The aircraft, BuNo. 161159, was the first of the 'retread' A-models to emerge from the Bethpage works as F-14Ds, and was redelivered to the Navy in late 1990.

improved defensive systems, including AN/ALR-67 RWR, a BOL chaff dispenser and a PTID programmable tactical information display in the rear cockpit.

These modifications brought the old versions up to a broadly similar avionics standard to the 53 remaining F-14Ds, resulting in the designations F-14A (Upgrade) and F-14B (Upgrade), or F-14A++ and F-14B MMCAP (Multi-Mission Capability Avionics Programme). At one time, it was hoped that this improved commonality would allow F-14s of all variants to be deployed in mixed squadrons. It soon became clear that mixing TF30- and F110-engined versions in single units would be impractical, but the integration of F-14Bs and F-14Ds seemed more realistic, and it came as a surprise when plans for mixed F-14B/D squadrons were quietly cancelled in 1997. It had been intended that VF-2, VF-102, VF-143, VF-103 and VF-31 would transition to a mix of F-14Bs and F-14Ds (in that order), with the 'Bounty Hunters' expected to be the first to deploy, in August or September 1999.

LANTIRN 'Bombcat'

Meanwhile work began on providing the F-14 with a rudimentary night/precision attack capability, using a FLIR and laser designator. The US Navy decided to see whether such a system could be integrated on the F-14 using funding originally set aside for the integration of JDAM on the Tomcat. This inferred the use of an off-the-shelf system, and the Navy carefully examined Loral's Nite Hawk pod (used by the F/A-18C) and the Martin-Marietta LANTIRN (Low-Altitude Navigation and Targeting Infrared for Night) pod used on the F-15E and F-16C. Lockheed Martin had been proposing a variant of the LANTIRN pod to the Navy since 1993, for use on the F-14, and in December 1994 a Navy report had urged the acquisition of such a system.

The Nite Hawk system naturally offered commonality advantages, but in the end, LANTIRN had a wider field of regard (a 150° cone around the boresight) and a 5.87° field of view for target acquisition, while Nite Hawk offered only 4°. LANTIRN also offered a higher degree of magnification.

Instead of following the usual route, commissioning industry to prototype a LANTIRN installation and then conducting trials at the Naval Air Warfare Center (with service evaluation following with VX-9), the US Navy adopted a more streamlined approach, managing the programme 'in-house' and achieving much greater input from the front-line at every stage. AIRLANT was then given the task of demonstrating the capabilities of the system, and the installation was trialled by a Fleet squadron. This was possible because LANTIRN was already a mature system, in use with the Air Force since the late 1980s.

Fairchild Defense produced design drawings for an interface between a hand controller in the F-14 cockpit and a LANTIRN pod. This was a virtually self-contained system, with minimal modification to the aircraft's existing software and hardware. The pod is not integrated into the F-14's computers and software, instead feeding images directly from the FLIR onto the RIO's PTID and onto the pilot's vertical display indicator (VDI) in the F-14A/B, or onto one of the two MFDs in the F-14D.

Other LANTIRN-equipped aircraft tended to use two separate LANTIRN pods, with an AN/AAQ-13 navigation pod combining a wide Field of View FLIR and Texas Instruments TFR, and an AN/AAQ-14 targeting pod combining a stabilised, steerable telephoto IR imager with a collimated laser designator. When integrating the LANTIRN system onto the F-14, Lockheed Martin decided to use only the AN/AAQ-14 targeting pod, albeit with increased stabilisation and accuracy, thanks to its new inertial measurement system. The pod also incorporated a built-in GPS/INU, so that the pod 'knew where it was' without having to interface with the aircraft's navigation system. Because the pod has a GPS, navigational accuracy of the Tomcat itself is also greatly improved. The pod computer also contained all necessary ballistics data.

With a pre-briefed known target, the pod's GPS allowed

the laser to be automatically cued onto the target, and could even generate steering cues in the pilot's HUD, in the VDI (Vertical Display Indicator) or superimposed on the FLIR picture. The pod could find targets without a radar or aircraft navigation system hand-off, and did not need to be accurately boresighted to the aircraft.

The RIO designates the target after the pilot 'pickles' the bomb, and the pod performs its own BDA, by video-taping the FLIR picture through to impact. The LANTIRN pod can be used against targets of opportunity, in 'Cue-to-HUD' or 'Snowplough' modes. In the former case, the laser's line of sight is locked to a particular spot in the HUD, which the pilot manoeuvres onto the target by pointing the nose of the aircraft at it. In the Snowplough mode, the pod's line of sight is similarly fixed, but depressed by 15°, and the pilot steers the 'dot' onto the target by reference to the FLIR picture.

Originally designated F-14A+, the F-14B introduced F110 engines but none of the other F-14D improvements. The MMCAP programme added a host of upgrades, the most important of which for the crew are the new HUD (pilot) and PTID (RIO). The latter provides an excellent display of LANTIRN and TARPS imagery.

This smart F-14A 'CAG-bird' from VF-14 participated in the April 2000 Fleet Week fly-by of New York.

With its wings still in the 'oversweep' position, a VF-2 F-14D taxis forward to the bow cat of Constellation. Its blotchy complexion reflects the continuous application of paint along chipped panel lines and fastenings in the never-ending war against saltwater corrosion.

With a live 'Buffalo' – as the AIM-54 is called – aboard, a VF-213 F-14D prepares to launch for an OSW mission. This squadron made the first (US) combat firing of a Phoenix, when two were fired at extreme range against Iraqi fighters.

On the Tomcat, the AN/AAQ-14 pod is carried on station #8B (the starboard wing station) and is controlled by the RIO in the rear cockpit, using a simple hand controller. These hand controllers were 'off-the-shelf' items, originally designed for the A-12, and similar in appearance to an F/A-18 stick top. The pod requires MIL STD 1553B databus architecture, so LANTIRN has to be fitted to an F-14D or an F-14 MMCAP (F-14A (Upgrade), F-14B (Upgrade) or F-14A++) aircraft, or to an aircraft which has been specially fitted with MIL STD 1553B databuses. PTID is not required, since LANTIRN imagery can be displayed (albeit with less fidelity) on the older display screens.

A VF-103 F-14B (BuNo. 161608, Modex 213) was chosen to be the LANTIRN testbed. The aircraft was returned to Northrop Grumman for modification and the test programme then began in March 1995, with the aircraft making its first flight with LANTIRN on 21 March, flown by Commander Alex Hnarakis (VF-103's XO) with Lt Cdr Larry Slade as RIO.

Trials went exceptionally well, and the F-14B MMCAP's PTIDS big screen gave a better LANTIRN picture than could be obtained in the F-15E or F-16. After a series of shake-down flights, in which pod controls were explored and fine-tuned, the aircraft was used to drop four Laser Guided Training Rounds and four inert GBU-16s on the Dare County Range, all but one of the LGTRs scoring direct hits. The exception was dropped outside the weapon's wind limits. Hnarakis and Slade then dropped four live GBU-16s at the Vieques range in Puerto Rico, scoring three bullseyes and one miss as a result of system failure.

By June testing was complete and Lockheed Martin was awarded a contract for production-standard systems for 10 aircraft. VF-103 was awarded the newly instituted Vice Admiral Allen Precision Strike Trophy (named after the Admiral who had driven the programme forward), and 10 squadron aircraft were modified to accept the six LANTIRN pods procured. These aircraft then carried out the further trials necessary before the system could be declared ready for deployment, including a 'mini-cruise' aboard the USS *Enterprise* during April-May 1996. The squadron used its new LANTIRN pods to 'spike' for RN Sea Harriers, and various other aircraft types.

On 14 June 1996, the LANTIRN-equipped F-14 Precision Strike Fighter was formally unveiled as the centrepiece of a lavish official roll-out ceremony in NAS Oceana's Hangar 23, at which Secretary of the Navy John Dalton officially accepted the first pod. Less than 10 months (actually 233 days) had elapsed between the initial signing of the contract and the system being ready for operational use.

Smart procurement

The F-14 LANTIRN program represented a textbook example of streamlined 'smart' acquisition, and has been hailed as "one of the most astonishingly successful military acquisition programme in recent history". The industry/Navy Department/front-line team worked together with brisk efficiency, achieving their goals within the set timescales and under budget. This F-14 Precision Strike team's achievement was officially recognised with the award of the Secretary of Defense Superior Management Award.

On 28 June 1996, VF-103 'Jolly Rogers' took nine LANTIRN-capable aircraft (and five non-LANTIRN TARPS-equipped jets) and six LANTIRN pods with them when they embarked on a Mediterranean cruise aboard the USS *Enterprise*. Because the LANTIRN hand-controller replaced the usual TARPS panel it was not then possible for aircraft to be both TARPS- and LANTIRN-capable, although a 'work-round' has since been developed, and aircraft can now be fully compatible with both systems. Six of the nine VF-103 LANTIRN-compatible aircraft were further modified to allow their crews to use MXV-810 'Cat's Eye' NVGs, which allowed pilots to 'look into the turn', while the LANTIRN FLIR kept looking forwards. These allowed the squadron's FAC(A)-qualified crews to practise their craft by

night, and proved entirely satisfactory, although in the event, the F-14 fleet has been provided with rival ANVIS-9 NVGs, which have a wider field of view, tripled light amplification performance and lower unit price.

Operational success

LANTIRN's first operational cruise was a triumph, and only seven failures were experienced in more than 460 sorties. Failures were quickly rectified, since Lockheed Martin contractors were on board the *Enterprise* throughout the cruise. The LANTIRN pod proved useful for reconnaissance (giving the Tomcat an 'after dark' recce capability) and even in the air-to-air role, proving better at identifying long-range targets than the usual TCS. As well as taking

Between 1993 and 1996 the US Navy slashed its Tomcat squadrons, reducing most air wings to just one F-14 unit instead of two. The training requirement was reduced accordingly, and was consolidated within one squadron (VF-101) at Oceana. The 'Grim Reapers' continue to train new Tomcat crews at both the home base (below) and on available carrier decks (above).

Many of the Tomcat modifications have been applied to the F-14A, allowing it to remain a viable warplane in its last years of service. This VF-41 aircraft, seen on its last cruise in 2001, displays the BOL Sidewinder launch rails which also house chaff dispensers.

part in missions over Bosnia the squadron flew a 690-mile (1110-km) round trip strike mission against targets in Israel as part of Exercise Juniper Hawk. The VF-103 Tomcats scored hits on their four assigned targets and were credited with killing all opposing aircraft, proving the Tomcat's formidable self-escort capability. During the same cruise, VF-103 took the LANTIRN pod to war over Bosnia.

Initially the Navy ordered 13 LANTIRN pods, and a shortage of pods was at first the only major problem with the Tomcat LANTIRN programme. During 1997, for example, both pods and modified aircraft were in such short supply that they had to be transferred from unit to unit as squadrons deployed, and while shore-based at NAS Oceana squadrons often had no suitably equipped aircraft for LANTIRN training. Thus, when VF-103 returned from

deployment on 20 December 1996, its LANTIRN pods and equipment were immediately transferred to VF-32 aboard USS *Theodore Roosevelt*, for use on the MMCAP-modified A-model Tomcats.

At least 25 more pods were quickly ordered, and there were soon sufficient pods for simultaneous deployed operations by several LANTIRN-equipped Carrier Air Wings. Next to deploy with LANTIRN were VF-41 and VF-14, who deployed to the Mediterranean and the Red Sea from spring 1997 until the late summer.

VF-2 became the first Pacific Fleet squadron (and the first F-14D unit) to deploy with LANTIRN, between 1 April 1997 and September 1997 on board USS *Constellation*. With 10 LANTIRN-equipped F-14Ds (which the 'Bounty Hunters' always insist on referring to as Super Tomcats), VF-2 modestly claimed to be "the most potent Strike-Fighter squadron to have ever deployed".

It was followed by VF-211 aboard the USS *Nimitz*, in September 1997. VF-102 deployed on board the USS *George Washington* in October 1997, while VF-154 at NAF Atsugi, Japan, received Upgrade- and LANTIRN-modified Tomcats in September 1997, before deploying to the Persian Gulf in January 1998. The deployment by VF-102 marked the first deployment by aircraft which could carry either TARPS or LANTIRN, three of its aircraft being so equipped.

LANTIRN at war

LANTIRN-equipped 'Bombcats' made their combat debut during Operation Desert Fox at the end of 1998. F-14Bs from VF-32 aboard the USS *Enterprise* were involved in the first wave of attacks, on 16 December 1998, dropping GBU-12s and GBU-24s on Iraqi air defence installations. USS *Carl Vinson* arrived in time for the F-14Ds of VF-213 to participate in the third day's strikes. An official release later stated that: 'The strength of the F-14/LANTIRN programme was ably demonstrated in Desert Fox, and has provided us with a firm bridge to the F/A-18E/F'.

LANTIRN Tomcats were soon in action again. Within nine days of embarking for a six-month Mediterranean cruise, the 'Black Aces' of VF-41 found themselves flying combat missions over Kosovo in support of Operation Deliberate Force. VF-41 flew 384 sorties, totalling more than 1,100 combat hours, and dropped more than 160 tons of laser-guided munitions. The squadron claimed an unprecedented 85 percent success rate.

Back in the Middle East, on 9 September 1999, VF-2's LANTIRN-equipped F-14D Tomcats led the rest of Carrier Air Wing Two in Operation Gun Smoke. The Carrier Air Wing destroyed 35 of the 39 Iraqi anti-aircraft artillery and surface-to-air missile site targets it was assigned, in a large-scale operation which marked the biggest expenditure of ordnance during a single day since Operation Desert Storm.

Above: VF-154's F-14As received individual nicknames, perhaps indicative of their distance from the centre of bureaucracy: they are forward-deployed at Atsugi. Being based in Japan provides less opportunities for carrier deck training during work-up periods.

Right: The 'Red Rippers' of VF-11 are significant in that, since the return of VF-14 and VF-41 in November 2001, they form part of the only air wing which retains two Tomcat squadrons – CVW-7 aboard John F. Kennedy. VF-11 has a LANTIRN speciality within the wing.

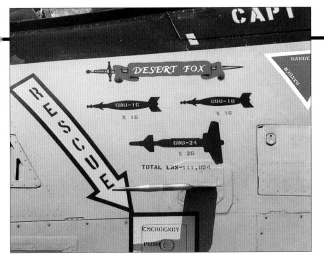

Despite this combat record, and even with the night and precision attack capabilities conferred by LANTIRN, the F-14 is not a true replacement for the A-6, nor even a real competitor to the F/A-18C. The FLIR's effectiveness can be severely constrained by the thinnest cloud or the lightest rain, and worse conditions can effectively ground the LANTIRN Tomcat.

Despite its limitations, LANTIRN is undergoing development to enhance its capabilities. Under the 'LANTIRN 40K' programme the Navy hopes to extend the firing limit from an altitude of 25,000 ft (7620 m) AMSL to 40,000 ft (12192 m), while achieving the specification ranges of 20 miles (32 km) (combat laser) and 12 miles (19.5 km) (training laser). Previously, the LANTIRN pod proved prone to arcing at higher altitudes, and required new, higher sensitivity laser receivers. 'LANTIRN 40K' components were laboratory-tested and installed in a targeting pod, and the laser was then successfully fired at simulated altitudes of up to 45,000 ft (13716 m) in a test chamber at Lockheed Martin's Orlando facility.

Flight testing of the prototype pods began in late August 2000, and 'LANTIRN 40K' component retrofit starting at the end of 2000. The first 'LANTIRN 40K' pods were scheduled for Fleet introduction in February 2001. LANTIRN Tomcats are also receiving new weapons, most recently the GBU-24E/B Enhanced Penetrating LGB and the GBU-31/32 Joint Direct Attack Munition (JDAM).

Modern weapons

Integration of the GPS-guided JDAM on the F-14 had been planned for many years, and the programme was even funded. In fact, LANTIRN integration was achieved using funding originally allocated for F-14/JDAM and, ironically, provided the F-14 with the GPS solution on which JDAM relies. Unlike an LGB, JDAM does not rely on laser designation, but instead has an INU, a GPS receiver and steerable tail surfaces, with the bomb being accurately 'flown' onto a given set of GPS co-ordinates. The weapon is therefore entirely unaffected by the weather and atmos-

pheric conditions which may affect a laser-guided weapon, although accuracy may be slightly reduced. JDAM 'kits' (with new tails and side fairings) will allow existing 'dumb' bombs to be converted simply and cheaply.

JDAM is now in widespread service, and was used 'in anger' during operation Allied Force in Kosovo. Some 87,000 JDAM kits have been ordered by the US DoD, and the weapon will be used by the USAF, USN and USMC. The JDAM programme for the F-14 is reportedly progressing well. The Naval Strike Aircraft Test Squadron (part of the Naval Air Warfare Center Aircraft Division at NAS Patuxent River) completed separation tests for an envelope of up to Mach 0.95 with a minimum number of drops, and Weapons Test at Point Mugu quickly authorised a full-up JDAM drop from an F-14B Upgrade aircraft. The weapon was soon cleared for service, transforming the Tomcat into a GPS weapons player and freeing it from its previous long-standing reliance on unguided or laser-guided weapons. VF-102 is believed to have deployed to the northern Arabian Sea with full JDAM compatibility, though it remains to be seen whether Tomcats used the weapon during Operation Enduring Freedom.

While making strenuous efforts to expand the scope of the Tomcat's air-to-ground 'bite', the US Navy has not ignored the aircraft's defensive capabilities. Swedish BOL chaff dispensers were added (in the four underwing LAU-138 missile launch rails) as part of the MMCAP upgrade, though integration of these with the Tomcat's AN/ALE-39 expendable dispensing system was primitive. An AN/ALE-47 retrofit programme was therefore devel-

Above: An F-14B from VF-102 'Diamondbacks' leaps from the waist cat of Roosevelt. F110-powered F-14s have sufficient thrust in military (non-afterburning) power to launch without reheat, whereas TF30-powered F-14As must use Zone Three reheat.

Above left: F-14B operator VF-32 was the first unit to use the F-14/LANTIRN combination in action, during three nights of attacks on Iraq during Operation Desert Fox in December 1998. The squadron's bomb log (16 GBU-10s, 16 GBU-12s and 26 GBU-24s) is faithfully recorded on the nose of the 'CAG-bird'.

Below: A LANTIRN-carrying F-14D of VF-213 recovers aboard the 'Starship Vinson' during February 2001 work-ups. By October the squadron's Tomcats were in action over Afghanistan.

Above: The VF-41 squadron commander's aircraft received this nose art after the unit's fine showing in Operation Allied Force. The Tomcat was especially useful in the FAC(A) role, being used to remain on-station over designated 'kill boxes' to direct and designate for other attack aircraft after it had dropped its own ordnance. In this role the extra pair of eyes is of inestimable value.

Above: With LGBs in the 'tunnel' and LANTIRN clutched to station 8B, a 'Black Aces' Tomcat prepares to launch from Theodore Roosevelt during Allied Force. This campaign saw the 'Bombcat' come of age and proved the success of the LANTIRN integration. One former A-6 B/N, now an F-14 RIO, stated that the task of acquiring targets for designation was much easier in the Tomcat, mainly as a function of the embedded GPS.

Many of VF-41's missions over Kosovo were conducted by night. Recent Tomcat upgrades have made the cockpit displays fully NVG-compatible.

oped, under which the new system will replace the existing AN/ALE-39 systems on all surviving F-14Bs and F-14Ds. The replacement will involve a 'box for box' swap, together with the removal of unnecessary AN/ALE-39 components and the loading of a platform-specific Mission Data File (MDF) within the ALE-47's own Operational Flight Program (OFP), which is common to all Navy Aircraft. A new NVG-compatible Digital Control Display Unit (DCDU) will be fitted in the rear cockpit.

Integration of AN/ALE-47 will provide a step change in capability and reliability, and may even reduce support costs. The AN/ALE-47 will provide greater programming flexibility, and an expanded inventory of expendables, including BOL chaff/IR cartridges. The AN/ALE-47 will be fully integrated with all four of the Tomcat's BOL launchers, enabling complex deployment sequences using expendables from the BOL rails and the fuselage-mounted 'buckets', as part of a combined dispensing programme. The OFP supports seven different dispenser programmes.

Functional and carrier suitability testing of the ALE-47 on the F-14 was carried out by the Strike Aircraft Test

Squadron during the summer of 2000, leading to full deployment during 2001.

Upgrades do not always make things better. This was the case with the new HUD installed in F-14B (Upgrade) aircraft as part of the MMCAP programme. This was found to be 'marginally effective' and, with the erosion of the head-down Vertical Display Indicator's (VDI) reliability, caused real concerns over the impact on F-14B flight safety, as well as making interoperability difficult. Together referred to as the Vertical Display Indicator Group (VDIG), the HUD and VDI were controlled by an analog Display Indicator, and it was decided that all needed to be replaced.

Display replacement programme

The Strike Aircraft Test Squadron at Patuxent River received an F-14B Upgrade aircraft – ('Vandy 241') from VX-9 det Point Mugu – to complete testing of the replacement VDIG(R), and this aircraft was also used to complete all other F-14B Upgrade testing, including GBU-24E/B, JDAM and AN/ALE-47.

The replacement VDIG consisted of an advanced but off-the-self Flight Visions Inc Sparrow Hawk HUD, a new head-down VDI and a new colour video camera. The original analog Display Indicator was replaced by a new Modular Mission Display Processor (MMDP). The new HUD retains F-14B(U)-type air-to-air symbology, and uses F-14D-type symbology for take-off, cruise and landing, but offers an even larger field of view than the HUD installed in the F-14D. A so-called 'power carrot', which serves as a predictor of the aircraft's future energy state, and which is a feature of the F-14D HUD, will be incorporated in all HUD modes. These changes significantly improved the quantity and quality of information presented, and improved overall system reliability.

Initial flight tests of elements of the new VDIG(R) were conducted from November 1999 by NAWC's Weapons Division at Point Mugu, before a Developmental Test (DT) flight clearance recommendation was issued, allowing full testing to begin at the NAWC's Aircraft Division at Patuxent River. VX-9 then conducted operational assessment of the system, resulting in a fleet clearance in the autumn of 2000. Some 82 surviving F-14Bs are receiving this upgrade.

Taming the 'Turkey'

Although generally possessed of excellent handling qualities, especially by contrast with its predecessors, the F-14 does have some extremely undesirable flying quality characteristics in both the high angle of attack regime and in the landing configuration, and over the years these have resulted in a number of aircraft and aircrew losses, with engine failure/asymmetric thrust/stall-spin departures proving a particular problem.

Late in the Tomcat's career, a new Digital Flight Control System, developed by GEC Marconi Avionics (and based on that of the Eurofighter Typhoon), was procured for the F-14 fleet, under a 1996 $84 million contract. The DFCS programme has been conducted by a combined, integrated project team consisting of Navy and Industry personnel. GEC-Marconi Avionics provided the DFCS computer hardware, operational flight programme software and technical support. Northrop Grumman supplied flight test support and system integration support and conducted flying quality and structural analyses. The Naval Air Warfare Center Aircraft Division (NAWC-AD) at Patuxent River was responsible for development, integration and flight testing.

The DFCS team used two testbed aircraft, an F-14A (modex SD/207) and an F-14D (modex SD/230), and these completed clearance testing of the DFCS's mode I on board the USS *Enterprise* (CVN 65) in a variety of wind and sea conditions.

Fleet introduction of the F-14 DFCS (in its initial fleet release software version OFP 4.1.1) began in July 1999, with VF-14 becoming the first unit to deploy with the DFCS F-14A. DFCS was subsequently incorporated into all remaining F-14A, B and D variants under an aggressive and rapid transition schedule. All front-line F-14 squadrons

have now completed DFCS integration, with VF-102 completing the last AFCS deployment in April 2000.

The new DFCS has already been a great success story, even in its initial release form. The system greatly increases departure resistance and provides improved recovery capabilities when the aircraft does depart. The new DFCS also significantly improves handling qualities on approach. As well as enhancing flight safety, the new DFCS has proved more reliable and more maintainable than the original analog AFCS that it was designed to replace

The final DFCS software version (OFP 4.4), with improvements to the existing control laws for the automatic carrier landing system (ACLS), was released in August 2000, having completed flight testing aboard the USS *Enterprise* (CVN 65) in April 2000.

The new software load also included new control laws for the roll SAS, which eased manoeuvring flight envelope restrictions, and expanded the FCS self-test fault reporting capability.

Having undertaken three nights of operations during Desert Fox in December 1998, Enterprise was nearing the end of its operational deployment when Allied Force was launched against Serbia and Kosovo. The carrier had its deployment extended and arrived in the Mediterranean on 20 April 1999, the 27th day of the NATO campaign. After three days the Pentagon decided not to call upon the air wing, which included the F-14As of VF-14, for combat missions.

Paveway II-carrying F-14A Tomcats are seen during Mediterranean operations aboard Enterprise in April/May 1999. The 'CAG-bird' (left) displays special markings for the squadron's 80th anniversary, the unit claiming to be the oldest US Navy squadron. After return to the US at the end of this deployment, VF-14 became the first unit to field F-14As with the DFCS (Digital Flight Control System) installed. Other A-model units (VF-41, VF-154 and VF-211) followed swiftly after, as did B/D squadrons.

Two views show VF-32 F-14Bs recovering aboard USS Harry S. Truman *during operations in the Persian Gulf during the carrier's first operational deployment in 2000/2001. The F-14 has always been somewhat tricky on the approach, even with the benefit of the DLC (direct lift control) which uses the automatic lowering and raising of spoilers to increase and decrease lift without altering aircraft attitude. Many of the problems arose from the high residual thrust of the turbofan engines, which required very low throttle settings where the engines are unresponsive, and a tendency to 'float' on the approach. Many of the approach problems have been alleviated by the DFCS.*

The final ACLS configuration includes hardware and software modifications and has replaced the original pitch attitude command system with a new vertical velocity, or 'h-dot', command system with integrated direct lift control (DLC) giving extremely smooth glideslope control.

The lady vanishes

Many had hoped that the F-14's new capabilities and new usefulness as a long-range multi-role strike fighter would see the fleet being maintained at its late 1980s level, with two squadrons on every carrier deck. For a brief period following the withdrawal of the A-6, this was achieved, with the composition of the standard Air Wing changing to incorporate two slimmed-down F-14 squadrons and three squadrons of F/A-18Cs (often including a USMC unit). In the event this was judged to be impossible to sustain, since attrition and an uneven distribution of flying hours/fatigue led to a severe shortage of F-14 airframes. It became clear that maintaining a single F-14 squadron within each Air Wing would be a more realistic target, and this became the new 'standard' Air Wing composition. Between the end of Desert Storm and the end of 1996, the US Navy lost 14 F-14 squadrons – more than half the total. With 12 squadrons and 10 Air Wings, Tomcat numbers were sufficient to retain two Air Wings at what Tomcat supporters saw as the 'optimum' composition, with two squadrons of F-14s augmented by two Hornet units. The remainder transitioned to a one-Tomcat VF/three-

Hornet VFA squadron mix. In practise, the use of the Hornet rather than the Tomcat had few disadvantages in the post-Cold War world, since the newer Hornet proved more reliable, more maintainable and more capable than the ageing F-14.

Experience showed that there was a strong likelihood that in any given strike package, at least one F-14 was likely to abort for technical reasons, while Hornets tended not to, while the maintenance hours required to sustain a single Tomcat sortie remained very high, making it difficult for F-14 squadrons to maintain a high sortie rate, and requiring their maintenance departments to be large and well-manned. Finally, even with LANTIRN and all of the other upgrades, the Tomcat was not as versatile nor as effective as the Hornet, and offered no advantages, except where payload/range was an issue or where an extra pair of eyes was relevant, such as in the forward air control role.

When the 1997 Quadrennial Defence Review (QDR) suggested that production of the Super Hornet should be cut by almost 50 percent, from just over 1,000 to 548 units, many saw this as an opportunity for revitalising the Tomcat, though in truth, the F-14's fate had long been decided, and the aircraft will retire by 2008. If fewer Super Hornets are procured, they will instead be replaced by the new F-35 Joint Strike Fighter.

Recce Tomcat

If the Tomcat remains something of a 'poor relation' in terms of the scope of its air-to-ground capabilities, it remains the only carrierborne tactical reconnaissance asset. However, to infer that the Tomcat's usefulness in the reconnaissance role is a function of the lack of any alternative would be extremely misleading, since the aircraft has always had a fine reputation as a recce platform, thanks to the excellence of the TARPS (Tactical Air Reconnaisance Pod System) reconnaissance pod, the skill and elan of Tomcat TARPS crews, and the professionalism and dedication of those who process and exploit TARPS imagery.

The success of TARPS is perhaps surprising, since it originated as an interim solution to the US Navy's requirement for a carrierborne recce aircraft to replace the RA-5C Vigilante and RF-8G Crusader. Initial studies looked at developing and deploying a dedicated RF-14 reconnaissance variant of the Tomcat, but by 1974 it was clear that such an aircraft could not be ready in time, and the 'interim' solution of a Tomcat recce pod was adopted. This, it was confidently predicted, would soon be replaced by a dedicated RF-18 version of the Hornet, with a reconnaissance pallet in the former gun bay.

Development of TARPS began in April 1976, using an off-the-shelf system originally developed for the A-7 Corsair, but never placed into production or service. Prototype pods began flight testing in April 1977, on the fifth YF-14A (BuNo. 157984). The original (finned) version of the pod was carried on the right-hand intake duct, in place of a drop tank. During development the pod was moved to the right-hand rear fuselage Phoenix station (no. 5) and became more streamlined and refined in appearance.

Weighing 1,750-lb (794-kg) and 17 ft (5.18 m) in length, the TARPS pod contained four bays, or stations, with the fourth bay containing the electronics required to relay information to the RIO's display in the rear cockpit, and to the AN/ASQ-172 data display set, which may be used to mark the film to allow easier interpretation. Station 1 in the nose of the TARPS pod was designed to accommodate the KS-87B framing camera, used in the vertical or forward oblique mode with a 3- or 6-in (7.62- or 15.24-cm) focal length lens. Following a TARPS upgrade, this could be replaced by a new KS-153T camera, or an LLTV video camera. Station 2 was designed to hold the KA-99, a low-altitude, panoramic camera with a focal length of 9 in (22.86 cm) giving horizon-to-horizon coverage. The KA-99 is the primary sensor on most reconnaissance missions and represents the heart of the TARPS system, but since the TARPS upgrade this can now be replaced by a KS-153A or KS-153L. An AN/AAD-5 infra-red line scanner completed the TARPS pod's array of sensors, in Station 3.

The pod and its sensors are monitored and controlled by the Naval Flight Officer/Radar Intercept Officer (NFO/RIO) in the rear cockpit, who has a new TARPS display although the pilot is also provided with a camera on-off control on the stick.

Although TARPS imposes only a minimal penalty on aircraft performance and makes little demand on the aircraft systems, it does require power, signal and environmental control connections that are not normally available at Station 5. Aircraft therefore have to be specially converted and wired to carry the pod. Initially, some 65 F-14As were wired to carry TARPS, some of which were subsequently converted to F-14B standards. The 38 new-build F-14Bs were not wired for TARPs, unlike the 37 new-build F-14Ds and the 18 F-14D conversions, although a handful from Block 160 (163412, 163415, 163416 and 163417) have since been de-modified as NF-14Ds.

The F-14 retains significant defensive capabilities with the pod attached, although underfuselage AIM-54s cannot be carried. Outboard missiles (usually two AIM-7s and two AIM-9s) can be carried, and the 20-mm cannon can be fired while the pod is being carried. When not carrying TARPS, the aircraft can quickly be re-roled to full Phoenix or 'Bombcat' configuration.

TARPS enters service

After successfully completing testing, procurement of TARPS began in 1978. The system underwent OPEVAL in 1979 and the first operational deployment was undertaken by VF-84 in 1981. Thereafter, one squadron aboard each carrier was always TARPS-capable, deploying with several TARPS-compatible aircraft and a number of pods. When Air Wings went down to a single Tomcat squadron, the remaining unit was either the TARPS squadron, or took over the TARPS role.

By the 1980s, wet-film sensors were becoming increasingly old-fashioned. Imagery could not be datalinked, and film had to be processed (and sometimes even printed)

The F-14B is the most numerous version remaining in front-line service, equipping five squadrons. Most have been fitted with full LANTIRN and TARPS capability, and they have undergone the F-14B Upgrade programme. Among the less-visible features of the upgrade is a structural life extension to 7,500 hours.

Expendable countermeasures are released by the AN/ALE-39 dispensers under the rear fuselage and from the CelsiusTech BOL missile rail launchers. The new AN/ALE-47 system will allow a fully integrated and programmable release of chaff bundles or flares from all of the dispensers, significantly enhancing the Tomcat's protection against missiles. The AN/ALE-50 towed decoy system is unlikely to be applied to the aircraft.

USS Enterprise (CVN 65) was nearing the end of a NorLant deployment when terrorists struck in the US on 11 September. The deployment was immediately extended as part of the US mobilisation response. The two Tomcat squadrons aboard were VF-14 (illustrated), and VF-41 both flying the F-14A. When they returned to the US in November, they became the first Tomcat units to transition to the Super Hornet.

before it could be interpreted and exploited. This all took time (and expensive manpower) and forced a reliance on environmentally damaging chemicals, and as the performance of electro-optical sensors improved, the reconnaissance community generally began looking more and more at EO-based systems.

As the troubled ATARS system stalled due to technical and political difficulties, attention turned towards updating TARPS, to allow it to remain viable and useful through to the end of the Tomcat's life. The obvious solution was to convert the TARPS pod to carry EO sensors.

The Tomcat's new 'Digital TARPS' reconnaissance pod has already proved extremely successful, its EO-based sensors offering faster turnaround of imagery, better performance in poor light, poor weather and haze, while offering cost and manpower savings in processing and exploitation. The first version of digital TARPS, known as TARPS-DI, entered service in 1996 with VF-32, which deployed with the system in November 1996. TARPS-DI contained a Pulnix digital camera in the former KS-87B station (Station 1). The new Pulnix uses only the downward-facing

window and can store up to 200 images onboard. The RIO can review these images and transmit them to the carrier or any other suitably equipped receiver within a 186-mile (300-km) range. The system is able to downlink imagery in near real time for battle damage assessment, although only by 'line-of-sight'. The next version, TARPS-CD, began testing in 1998, adding real-time EO step-framing.

Both attack and reconnaissance operations have been revolutionised by the introduction of FTI (Fast Tactical Imagery), a real-time tactical datalink, first deployed with VF-14 and VF-41 in April 1999. This allows TARPS, TCS or LANTIRN imagery to be transmitted from 'stand-off range' to the carrier or to any other FTI-equipped platform. Moreover, LANTIRN can be used to obtain GPS-quality target co-ordinates, which can then be transmitted (with imagery) to other aircraft.

Tomcat today

Although the US Navy's Tomcat fleet is at its smallest ever size, and although the first front-line units have already begun conversion to the Super Hornet, and even despite its

A VF-41 F-14A refuels from a VS-24 S-3B on 5 October 2001, two days before Tomcats led the first US Navy strikes into Afghanistan as part of Operation Enduring Freedom. As well as delivering Paveway laser-guided bombs, the F-14s have also performed the 'fast-FAC' mission, using LANTIRN to designate targets for Hornets.

Clutching a pair of GBU-16s to its belly, a VF-41 F-14A launches from Enterprise for an Enduring Freedom mission on 18 October, while the squadron's 'CAG-bird' manoeuvres into position behind. After heavy involvement in the opening phase of the campaign, Enterprise and its two F-14 squadrons were withdrawn, replaced by Roosevelt.

Below: Along with Enterprise, initial Enduring Freedom missions were launched by Carl Vinson, whose single F-14D squadron (VF-213) was heavily involved. This scene from the third night of the war shows JDAMs (for F/A-18s) and GBU-16s, although the Tomcat appears to be armed with Mk 20 Rockeyes.

limited operational capabilities, the F-14 has continued to provide the US Navy with a vital asset, and one which has seen action on a number of occasions.

On 6 January 1999, an F-14D of VF-213 from the USS *Carl Vinson*, participating in Operation Southern Watch, fired two AIM-54 Phoenix AAMs at a pair of Iraqi MiG-25s, marking the first USN combat use of the Tomcat's big missile (it had been used in anger by Iranian Tomcats). The weapons missed their targets, which were able to turn away outside the Tomcat's relatively narrow radar gimbal limits at the long ranges involved, though parametric details of the engagement are naturally highly classified. The poor combat record of the AIM-54 in US Navy service has been echoed during exercises where, even in apparently ideal conditions, the AIM-54 seems to have a relatively poor 'strike rate'. Supporters of the Phoenix inevitably quote the results of the 'Six-on-Six' ripple fire test carried out by Commander John 'Smoke' Wilson, with Lt Cdr Jack H. Hawver in the back seat, at Point Mugu on 21 November 1973. The test was taken as proof that the Tomcat/Phoenix could successfully make a simultaneous interception of six targets, flying at different heights and airspeeds.

Others remain unconvinced even by the test, not least because only four of the drone targets were downed. One BQM-34E 'lost augmentation' and the missile missed, while another suffered a failure and missed the QT-33 drone it was fired at. Critics doubted the validity of a test which had been studiously pre-rehearsed (with drones flying at the same speeds and heights, and on the same headings in order to allow the crew to work out and practise the appropriate launch sequence). Others questioned the realism of the narrow 15-mile (24-km) front along which the targets

approached and the 2,000-ft (610-m) maximum separation between targets. It was also pointed out that the targets all had augmentation (to make them better radar targets) and were flying at 'easy' speeds of between Mach 0.6 and Mach 1.1, with no evasive manoeuvring, jamming or chaff. The test, they averred, presented a modest challenge, while no-one could expect an enemy bomber formation to behave so co-operatively.

Whether or not the test was the success which Grumman, Westinghouse, Hughes and the Navy claimed, it

Below and below left: When Theodore Roosevelt arrived in the war zone it brought with it the F-14Bs of VF-102 'Diamondbacks', these aircraft being JDAM-capable. Below is a night launch from 21 October, during the period in which F-14s flew combat missions from three carriers.

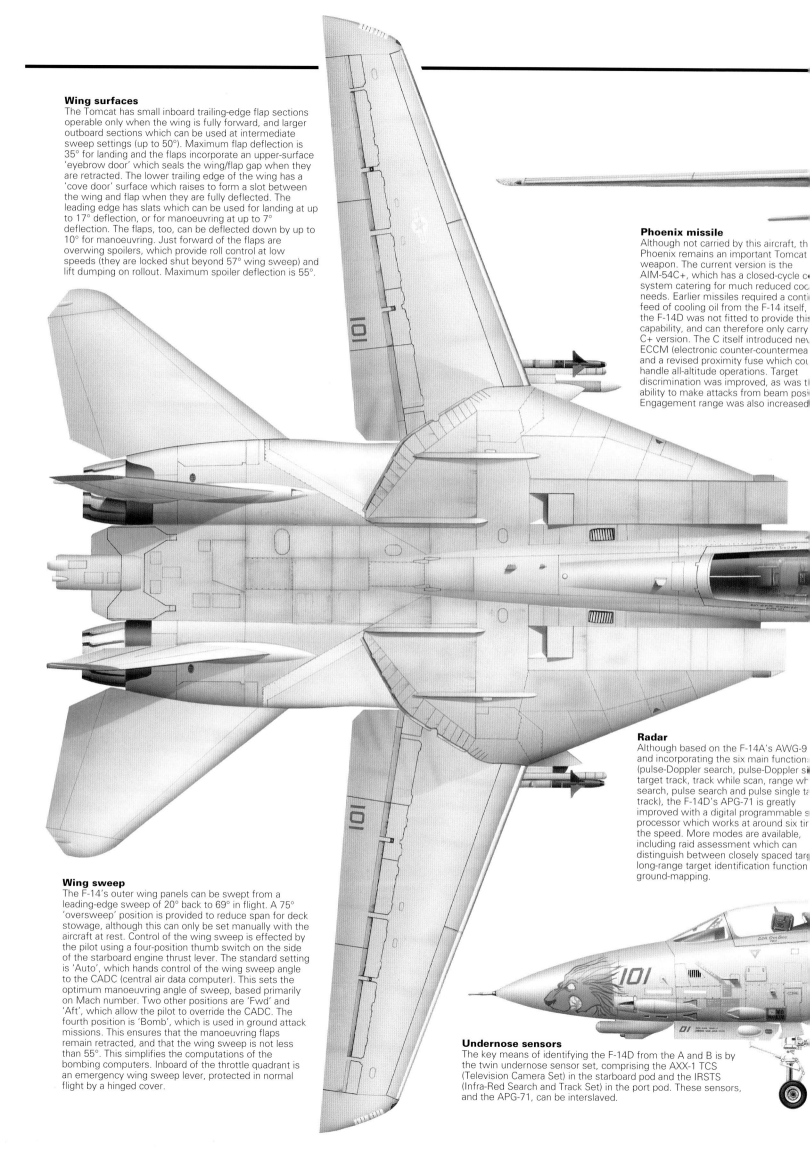

Wing surfaces
The Tomcat has small inboard trailing-edge flap sections
operable only when the wing is fully forward, and larger
outboard sections which can be used at intermediate
sweep settings (up to 50°). Maximum flap deflection is
35° for landing and the flaps incorporate an upper-surface
'eyebrow door' which seals the wing/flap gap when they
are retracted. The lower trailing edge of the wing has a
'cove door' surface which raises to form a slot between
the wing and flap when they are fully deflected. The
leading edge has slats which can be used for landing at up
to 17° deflection, or for manoeuvring at up to 7°
deflection. The flaps, too, can be deflected down by up to
10° for manoeuvring. Just forward of the flaps are
overwing spoilers, which provide roll control at low
speeds (they are locked shut beyond 57° wing sweep) and
lift dumping on rollout. Maximum spoiler deflection is 55°.

Phoenix missile
Although not carried by this aircraft, th
Phoenix remains an important Tomcat
weapon. The current version is the
AIM-54C+, which has a closed-cycle coc
system catering for much reduced coc
needs. Earlier missiles required a conti
feed of cooling oil from the F-14 itself,
the F-14D was not fitted to provide this
capability, and can therefore only carry
C+ version. The C itself introduced nev
ECCM (electronic counter-countermea
and a revised proximity fuse which cou
handle all-altitude operations. Target
discrimination was improved, as was tl
ability to make attacks from beam posi'
Engagement range was also increased

Radar
Although based on the F-14A's AWG-9
and incorporating the six main function
(pulse-Doppler search, pulse-Doppler si
target track, track while scan, range wh
search, pulse search and pulse single ta
track), the F-14D's APG-71 is greatly
improved with a digital programmable s
processor which works at around six tin
the speed. More modes are available,
including raid assessment which can
distinguish between closely spaced targ
long-range target identification function
ground-mapping.

Wing sweep
The F-14's outer wing panels can be swept from a
leading-edge sweep of 20° back to 69° in flight. A 75°
'oversweep' position is provided to reduce span for deck
stowage, although this can only be set manually with the
aircraft at rest. Control of the wing sweep is effected by
the pilot using a four-position thumb switch on the side
of the starboard engine thrust lever. The standard setting
is 'Auto', which hands control of the wing sweep angle
to the CADC (central air data computer). This sets the
optimum manoeuvring angle of sweep, based primarily
on Mach number. Two other positions are 'Fwd' and
'Aft', which allow the pilot to override the CADC. The
fourth position is 'Bomb', which is used in ground attack
missions. This ensures that the manoeuvring flaps
remain retracted, and that the wing sweep is not less
than 55°. This simplifies the computations of the
bombing computers. Inboard of the throttle quadrant is
an emergency wing sweep lever, protected in normal
flight by a hinged cover.

Undernose sensors
The key means of identifying the F-14D from the A and B is by
the twin undernose sensor set, comprising the AXX-1 TCS
(Television Camera Set) in the starboard pod and the IRSTS
(Infra-Red Search and Track Set) in the port pod. These sensors,
and the APG-71, can be interslaved.

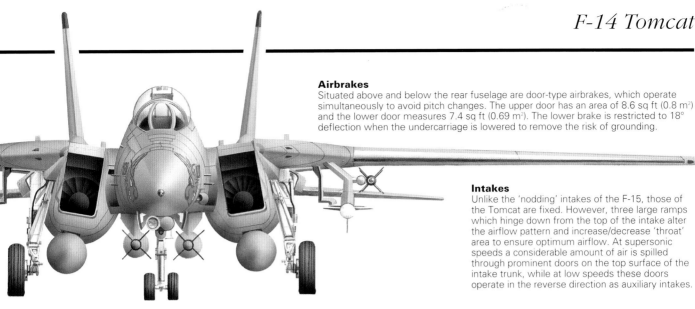

Airbrakes
Situated above and below the rear fuselage are door-type airbrakes, which operate simultaneously to avoid pitch changes. The upper door has an area of 8.6 sq ft (0.8 m²) and the lower door measures 7.4 sq ft (0.69 m²). The lower brake is restricted to 18° deflection when the undercarriage is lowered to remove the risk of grounding.

Intakes
Unlike the 'nodding' intakes of the F-15, those of the Tomcat are fixed. However, three large ramps which hinge down from the top of the intake alter the airflow pattern and increase/decrease 'throat' area to ensure optimum airflow. At supersonic speeds a considerable amount of air is spilled through prominent doors on the top surface of the intake trunk, while at low speeds these doors operate in the reverse direction as auxiliary intakes.

...ser-guided bombs
...s aircraft is depicted carrying two GBU-24A/B ...nbs, the penetrating warhead version of the ...00-lb (907-kg) class Paveway III. The Paveway III ...apons, distinguished by their fixed seeker heads ...larger wing assemblies, are considerably more ...urate than the Paveway IIs as they use ...portional guidance rather than full deflection of ...control surfaces. This, in turn, means they ...noeuvre less, and can convert more of the kinetic ...rgy imparted by the launch aircraft into stand-off ...ge. Another feature is the ability to follow a pre-...grammed attack profile, depending on the target. ...eway III kits have only been applied to to ...00-lb warheads, whereas the Paveway II kit is ...ilable for a range of warhead weights.

...werplant
...e Pratt & Whitney TF30 turbofan had always been regarded as the ...hilles heel of the F-14A, particularly in its susceptibility to compressor ...lls. Although successive versions, culminating in the -414, alleviated ...ny of the problems, a new engine in the form of General Electric's ...10-GE-400 fully ended the Tomcat's long-running engine saga. Fitting the ...10 (which has an 82 per cent parts commonality with the F110-GE-100 ...ed in the F-16) proved straightforward, with only minor changes to ...condary structures. The engine itself has a 50-in (1.27-m) section added ...wnstream of the turbine, which moves the intake face further forward ...compared with the TF30) and the nozzle further aft.
...Mass flow through the engine rises from the TF30's 250 lb (113.4 kg) ...second at take-off to 270 lb (122.5 kg), while thrust is theoretically ...reased to 29,000 lb (129.05 kN), although in the Tomcat the thrust is ...uced to 27,000 lb (120.15 kN) to match the engine better to the F-14's ...uirements. The extra thrust allows the Tomcat to launch without using ...erburner unless at high weights. Further advantages of the F110 are ...efree throttle handling, greater reliability and TBO (time between ...erhaul), and a significant reduction in fuel burn, equating to an average ...ssion radius increase of around 62 per cent. The engine itself has a ...ee-stage bypass fan and a nine-stage compressor providing a ...mpression ratio of 31. Ahead of the fan is a bullet spinner and 20 fixed ...es, each with a variable flap on the trailing edge.

Northrop Grumman F-14D Tomcat

VF-213 'Black Lions'
CVW-11, USS *Carl Vinson* (CVN 70)

USS *Carl Vinson* and Air Wing Eleven were among the first US forces to be assigned to Operation Enduring Freedom, the US government's 'war on terrorism' launched after the attacks of 11 September 2001. While on a WestPac cruise, the carrier received orders to take up station in the Arabian Sea off the coast of Pakistan, where it awaited the call to launch raids into Afghanistan against Al Qaeda terrorist training camps and Taliban military positions. Such operations began on 7 October. At the forefront of the raids were the Tomcat squadrons of *Carl Vinson* (VF-213) and *Enterprise* (VF-14 and VF-41), the latter carrier having had its NorLant deployment extended to allow its participation in Enduring Freedom.

In the attack role the principal weapon of the Tomcat is the laser-guided bomb, aimed using the LANTIRN forward-looking infra-red/laser designator pod carried on the lower starboard pylon (station 8B). This aircraft is shown carrying a typical 'laser-bomber' loadout, with bombs carried on modified Phoenix pallets in the 'tunnel', as the underfuselage area between the engine trunks is known. It is assigned to the squadron commander, and carries the lion nose marking which appeared in early 2001.

Electronic defences
As one would expect, the F-14 is well protected against a variety of threats. The principal warning system is the ALR-67, which receives across a 1 GHz to 16 GHz range. It can identify radars by cross-checking received signals with an onboard threat library, and presents an annotated display with azimuth and type details on a screen in the rear cockpit. Jamming equipment consists of the ALQ-165 ASPJ (Airborne Self Protection Jammer) in some aircraft or the older ALQ-126 DECM (deception ECM). ASPJ was to be fitted to all Navy aircraft, but these plans were cancelled. However, F-14Ds continue to use the equipment, even it does not meet its full specification. Some of the ALR-67 and ALQ-165 antennas are housed in a reprofiled leading-edge extension. Mechanical countermeasures include ALE-39 dispensers under the tail, and BOL Sidewinder launch rails which contain a dispenser in the rear. The ALR-43 ECA (Expanded Chaff Adaptor) can also be carried.

Internal fuel
The total internal capacity of 2,397 US gal (9074 litres) is carried in five main areas (left and right outer wing interspar voids, forward fuselage cells, rear fuselage cells and wing box carry-through). The left engine is usually fed by fuel in the left wing, rear fuselage and left side of the wing box, while the right engine draws from the right wing, forward fuselage and right side of the wing box.

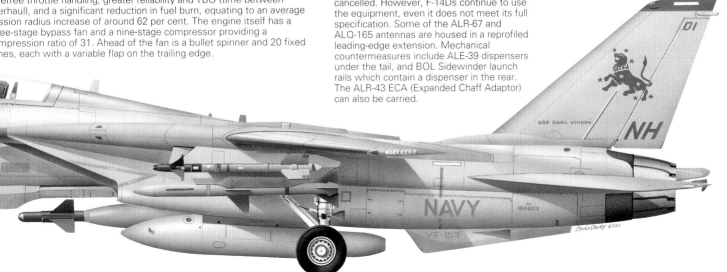

Considering its role and the amount of time it has been in service, it is somewhat surprising that the F-14 has only one confirmed air-to-air 'kill' in US Navy service – and that was over an Mi-8 helicopter during Desert Storm. This should not disguise the fact that the F-14 remains in the top drawer of air combat fighters. US Navy air combat training remains among the best in the world, although F-14 crews now have to work even harder to achieve the requisite skill levels in both air fighting and ground-attack regimes, and all the while operating a notoriously 'difficult' aircraft from a boat in the middle of the ocean. Compared with the F/A-18C, the Tomcat's two-man crew certainly aids air-to-ground work.

was certainly expensive – the 38-second sequence being costed at a staggering $154,000 (in 1973 dollars!) per second. "It was like setting fire to a 10-storey car park filled with brand new Cadillacs" recalled pilot Wilson later.

Testing of the improved AIM-54C began at Point Mugu in 1979, at the same time that Iran's F-14As and some 200 Phoenix missiles were falling into revolutionary hands. Point Mugu was forced to develop counter-countermeasures against its own AIM-54, and had to ensure that the capabilities of the new F-14A/AIM-54C would not be compromised by enemy knowledge of the earlier system. Development testing at Point Mugu included another spectacular 'Six-on-Six' test, this time conducted before a congressional committee. This demonstrated that the weapon system could simultaneously acquire and track six independent targets, and then launch and guide six missiles, each to a selected target, although it is not known whether the new test repeated the unrealistic test conditions of the first.

Although the AIM-120 AMRAAM cannot match the 'brochure range' figures claimed for the Phoenix, the missile is widely believed to be very much more effective. This seemed to be acknowledged when the US Navy opted to add AIM-120 AMRAAM capability to the F-14D when its computer software was updated. This plan was subse-

quently cancelled and the shorter-range F/A-18C, which does enjoy full AMRAAM capability, has assumed an increasing share of the air defence burden. Moreover, advanced derivatives of the AMRAAM have been developed with ramjet boosters which dramatically increase range, probably to beyond the reach of the Phoenix.

The AIM-54C was given another chance to prove its mettle in September 1999, when a VF-2 F-14D fired a single AIM-54 at a pair of Iraqi MiG-23s (or MiG-25s, according to some sources) during Operation Gun Smoke, missing again.

Enduring Freedom

Regular bombing and reconnaissance missions have continued over Iraq, and more recently over Afghanistan. When the USA launched retaliatory strikes following the terrorist attacks on the World Trade Center and Pentagon on 11 September 2001, they relied principally on ship- and submarine-launched cruise missiles, and on B-52 and B-1B bombers forward deployed to Diego Garcia, together with two Carrier Air Wings operating from aircraft-carriers in the northern Arabian Sea. Politically prevented from using most nearby land-bases in the Persian Gulf and in Iran and India, and unwilling to over-use bases in front-line Pakistan and Uzbekistan, aircraft-carriers proved the only way of applying tactical air power in Afghanistan, though their aircraft were operating at the limit of their range, and relied on air-to-air refuelling en route to and from the target. The air war over Afghanistan has a remarkably low profile, and very few details were released about its conduct, let alone about its effectiveness.

After an initial brief phase of night attacks, the carriers launched a handful of sorties on most days of the campaign, with the F/A-18Cs and F-14s operating in conditions of total air supremacy and with only the most primitive surface AA threat. They attacked targets from medium altitude, mainly using Paveway laser-guided bombs, partly switching to CBUs when attacks switched to the Taliban front line. Despite a low intensity of operations, carrier-based tankers were unable to meet the demand for fuel, and RAF and USAF tankers were active in supporting operations by the carriers' Tomcats and Hornets.

When Operation Enduring Freedom began, the US Navy could call upon USS *Carl Vinson* (with CVW-11 embarked, including the F-14Ds of VF-213) and USS *Enterprise* (with CVW-8 embarked, including the F-14As of VF-41 and

VF-14). *Enterprise*'s place was then taken by USS *Theodore Roosevelt*, whose CVW-1 included the F-14Bs of VF-102. These were the first F-14s to deploy with JDAM. A fourth carrier, USS *Kitty Hawk*, was involved in Enduring Freedom, but operated as a Special Forces helicopter platform, and only embarked with some of CVW-5 (including F/A-18s and S-3s) but without the F-14 element, VF-154. In the last days of the war USS *John C. Stennis* arrived to take part in combat operations and the ensuing mopping-up operations.

Quite apart from combat operations, the F-14 squadrons have also undertaken some useful and realistic training exercises. In September 1999, for example, F-14s from VF-2, VF-41, VF-143 and VF-211 sank the redundant cruiser *Belknap* using only free-fall, unguided bombs. One VF-2 pilot put two such weapons down the ship's smokestacks, proving the ability of the Tomcat to deliver unguided ordnance with great accuracy.

Iraq – the last war?

In March 2003 the US and UK launched Operation Iraqi Freedom to oust Saddam Hussein from power. As would be expected, the F-14 was heavily involved from the first day. Carrier forces amassed for the initial onslaught comprised *Abraham Lincoln* (with VF-31 F-14Ds aboard), *Constellation* (VF-12 F-14Bs) and *Kitty Hawk* (VF-154 F-14As) in the Arabian Gulf, while *Theodore Roosevelt* (VF-213 F-14Ds) and *Harry S. Truman* (VF-32 F-14Bs) operated from the eastern Mediterranean. *Nimitz* subsequently joined the fray, but for the first time it carried Super Hornets in place of Tomcats. The five Tomcat-operating carriers operated a combined force of 56 F-14s.

Prior to the conflict only the F-14As and Bs were JDAM-capable, but in the run-up to war the deployed F-14D units modified their aircraft to drop the near-precision weapon. This provided a significant boost to the Tomcat's potential, and JDAMs were widely used by all five units during the war. They were also heavily employed as laser bombers, the Tomcat's LANTIRN system being widely regarded as superior to the Nite Hawk used by F/A-18Cs and Es. Tomcats also flew a few air superiority and escort missions, especially in the early days of the campaign, although there

For the time being it would appear that the sun is finally setting on the F-14. Whether the Super Hornet can adequately fill the vacant space on US Navy decks left by the F-14's passing remains to be seen. Above is a VF-102 F-14B, while below is a VF-2 F-14D.

Right: LGB-armed F-14Bs from VF-32 aboard Harry S. Truman (CVN 75) fly in formation off the wing of a KC-10 Extender in April 2003. USAF tanker support was vital for the two air wings which flew from the Mediterranean during Iraqi Freedom.

Below: An F-14B from VF-32 traps aboard Harry S. Truman on 22 March 2003, the day Truman's air wing joined the Iraqi Freedom air campaign following approval by the Turkish government for overflights. This was the third day of the conflict.

now infamous engagement at Karbala. US forces attempted to destroy the downed helicopter, at first with artillery and then with LGBs guided by F-14Ds. These aatcks were unsuccessful, as a few days later the Apache was seen on TV being paraded through the streets of Baghdad. *Roosevelt*'s aircraft covered the large paradrop on 26/27 March which occupied Harir airfield near Bashur in northern Iraq.

In the early hours of 2 April an F-14 went down, the coalition's first fixed-wing loss inside Iraq. The F-14A from VF-154 suffered an engine failure and fuel transfer problems as it prepared to refuel from a tanker – the crew ejected and was rescued by helicopter. They were taken, with only minor injuries, to Ahmed al Jaber in Kuwait, and then back to *Kitty Hawk*.

The end of the line

The process of replacing the Tomcat with the Super Hornet began in November 2001. When *Enterprise* returned from Afghanistan war duty its two F-14A squadrons – VF-14 and VF-41 – stood down for conversion to the new type. While the 'Black Aces' transitioned to the two-seat F/A-18F, (becoming VFA-41), the 'Tophatters' adopted the single-seat F/A-18E as VFA-14. Both squadrons stayed together, and joined *Nimitz*'s Air Wing 11.

The next squadron to convert was VF-102. The 'Diamondbacks' had also been involved in operations over Afghanistan, flying F-14Bs from *Roosevelt*. When they returned to the US in the spring of 2002 the squadron began its conversion to the F/A-18F, a process completed in time to deploy to Atsugi in November 2003 to jopin the forward-deployed Air Wing Five. In the reverse direction, VF-154's F-14As returned to the US from CVW-5 (and Iraqi Freedom) duty at the end of September. With its transition to the F/A-18F complete, the squadron then joined CVW-9 aboard *Carl Vinson* as VFA-154.

Preceding VFA-154's conversion were the 'Bounty Hunters' of VF-2. They had been flying F-14Ds from *Constellation* before flying ashore to begin learning to fly

was no aerial opposition. At about this time the Department of Defense announced that it was withdrawing the Phoenix missile from the inventory due to the high costs of maintaining it and the small number of scenarios in which it could be employed. Standard rules of engagement require the kind of positive identification of a target that is very difficult to achieve at the long ranges at which Phoenix is typically used.

Tomcats were involved from the first day of the war, *Constellation* launching a strike in the evening of 20 March. On 24 March the US Army lost an AH-64 Apache in the

This scene aboard Truman *shows ordnancemen preparing to load 2,000-lb (907-kg) GBU-31 JDAMs on to the waiting Tomcats of VF-32. The date was 21 March, the day before the 'Swordsmen' went to war.*

1980s), and this will remain the standard Air Wing composition until the F/A-18C/Ds are replaced by F-35C in the following decade. By 2008, the Tomcat is due to have disappeared from front-line service altogether, and the 'Mighty Turkey' will soon be no more than a memory.

Many may bemoan the retirement of the Tomcat and its replacement by the shorter-ranged F/A-18F, but with the US Navy's shift from 'blue-water' to littoral operations, and with a diminished long-range bomber threat, the F/A-18E/F represents a better tool for the carrier air wing, and one which will, in any case, be augmented by CALCMs for longer range strikes.

Jon Lake: additional material by David Donald

Above: VF-101 at Oceana continues to train Tomcat aircrew. Here one of the squadron's aircraft traps aboard Enterprise *during a carqual campaign in May 2004, in what is almost certainly the last Tomcat deployment to the 'Big E'.*

Above left: F-14As from VF-154 return to Kitty Hawk *on 3 April 2003. On the previous day the squadron had lost an aircraft over Iraq.*

the F/A-18F. They returned to Air Wing Two in 2003, which was by then assigned to *Abraham Lincoln*. The remainder fo the fleet was originally due to convert to the Super Hornet up to the end of 2007, but in 2004 the process was accelerated due to the number of Super Hornets being delivered. In 2004 the expected out-of-service date was spring 2006, with squadrons converting as they complete their current carrier deployment schedules. VF-211 was due to begin transition in 2004: having earlier been pencilled in for upgrade to the F-14D, the last F-14A squadron will now convert straight to the F/A-18F.

A front-line CVW's offensive/defensive capability will then be provided by four Hornet squadrons (like the experimental *Coral Sea* Air Wing deployed in the early

Above: VF-211 undertook the last operational F-14A cruise in the winter of 2003/04, sailing aboard Enterprise *on Iraqi Freedom policing duties. The F-14A always launched with full afterburner.*

Left: In a scene that will disappear all too quickly from the US Navy, an F-14 launches from USS George Washington, *sailing off Iraq in April 2004. Air Wing Seven is the last in the Navy to boast two Tomcat squadrons (VF-11 and VF-143), each with 10 aircraft. A total of 15 is visible in this view.*

Tomcat stores and weapons

Air-to-air missiles

The AIM-54C Phoenix remains the F-14's most powerful air-to-air weapon, and is scheduled to see out the Tomcat's career. AIM-54s can be carried from the lower wing pylons (below) or from four dedicated pallets under the fuselage. At the other end of the AAM spectrum is the AIM-9M Sidewinder, fitted to the shoulder rails.

Lacking AMRAAM capability, the F-14 still employs the AIM-7 Sparrow (above) for medium-range engagements.

Laser-guided bombs

Paveway II bombs (identified by the gimbal-mounted seeker head) available to the Tomcat are the 500-lb (227-kg) GBU-12 (below), 1,000-lb (454-kg) GBU-16 and 2,000-lb (907-kg) GBU-10. All bombs are carried under the fuselage on adapted Phoenix pallets.

The GBU-27 Paveway III is available in standard or penetrating (above) forms. The Paveway III seeker offers greater accuracy and increased flexibility.

Training weapons

For dumb bombing practice various small-scale stores can be carried on Triple Ejector Racks (TERs). They mimic the ballistics of the Mk 80 series weapons. This is a Mk 76 simulator for the Mk 82 weapon. Full-size inert weapons are also routinely used.

For laser-bombing training the Tomcat can carry the LGTR (Laser-Guided Training Round). This has a Paveway seeker head, and its ballistics mimic those of a full-size bomb.

TARPS pod

Carried under the rear right Phoenix station, the TARPS pod provides multi-sensor reconnaissance. The Digital TARPS pod has replaced the traditional wet-film system used previously.

LANTIRN targeting pod

LANTIRN is carried on the starboard wing pylon. This aircraft (above) is also fitted with the BOL Sidewinder rail which incorporates a chaff/flare launcher in the rear.

The LANTIRN pod gives the Tomcat its precision targeting capability. A laser designator is boresighted with an acquisition FLIR, which has two fields-of-view available: wide (5.87°) and narrow (1.68°). Normal magnifications are x4.1 (wide) and x10 (narrow), although x20 is available.

Electronic countermeasures pod

The ALQ-167 'Bullwinkle' reconfigurable jamming pod is occasionally carried from an adapted Phoenix pallet for use against specific threats. It can also be used to provide an EW threat environment during training exercises.

United States Navy

Between the end of Desert Storm in 1991 and the end of 1996, the US Navy lost 14 F-14 squadrons – more than half the then total – leaving just 12 front-line squadrons, a training unit and a single USNR unit, which itself converted to the F/A-18 in 1999. F-14 units which have disbanded are as follows:

VF-1 'Wolfpack'	disestablished 1 October 1993
VF-21 'Freelancers'	disestablished January 1996
VF-24 'Renegades'	disestablished August 1996
VF-33 'Starfighters'	disestablished October 1993
VF-51 'Screaming Eagles'	disestablished 31 March 1995
VF-74 'Bedevilers'	disestablished 28 or 30 April 1994
VF-84 'Jolly Rogers'	disestablished October 1995
VF-111 'Sundowners'	disestablished 30 March 1995
VF-114 'Aardvarks'	disestablished 30 April 1993
VF-124 'Gunfighters'	disestablished 30 September 1994
VF-142 'Ghostriders'	disestablished 7 April 1995
VF-191 'Satan's Kittens'	disestablished 30 April 1988
VF-194 'Red Lightings'	disestablished 30 April 1988
VF-201 'Hunters'	to F/A-18 1999
VF-202 'Superheats'	disestablished 31 December 1994
VF-301 'Devil's Disciples'	disestablished 31 December 1994
VF-302 'Stallions'	disestablished 31 December 1995

The remaining squadrons are now converting to the F/A-18E/F Super Hornet. This process began with the squadrons of Air Wing Eight, which returned from duty over Afghanistan in late 2001. VF-14 re-equipped with the single-seat F/A-18E, while VF-41 received two-seat F/A-18Fs. Next to convert to the F/A-18F was VF-102 in early 2002, followed by VF-2 and VF-154.

During the course of the 2000s the F-14 will give way to the F/A-18E/F. The process began in late 2001 when VF-14 and VF-41 transitioned to the Super Hornet, becoming VFA-14 and VFA-41 in the process.

According to the original Navy plans, VF-32 and VF-103 were to convert in 2005, VF-211 and VF-213 in 2006, and the remaining three units (VF-11, VF-31 and VF-143) in 2007. In the meantime, VF-211 – the last F-14A squadron – was slated to receive F-14Bs in 2004.

However, Boeing has been producing Super Hornets faster than the squadrons have been converting. In answer to this, a new, drastically accelerated schedule has been produced, under which Tomcat squadrons will convert once their current deployment cycles have been completed. Under the new programme VF-211 will go straight to the F/A-18F in 2004, having returned from the A's last cruise. CVW-1 is deploying in the meantime without an F-14 or F/A-18F squadron aboard. The remaining units will follow and all are due to have given up the Tomcat by spring 2006. VF-11 is unusual in that it will adopt the F/A-18E rather than the F.

Although F-14s still deploy aboard both Pacific and Atlantic Fleet carriers, Commander, Fighter Wing, US Atlantic Fleet provides logistics and administrative support to all fleet F-14 Tomcat squadrons, and the F-14 Fleet Replacement Squadron (FRS), all of which are shore-based at NAS Oceana, Virginia. The conversion to the Super Hornet has favoured the Pacific Fleet, which now only has one Air Wing equipped with Tomcats.

The six remaining front-line squadrons equip five regular CVWs, one of which (Air Wing Seven aboard *George Washington*) still embarked two F-14 squadrons in 2004.

CVW-3	**VF-32** (F-14B)	*Harry S. Truman* (CVN 75)	Lant
CVW-7	**VF-143**, **VF-11** (F-14B)	*George Washington* (CVN 73)	Lant
CVW-11	**VF-213** (F-14D)	*Theodore Roosevelt* (CVN 71)	Lant
CVW-14	**VF-31** (F-14D)	*John C. Stennis* (CVN 74)	Pac
CVW-17	**VF-103** (F-14B)	*John F. Kennedy* (CV 67)	Lant

In addition to the regular fighter squadrons, FRS unit and operational evaluation squadron described below, a handful of Tomcats also serve with the Naval Air Warfare Center's test fleet at two sites: Patuxent River (VX-23) and Point Mugu (VX-30). This NF-14B is allocated to NAWC-AD at the former.

VF-2 'Bounty Hunters'

Dormant since World War II, Fighting Two became the US Navy's second F-14 squadron in October 1972. As a Tomcat squadron, VF-2 won a succession of high-profile awards and established a reputation as one of the Navy's premier fighter squadrons. The awards included two COMNAVAIRPAC Battle 'E's, an unprecedented three consecutive Boola-Boola Awards from 1985 to 1987, and numerous victories in the West Coast High Noon Gunnery, TARPS, ECCM and Fighter Derby competitions.

VF-2 flew more than 550 combat missions and 1,900 combat flying hours during Operation Desert Storm – more than any other tactical squadron flying in-theatre during the 43-day war. VF-2 transitioned to the new F-14D in February 1993, and in July the squadron cross-decked to the USS *Constellation* (CV 64) when the ship returned to San Diego after completing its Service Life Extension Program. A 1994 deployment to the Arabian Gulf saw VF-2 achieving nearly 800 operational sorties and more than 2,050 flying hours, shooting more than 85,000 ft (25908 m) of TARPS film, and producing 12,000 8 x 10 prints.

In May 1996 VF-2 'led the pack', becoming the first West Coast F-14 squadron to relocate to NAS Oceana. VF-2's next cruise began in April 1997 – this time using its F-14Ds as 'Bombcat' strike-fighters, using the LANTIRN targeting pod, LGBs and 'dumb' bombs. With 10 of its 14

F-14Ds (which the 'Bounty Hunters' always call Super Tomcats) equipped for LANTIRN, VF-2 modestly claimed to be "the most potent strike-fighter squadron to have ever deployed". Equally notably, the squadron's remaining four F-14Ds deployed with the new Digital TARPS pod, using these operationally over Iraq, and transmitting imagery back to the ship in near real time. The squadron deployed again in June 1999, with *Constellation* taking over the Operation Southern Watch commitment from *Kitty Hawk* on 28 August 1999. This cruise marked the first use by the Tomcat of the Fast Tactical Imagery (FTI) system, demonstrating near real time targeting in-theatre for the first time, sending FTI imagery to an airborne F-14D aircraft to give the aircrew minute-old satellite imagery.

VF-2 encountered Iraqi anti-aircraft fire on almost every mission flown and, on one occasion, launched an AIM-54 against a pair of incoming MiG-23 'Floggers'. On 9 September 1999 LANTIRN-equipped VF-2 Tomcats led Carrier Air Wing Two in Operation Gun Smoke, destroying 35 of the 39 Iraqi anti-aircraft artillery and surface-to-air missile site targets assigned. The operation marked the biggest expenditure of ordnance in a single day since Operation Desert Storm.

Meanwhile, VF-2 continued its award-winning prowess, scooping the 1995, 1997, and 1999 COMNAVAIRPAC Battle 'E's, the

1995 and 1997 Boola-Boola Awards, the 1996 Bombing Derby Award and the 1997 and 1999 Safety 'S' Awards.

Until recently, VF-2 formed part of Air Wing Two aboard the USS *Constellation* (CV 64), and its aircraft wore the tailcode 'NE' and modexes 100-107 and 110-116. As the only Tomcat unit in CVW-2, VF-2 operated in the TARPS and LANTIRN roles.

As a reminder of VF-2's rich history, VF-2's aircraft originally retained the red, white, and blue 'Langley Stripe', which is similar to the markings used by the original

VF-2 when deployed aboard the USS *Langley* in 1925, though since the toning down of unit markings, this was only seen in full colour on CAG-birds and CO's aircraft, and in miniature form as a background to the unit badge on the tail.

In early 2003 VF-2 became the fourth Tomcat squadron to begin Super Hornet conversion before joining CVW-2.

VF-2's Tomcats wore the 'Langley' stripe, albeit in toned-down form. Two stars adorned the rudder.

VF-11 'RED RIPPERS'

Flying F-14As since 1980, VF-11 is the US Navy's longest continuously serving fighter squadron (VF-14 has served longer, but was briefly assigned a bomber role). The 'Red Rippers' joined Carrier Air Wing 14 (CVW-14) on 12 July 1992, and converted to the F-14D, becoming the first Fleet F-14D unit. The 'Red Rippers' were awarded the 'Mutha' award in 1993 for being the most outstanding and spirited fighter squadron at NAS Miramar. The squadron made the F-14D's first cruise, deploying on board USS *Carl Vinson* (CVN 70) for WestPac '94, during which the squadron flew missions in support of Operation Southern Watch. In 1994 VF-11 pioneered an NVG upgrade for the F-14, developing the necessary instrument/

VF-11 F-14Bs wear the unit's hog's head and lightning flash badge in toned-down colours on the fin. The insignia has barely changed since 1927.

lighting filters in-house, and then testing the modification on a squadron aircraft. The squadron deployed to the western Pacific with six NVG-compatible aircraft, and long-term Navy plans envisage the system being fitted to all F-14s. VF-11 deployed aboard the *Vinson* again in May 1996 for the ship's last cruise with CVW-14. During the cruise, VF-11 again flew missions in support of Operation Southern Watch and escorted B-52 bombers during Operation Desert Strike in early September 1996.

Like all Pacific Fleet F-14 squadrons, VF-11 moved to NAS Oceana during early 1997, and almost immediately

started to convert from the F-14D Tomcat to the older, less capable F-14B, completing the process in May 1997. The limited number of F-14D airframes available seemed to make it impossible to support three active squadrons, as well as the RAG and various test units. The 'Red Rippers' joined CVW-7 for its 1998 cruise, which was also the first operational deployment of the USS *John C. Stennis* (CVN 74), then the Navy's

newest carrier. *Stennis* relieved *George Washington* in the Persian Gulf.

VF-11 currently forms part of Air Wing Seven aboard the USS *George Washington* (CV 67), and its aircraft wear the tailcode 'AG' and modexes 200-216. While VF-143 handles CVW-7's TARPS requirements, VF-11 has a LANTIRN commitment. The squadron is due to convert to the F/A-18E single-seat Super Hornet in 2005.

VF-14 'TOPHATTERS'

VF-14 claims to be the oldest US Navy squadron in existence, tracing its lineage back to 1919, through many re-designations. Before becoming VF-14 on 15 December 1949, the 'Tophatters' were known as VF-1, VS-41, VB-4, VA-1A and VA-14. VF-14 converted to the F-14 in September 1974, the first Atlantic squadron to deploy with the F-14A and followed much the same pattern as other Tomcat units, including participation in Operation Desert Storm. VF-14 began to work up an air-to-ground capability in December 1991, starting with the Tomcat Advanced Strike Syllabus (TASS) and progressing to air wing workups at NAS Fallon. Though VF-14 was not the first unit to become 'Bombcat'-qualified (VF-24 and VF-211 practising the role even before Desert Storm) it was the first to make a 'Bombcat' carrier deployment. *Kennedy* and its squadrons were emergency-deployed in July 1992 as tensions in the Persian Gulf increased, but the carrier was recalled within days as the problems cooled. The scheduled cruise began in October 1992 and VF-14 participated in Operation Deny Flight sorties over former Yugoslavia.

VF-14 left CVW-3 in late 1995, and was directly assigned to Fighter Wing Atlantic at NAS Oceana, awaiting reassignment. At one time it seemed likely that the squadron would convert to the F/A-18 Hornet and become VFA-14. During this period, the 'Tophatters' continued to work up in the air-to-ground

role and served as the testbed unit for the Tomcat air-to-ground rocket programme. However, the decision was taken to retain VF-14 as an F-14 squadron and, in 1996, the squadron participated in its first cruise for several years, joining CVW-8 aboard the USS *John F. Kennedy* for a Mediterranean cruise. This finally restored CVW-8 to two F-14 squadrons, VF-14 operating alongside VF-41. VF-14 made another Mediterranean Sea/Arabian Gulf cruise in spring 1997, participating in Operation Allied Force. Both CVW-8 F-14 squadrons had by then received LANTIRN-capable Tomcats.

At the end of 1998 VF-14 re-equipped with the new F-14A DFCS, deploying with these on 26 March 1999 aboard USS *Theodore Roosevelt* for a scheduled six-month cruise to the Mediterranean

and the Gulf. During this deployment, VF-14 was successfully involved in NATO's Operation Allied Force and in Operation Southern Watch.

VF-14 has continued to add to its haul of awards, which already include two Presidential Unit Citations, the Navy Unit Commendation, two Meritorious Unit Commendations, five Battle stars, four CNO Aviation Safety awards, and seven COMNAVAIRLANT Battle Efficiency 'E' awards – in 1998 VF-14 gained the Admiral Joseph C. Clifton award and the Arleigh Burke Fleet Trophy, awarded annually to the most improved combat unit (ship, submarine or squadron) in the US Atlantic Fleet (CINCLANTFLT). This award had never before been won by an F-14 squadron.

For its last cruise VF-14 formed part of Air Wing Eight aboard the USS

Enterprise (CVN 65), and its aircraft wore the tailcode 'AG' and modexes 200-216. It is partnered by VF-41 'Black Aces' and two F/A-18C units – VFA-15 and VFA-87. Unusually, both of CVW-8's Tomcat units had a LANTIRN capability.

Enterprise departed from Norfolk for a six-month Mediterranean/Gulf deployment on 27 April 2001, transiting via the UK for exercises in the North Sea. The carrier entered the Persian Gulf on 1 August 2001, and relieved *Constellation* on Operation Southern Watch on 4 August 2001. *Enterprise* was itself relieved by *Carl Vinson* on 16 September, but then moved to the northern Arabian Sea in support of Operation Enduring Freedom.

Between 21 and 22 October *Enterprise* completed a complex resupply operation, transferring the remaining ordnance to *Roosevelt*, before leaving the northern Arabian Sea. The carrier completed passage through the Suez Canal on 28 October, and passed through the Straits of Gibraltar on 3 November.

After completing this final cruise aboard *Enterprise* (between 25 April 2001 and November 2001), including participation in operations over Afghanistan, VF-14 returned to Lemoore to begin transition to the F/A-18E, one of two F-14 units to transition to the single-seat version of the Super Hornet.

Two bomb-carrying VF-14 F-14As are seen in January 2001 during exercises with the Royal Navy off Scotland.

VF-31 'TOMCATTERS'

VF-31 is usually said to be the US Navy's second oldest fighter squadron, and enjoys the unique distinction of having scored kills in World War II, Korea and Vietnam. The squadron received F-14s in 1981, and transitioned to the F-14D in 1992, joining CVW-14 that July. Partnered with VF-11, the 'Tomcatters' embarked on USS *Carl Vinson* for another WestPac deployment in 1995, and then again in 1996. During this latter deployment, the *Carl Vinson* Task Group took part in Operation Southern Watch and in Operation Desert Strike, during which USN and USAF forces conducted TLAM and CALCM strikes against Iraq in response to Baghdad's invasion of Kurdish-held territory in northern Iraq. VF-31 escorted B-52 aircraft in support of their CALCM strikes and subsequently flew numerous sorties to enforce the

VF-31's 'Felix' badge is one of the best-known military aircraft markings, dating back to the late 1920s. Here it is worn in 2001 by a Phoenix-toting F-14D.

'no-fly' zone which had been expanded to 33° north.

VF-31 became CVW-14's only F-14 unit in 1998, when VF-11 joined CVW-11. The 'Tomcatters' deployed on USS

Abraham Lincoln again for WestPac 98, participating in Operation Southern Watch and in maritime interdiction operations in the Arabian Gulf.

VF-31 still forms part of Air Wing

Fourteen, aboard USS *John Stennis* (CVN 72), and its aircraft wear the tailcode 'NK' and modexes 100-116. It is partnered by three F/A-18C units – VFA-25, VFA-113 and VFA-115.

VF-32 'SWORDSMEN'

Like most 'CAG-birds, that of VF-32 wears colourful markings. The squadron flies the F-14B from Truman.

VF-32 remained with CVW-3 even after long-time partner unit VF-14 moved across to CVW-8 to join VF-41. Air Wing Three itself moved from *Kennedy* to *Eisenhower* for a 1994-95 cruise, and then on to *Roosevelt* for cruises which took place between November 1998 and May 1999, and between November 2000 and May 2001. In the course of the first of these cruises, VF-32's Tomcats exercised with Israeli F-16s in March 1999. VF-32, a long-term home of recce expertise and excellence within the Tomcat community, was among the first units to receive the new digital TARPS

reconnaissance pod, carrying out much of the trials and development work.

VF-32 currently forms part of Air Wing Three aboard USS *Harry S. Truman* (CVN 75), and its aircraft wear the tailcode 'AC' and modexes 100-116. As the only Tomcat unit in CVW-3, VF-32 operates in the TARPS and LANTIRN roles. The carrier's first deployment in 2001 involved a period of duty on Operation Southern Watch in the Persian Gulf and its Air Wing later flew in OIF. VF-32 is due to convert in 2005.

VF-41 'BLACK ACES'

The 'Black Aces' transitioned to the F-14A Tomcat in 1976 and joined Carrier Air Wing Eight aboard USS *Nimitz* (CVN 68) in January 1978. The squadron participated in Operation Desert Storm, but did not deploy during the March-September 1993 cruise aboard *Roosevelt*, its place being taken by VMFA-312. VF-41 remained part of CVW-8, ready to deploy if required, though many expected that this was the prelude to disestablishment. In fact, VF-41 conducted intensive training, including participation in Exercises Red and Maple Flag, and in early 1994 the 'Black Aces' grew to a 14-aircraft squadron and received its first TARPS-equipped aircraft and additional

personnel. Under the command of Captain 'Sodbuster' Benson, skipper from February 1992 to May 1993, VF-41 led the Tomcat community into the multi-mission strike role. Fighting Forty-One played a pivotal role in Kosovo as a result, and Benson was later voted 'Black Ace of the Century'. Some had expected VF-41's departure to be the beginning of a permanent arrangement, with VF-84 continuing as CVW-8's sole F-14 unit. Instead, VF-41 rejoined *Roosevelt* as an integral part of CVW-8, deploying for a six-month deployment to the Mediterranean Sea, Red Sea, Arabian Sea, Arabian Gulf, Persian Gulf and Adriatic Sea from 22 March 1995. During this deployment, VF-41 participated in Operations Deliberate Force and Deny Flight over Bosnia-

Herzegovina and in Operation Southern Watch over Iraq, amassing 530 sorties and logging more than 600 combat flying hours. During Deliberate Force VF-41 became the first F-14 unit to drop bombs 'in anger'.

VF-84 did not deploy, its place taken by a Marine F/A-18 unit, and it was disestablished after the cruise. In March 1996, VF-41 then made a brief deployment aboard *Stennis*, as part of the new CVN 74's shakedown cruise. VF-41 was not destined to remain as the sole Tomcat unit within CVW-8, however, being partnered by VF-14, previously part of Air Wing Three. VF-14 and VF-41 have remained partnered within CVW-8 ever since.

On 26 March 1999 VF-41 embarked for a six-month deployment, and was flying combat missions over Kosovo within nine days of leaving home, operating in support of Operation Allied Force. The squadron undertook 384 sorties and logged over 1,100 combat flying hours, dropping more than 160 tons of LGBs and achieving an

In its final Tomcat deployment, VF-41 undertook bombing missions over Afghanistan in the opening three weeks of Enduring Freedom.

unprecedented 85 per cent success rate. In doing so the 'Black Aces' became the first Tomcat squadron to prove LANTIRN in combat. VF-41's Tomcats also operated in the forward air control role, guiding the crews of other aircraft as they delivered more than one million pounds of ordnance. During the same cruise, USS *Theodore Roosevelt* was ordered to the Persian Gulf where VF-41 operated in support of Operation Southern Watch, dropping bombs in two theatres in a single cruise. When the squadron returned to Oceana in late September it had flown more than 1,200 combat sorties, and had dropped over 200,000 lb of ordnance, including 400 laser-guided bombs.

VF-41's last assignment as an F-14 unit was as a part of Air Wing Eight aboard *Enterprise* (CVN 65), and its aircraft wore the tailcode 'AG' and modexes 100-116. Its aircraft had both LANTIRN and TARPS capabilities, and were partnered by VF-14 'Tomcatters' and two F/A-18C units, VFA-15 and VFA-87. VF-41 participated in Operation Enduring Freedom, following a similar pattern of operations as VF-14, as described in the 'Tophatters' entry. On return to the US in 2001 the squadron began conversion to the F/A-18F.

VF-101 'GRIM REAPERS'

VF-101, then the Atlantic Fleet F-4J Readiness Squadron, assumed the additional role of training F-14 aircrews and maintenance personnel in January 1976, convening its first conversion course (for aircrew from VF-41 and VF-84) that June. On 5 August 1977, VF-101 split in two, with the F-4 element becoming VF-171.

As the East Coast F-14 FRS VF-101 kept abreast of every development in the wider Tomcat community, thus in April 1988, VF-101 received its first F-14B, and in September 1990 began training the fleet in strike warfare. VF-124 'Gunfighters' (the west coast F-14 FRS) disestablished on 30 September 1994, leaving VF-101 as the sole F-14 Fleet Replacement Squadron. VF-101

maintained aircraft on the west coast (Det Miramar) while front-line units were still based there. The squadron's aircraft wear a stylised 'grim reaper' insignia, in which the skeleton is said to represent sudden death to the USA's enemies, with the scythe being symbolic of the Tomcat's powerful armament.

While it may be a training unit, VF-101 has a front-line ethos, exemplified by its oath: "To engage the enemy whenever and wherever he is met with a fury and aggressiveness that will ensure the success of our mission and to do this not with the thought of attaining personal honor, but because by our actions, we will contribute to the ultimate defeat of our enemy and the glory of the US Navy. Mow 'em down!"

VF-101 operated all three front-line Tomcat variants for type conversion. It is due to disband in 2005 as there is no further need for Tomcat aircrew.

VF-102 'DIAMONDBACKS'

Following participation in Operation Desert Storm and the usual round of carrier deployments with CVW-1, VF-102 'Diamondbacks' became Carrier Air Wing One's sole Tomcat squadron following the disestablishment of VF-33 in July 1993. VF-102 received four additional aircraft, taking its complement to 14 F-14As.

During the Mediterranean deployment which began in early August 1993, CVW-1 supported Operations Provide Promise and Deny Flight, transiting the Suez Canal in late October to participate in Operation Restore Hope in Somalia.

The Air Wing then went on to support Operation Southern Watch in Iraq from mid-December, breaking records in total flying hours and sorties flown.

After an Orange Air detachment to Roosevelt Roads, Puerto Rico, in June 1994, VF-102 returned to Oceana and began conversion to the F-14B. The squadron completed carrier qualifications aboard USS *America* in July and USS *Enterprise* in October.

The squadron embarked aboard USS *America* in December 1994 for Refresher Training (REFTRA) prior to an August 1995 cruise. VF-102 became the

first Tomcat squadron to deploy to MCAS Yuma for SFARP in 1995, and provided students for the Navy's first ever FAC(A) training course, producing four fully qualified crews.

During its final 1995-96 Mediterranean cruise USS *America* made an emergency diversion to the Adriatic to take part in Operation Deliberate Force. Most of the cruise was then spent in the Adriatic, although in November the Air Wing participated in Exercise Bright Star with the Egyptians. Reaching the Persian Gulf, VF-102 flew missions in support of operation Southern Watch, but these were cut short when the deployment of US ground forces in Bosnia led to a quick

dash back to the Adriatic in December.

VF-102 transitioned to the F-14B Upgrade during the 1996-97 turnaround cycle. The new sub-variant featured a number of software upgrades and full compatibility with the LANTIRN targeting pod. At the annual 'Fighter Fling', VF-102 won the prestigious new VADM 'Sweetpea' Allen Precision Strike Award for its role in expanding the F-14's strike warfare capabilities and tactics.

Between October 1997 and April 1998, CVW-1 made a Mediterranean cruise aboard USS *George Washington*, and VF-102 again participated in Bright Star. *Washington*'s Battle Group was sent to the Arabian Gulf in November to

reinforce Southern Watch, following worsening relations with Iraq as the UN's Weapons Inspection Process began to disintegrate.

Between September 1999 and March 2000, CVW-1 deployed aboard USS *John F. Kennedy*, and then aboard *Theodore Roosevelt*. Its aircraft wore the tailcode 'AB' and modexes 100-116. As the only Tomcat unit in CVW-1, VF-102 operated in the TARPS and LANTIRN roles.

A 'Diamondback' F-14B cruises over the Adriatic during operations over Bosnia. In 2001 the unit went to war again over Afghanistan, its Tomcats being the first equipped to employ JDAM.

Roosevelt reached the northern Arabian Sea in late October 2001, and began combat operations over Afghanistan in support of Enduring Freedom, relieving *Enterprise*. After the

completion of the Tomcat's last cruise aboard *Roosevelt*, VF-102 began its transition to the new F/A-18F Super Hornet at NAS Lemoore in April 2002.

As VFA-102, the squadron then joined CVW-5 which is forward-deployed in Japan, replacing the F-14As of VF-154 in late 2003.

VF-103 'JOLLY ROGERS'

VF-103 was originally known as the 'Sluggers' before it adopted the historic 'Jolly Rogers' name and symbol in late 1995. As the 'Sluggers', VF-103 pioneered the use of the LANTIRN targeting pod on the F-14, conducting extensive trials in March/April 1995. The squadron deployed to the Mediterranean on 28 June aboard *Enterprise*, taking nine LANTIRN-capable aircraft and six pods. This marked the first operational deployment of LANTIRN for the US Navy.

When VF-84, the original 'Jolly Rogers', disestablished as part of planned (budget-driven) cuts on 29 September 1995, VF-103 requested permission to adopt the 'Jolly Rogers'

name, traditions and insignia, and formally took them over the next month.

In May 1997 VF-103 moved over to USS *Dwight D. Eisenhower* (CVN 69), and in June the next year deployed aboard 'Ike' for a cruise to the Adriatic, ready to undertake possible air strikes to protect the province of Kosovo.

VF-103 currently forms part of Air Wing Seventeen aboard USS *John F. Kennedy* (CV 67), and its aircraft wear the tailcode 'AA' and modexes 100-116. As the only Tomcat unit in CVW-17, VF-103 operates in the TARPS and LANTIRN roles. It is due to convert to the F/A-18F Super Hornet some time in 2005.

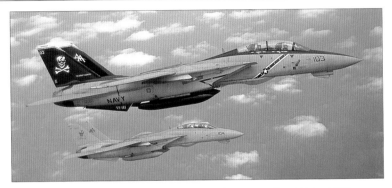

Two 'Jolly Rogers' Tomcats display the standard (background) and high-visibility schemes used by the squadron, the full-colour aircraft also wearing the unit-significant modex of '103'. 'AA' tailcodes are worn on the inner sides of the fins.

VF-143 'PUKIN' DOGS'

In August 1992, the 'World Famous Pukin' Dogs' and the rest of Carrier Air Wing Seven were reassigned to USS *George Washington* (CVN 73), then the Navy's newest aircraft-carrier. Despite

its 'politically incorrect' name, VF-143 survived the reduction of CVW-7 to a single F-14 squadron in April 1995. The squadron was directed to remove the 'Pukin' from its name, though VF-143

never seems to have complied.

VF-143 deployed aboard *Washington* on its maiden 'shakedown' cruise, and then again for the first full Mediterranean deployment in May 1994. In December 1995, the 'Pukin' Dogs' departed on another cruise

aboard CVN 73, and soon began flying missions over Bosnia in support of Operation Decisive Endeavor, and later over Iraq in support of Operation Southern Watch.

CVW-7 (with the 'Pukin' Dogs') transferred to USS *John C. Stennis* (CVN 74) for the new carrier's maiden deployment. VF-143 was by then equipped with LANTIRN, night vision goggles and digital TARPS. At the same time, CVW-7 gained a second F-14 squadron, in the shape of VF-11. Air Wing Seven's next cruise (beginning in February 2000) was aboard USS *Dwight D. Eisenhower* (CVN 69).

VF-143 now forms part of Air Wing Seven, back aboard USS *George Washington*, and its aircraft wear the tailcode 'AG' and modexes 100-116. Its aircraft include some equipped with the digital TARPS pod. It is partnered by VF-11 'Red Rippers' and two F/A-18C units – VFA-131 and VFA-136.

By the end of 2001 CVW-7 was the only air wing with two Tomcat squadrons. VF-143 flies the air wing's TARPS-capable aircraft.

VF-154 'BLACK KNIGHTS'

When VF-21 disestablished in January 1996, VF-154 was left as the sole F-14 squadron within Air Wing Five. CVW-5 was attached to USS *Independence* (CV 62), home-ported at Yokosuka, Japan, and its units were forward-deployed at nearby NAS Atsugi. *Independence* was replaced by USS *Kitty Hawk* (CV 63) during 1998.

1999 was a particularly busy year for VF-154, with training detachments in the USA, two Phoenix missile shoots, and Exercise Tandem Thrust all taking place before the end of March. The period saw VF-154 making its first tactical use of FTI, the employment of two GBU-16s, and the first-ever FAC(A) participation in a Naval Gun Fire Exercise, controlling live fire from USS *Chancellorsville* (CG 62). Next the squadron deployed to the Gulf to take part in Operation Southern Watch, doing so with aircraft just modified with the Digital Flight Control System (DFCS),

A VF-154 F-14A rests on the deck of Kitty Hawk during a 2001 visit to Australia.

making the 'Black Knights' the first F-14 squadron to deploy with the new system. The aircraft also featured the new Fast Tactical Imagery system, giving F-14 crews the ability to transmit and receive imagery and bomb damage assessment in near real-time. During the cruise, VF-154 flew 397 sorties in support of Operation Southern Watch, and participated in three separate strikes against Iraqi targets, destroying 67 per cent of assigned targets. The cruise gave the opportunity for exercises with the Royal Air Force of Oman, before the F-14s returned to NAF Atsugi in August.

In October VF-154 again deployed as part of CVW-5, participating in Exercises Foal Eagle and ANNUALEX. All VF-154 FAC(A) aircrew participated in close air support missions in South Korea, including operations to within 10 nm of

the DMZ, co-operating with other Navy, Air Force and ROK assets. VF-154 also developed innovative tactics using the F/A-18's Laser Spot Tracker in conjunction with the F-14's LANTIRN.

When *Kitty Hawk* departed from Yokosuka to take part in Operation Enduring Freedom, it did so for primary use as a floating base for special

operations helicopters and troops. Much of its air wing was left behind, including VF-154. However, VF-154 (with the tailcode 'NF' and modexes 100-107 and 110-116) was aboard for Operation Iraqi Freedom. In September 2003 the squadron flew its F-14As back to the US where it began conversion to the Super Hornet and reassignment to CVW-9.

VF-211 'CHECKMATES'

VF-211 originally transitioned to the F-14A in 1975, converting to the more powerful F-14B in 1989. Following participation in Operation Desert Storm, the 'Fighting Checkmates' transitioned back to the F-14A in 1992, when it was decided to concentrate all F-14Bs within the Atlantic Fleet. The squadron moved from NAS Miramar to Oceana in August 1996, and became Carrier Air Wing

Nine's sole Tomcat unit when VF-24 disestablished on 31 August 1996. VF-211 made one 'solo' deployment aboard USS *Nimitz* before CVW-9 transferred to USS *Stennis*, making a first deployment from January 2000.

Until 2004 VF-211 formed part of Air Wing One aboard USS *Enterprise* (CVN 74), and its aircraft wear the tailcode 'AB' and modexes in the 1xx

VF-211's 'CAG' aircraft has the fin checkers in red/white. Regular squadron aircraft have a checkerboard in toned-down greys.

range. It operated in both in the TARPS and LANTIRN roles. It is partnered by three F/A-18C units – VFA-146, VFA-147 and VMFA-314.

In 2004, after the completion of the

F-14A's last cruise, VF-211 began its transition to the new F/A-18F Super Hornet at NAS Lemoore. It is due to return to the fleet as VFA-211 in March 2005.

VF-213 'BLACK LIONS'

After participation in Desert Storm, VF-213 deployed aboard USS *Abraham Lincoln* for the second time in 1993, participating in Operation Southern Watch over Iraq and Operation Restore Hope in Somalia. VF-154 became the only Tomcat unit within CVW-11 with the disestablishment of VF-114 'Aardvarks' on 30 April 1993. From April to October 1995, VF-213 made another cruise aboard the 'Honest Abe', again flying in support of Operation Southern Watch.

VF-213 then moved (with the rest of CVW-11) to the USS *Kitty Hawk*, deploying for six weeks for Exercise RIMPAC '97 and for six months for a WestPac '97 cruise. During RIMPAC '97, VF-213 fired twenty-six Phoenix and six Sidewinder missiles, including an unprecedented simultaneous six-Tomcat, 12-missile Phoenix shoot.

On returning from the WestPac cruise in April 1997, VF-213 disembarked to NAS Oceana, the unit's new home. A shortage of F-14As forced

The 'Black Lions' have been busy recently, with time spent on Southern Watch and now Enduring Freedom.

the squadron to re-equip, even though the US Navy had previously gone from three to two F-14D units because of a similar shortfall. Nevertheless, the 'Black Lions' immediately began conversion to the F-14D, completing the process in December 1997. Air Wing Eleven and VF-213 then moved to *Carl Vinson*. A RIMPAC '98 exercise followed, during which one Sidewinder and six Phoenix missiles were expended, one AIM-54C being launched at night by a crew using NVGs.

Two months into *Vinson*'s 1998/99 WestPac deployment to the Arabian Gulf, the carrier participated in Operation Desert Fox. VF-213 became the first unit to launch an AIM-54C in anger, firing two missiles against Iraqi fighters violating the Iraqi 'no-fly' zone. Both missiles missed their targets.

Vinson departed from Bremerton for

a six-month WestPac/Gulf deployment on 25 July 2001, subsequently embarking VF-213 as part of Air Wing 11. The carrier relieved *Enterprise* on Operation Southern Watch on 16 September 2001, moving to the northern Arabian Sea in early October to take part in Operation Enduring Freedom.

VF-213 was subsequently transferred to Air Wing Eight ('AJ' tailcode, 1xx Modexes) aboard *Theodore Roosevelt* (CVN 71). From this carrier the squadron undertook combat operations over Iraq in March/April 2003. It remains assigned to CVW-8, and is due to be one of the last squadrons to fly the F-14.

VX-9 'VAMPIRES'

VX-9, a test and evaluation unit based at NAS China Lake, is a tenant command of NAWS China Lake, and was formed on 29 April 1994 by combining VX-4 at Point Mugu and VX-5 at China Lake. It is tasked with the operational evaluation of aircraft, weapons systems and equipment, and to develop tactical procedures for their employment. China Lake incorporates massive ranges, lying under some 17,000 square miles (44000 km²) of joint-service restricted airspace. At China Lake, VX-9 operates all versions of the F/A-18 Hornet, the AV-8B Harrier II, the Grumman EA-6B Prowler and the Bell AH-1W. The unit's F-14s (drawn from all variants) were operated from NAS Point Mugu, by a separate permanent detachment. The main element of VX-9 at China Lake essentially took over the role (air-to-ground ordnance and tactics testing and trials) and duties of the former VX-5, while the Point Mugu detachment took

over the responsibilities of the former VX-4.

Like VX-4, the VX-9 Detachment at NAS Point Mugu conducted testing on all facets of the air-to-air fighter role, including weapons, aircraft systems and software. In effect, this restricted the

scope of the squadron's activities to the F-14 Tomcat, the US Navy's only dedicated interceptor.

VX-9's aircraft wear the traditional Vampire bat insignia of VX-5, with four stars added in acknowledgement of the absorption of VX-4.

Two VX-9 F-14Bs display the black-finned and black-tanked scheme adopted as standard by this operational evaluation and trials unit.

VX-4 had for many years operated a number of 'flagship' aircraft in an overall glossy black paint scheme, as 'Black Bunnies'. This tradition was continued by VX-9's Point Mugu detachment, although the 'Vampires' most recent flagship, a gloss black F-14D (callsign 'Vandy One') had the unit's bat insignia in place of the traditional Playboy bunny.

Another VX-9 Det. Point Mugu F-14B ('Vandy 240') had its tails, ventral fins and external tanks painted black to match those of the flagship, and was followed by another F-14B (upgrade), 'Vandy 241'.

On 23 June 2004 VX-9 Det. Point Mugu closed down and its Tomcats were retired. 'Vandy One' (which was the last F-14 built and which never made an arrested landing) was due to go on display at NAS Oceana.

NSAWC

NSAWC (pronounced 'N-Sock') formed through the merger of three separate units on 11 July 1996. NSAWC's components are the former Naval Strike Warfare Center ('Strike U') at Fallon (and latterly Lemoore), the Naval Fighter Weapons School ('Top Gun') at NAS Miramar and the Carrier Airborne Early Warning Weapons School ('Top Dome') also from NAS Miramar. Consolidation of these three units brought with it efficiency savings, but also helped to standardise and co-ordinate training and communication between various naval aviation communities.

Until recently, NSAWC flew a mix of about six F-14As, and about 20 F/A-18As and F/A-18Bs, together with with three or four SH-60F/HH-60Hs forming a

Combat Search and Rescue element. When NSAWC received an influx of F-16As from the embargoed Pakistani order, the Tomcat was withdrawn from the adversary role.

NSAWC's mission is two-fold, providing 'graduate training' in tactics for selected front-line aircrew (who then

return to their units to pass on their newly acquired knowledge and expertise as instructors) and also providing pre-deployment training for Carrier Air Wings in air-to-air and strike warfare. CVW Integrated and Advanced Training Phases (ITP/ATP) conducted at NAS Fallon are large-scale exercises,

and may involve as many as 50 aircraft, serving as invaluable 'dress rehearsals' for scenarios which the Air Wing might meet 'on deployment'. This dual task has remained basically unchanged since NSAWC's three elements were separate units, although new courses have been added. NSAWC also provides *ad hoc* adversary training for Fleet units.

NSAWC Tomcats wore the traditional and long-standing 'Top Gun' 'MiG in the pipper' badge, though this is superimposed on the lightning bolt insignia traditionally associated with 'Strike U'.

A 'plain Jane' NSAWC F-14A (foreground) flies in company with VX-9's all-black F-14D. Since the arrival of F-16As – originally built for Pakistan – the F-14A has been retired.

41

Super Hornet production Lot numbers follow on from those of the 'legacy' Hornet, but to all intents the F/A-18E/F is no more than a derivative design, sharing few common parts apart from the baseline avionics suite, which is in the process of being largely replaced by newer items. The new aircraft has gained the nickname of 'Rhino' on account of its larger size and grey colour. Given enough imagination it can also be suggested that the Super Hornet has a horn, in the shape of the AIFF fairing forward of the windscreen. VFA-14 'Tophatters' was the second squadron to get the single-seat F/A-18E, and one of its aircraft is seen here in the 'five-wet' tanker configuration. Note the spinning turbine which provides power for the A/A42R-1 refuelling pod on the centreline.

Boeing
F/A-18E/F
Super Hornet

Born out of the procurement mire of the late 1980s/early 1990s which saw the cancellation of several important naval aircraft programmes, the Super Hornet has not introduced any radical new technology, nor any quantum leap in performance. Instead, it has been developed on time and to a tight budget, and is a highly adaptable and versatile aircraft for the US Navy to operate in the post-Cold War combat environment. Furthermore, it represents a considerable improvement over its predecessor in terms of range/load characteristics, reliability and affordability. It is slated to receive the latest in sensor, weapons and communications technology, and has the room for growth which allows it to be at the cutting edge of the development of netcentric warfare, and a key platform in the race to cut 'sensor to shooter' times to a minimum.

Now the centrepiece of naval aviation, the Boeing F/A-18E/F strike fighter is flying fighter, attack, reconnaissance, refuelling and suppression of enemy air defences (SEAD) missions for the US Navy's carrier fleet. Derived from an already versatile and flexible platform – the F/A-18 Hornet – the Super Hornet is the culmination of years of work to perfect the Hornet design. Indeed, the Super Hornet in many respects represents what the original Hornet should have been, as it specifically addresses and resolves deficiencies in range, payload and bring-back capability that plagued the earlier machine, while at the same time providing the Navy with a renewed growth clock to incorporate new technologies.

The Super Hornet is now operational with several fleet squadrons and has already seen combat in operations over Iraq and flown patrol missions over Afghanistan. Although still not representative of what the Super Hornet will ulti-

mately bring to the table, these aircraft performed outstandingly and confirmed the predictions of their proponents. According to Captain B.D. Gaddis, NAVAIR F/A-18 Program Manager, "All of our debriefs from the commanders and CAGs are saying that the Super Hornet is exceeding all expectations in performance and capability." Captain Gaddis pointed out, "These reports are even more significant in the context of the Super Hornet because they are coming not only off the aircraft's maiden deployment, but also from its first combat deployment, and an extended one at that." As planned systems such as the Advanced Tactical Forward-Looking Infra-red (ATFLIR) pod, the Multi-functional Information Distribution System (MIDS), the Joint Helmet-Mounted Cueing System (JHMCS), and SHAred Reconnaissance Pod (SHARP) enter service over the next five years, the Super Hornet will prove even more lethal, making it the definitive strike fighter – one that no opponent will want to meet in combat.

The Super Hornet will also serve as the Navy's new electronic warfare/electronic attack platform, offering a combination of speed and functionality far surpassing that of the EA-6B. Scheduled to enter service in 2009, the EA-18G will fly the same mission profiles as its -E/F stablemates and also carry a robust self-defence capability. Moreover, the incorporation of new technology allows the two-person EA-18G crew to perform the mission currently handled by four EA-6B crew members.

The advent of the Super Hornet brings with it a change of face for naval aviation. The aircraft-carriers of 2015 and beyond will be stocked with at least three strike fighter squadrons of F/A-18E/Fs flying a range of missions including strike, fighter, SEAD, reconnaissance and sea control, as well as providing organic tanking services to carrier aircraft. A squadron of five or six EA-18G aircraft will provide jamming and offensive electronic warfare support, while a squadron of the new F-35 Joint Strike Fighter (JSF) will give the carrier stealthy, deep-strike capabilities. Long-range airborne early warning duties will be flown by the latest version of the E-2C Hawkeye, and anti-submarine duties will be filled by the MH-60R Seahawk.

Captain Gaddis told *International Air Power Review* that he considers two features to be key to the Super Hornet design. "The Advanced Mission Computer and Displays are the heart of the aircraft that allow it to connect to and fuse the data. The ability to move data from sensor to display and process that data into a usable format has vastly increased. The second aspect is the APG-79 AESA radar. In terms of raw capabilities, the radar is phenomenal. But the real capability comes when you mate the radar with the various sensors – ATFLIR, SHARP, the EW suite – and from those build a high-resolution map and get that map to the commanders on the ground. These systems literally revolutionise how we fight today." Captain Gaddis added, "[the] advanced sensors are critical to developing the powerful network that the Navy is trying to achieve."

The Navy is currently in the fourth year of its first multi-year purchase contract, and approximately 87 of the 222 ordered Super Hornets have been delivered. A second multi-year contract is approaching, which will result in another 210, 90 of which will be built as EA-18Gs.

Birth of the Super Hornet

The late 1980s and early 1990s were very turbulent times for military aircraft procurement, characterised by ever-growing budgetary constraints and a major refocusing of US war-fighting strategy and force structure. These forces worked together to produce the programme that today is the F/A-18E/F Super Hornet. As the 1980s began, the Navy found itself with several ageing airframes in need of replacement. Many aircraft, such as the F-4, RF-8 Crusader and A-7 Corsair II, had been flying since the late 1960s and were approaching, if not surpassing, the end of their useful lives. Other airframes, such as the A-6E – although performing well at the time – were not technologically advanced enough to survive in the projected air defence climate of the 21st century. Moreover, their airframes were limited in growth capacity. What was needed were follow-on aircraft for all three major missions: attack, fighter and strike fighter.

Cold War plans called for high-end follow-ons to both the F-14 Tomcat fleet defence fighter and the A-6E Intruder attack aircraft that would incorporate high levels of stealthiness and ensure continued US naval air dominance well into the 21st century. A navalised F-22, called the Naval Advanced Tactical Fighter (NATF), was slated to succeed the F-14, and the flying-wing A-12 Avenger II was to replace the venerable Intruder. Yet, both programmes were costly and technologically a long way from fruition.

In July 1987, the Department of Defense ordered the Navy and the Air Force (which at the time was pursuing the proposed F-22 ATF) to investigate possible derivatives of the F/A-18 and F-16 as a stopgap measure until the F-22

and A-12s began to enter service in the early 2000s. McDonnell Douglas responded with the Hornet 2000 programme in 1987, which was essentially a further evolution of the original F/A-18, and which further corrected some of the deficiencies of the baseline F/A-18A such as its poor range and payload. The Hornet 2000 featured a larger wing and stabilators, additional internal fuel and more powerful engines. The programme was actually marketed abroad, with little interest, and was temporarily shelved. At about the same time, and in anticipation of the NATF and A-12, the Navy scrapped plans to introduce the improved A-6F Intruder II and limited production of the advanced F-14D to just 54 aircraft.

Shortly after McDonnell Douglas began its Hornet programme, two related events occurred that perhaps are the most significant factors in the ultimate decision to pursue the F/A-18E/F – the collapse of the Soviet Union and the end of the Cold War. With these events came both a major restructuring of the US military and massive budget cuts that ultimately spelled the end for both the NATF and the A-12. Of course, the latter programme had significant cost issues of its own that contributed significantly to its demise. With America's chief enemy now gone, strategy shifted from fighting open seas, 'blue-water' engagements with the Soviet fleet to operations in 'white water', or the littoral regions – targets within a few hundred miles of the coastal areas. This, in turn, negated the need for a naval long-range strike aircraft. Likewise, with no threat posed by vast fleets of missile-carrying Soviet bombers or submarines, the need diminished for a long-range high-end interceptor. Moreover, in addition to strategic considera-

A bigger, smarter, stealthier Hornet – this view of the prototype F/A-18E highlights the enlarged wing of the Super, and the trapezoidal intakes which help reduce the type's RCS.

With two extra pylons, enhanced weapons capability and the routine use of asymmetric loads, the number of weapon loadouts for the Super Hornet is vast. Two EMD aircraft were assigned to initial weapons separation trials to investigate some of the Super Hornet's huge repertoire. E5 and F2 were sent to the Navy's main weapon test base at China Lake for this work, the pair being the first Super Hornets with a working avionics suite that included APG-73 radar. Both were liberally covered with photo-calibration marks, and here E5 carries inward-facing cameras on wingtip-mounted test rigs, and an aft-facing camera under the forward fuselage.

EMD aircraft

E1 – BuNo. 165164
F/f – 29 November 1995

Charged with investigating flying qualities and flight envelope expansion. Tests on E1 confirmed the aircraft's compliance with flutter safety margins. E1 concluded its test flights on 23 October 1998, and tallied 408 sorties and 757.9 flight hours during the EMD.

E2 – BuNo. 165165
F/f – 26 December 1995

E2's EMD tasks included engine and performance testing; the aircraft flew 486 sorties and 847.9 flight hours in the period from 19 February 1996 through 30 April 1999. Here the aircraft is seen during trials at Patuxent River.

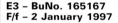

E3 – BuNo. 165167
F/f – 2 January 1997

Last of the EMD aircraft to take to the air, E3 handled the load testing portion of the EMD, during which it flew 354 sorties and 552.5 flight hours. Like E1 and E2, the aircraft did not have radar installed and was fitted with an air data instrumentation boom in the nose.

E4 – BuNo. 165168
F/f – 2 July 1996

E4 was assigned to high angle-of-attack trials. During EMD it amassed 402 sorties and 570.4 flight hours. The aircraft received a red and white scheme for maximum conspicuity during its aerodynamic trials, and for most sorties carried a spin recovery chute mounted on a gantry above the jetpipes.

E5 – BuNo. 165170
F/f – 27 August 1996

E5 was the first Super Hornet to possess mission capability, and was fitted with APG-73 radar. The aircraft made numerous 'firsts' during weapons evaluations, and ended the EMD phase with 480 flights and 594.1 flight hours. It initiated the stores separation trials on 19 February 1997 when a fuel tank was jettisoned.

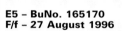

F1 – BuNo. 165166
F/f – 1 April 1996

The first two-seat aircraft was the third EMD aircraft to fly. As well as aerodynamic evaluation of the two-seat aircraft, it was assigned to carrier suitability and weapons testing. F1 tallied 508 sorties and 601.8 flight hours, the most flight time of all EMD aircraft.

F2 – BuNo. 165169
F/f – 11 October 1996

F2 was also assigned to some carrier qualification duties, joining F1 in an intensive trials campaign on *Truman* in March 1999. As it was the second Super Hornet with a full avionics suite, F2 spent much of its time flying alongside E5 performing weapons testing at China Lake, including launches of AIM-9 and AIM-120 AAMs.

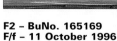

tions, the defence budget was curtailed significantly as the US began a force draw-down, resulting in less money.

Thus, as the 1990s began, the Navy found itself with a tough choice. Although it needed to replace both its fighter and attack aircraft, it simply did not have the funds to pursue a new aircraft for each mission. The Navy therefore decided to pursue one major system upgrade and one new aircraft. Navy strategy at that time still focused on power projection as outlined in the paper *... From the Sea*, so the Navy sought a new aircraft to replace the Intruder; this came through a new programme, dubbed the A-X (later redesignated A/F-X). In turn, the Navy undertook a major upgrade to replace the fighters, and McDonnell Douglas's Hornet 2000 provided the catalyst for the aircraft that became the F/A-18E/F.

As the Navy moved from power projection to littoral missions, the NATF and the A-12 were no longer deemed viable equipment. Moreover, the Bottom-Up Review of 1993 concluded that the US simply could not afford all of the high-end programmes that had emerged from the Cold War days of the 1980s. This meant that costly and inefficient programmes had to be trimmed or cancelled altogether. The Navy's A/F-X (a planned replacement for the A-6E and F-14) and the Air Force's Multi-Role Fighter (its planned replacement for the A-10 and F-16) programmes met with a similar fate. Navy officials, as well as their counterparts in the Air Force, then had to select which aircraft system they would pursue. In the end, the Navy chose the F/A-18E/F upgrade based on the original Hornet 2000, to be complemented by the Joint Service Fighter (later known as the Joint Strike Fighter and now the F-35). The Air Force decided to support the F-22, with a complementary JSF force.

Super Hornet comes to fruition

Navy support for the Super Hornet came in late 1991, followed by a formal declaration of an 'intent to procure' on 12 May 1992. Total cost of the programme was estimated to be $US63,090 million (in FY96 dollars), with $US5,783 million slated for development costs. Initial Operational Capability (IOC) was scheduled for 2000, with the first carrier-based squadron to deploy in 2003. Congressional approval was received in June 1992, culminating in a $US4.88 billion (in FY92 dollars) contract for engineering and development (EMD). Of this contract, $US3.7 billion went to McDonnell Douglas; the remaining amount went to General Electric for development of the F414 engine. Congress placed a cap on the overall Super Hornet cost of 125 per cent of an F/A-18C. The Navy signed the final F/A-18E/F contract on 7 December 1992, authorising McDonnell Douglas and Northrop Grumman to produce three ground test airframes (ST-50 for static tests; DT-50 for drop tests; and FT-50 for fatigue tests), five single-place F/A-18Es, and two dual-place F/A-18Fs.

The E/F programme underwent a successful Preliminary Design Review from 28 June through 2 July 1993, resulting in only 53 relatively minor action items, all of which were subsequently resolved. A more thorough Critical Design Review was held from 13 to 17 June 1994, with the Super Hornet passing all of the Navy's schedule, cost, technical, reliability and maintainability requirements. Northrop Grumman commenced production of the centre/aft fuselage for E1 (BuNo. 165164) on 24 May 1994 at its Hawthorne, California, facility and McDonnell Douglas began work on the forward fuselage in St Louis, Missouri, on 23 September that same year. The first Super Hornet, E1, debuted in a highly-touted roll-out ceremony at McDonnell Douglas's St Louis facility on 18 September 1995, and made its first flight on 29 November. Speaking at the ceremony, then-Secretary of the Navy John H. Dalton said that the aircraft represented a "remarkable achievement" that had come in "on schedule, on budget and under weight". Company test pilot Fred Madenwald piloted the maiden voyage. E1 left for Patuxent River, Maryland, in February 1996 to begin its flight tests.

VX-9 'VAMPIRES'

Air Test and Evaluation Squadron (AIRTEVRON) Nine was formed at China Lake on 29 April 1994 by combining the operations of VX-4 (established 15 September 1952) and VX-5 (established 18 June 1957) – hence the new unit number. VX-4 was previously at Point Mugu, where it undertook air-to-air evaluation work, while VX-5 at China Lake was the Navy's main air-to-ground and tactical evaluation unit. Although the China Lake squadron now oversees both elements, it maintains a detachment at Point Mugu. VX-9 was the first Navy squadron to have Super Hornets assigned, and was responsible for conducting the OPEVAL. Markings consist of the bat and lightning bolts from VX-5's old badge, with four stars from VX-4.

A procurement contract for low-rate initial production (LRIP) was signed in March 1997. This agreement called for a total of 62 aircraft to be delivered in three lots (12 aircraft in LRIP 1 during FY97; 20 in LRIP 2 during FY98; and 30 in LRIP 3 during FY99). The last of the LRIP-1 aircraft (eight Es and four Fs) was delivered on 9 November 1999 – ahead of schedule. LRIP-2 aircraft (8 Es and 12 Fs) were delivered between January and October 2000, and LRIP-3 deliveries (14 Es and 16 Fs) ended in July 2001. These aircraft were flown during the initial Operational Evaluation (OPEVAL) and were also used to form the new fleet readiness squadron (FRS), VFA-122, and the first operational Super Hornet squadron, VFA-115. Full-rate production began in September 2000, with 36 Super Hornets (15 Es and 21 Fs), followed by 39 aircraft in 2001. Of this latter production, 14 aircraft were Es and 25 were F models. The five-year contract signed on 15 June 2000 authorised an additional 222 aircraft through FY04.

Although a total of 548 Super Hornets was planned, this procurement was trimmed in 2003, with production scheduled to drop from 48 aircraft per year in 2002 to 45 in 2003 and 42 in 2004. In part, the uncertainty arises from the Marine Corps' initial decision not to adopt the Super

Above: BuNo. 165533 was the first Super Hornet from Low-Rate Initial Production. It first flew in unpainted state (with 'F/A-18E6' on the tail) on 6 November 1998, six weeks ahead of schedule. It was subsequently painted in VX-9's markings, and was handed over to the US Navy on 18 December.

Hornet as a replacement for its F/A-18C/Ds. It further stems from the decision to build the EA-18G as a replacement for the EA-6B electronic combat aircraft. As discussed later in this article, the Navy plans to purchase as many as 90 reconfigured two-place Super Hornets to perform fleet jamming and electronic attack missions. The Marines may follow suit as well, although they are also evaluating a proposed EW variant of the F-35.

Compromises on mission and stealth

Before discussing the aircraft itself, a few points must be made concerning the overall F/A-18E/F programme. During the late 1980s, a major re-thinking occurred as to how to approach aircraft design. Budget constraints were making it very difficult to develop a high-end, all-around aircraft that maximised all available technologies, such as stealth. Cost had to be a driving factor. In an interview in late 2000, Vice Admiral Joe Dyer, then-Commander Naval Air Systems Command and former F/A-18 Program Manager from 1994 through 1997, explained, "[there] was a recognition in the late 1980s that we simply could not do things the same way in procurement." Given this realisation, Dyer maintained, the Navy needed to replace a

Although assigned to VX-9 at China Lake, the first production aircraft was initially dispatched to NAWC-AD at Patuxent River (in the background) for flight trials. After a few months at the Maryland base it was transferred to China Lake to begin VX-9's OPEVAL work.

In its two-seat F/A-18F form, the Super Hornet is replacing the F-14 in the fleet. Providing a comparison between the two is an F/A-18F from VX-9 and an F-14D from the squadron's Point Mugu detachment. The Tomcat is the latest in a line of VX-4/VX-9 aircraft to be painted gloss black, which operate with the callsign VANDY 1.

VX-9 currently flies a number of Super Hornets at China Lake on weapons and tactics evaluation duties.

Three VX-9 aircraft fly with the CAG and CO jets from VFA-122. The Super Hornet training squadron worked very closely with VX-9 during its early months to establish a training syllabus for the new type, and to train up a cadre of pilot and WSO instructors. VFA-122 was in existence for nearly a year before it received its own aircraft.

certain number of aircraft within a certain price. "They looked at how much money was available at the time and at how many aircraft were needed to do the job the Navy needed done. This allowed us to fix a number, then work to develop a design that fell within it."

Coupled with these considerations, Dyer continued, there had been an overall move away from single-mission aircraft to more of a force composition structure wherein aircraft could rely on other assets to accomplish the overall mission. This was demonstrated during Operation Allied Force over Kosovo in 1999, and in later operations over the Persian Gulf region in Operation Iraqi Freedom. Today, strike fighters co-ordinate missions with F-15Es, EA-6Bs, tankers, and reconnaissance aircraft, and even stealthy F-117s and B-2s. Vice Admiral Dyer stressed that "by focusing on a design in isolation, without reference to the systems at large, we took affordability out of the picture."

Vice Admiral Dyer added that the acceptance of these concepts led to a more open attitude towards trade-offs, and said, "We applied this to the question of stealth and survivability. We saw the crucial question as 'how much stealth is enough' for this design? Our answer was simple – enough to deliver stand-off weapons and survive to fight another day." Certainly, the admiral's comments are well taken. Stealth can be achieved in a number of ways, at varying costs, and this is exemplified by the different approaches taken with low-observability by the so-called 'stealth designs', the F-117, F/A-22 and B-2. The F/A-18E/F achieved its stealthiness through a combination of radar-absorbing materials, electronics and innovative use of stand-off weapons. Admiral Dyer concluded, "[the] key is finding the right balance, within the confines of affordability."

These comments dove-tailed with those made by Rear Admiral Dennis V. McGinn, Director of Air Warfare in the

Office of the Chief of Naval Operations, who commented in 1998 concerning the 'perishability' of stealth. "If you try to place your mission effectiveness in one specific area, you can get yourself in a situation ... if the enemy comes up with a countermeasure..." McGinn noted that the Super Hornet's design offers "the flexibility ... to shift your strategy ... more toward electronics, or more toward missile performance, or more toward onboard or offboard sensor components. That's the key to staying two steps ahead of potential adversaries."

This compromise approach also surfaced in the design of the overall Super Hornet mission. Conceived as a strike fighter, the proposed design had to accommodate both roles, much as the venerable F-4 did during the 1960s in the skies over Vietnam. Yet, as a strike fighter, it is obvious that no design can perform all missions across the operational spectrum with equal proficiency. Many of the attributes that make for a quality high-end interceptor make for a poor attack aircraft, and vice versa. "What the Super Hornet does," Dyer stated, "is to stake out the middle of the spectrum, expanding out as far towards the ends as possible." This creates the flexibility that air commanders want to prosecute their air campaigns.

F/A-18E/F versus the F/A-18C/D

The Super Hornet represents a design compromise of five variables, each intended to cure perceived shortcomings of the original Hornet – range, payload, bring-back, survivability and growth room. Of these five, perhaps the two most important variables were range and bring-back. Hornets had long been criticised for having 'short legs'. The Navy Operational Requirements (OR) called for the original F/A-18A to have an unrefuelled 400-nm (741-km) range for fighter and a 450-nm (833-km) range for attack missions. The -A/B performance, however, came in at 366 and 415 nm (678 and 769 km), respectively, figures that only got worse over time as new components added more and more weight to the airframe. In all, the Super Hornet promised an increase of approximately 40 per cent in range over the current F/A-18C/D. The Navy's 1992 OR called for ranges of 410 nm (759 km) in the fighter role and 430 nm (796 km)

in the attack role, figures which the -E/F has beaten at 420 and 490 nm (778 and 907 km).

To create room for the extra fuel, the -E/F fuselage was stretched by 2 ft 10 in (0.86 m) and its wings enlarged by 25 per cent. This represented an increase of 4 ft 3.5 in (1.31 m) and 100 sq ft (9.29 m²) over the C/D, and provided an additional 3,000 lb (1361 kg) of fuel (approximately 33 per cent more than the F/A-18C). According to projected figures (and subsequently confirmed), in an air defence role the -E/F has 40 per cent greater combat radius than the -C/D (1.8 hours versus 1.0 hours) while operating 200 nm (370 km) from the carrier. Similarly, the -E/F in an escort role posts an increase in range of nearly 38 per cent. Range for self-escorted strike missions improved from 277 to 475 nm (513 to 880 km), an increase of over 70 per cent. These were confirmed through subsequent test flights.

The larger wings brought additional benefits to the aircraft, including two new weapons stations and an overall payload rating of 17,000 lb (7711 kg) (an increase of 20 per cent). Rated at 1,250 lb (567 kg) each, the additional hardpoints (Nos 2 and 10) permit more flexible mission loads, which translates into fewer missions, fewer aircraft per mission and more target options. All of these factors contribute to a more survivable and more flexible platform.

Top: VFA-122's first aircraft were from the LRIP batches. The squadron spent the first 18 months of its existence hammering out the syllabus and training instructors so that it could open for business in June 2000.

Above: As well as providing a shore base for fleet squadrons, NAS Lemoore is the centre of the Super Hornet training effort. The airfield has been a major training location for decades.

Located in the Californian Central Valley, Lemoore is surrounded by open, flat land – ideal for initial conversion training. For more challenging flying the mountains and desert are not far away.

VFA-122 'Flying Eagles'

Attack Squadron 122 was created by the renumbering of VA(AW)-35 on 29 June 1959. The unit was first assigned to its present base at NAS Lemoore in January 1963, when it was acting as the West Coast FRS for the A-1 Skyraider. In 1966 it began training A-7 Corsair II pilots, a role which ended with the disestablishment of the squadron on 31 May 1991. The nickname 'Flying Eagles' was in use from 1971. The squadron was reactivated as VFA-122 on 1 October 1998 to act as the Super Hornet FRS, and was ceremonially stood up on 15 January 1999. It did not receive its first aircraft until November, allowing the task of training sufficient instructors to staff the squadron to begin. VFA-122's motto is 'We train the experts', and it uses the EXPERT callsign. The badge consists of a bald eagle clutching three arrows, and the tail marking consists of the bird's head. The 'NJ' tailcode is that of the Pacific Fleet training wing.

VFA-122 has 37 Super Hornets assigned, of which 11 are single-seaters. Of the F/A-18Fs, eight are configured as twin-stickers to provide initial type conversion training before students progress to mission-based training on the E or single-stick F. The squadron has two 'boss-birds' (Modexes 101 and 201) which wear high-visibility markings. Due to the Super Hornet's improved aerodynamics and more forgiving handling, basic conversion from older Hornets or Tomcats is considered straight-forward. However, learning to use the more advanced weapons system takes some time due to the capabilities of the avionics.

Opposite page, bottom: This VFA-122 F/A-18F carries a test round of the AGM-154 JSOW. Guided by GPS, the AGM-154A version provides the Super Hornet with a stand-off attack capability against area targets. The A-model JSOW dispenses 145 BLU-97 sub-munitions as it glides over the target area. JSOW has been widely used against Iraqi air defence sites.

A Super Hornet can now fly with a load of two AIM-9s, an AMRAAM, a FLIR pod, two high-speed anti-radiation missiles (HARMs), two precision-guided munitions (PGMs), and two 480-US gal (1817-litre) fuel tanks. F/A-18Cs would be limited to a single PGM and HARM, or two of either, and two 330-US gal (1249-litre) tanks, and have reduced overall range.

The strengthened wings also gave the Super Hornet added lift, thereby allowing a slower approach speed. At 128 kt (237 km/h), Super Hornets handle better behind the carrier. The larger wings further permit use of the larger 480-US gal (1817-litre) external tanks, which current models could only carry in a land-based role. The larger

wings and strengthened fuselage also helped alleviate another significant criticism of the Hornet: bring-back capability. As new systems were added to the Hornet, its heavier weight decreased operational warloads and, more importantly, decreased the amount of unexpended ordnance that the Hornet could safely bring back to the carrier. One company official estimated as much as 0.33 lb (150 g) per day was added to the Hornet over its life. Although Hornets could overcome this problem on take-off by launching with less fuel, then immediately tanking, there were few options when aircraft returned from missions with full loads and had to jettison unexpended ordnance into the ocean. Such practice was common during operations over Bosnia, Kosovo and the No-Fly Zones in Iraq. In fact, during Allied Force operations over Kosovo, an F/A-18C launching with four AGM-154 Joint Stand-Off Weapons could bring only two back onboard. This wasted significant amounts of money. An F/A-18C has a bring-back capability of approximately 5,500 lb (2495 kg); the E can bring back 9,900 lb (4490 kg) and the F about 9,000 lb (4082 kg). This increased ability factored large in recent operations over Afghanistan and Iraq.

Enhanced survivability

Increasing overall survivability was another chief concern of the Super Hornet's design team, and it has been placed by some analysts at more than five times that of the original -C/D. Interestingly, the increase was obtained not by stealth, but by a combination of factors that includes incorporation of radar cross-section reduction techniques, improved electronic countermeasures, reduced system vulnerability and improved stand-off weapons delivery tactics. While not depending on F-117 stealth design techniques, a significant radar cross-section reduction was obtained by a combination of radar-absorbing materials (RAM) and the redesign of panels and engine inlets. Some 154 lb (70 kg) of RAM is used throughout the aircraft, most notably on the leading-edge surfaces, the pivot point of the tail-hook and the aileron actuator fairings and hinges.

Access panels and landing gear doors now feature jagged or saw-toothed edges to redeflect radar waves. The formerly D-shaped engine outlets of the -C/D were recon-figured to an angled box (similar to those of the F/A-22). These inlets not only help deflect radar waves, they permit greater airflow to the engines. Other measures included tightening tolerances and better aligning planforms. Boeing also looked at ways of hiding the tailhook, but ultimately declined to vary from proven prior practice. Although figures are classified, radar signature has been reduced by an order of magnitude.

Improved countermeasures systems were also added to increase the -E/F's effectiveness against surface-to-air and air-to-air missiles. Centred around the Integrated DEfence CounterMeasures (IDECM) system designated ALQ-214, this suite comprises the enhanced ALR-67(V)3 radar warn-ing receiver, the ALQ-214 countermeasures system and the fibre-optic towed ALE-55 deceptive jammer. Super Hornets have initially deployed with Raytheon's ALE-50 towed decoy pending the final development of the ALE-55. The number of flare/chaff dispensers was doubled from 60 to 120 units, using the BAE Systems Integrated Defence Solutions (formerly Tracor) ALE-47, which is also capable of dispensing POET and GEN-X active expendable decoys.

Reduced vulnerability

Loss figures will be lower because vulnerable areas are decreased by more than 14 per cent compared to the -C/D. Dry-bay fire suppression gear was added to reduce the incidence of fire and explosion. Consisting of 14 optical sensors and seven extinguishing heads that automatically sense heat then release inert gas to counter fires, the dry-bay system is located in the bottom of the fuselage near the hydraulic lines and flight control circuits. Boeing designers consider this the single greatest factor in lowering overall -E/F vulnerability. "It makes the -E/F harder to bring down when it is hit," one spokesperson said. A quadruply-redundant fly-by-wire flight control system was also included to ensure the retention of flight control in the event of a missile strike. These improvements are maximised when coupled with new stand-off weapons such as the JSOW (Joint Stand-Off Weapon), JDAM (Joint Direct Attack Munition) and JASSM (Joint Air to Surface Stand-off Missile), which allow Super Hornet crews to stay far outside the effective range of various enemy air defences. Also, as mentioned earlier, the two additional hardpoints mean that Super Hornets can carry more ordnance and so, perhaps, fly fewer missions.

Overall, improved survivability systems reduced -E/F combat losses by 87 per cent in a simulation run by Boeing, compared against F/A-18Cs. For that simulation, 10 -E/Fs flew anti-air defence system strike missions. In an interview reported in *Aviation Week & Space Technology*, Boeing offi-cials noted, "[aircraft] participating in the strike simulation had 45 per cent fewer encounters with hostile aircraft during missions due to signature reductions and improved

jamming, and improved countermeasures reduced the lethality from ground-launched missiles by 80 per cent."

Finally, one of the most desired features of the Super Hornet is its expanded room for growth. Provisions for upgrades have been designed into the Super Hornet such that it will enter service with about 40 per cent growth capacity in electrical power, cooling and equipment volume. The -C/D has less than 0.2 cu ft (0.0056 m^3) left for systems growth; the -E/F entered service with 17 cu ft (0.4813 m^3) of growth space. This new lease on life essen-tially restarts the growth clock that had all but stopped in the original model. The lack of growth space in the -C/D was one of the chief reasons for looking at a new variant.

Several other areas were modified as a result of these primary changes. To accommodate the heavier aircraft, the more powerful General Electric F414-GE-400 engines were installed, providing 35 per cent more thrust than the F404.

The F/A-18E/F has full night capability and the training syllabus includes a fair proportion of night work. Both cockpits of the F have a large multi-purpose display (above, showing a moving map) and two flanking displays. The small screen at lower left shows fuel and engine information. Low-voltage 'slime' lights and the use of night vision goggles allow pilots to fly in close formation (top) even in darkness.

A key part of the VFA-122 syllabus is carrier qualifications. From its Lemoore base the squadron regularly sends small training detachments of aircraft and pilots to carriers operating off the southern California coast. Carriers usually sail specifically for these training periods, which also involve other aircraft types from the other FRSs on the West Coast. These F/A-18Fs were conducting CarQuals in October 2000 aboard USS Carl Vinson (CVN 70). At the time VFA-122 was training its first students – an advanced guard of pilots fresh from flight school (CAT 1) and destined for service with VFA-115.

Each capable of delivering up to 21,890 lb (97.36 kN) of thrust, the F414s were derived from the F404 used in the original Hornet and modified with technologies from the F412 engine developed for the cancelled A-12. The new engines have a 16 per cent higher airflow than the F404, a 30:1 pressure ratio and a 9:1 thrust ratio, all within the same length and aft diameter as the F404. The increased performance is due largely to use of an integrally-bladed disc in the compressor, called a blisk. The -E/F is the first system to use dual-channel full authority digital engine control.

Additional structural changes included enlarging the rudders by 54 per cent, increasing the horizontal stabilators by 36 per cent, enlarging the vertical tails by 15 per cent and expanding the LEX by 34 per cent. The enlarged wings, discussed above, were expanded to 500 sq ft (46.45 m²). Internally, commonality with the -C/D is just 10 per cent. Most changes concerned redesigning features in order to save weight and cost. Carbon-fibre composite use has doubled compared to the -C/D, to 22 per cent of the structural weight, most of which is applied to the centre and aft fuselage, wings, and leading- and trailing-edge flaps. IM7, an improved stiffness/strength carbon-fibre, was used extensively in the wings and tail skins. Use of aluminium alloys decreased from 50 per cent in the -C/D to 29 per cent in the -E/F. The landing gear was strengthened by using Aermet 100 steel, which has a higher damage tolerance.

Overall, the -E/F has 8,100 structural parts compared to the -C/D's 14,100. In fact, easier assembly and parts reduction was a guiding design principle of the product definition teams. One example can be found in the nose barrel bulkhead, where a formerly 90-piece assembly in the -C/D was reduced to a one-piece machined part in the Super Hornet by using high-speed machining tools. Fuselage splicing was also modified in order to reduce tolerance problems; assembly is now accomplished using a new Boeing-designed splice tool, which uses a laser tracker to guide the two sections together for a nominal fit.

Cockpit improvements

The cockpit gained new features as well. Cockpit displays were modified by substituting a new Kaiser 8 x 8-in (20.3 x 20.3-cm) flat-panel active matrix LCD display for the C/D's 5 x 5-in (12.7 x 12.7-cm) central display and by replacing the C/D's two 5 x 5-in (12.7 x 12.7-cm) MRDs with two multipurpose CRT touch-screens. The up-front control panel display was also replaced with a monochrome touch-sensitive screen. A new feature included an engine/fuel display featuring a programmable monochrome active-matrix LCD that graphically displays nozzle positions and fuel tank capacity, and fuel tank 'bingo' in pounds. At the time the first Hornet was delivered, the F/A-18C Lot 19 served as the avionics baseline for the E/F. Thus, avionics retained about 90 per cent commonality with the C/D models. Controls remained at 85 per cent commonality and the flight control systems at 67 per cent. As for avionics, the decision to begin with commonality represented Boeing's effort to contain costs and reduce programme risks.

As production of the seven contracted EMD Super Hornets went on, programme focus shifted to demonstrating that the aircraft could perform as advertised. The primary objectives of the engineering, manufacturing and development phase were to "translate the most promising design into a stable, producible, cost-effective design; validate the manufacturing processes; and demonstrate system capabilities through testing". Essentially, the goal was to "detect what was not predicted and to fix what goes wrong". After initial test flights in St Louis, the Super Hornet headed to the Naval Air Warfare Center at NAS Patuxent River, Maryland, for the development flight test programme. Seven Hornets – five single-seat E models and two dual-place F models – were used for these tests, as were three ground test articles. An F/A-18D was fitted with new avionics and served as an avionics testbed. Clearly indicative of the programme's attention to detail, the Super Hornet entered EMD flight testing 1,000 lb (454 kg) under projected weight.

Pax River adventures

The development flight test phase of the EMD began on 4 March 1996 under the guidance of the Navy/Industry Integrated Test Team (ITT). The -E/F's EMD phase differed from prior test programmes in that it combined Navy and contractor flight testing under one programme, rather than having two independent tests proceed consecutively. The Navy's Operational Test and Evaluation Squadron, VX-9, also provided support for testing activities. Having engineers and test pilots from both groups working side by side, interacting directly with their impressions and findings, reduced the EMD test flight phase by as much as one year. Overall, the EMD Super Hornets accumulated 3,000 flight hours and expanded the flight envelope to 49,500 ft (15088 m), speeds greater than Mach 1.5, and +7/-1.7 g.

The ITT's work at this stage sought to show that "the aircraft can fly, that it can fight, and that its systems can work together". Each aircraft in the test programme was given specific duties: aircraft E1 made its maiden flight on 29 November 1995 and was charged with investigating flying qualities and flight envelope expansion. E1 made its initial flight with stores on 21 February 1997; its load consisted of three external tanks, two Mk 84 bombs, two AIM-9 Sidewinders, and two AGM-88 HARMs. Total weight reached 62,400 lb (28304 kg). E2 first flew on 26 December 1995 and was used for engine and performance testing. E3 handled the load testing portion of the EMD, while high angle-of-attack (AoA) evaluations were assigned to E4. E5 was the first Super Hornet to possess full mission capability and was used for weapons work.

The two dual-place Super Hornets were also busy. F1 was assigned carrier suitability and, later, weapons testing. First flying on 1 April 1996, F1 racked up 508 sorties and 601.8 flight hours, the most flight time of all EMD aircraft. F2 (BuNo. 165169; first flight 11 October 1996), was also assigned to some carrier qualification duties, but spent much of its time with E5 performing weapons testing at

China Lake. F2 was the second Super Hornet to have a full avionics suite.

Static tests were performed on ST50 commencing in August 1995. It was later sent to Lakehurst, New Jersey, for emergency barricade testing. The airframe completed three tests before being damaged on 23 September when a restraining cable failed and the aircraft overturned into a wooded area. ST50 was subsequently repaired at Boeing and transferred to China Lake for live-firing testing using large armour-piercing incendiary projectiles. DT50 began its shock loading assessment in February 1996, and FT50 began its fatigue testing in June 1997. FT50 completed its first lifetime (6,000 hours) one month ahead of schedule. The second ran from January 1997 through November 1999.

The first segment of the Super Hornet's sea trials began on 6 August 1996 at NAS Patuxent River, Maryland, when Commander Tom Gurney made the Super Hornet's first catapult launch from a land-based, steam-powered MR-7 catapult in F1. Fifteen days later, F1 made its first arrested landing. F/A-18F1 headed out to USS *John C. Stennis* (CVN 74) in January 1997 for the Super Hornet's initial sea trials. In cold and snowy weather, F1 made the two-hour flight from the Naval Air Warfare Center at Patuxent River and landed in what were considered 'marginal' weather conditions for an aircraft at this stage of its flight tests. The

VFA-115 'Eagles' landed the honour of becoming the fleet's first Super Hornet squadron, and the first unit to pass through the VFA-122 'schoolhouse'. VFA-115's aircraft were from the third and final LRIP batch, the last aircraft built before full production got under way. Several features of full production aircraft were missing, and their avionics suite was roughly comparable to that of the F/A-18C – lacking MIDS, SHARP and JHMCS capability. The squadron did receive four LRIP ATFLIR pods, but they were not used when the squadron went into combat due to reliability issues associated with the early-production equipment.

Above: VFA-115's 'boss-bird' traps aboard Lincoln *in August 2002, during the squadron's first operational deployment. The carrier was sailing off Hawaii at the time. The commander's aircraft wears less colourful markings than the CAG jet.*

Left: VFA-115 F/A-18Es share deck space on Lincoln *with a VF-31 F-14D. At the time Air Wing 14 was undergoing a COMPTUEX prior to its operational cruise (the first with the Super Hornet).*

Inside the F/A-18E/F

F414 engine

The F414 is a direct descendant of the F404 which powers the 'legacy' Hornet, offering considerable advances throughout the engine and more power. It has a larger fan for increased mass flow. The engine is a two-shaft powerplant built around a core which was similar to that developed for the F412 engine for the cancelled A-12, and features an afterburner section based on technology from the YF120 engine developed for the F-22/F-23. Upstream of the three-stage fan is a row of inlet struts and one of variable stators. The compressor has seven stages, while the low-pressure and high-pressure turbines each consist of a single stage.

Boeing F/A-18E cutaway

1. Composite radome
2. Radome open position for access
3. Raytheon AN/APG-73 multi-mode radar
4. Radome hinge
5. Scanner tracking mechanism
6. Radar mounting bulkhead
7. AN/APG-79 AESA radar for future integration
8. Low-band antenna
9. Radar equipment module
10. Electro-luminescent formation lighting strip
11. Cannon barrels
12. Cannon port and blast-diffuser vents
13. Flight refuelling probe, extended
14. Probe actuating link
15. Upper combined IFF interrogator antenna
16. M61A2 Vulcan 20-mm cannon
17. Cannon ammunition drum, 570 rounds
18. Incidence transmitter
19. Lower VHF/UHF/L-band antenna
20. Pitot head
21. Gun gas vents
22. Cockpit front pressure bulkhead
23. Nosewheel door
24. Ground power socket
25. Avionics ground cooling air fan and ducting
26. Rudder pedals
27. Instrument panel, full-colour multi-function CRT displays
28. Instrument panel shroud
29. Frameless windscreen panel
30. Head-up display (HUD)
31. Upward hingeing cockpit canopy
32. Martin-Baker NACES 'zero-zero' ejection seat
33. Starboard side console panel
34. Control column, digital fly-by-wire flight control system
35. Port side console with engine throttle levers, full HOTAS controls
36. Sloping seat-mounting bulkhead
37. Boarding step
38. Forward fuselage lateral equipment bays, three per side
39. Nosewheel leg pivot mounting
40. Landing light
41. Deck approach signal lights
42. Nosewheel steering unit
43. Catapult shuttle link
44. Twin nosewheels, forward retracting
45. Torque scissor links incorporating holdback fitting
46. Folding boarding ladder
47. Nosewheel retraction jack
48. AN/ALQ-165 EW transmitting antenna
49. Boarding ladder stowage
50. LEX equipment bay
51. Cockpit rear pressure bulkhead
52. Cockpit avionics equipment bay
53. Canopy rotary actuator
54. Starboard AN/ALQ-165 transmitting antenna
55. Canopy actuating strut
56. Canopy hinge point
57. No. 1 fuselage bag-type tank
58. Sloping bulkhead, structural provision for two-seat F/A-18F
59. EW receiver
60. LEX rib structure
61. Port leading-edge extension (LEX) chine member
62. 480-US gal (1817-litre) external fuel tank, centreline refuelling store as alternative
63. Port position light
64. Liquid cooling system equipment, reservoir, heat exchanger and ground running fan
65. Forward slinging point
66. Forward tank bay access panel
67. Starboard position light
68. Starboard LEX avionics equipment bay
69. Spoiler panel
70. LEX vent, operates in conjunction with leading-edge flap
71. Intake boundary layer spill duct
72. GPS antenna
73. No. 2 tank bay access panel
74. No. 2 bag-type fuel tank
75. Port spoiler
76. Spoiler hydraulic actuator
77. Boundary layer bleed air ducts
78. Bleed air spill duct
79. Port LEX vent
80. Perforated intake wall bleed air spill duct
81. Port fixed-geometry air intake
82. Mainwheel leg door
83. Main undercarriage leg strut
84. Trailing axle suspension
85. Port mainwheel
86. Shock absorber strut
87. Mainwheel door
88. LAU-116 missile carrier/launch unit
89. Mainwheel leg pivot mounting
90. Hydraulic retraction jack
91. Intake duct framing
92. Wing panel attachment joints
93. Machined titanium fuselage main bulkheads
94. No. 3 bag-type fuel tank
95. No. 4 bag-type fuel tank
96. No. 3 tank access panel
97. IFF antenna
98. Dorsal fairing access panels
99. Upper VHF/UHF/L-band antenna
100. Starboard wing panel bolted attachment joints
101. Starboard wing integral fuel tank
102. Leading-edge flap hydraulic drive unit and rotary actuator
103. Wing carbon-fibre composite (CFC) skin panelling
104. Starboard stores pylons, wing pylons canted 4° outboard
105. Leading-edge dogtooth
106. Wing-fold hinge fairing porous panel
107. Outboard leading-edge flap rotary actuator
108. Two-segment leading-edge flap
109. Outer wing panel dry bay
110. Wing tip position light
111. Formation light fairing
112. Wing tip missile installation
113. Starboard outer wing panel folded position
114. Drooping aileron
115. Aileron hydraulic actuator
116. Wing-fold hydraulic jack
117. Aileron and flap opposed movement as airbrake function
118. Starboard single-slotted trailing-edge flap
119. Hinged flap shroud
120. Flap hydraulic actuator
121. Dorsal equipment bay
122. No. 4 tank bay access panel
123. Ram air from intake duct for ECS
124. Rear fuselage slinging points
125. Environmental control system (ECS) equipment bay
126. ECS hinged auxiliary intake doors
127. Fuselage fuel vent tanks, port and starboard
128. Primary (starboard) and secondary (port) heat exchangers
129. Heat exchanger exhaust ducts
130. Engine pressure balance vent
131. Starboard fin bolted attachment joints
132. Fin integral vent tank
133. Multi-spar fin structure
134. Leading edge structure, CFC skin with honeycomb core
135. Fin CFC skin panelling
136. CFC fin tip fairing
137. Rear position light
138. Aft AN/ALQ-165 receiving antenna
139. AN/ALR-67 RWR antenna
140. Fuel jettison

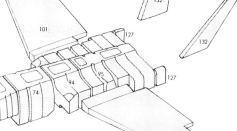

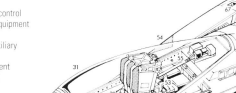

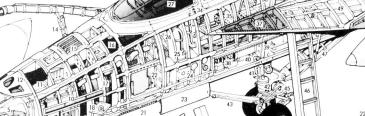

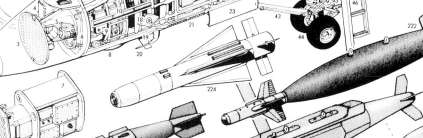

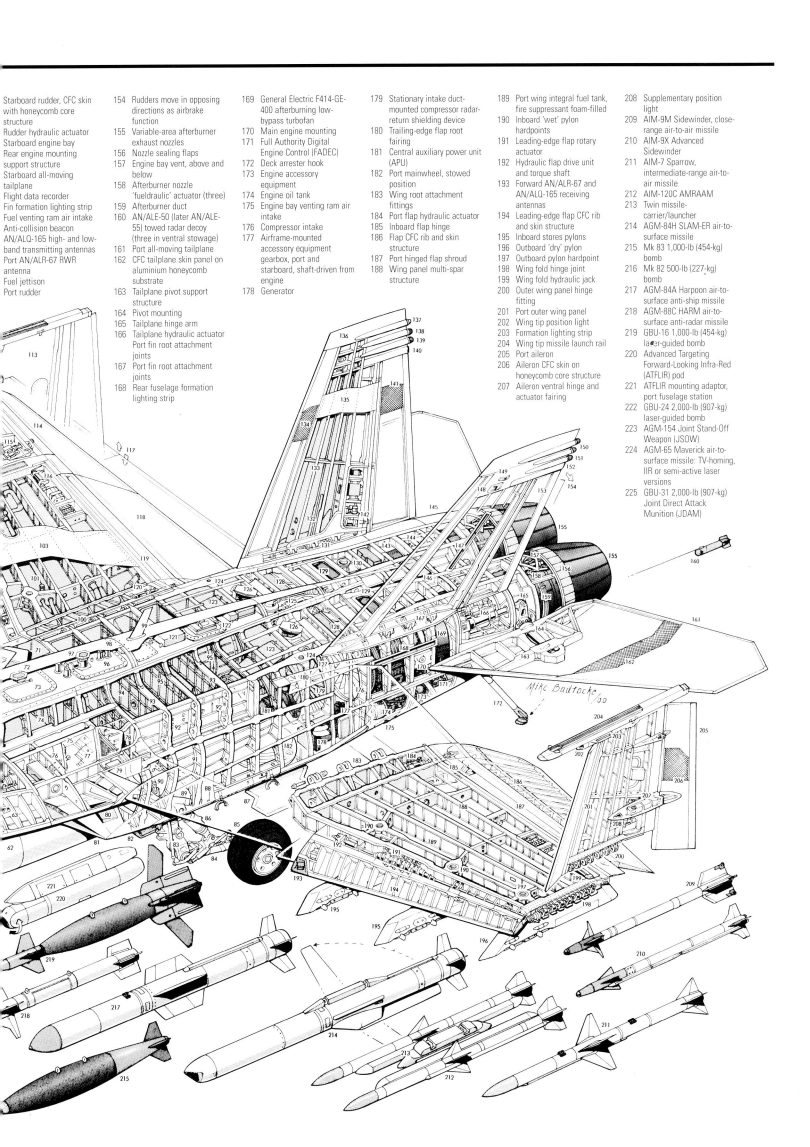

Starboard rudder, CFC skin with honeycomb core structure
Rudder hydraulic actuator
Starboard engine bay
Rear engine mounting support structure
Starboard all-moving tailplane
Flight data recorder
Fin formation lighting strip
Fuel venting ram air intake
Anti-collision beacon
AN/ALQ-165 high- and low-band transmitting antennas
Port AN/ALR-67 RWR antenna
Fuel jettison
Port rudder

154 Rudders move in opposing directions as airbrake function
155 Variable-area afterburner exhaust nozzles
156 Nozzle sealing flaps
157 Engine bay vent, above and below
158 Afterburner nozzle 'fueldraulic' actuator (three)
159 Afterburner duct
160 AN/ALE-50 (later AN/ALE-55) towed radar decoy (three in ventral stowage)
161 Port all-moving tailplane
162 CFC tailplane skin panel on aluminium honeycomb substrate
163 Tailplane pivot support structure
164 Pivot mounting
165 Tailplane hinge arm
166 Tailplane hydraulic actuator
Port fin root attachment joints
167 Port fin root attachment joints
168 Rear fuselage formation lighting strip

169 General Electric F414-GE-400 afterburning low-bypass turbofan
170 Main engine mounting
171 Full Authority Digital Engine Control (FADEC)
172 Deck arrester hook
173 Engine accessory equipment
174 Engine oil tank
175 Engine bay venting ram air intake
176 Compressor intake
177 Airframe-mounted accessory equipment gearbox, port and starboard, shaft-driven from engine
178 Generator

179 Stationary intake duct-mounted compressor radar-return shielding device
180 Trailing-edge flap root fairing
181 Central auxiliary power unit (APU)
182 Port mainwheel, stowed position
183 Wing root attachment fittings
184 Port flap hydraulic actuator
185 Inboard flap hinge
186 Flap CFC rib and skin structure
187 Port hinged flap shroud
188 Wing panel multi-spar structure

189 Port wing integral fuel tank, fire suppressant foam-filled
190 Inboard 'wet' pylon hardpoints
191 Leading-edge flap rotary actuator
192 Hydraulic flap drive unit and torque shaft
193 Forward AN/ALR-67 and AN/ALQ-165 receiving antennas
194 Leading-edge flap CFC rib and skin structure
195 Inboard stores pylons
196 Outboard 'dry' pylon
197 Outboard pylon hardpoint
198 Wing fold hinge joint
199 Wing fold hydraulic jack
200 Outer wing panel hinge fitting
201 Port outer wing panel
202 Wing tip position light
203 Formation lighting strip
204 Wing tip missile launch rail
205 Port aileron
206 Aileron CFC skin on honeycomb core structure
207 Aileron ventral hinge and actuator fairing

208 Supplementary position light
209 AIM-9M Sidewinder, close-range air-to-air missile
210 AIM-9X Advanced Sidewinder
211 AIM-7 Sparrow, intermediate-range air-to-air missile
212 AIM-120C AMRAAM
213 Twin missile-carrier/launcher
214 AGM-84H SLAM-ER air-to-surface missile
215 Mk 83 1,000-lb (454-kg) bomb
216 Mk 82 500-lb (227-kg) bomb
217 AGM-84A Harpoon air-to-surface anti-ship missile
218 AGM-88C HARM air-to-surface anti-radar missile
219 GBU-16 1,000-lb (454-kg) laser-guided bomb
220 Advanced Targeting Forward-Looking Infra-Red (ATFLIR) pod
221 ATFLIR mounting adaptor, port fuselage station
222 GBU-24 2,000-lb (907-kg) laser-guided bomb
223 AGM-154 Joint Stand-Off Weapon (JSOW)
224 AGM-65 Maverick air-to-surface missile: TV-homing, IIR or semi-active laser versions
225 GBU-31 2,000-lb (907-kg) Joint Direct Attack Munition (JDAM)

Cockpit

Each cockpit (front, above left, and rear, above right) has four main screens. The larger screen is a Multi-Purpose Color Display (MPCD), while the two either side are monochrome. In the front cockpit the upper centre screen is the Active Matrix Liquid Crystal Display (AMLCD), which is touch-sensitive. AMLCDs have replaced the two side screens, while the MPCD is also due to be replaced in later production aircraft. A fifth screen in the front cockpit, below the left-hand display, shows engine and fuel information. Among the many displays which can be called up on the MPCD is a moving map (right). In this instance the aircraft (as represented by a simple symbol in the centre) is flying over Iraq, to the south of Baghdad. The front cockpit has a wide-angle head-up display (left) which displays flight and targeting data.

Undercarriage

The Super Hornet's undercarriage is similar in design to that of the F/A-18C/D, but is beefed up to cater for the higher weights. There is also more ground clearance to allow the aircraft to carry a large fuel tank on the centreline. The undercarriage retracts in the same way, swinging up and in so that stores can still be carried on the fuselage sides. When stowed the wheels lie flat beneath the intake trunking. The arrester hook fairing was identified as a key radar 'hot-spot', and has been treated with radar-absorbent material accordingly.

Defences

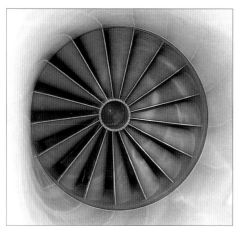

Rendering the Super Hornet more survivable in combat has been accomplished by the adoption of RCS reduction techniques and the use of advanced countermeasures. Although not a true 'stealth' aircraft, the Super Hornet has many RCS-reducing features, such as sawtooth edges on opening panels, application of RAM in key areas, and the adoption of radar 'blockers' in the intakes (left), which stop radar energy reaching the highly reflective fan face. The integrated electronic protection suite includes a towed radar decoy carried between the engines. In initial production aircraft this is the AN/ALE-50 (right), but this will be superseded in later aircraft by the AN/ALE-55. The AN/ALQ-214 system provides jamming, while a variety of mechanical countermeasures are available for decoying both IR- and radar-guided missiles away from the aircraft.

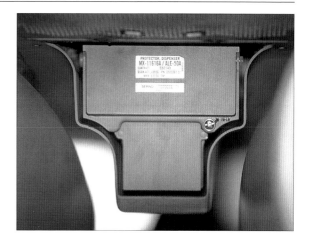

Stations and loadouts

The F/A-18E/F is equipped with 11 stations for the carriage of stores. On each wing is a wingtip Sidewinder missile launch rail and three underwing pylons. The outboard pylons can carry weapons in the 500-kg (1,100-lb) class, while the inboard and intermediate pylons can carry the larger stores, including fuel tanks. The fuselage has a centreline hardpoint for weapon, fuel tank or refuelling store carriage, either side of which is a hardpoint for the carriage of sensor pods or MRAAMS (AIM-7 or AIM-120). The number of hardpoints available allows a bewildering array of possible loadouts. By the use of twin racks on the two inner wing pylons the maximum number of weapons that can be carried is 14 (12 AIM-120s and two AIM-9s) for the air-to-air role, or 11 (Mk 82s or 83s, plus two AIM-9s) in the attack role.

When carrying asymmetric loads, the weights/moments on each wing have to be roughly equalled out. Here three Mk 83s are counterbalanced by a GBU-16 LGB and an AIM-120 AMRAAM.

Up to four GBU-31 JDAMs can be carried. A single AMRAAM is usually carried on the fuselage side pylon, but can be moved to the outer wing pylon if needed for balance purposes.

This 'five-wet' tanker (four 480-US gal/1817-litre tanks plus refuelling store) configuration leaves capacity for a baggage pod on the outer wing pylon and an AMRAAM for self-defence on the fuselage.

Air-to-air missiles

For the time being the AIM-9M is the standard wingtip missile, but it is being replaced by the Raytheon AIM-9X, an example of which is seen below on a VX-9 Super Hornet. The '9X' uses the motor and warhead from existing Sidewinders, but has a new imaging seeker and thrust-vectoring control. Although it has a small motor compared to other short-range air-to-air missiles, it has very low drag and its seeker allows engagements at beyond visual ranges.

The primary air-to-air weapon is the AIM-120C AMRAAM (above), which can be carried from any pylon apart from the centreline and wingtips. The four inner wing pylons can mount twin-rail launchers for AMRAAM. An air-to-air alternative to AIM-120 is the older AIM-7 Sparrow, of which up to eight can be carried. As the Super Hornet is tasked with fleet defence, it is a likely early candidate to receive any ramjet-powered AMRAAM follow-on, especially as the APG-79 AESA radar will greatly increase the Super Hornet's lethal range in the air-to-air role.

Air-to-surface

In the attack role the Super Hornet carries an array of unguided, near-precision and precision weapons. GPS-guided weapons such as the GBU-31 (2,000-lb/907-kg, of which four can be carried), GBU-32 (1,000-lb/454-kg, six) and AGM-154 JSOW (1,000-lb/454-kg, six) are widely used in guided attacks in all weathers. For greater precision laser-guided bombs are available from the Paveway II family, and the GBU-24 Paveway III is shortly to be cleared for service. Guided missile options include the AGM-65 Maverick (six) and the larger AGM-84H SLAM-ER stand-off weapon (four). Specialist weapons are the anti-ship AGM-84 Harpoon (four) and the AGM-88 HARM (six). Unguided munition options cover the range of Mk 80 series bombs and rocket pods.

The AGM-88 HARM (above and right) is used by the F/A-18E/F for attacking radars, although it is due to be replaced by the AARGM, which is designed to be better at attacking radars after they have shut down. For attacks against known radar site locations the AGM-154 JSOW (left) is often used, as this has proved far less likely to deviate from its target, with a consequent reduced risk of collateral damage.

After its work-up phase, VFA-115 deployed to Abraham Lincoln *on 24 July 2002 for the Super Hornet's first operational cruise. This took the carrier and Air Wing Fourteen to the Arabian Sea for operations over Afghanistan. At the time US forces were still conducting large-scale 'mopping-up' exercises against Taliban/al Qaeda forces, and VFA-115's Super Hornets provided top cover for these operations, although they did not drop any weapons. During their patrol in the Arabian Sea the 'Eagles' suggested changing their name back temporarily to the original 'Arabs'.*

first carrier landing was made by Navy Lieutenant Frank Morley on 18 January at approximately 10:00 a.m. EST off the coast of Cape Hatteras, North Carolina. Commander Tom Gurney then switched places with Morley and piloted F1 on its first carrier catapult launch, at approximately 2:30 p.m. that same day.

A total of 61 daytime launches and recoveries was made during the six-day deployment. Flights explored flying qualities from behind the ship, dual- and single-engine handling, and trim and crosswind effects while launching from the bow and waist catapults. A total of 54 touch-and-go landings confirmed the -E/F's landing approach speed to be 10 kt (18.5 km/h) slower than the -C/D's. The pilots described the Super Hornet as having "great hands-off fly-away characteristics off the catapult" and commented that it "[flew] well on approach, as expected, despite challenging wind conditions".

Weapons separation tests

Super Hornets E5 and F2 were assigned to weapons separation testing duties. The first such test occurred on 19 February 1997 as F2 successfully released an empty 480-US gal (1817-litre) fuel tank from 5,000 ft (1524 m). Two days later, E1 flew an Aero Servo Elasticity stores configuration comprised of three 480-US gal (1817-litre) tanks, two AIM-9s, two Mk 84 iron bombs and two HARMs, marking the first time a Super Hornet carried a simulated warload. At some 62,400 lb (23800 kg), it also represented the largest gross weight of the programme to date. Northrop Grumman test pilot Jim Sandberg, who flew E2 during the test, stated that "[the] airplane flew effortlessly

throughout the flight" and "performed as if it were flying clean".

F2 launched the first air-to-air missile – an AIM-9 Sidewinder – in April, followed by the launch of an AIM-120 on 5 May. Additional tests followed, and by the end of May the Super Hornet had successfully released a sampling of the typical Hornet warloads – AIM-7, ALE-47 flares, Stand-off Land Attack Missile (SLAM), Harpoon, a ripple of 10 Mk 82s, Mk 83s, a dual load of CBU-100s – and ejected 480-US gal (1817-litre) tanks from both wing and the centreline stations. Tests were also performed with the ALE-50 towed decoy. Live firings of HARMs followed in December 1998, then a Harpoon launch against a moving ship in January 1999. Twenty-five missiles and over 500,000 lb (226796 kg) of ordnance had been expended by the squadron before the end of the EMD weapons separation phase. Twenty-nine weapons configurations were cleared and made available for the OPEVAL.

Final CQs

The Super Hornet's final carrier qualifications before OPEVAL took place in February and March 1999 aboard USS *Harry S. Truman* (CVN 75) off the coast of Florida. This time, both -Fs were taken to sea. Navy pilot Lieutenant Commander Lance Floyd made the F/A-18F's first nighttime carrier landing. The two -Fs successfully launched off the bow with 15 kt (28 km/h) of crosswind and off the waist catapult with 10 kt (18.5 km/h) of crosswind. Launches and traps were also made with various asymmetrical weapons configurations and using the automatic carrier landing approach system from distances of 4 and

VFA-115 'EAGLES'

VA-115 was formed by the renumbering of VA-12A on 15 July 1948. It flew TBM Avengers, AD Skyraiders and A-6 Intruders before it transitioned to the F/A-18C in 1996, redesignating as VFA-115 in the process. From the 1950s the squadron used the nickname 'Arabs', although this was changed to the potentially less controversial 'Eagles' in 1979. The unit's time with the 'baby' Hornet was brief, as it was chosen to become the first front-line Super Hornet unit. Conversion began in late 2000 and was completed in the first half of the next year. The squadron badge, approved for use on 17 September 1956, consists of a stylised wing and globe design. The 'NK' tailcode signifies assignment to CVW-14 (formerly *Abraham Lincoln*/CVN 72, but from mid-2003 assigned to *John C. Stennis*/CVN 74).

8 miles (6.5 and 13 km). Other flights included minimum end speed tests with military power and full afterburner. At its maximum gross weight (66,000 lb/29937 kg), the -F was able to launch with full afterburner at 142 kt (263 km/h), and reportedly sank only 10 ft (3 m) below the bow before recovering. The aircraft was noted to handle superbly and was considered very responsive to last-minute corrections.

EMD problems

As is not unusual in a test programme, the ITT soon identified over 400 deficiencies, the most significant of which concerned the aircraft's flying qualities, service life, engine performance and weapons separation. Fortunately, only two delays occurred. The first came during the summer of 1996 and involved the delivery of the final three EMD aircraft, due to a three-month machinists' strike at one of the major contractors' facilities. The second delay followed an inflight engine failure, which ended all Super Hornet flight tests (except those of F1 to determine carrier suitability) for two months.

Perhaps the most publicised problem of the EMD was the wing drop phenomenon. First appearing in March 1996, this phenomenon is formally described as "an unacceptable, uncommanded abrupt lateral roll that randomly occurs at the altitude and speed at which air-to-air combat manoeuvres are expected to occur". In its simplest terms,

wing drop is caused by airflow separating on one wing before the other and typically occurred when the Super Hornet was manoeuvred at relatively high angles of attack and high g forces. First noticed during the 1950s during test flights on the F-86, it is a common event associated with high-performance, swept-wing aircraft.

Work towards resolving the problem continued until mid-1997, and isolated the wing drop in the centre of the Super Hornet's flight envelope – between Mach 0.70 and 0.95 at altitudes of 10,000 to 40,000 ft (3048 to 12192 m) and AoA between 6° and 12°. ITT members working with Navy and Boeing engineers, as well as NASA, eventually settled on an interim solution based on modifications to the leading-edge flaps and flight control software. The final solution was achieved through porous wing-fold fairings, which, according to Boeing documents, comprise "many small holes that influence the airflow over the wing, eliminating wing drop throughout the manoeuvring envelope".

Early wind tunnel tests conducted during July and August 1993 showed that some stores would collide with the side of the fuselage or with other stores when released. This problem resulted from adverse airflow created by the aircraft's airframe. To cure the problem, the pylons were redesigned and canted outward at 3°. Testing during the EMD confirmed the redesign had corrected most of the problem. Another related deficiency concerned unwanted

The two-seat F/A-18F enjoys the same combat capability as the single-seater, although its heavier weight reduces its 'bring-back' capacity slightly. Early production aircraft have coupled cockpits, but F/A-18Fs are now being produced with advanced displays in the rear cockpit and the ability to decouple the two work-stations, allowing independent targeting by front- and back-seaters. In most cases this would entail the pilot concentrating on the air threat while the WSO focuses on air-to-ground attacks. The F/A-18F expands further on work done previously by Boeing in this field on the F-15E and the F/A-18D for the USMC.

The capability of the Super Hornet in the tanker role cannot be overestimated, and in the future it will become the air wing's only organic refuelling capacity when the S-3 is retired. The Super Hornet offers a greater offload ability, although its endurance time is reduced, and pound for pound it is more expensive to operate. However, it can stay with the strike force, and during operations over Iraq routinely 'crossed the beach', taking strike aircraft to about 150 miles from their targets. Here a VFA-41 F/A-18F buddy refuels another tanker-configured aircraft.

During a visit to the UK for the Farnborough air show in 2002, VFA-41's 'boss-bird' flies past the cliffs of Beachy Head, with Eastbourne Pier in the background. A concerted sales effort has seen the Super Hornet attend most of the world's major trade shows, where its displays have focused on the type's excellent low-speed manoeuvrability and high-Alpha controllability.

VFA-41 'BLACK ACES'

The 'Black Aces' (callsign FAST EAGLE) transitioned from F-4Ns to F-14As in April 1976, and subsequently took the Tomcat into action against Libya (downing two Su-22s), and in Operations Desert Storm, Allied Force and Enduring Freedom. The final Tomcat cruise, which included combat action over Afghanistan, was made with CVW-8 aboard USS *Enterprise* (CVN 65). After its return in November 2001, the squadron was stood down for conversion to the F/A-18F, the first fleet unit to be equipped with the two-seat version. The squadron is now assigned to CVW-11 (tailcode 'NH') aboard USS *Nimitz* (CVN 68) alongside VFA-14.

noise and vibration created with certain stores configurations. To prevent structural damage in the short-term, speed limitations were placed on the Super Hornet while carrying certain weapons stores. Although a few of these limitations remain in place today (these were noted during the subsequent OPEVAL), the Navy and Boeing have come upon a more economical solution – redesigning the weapons to minimise the noise.

OPEVAL – the last step

Following completion of the successful EMD phase, the Super Hornet moved into the Operational Evaluation phase, the last test prior to fleet introduction. From a conceptual standpoint, the OPEVAL has a different focus than EMD flights, which seek to "test and confirm the aircraft's performance, as well as test new parameters". The OPEVAL, conversely, "looks to test the aircraft's ability to perform operationally and tactically in a realistic wartime environment". Former VX-9 OPEVAL Test Director, Commander Jeff Penfield, USN, described the process as follows: "[we] evaluate the aircraft [in OPEVAL] to determine how it will fit into real world operations. Operational pilots look at things differently than flight test pilots. If I took a Super Hornet into battle tomorrow, how would the aircraft perform?" The best rating for any unit or system entering an OPEVAL is a finding of 'operationally effective' and 'operationally suitable'. Operationally effective means that the aircraft is able to perform its prescribed mission in a fleet environment, and in the face of unexpected threats; operationally suitable means that the aircraft, when operated and maintained by typical fleet personnel in the expected numbers and of the expected experience level, is supportable when deployed.

With the arrival of VFA-14 and VFA-41, CVW-11 became the first and only air wing to operate all four operational US Navy Hornet versions (A, C, E and F), and the first to operate the Navy's preferred mix of two Super and two 'legacy' squadrons. Once aboard the operational carrier (Nimitz), Air Wing Eleven headed for the Persian Gulf for operations over Iraq.

The Super Hornet OPEVAL officially began on 27 May 1999 and ran through 19 November that year. Guidelines for the OPEVAL stemmed from the 1991 Navy Operation Requirement Document (ORD) for the F/A-18E/F Upgrade, which mandated numerous areas of improvements over the existing F/A-18C/D: (1) increased mission radius; (2) increased payload flexibility; (3) increased carrier recovery or bring-back; (4) increased survivability; and (5) decreased vulnerability. Improvements in combat performance over the Lot XII F/A-18 C/D (turn rate, climb rate and acceleration) and growth capability for general avionics (electrical, environmental control, flight control, and hydro-mechanical systems) were considered vital.

The OPEVAL was conducted by Test and Evaluation Squadron Nine (VX-9) based at NAWC China Lake, California, using three F/A-18Es and four F/A-18Fs. These aircraft were the first delivered under the LRIP Lot 1 contract, and all incorporated the modifications resulting from the EMD. The OPEVAL tests were flown by a team of 14 pilots and nine WSOs with diverse backgrounds, including the F/A-18A/B/C/D, F-14, A-6E, A-7E and S-3B communities; all had a significant amount of flight time and were regarded as outstanding crews. Approximately 70 Navy maintenance personnel were assigned to evaluate the aircraft's maintainability during the OPEVAL.

F/A-18E/F evaluated 'as is'

The F/A-18E/F OPEVAL was performed without reference to any of the new capabilities penned for the Super Hornet. Thus, systems such as the Active Electronically Scanned Array (AESA) radar, the AIM-9X Sidewinder off-boresight air-to-air missile, or the Joint Helmet-Mounted Cueing System (JHMCS) were not factored into the overall

VFA-14 'TOPHATTERS'

Despite only becoming VF-14 on 15 December 1949, the 'Tophatters' claim to be the oldest US Navy squadron with a lineage tracing back to 1919. With Tomcats, VF-14 (callsign CAMELOT) flew in Operations Desert Storm, Deny Flight and Enduring Freedom. For the last cruise aboard *Enterprise* the squadron partnered VF-41 in CVW-8, and was heavily committed to 'Bombcat' operations over Afghanistan. At the end of the cruise in November 1991 the squadron began conversion to the F/A-18E, one of two Tomcat units planned for transition to the single-seat Super Hornet. After re-equipment and training, VFA-14 was assigned alongside VFA-41 to *Nimitz*'s CVW-11 ('NH'), the first wing to have its full complement of Super Hornets allocated.

rating. Moreover, no consideration was given to follow-on systems – such as the Advanced Tactical FLIR (ATFLIR) or SHAred Reconnaissance Pod (SHARP) – designed to replace ageing legacy systems carried over from the current -C/D models. Commander Dave Dunaway, one of the lead VX-9 test pilots and a liaison to the EMD Integrated Test Team, described the OPEVAL as "taking an immature aircraft, one in its infancy, and pitting it against established threat systems". Given this, it is clear that the aircraft as tested did not represent the full range of the Super Hornet's tactical capability.

Multi-phase test program

The OPEVAL consisted of a five-phase test programme designed to evaluate the Super Hornet under realistic operating conditions to determine the effectiveness and suitability of the aircraft, its systems, and its weapons for combat. With the exception of reconnaissance (which was evaluated in a subsequent follow-on OPEVAL during 2002), all principle missions of the -E/F – interdiction, war-at-sea, fighter escort, combat air patrol (CAP), alert interceptor, suppression of enemy air defences (SEAD), close air support (CAS), tanker, and forward air control-airborne (FAC-A) – were evaluated. The OPEVAL aircrews initially

familiarised themselves with the aircraft at China Lake before completing carrier qualifications refreshers aboard USS *Abraham Lincoln*.

■ **Air-to-ground phase:** Evaluations of various air-to-air weapons and air-to-air sensors began on 27 May at China Lake. VX-9 aircrews also evaluated the E/F's air combat manoeuvring (ACM), defence suppression capabilities and the aircraft's overall survivability. Twenty-nine of the weapons planned for the E/F were cleared for OPEVAL, which represented those planned for the aircraft's initial deployment. As a comparison, the original Hornet had just two configurations at OPEVAL. The Super Hornets deliv-

These photos show VFA-14 F/A-18Es in the 'five-wet' configuration. Typically an embarked E squadron would have four aircraft configured as tankers. Standard procedure would be to launch the tankers twice during a strike, once to escort the outbound strike aircraft and then again to provide cover for the recovery.

The first operational deployment for the Super Hornet came in the latter part of the Enduring Freedom campaign over Afghanistan, although the aircraft did not drop any weapons. On 29 October 2002 VFA-115 began flying Southern Watch duties over Iraq. Here one of the squadron's aircraft refuels from a USAF KC-10A during an OSW mission. Armament comprises AIM-9 Sidewinders, AIM-120 AMRAAM and GBU-12 LGBs.

Lieutenant John Turner taxis on the deck of Lincoln after returning from a mission in which the Super Hornet had dropped its first bomb drops in anger. The date was 6 November 2002 and the target was a command centre at Tallil. Two Super Hornets released four GBU-31 JDAMs in the attack, and all guided precisely.

ered Mk 82 (500 lb/227 kg), Mk 83 (1,000 lb/454 kg), and Mk 84 (2,000 lb/907 kg) iron bombs during this phase, as well as cluster bomb units (CBUs). A variety of range profiles was also flown to verify the flight performance database predicted by Boeing. The Super Hornet's ability to serve as a tanker was also explored during day and night tanking missions, with the Super Hornet performing as expected.

■ **Air combat phase:** This was conducted during a two-week detachment at NAS Key West, Florida, from 14-25 June. VX-9 evaluated the Super Hornet in a variety of fighter escort and CAP profiles and ACM regimes, assessing both tactics and survivability. At Key West, the evaluators focused mainly on air-to-air critical operational issues (COIs) – fighter escort and air combat manoeuvrability. "The tactics COIs specifically tasked the evaluators to determine if the F/A-18E/F could execute current tactics." Adversary services were provided by F-16Cs from the 185th Fighter Squadron, Air National Guard of Sioux City, Iowa, which flew a series of realistic threat tactics emulating the latest-generation MiG-29. Scenarios pitted up to four Super Hornets against an equal or larger number of threat adversaries. In others, mixed sections of Hornets and Super Hornets were flown to compare the performance of the two aircraft under similar conditions.

■ **Carrier operations performance:** Given that the Super Hornet will live and fight from the decks of an aircraft-carrier, a crucial aspect of the OPEVAL evaluated

the aircraft's flight characteristics around the boat and assessed its overall integration with a carrier air wing during routine operations. During the two weeks from 12-28 July, a VX-9 detachment took a group of Super Hornets to USS *John C. Stennis* (CVN 74). After spending the first week qualifying the aircraft, VX-9 personnel operated the Super Hornets as a small squadron with other Air Wing Nine (CVW-9) aircraft, allowing the evaluators to critique the Super Hornet's performance and its ability to integrate with other carrier assets. Missions flown included simulated deck-launched intercepts, tanking, mining and war-at-sea strikes.

The anti-carrier and mining operations were conducted off the southern California operations area, while the long-range offensive strikes were flown from the *John C. Stennis* against the Fallon and China Lake ranges. Aircrews stated that the Super Hornet integrated well and fulfilled all tasked missions. Moreover, its greater range and flight time allowed planners to increase cycle time, which means that the Super Hornet will not be as limited as its predecessor in cyclic operations.

■ **Combined joint operations:** The final OPEVAL detachment went to Nellis AFB, Nevada, from 16-27 August. There, Super Hornets participated in a multinational Combined/Joint Red Flag Exercise with over 60 aircraft from the Air Force, Marine Corps, Navy, and several foreign countries. Flying strike, SEAD, fighter escort, interdiction, and FAC-A missions representative of current NATO operations, most flights used instrument pods that allowed later analysis. A limited number of flights used live ordnance. During the exercises, the Super Hornet's tanking ability was again assessed.

■ **Survivability, air-to-air missiles and smart weapons:** The final stage of the OPEVAL was conducted at China Lake from September through November 1999, and focused on survivability. Operationally representative flights were flown against actual and simulated threat surface-to-air missile (SAM) systems, followed by air-to-ground gunnery and air-to-ground sensor flights. Air-to-surface weapons tested included the Mk 80 series iron bombs, Rockeye, SLAM, Harpoon and Maverick. VX-9 crews found the -E/F's additional fuel significant because it allowed the use of routing alternatives, lower altitudes and more frequent use of afterburner to maintain energy during combat manoeuvring. During this phase, an actual side-by-side comparison was made between the -E/F and the Lot XII or later F/A-18C. Prior segment comparisons had been either quantitative (with a specific number in mind) or qualitative (in which the issue was whether the -E/F could execute in the particular mission area). Test data confirmed that the -E/F was more survivable than the F/A-18C/D.

The OPEVAL officially ended on 19 November. Some 850 sorties and 1,233 flight hours had been amassed and approximately 400,000 lb (181440 kg) of ordnance expended over the course of the six-month test programme. Rear Admiral John B. Natham, then-Director of Air Warfare in the Office of the Chief of Naval Operations, announced the OPEVAL results on 15 February 2000 during a ceremony at the Pentagon in Washington, DC. The Super Hornet was "operationally effective and operationally suitable". VX-9 therefore recommended the aircraft's introduc-

Right: As well as refuelling from USAF tankers and Air Wing 14's S-3B Vikings (VS-35 'Blue Wolves'), VFA-115's Super Hornets also 'buddy'-tanked during Operation Southern Watch missions. Following the 6 November combat debut, F/A-18Es were in action again the following day, and then three days later. The attacks were made in response to Iraqi sites threatening OSW aircraft.

Even though CVW-14 had Viking tankers, VFA-115 put up four F/A-18Es in tanker configuration during OIF. Their use permitted over 430 sorties to be flown that would otherwise not have been possible.

Above: VFA-115's CAG-bird peels away from the camera platform during Operation Iraqi Freedom. The aircraft carries two JDAMs and the AAS-38B Nite Hawk pod. This view highlights the 3° outward canting of the weapons pylons, introduced to cure a separation problem.

tion into fleet service. Commenting on the results, Rear Admiral James Godwin III said, "[there] were no surprises with what we saw out of the OPEVAL report, and what we predicted we would see during the developmental testing that we had ongoing prior to OPEVAL is precisely what we saw during the OPEVAL." Godwin continued, "We did not experience anything that was unexpected."

Areas of significant enhancement

The OPEVAL concluded the -E/F possessed several areas of "significant enhancement" over the F/A-18C/D, ranging from increased tactical and payload flexibility to carrier performance and survivability. The Super Hornet's ability to fly a wide variety of missions creates more options for war-planners in executing both combat and support missions. The evaluators found that when flying as a tanker, the Super Hornet can match the altitude and speed of the strike package, which leads to optimisation of flight profiles and resultant fuel efficiency.

Payload flexibility addresses the Super Hornet's ability to carry a wider variety and greater number of weapons than the current Hornet. The -E/F's two additional weapons stations increase mission effectiveness in two ways: more offensive weapons means that an F/A-18E/F can achieve the desired probability of destruction with fewer sorties flown, and the two additional weapons stations can be used to carry more self-defence weapons. Both options further enhance the -E/F's survivability and serve to reduce the number of sorties needed to reach a desired objective.

Two additional areas were noted concerning the Super Hornet's performance around a carrier – the -E/F's slower approach speed and its increased bring-back capability, both of which make the aircraft safer during landings. The enhanced bring-back amounted to an additional 3,400 lb (1542 kg) of ordnance for the -E and an additional 2,400 lb

(1087 kg) for the -F, as compared to the Lot XIX F/A-18C. These increases are ever-more significant in air operations such as those over Iraq and Afghanistan, where US pilots fly dozens of ground support missions and routinely return to the carrier with unspent ordnance.

The -E/F's manoeuvring and handling qualities were rated high and the aircraft was noted to resist departure even under aggressive high-AoA manoeuvring. Evaluators also relished the aircraft's 'positive nose pointing' – how

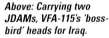

Above: Carrying two JDAMs, VFA-115's 'boss-bird' heads for Iraq.

Left: A VFA-115 jet launches from Lincoln, carrying an asymmetric load of one GBU-16 LGB, one AIM-120 AMRAAM plus three 500-lb Mk 82 GP bombs. Such loads were commonplace during the latter part of Iraqi Freedom, when aircraft were often launching without any pre-planned targets, and carried a mix of ordnance to cover several eventualities. Free-fall weapons were used mainly against troop concentrations, where precision was not required.

Above: VFA-115's 'war duck' goes into action during OIF. For most missions the Super Hornets carried AIM-9s for self-defence, plus an AMRAAM on the fuselage.

Above right: A VFA-41 F/A-18F tanker catches the wire on Nimitz shortly before the squadron entered the fray over Iraq.

Right: For VFA-115 operations continued round the clock in OIF. Most aircraft carried nose markings relating to the Twin Towers attacks.

Below: The CAG jet is about to launch on a combat sortie with a mixed weapon load. Twin-rail adapters are used with a variety of the smaller diameter weapons, including Mk 82 bombs (as here) and AIM-120 AMRAAMs, of which 12 can be carried in the maximum loadout.

quickly a pilot can put the aircraft's nose on a 'bogie' – which translates into who can take the first shot during an engagement. This quality has been described as outstanding by OPEVAL pilots. Weapons delivery accuracy was reported to be excellent, exceeding the ORD accuracy requirements and achieving results equal to or better than those of the F/A-18C.

Noted areas of concern

The OPEVAL identified nine areas of concern, although by that time most were being addressed or had been reme-

died. One concern noted the limited number of specific stores configurations that had been cleared and argued for the expedited removal of the restrictions placed on the carriage and release of those configurations. Although only 29 weapons configurations were available at the time of OPEVAL, this compared favourably to the two configurations available during the F/A-18A/B OPEVAL. Phillip E. Coyle III, Director, Operational Test & Evaluation for the Navy, in his statement to the Senate Armed Services Committee, AirLand Forces Subcommittee on 22 March 2000, noted, "Air-to-air missiles could not be employed if they were carried on a store station adjacent to air-to-ground ordnance. Numerous munitions could be carried and/or employed only from selected stores stations, although the plan is to bear these munitions from other stations as well."

Because of this, Coyle observed, "many of the load advantages planned for the F/A-18 E/F were not demonstrated during OPEVAL". Even so, many of the configurations which were presented were significantly beyond the capabilities of current F/A-18Cs.

Other areas concerned were minor and can be summarised as follows: (1) more severe noise and vibration environment under the wing compared to F/A-18 C/D; (2) a diminished specific excess power (Ps) rating; (3) buffet during 1g transition flight; and (4) residual lateral activity, albeit minimum. From a performance standpoint, the -E/F was considered comparable or superior to the -C/D in turns, climbs and deceleration at subsonic speeds. Large decelerations (airspeed bleed-off), however, were experienced in the transonic/supersonic regime during manoeuvres. From a tactical standpoint, this is insignificant, because most manoeuvring during an engagement quickly migrates to the 'current of the flight envelope' (approxi-

mately Mach 0.86 at 15,000 ft/4572 m). Moreover, since the Super Hornet is virtually immune to departure, it is extremely capable during a close-in fight.

KPPs confirmed during OPEVAL

Three key performance parameters were identified in the Congressional mandate for the F/A-18E/F programme which required it to exceed the F/A-18A-D's range and payload performance in specified associated flight profiles. Profiles evaluated included the E/F's combat radius in the fighter escort mission and interdiction mission roles, using two and three 480-US gal (1817-litre) external fuel tanks. The -E/F exceeded all threshold range requirements, posting a 425-nm (787-km) radius in the fighter escort mission and 400 nm (741 km) (two external tanks) and 450 nm (833 km) (three external tanks) in the interdiction mission.

Although the Super Hornet was projected to surpass these threshold requirements by Boeing and Navy officials, based on a flight performance database constructed from theoretical calculations, wind tunnel and engine-run tests, and developmental flight test data, these numbers needed to be confirmed. VX-9 aircrews undertook a calibration of the performance database by using a 'flight segment' approach. Under this system, fuel consumption data was collected in small, dedicated portions of many flights using a variety of aircraft configurations, gross weights and flight loads. As testament to the methodology employed by Boeing and the Navy, the deviations between actual and projected fuel consumption were insignificant, and the OPEVAL crews were able to confirm the database numbers as accurate. Based on this confirmation, OPEVAL crews were able to compute the range performance of the F/A-18E/F for the three profiles defined by the ORD and

the nine profiles defined by the Chief of Naval Operations. The nine CNO-defined operational missions were computed using a 4,000-lb (1815-kg) fuel reserve; the ORD-defined operational missions were computed using a 2,000-lb (907-kg) reserve.

Several recommendations stemmed from the OPEVAL, the most significant of which involved the correction of underwing noise and vibration. Addressing such problems is critical, Coyle noted in his statement to the Senate, because if left uncorrected it can impede the attainment of full weapons life. OPEVAL further recommended the immediate introduction of new systems such as the all-aspect high off-boresight AIM-9X missile and the JHMCS, the electronically scanned array radar (now designated APG-79), the ATFLIR, a positive identification capability such as the

Wings and fuel tanks
Based on the design of the original Hornet, the Super Hornet's wing is a multi-spar structure attaching to the fuselage by six main bolts. The interspar area forms an integral fuel tank, as does the interspar area of the twin fins. The remainder of the fuel is housed in a series of tanks in the upper fuselage. To the main wing structure is attached the trailing-edge flaps and leading-edge slats, and the outer folding panels. The latter also mounts control surfaces, and is attached to the main wing by a multiple ring/pin locking system. The actuating jacks are located in the inner panel near the trailing edge. The wingfold joint is covered by a porous fairing introduced to cure a wing-drop problem discovered during flight testing. This increases drag slightly, as does the toeing-out of the weapons pylons which was introduced to resolve stores separation problems.

Radar
The first production Super Hornet lots are fitted with the Raytheon APG-73 radar, as installed in the later production F/A-18C/Ds. From 2007 the APG-79 AESA will become available as both a new-build and retrofit option. AESA will not, however, be available for aircraft built prior to Lot 26 as they do not have the redesigned forward fuselage necessary for AESA installation. They will retain APG-73 throughout their lives unless they undergo a structural modification.

Cockpit
The F/A-18E's pilot sits on a Martin-Baker SJU-17/A ejection seat, inherited from the later F/A-18C/D production models. As well as its state-of-the-art touch-screen displays, the cockpit is configured for the use of night-vision goggles and the JHMCS helmet-mounted sight and sensor-cueing system. Access is made via a ladder which extends from below the forward part of the LEX.

AGM-88 HARM
HARM has been in service for 20 years, and remains the West's primary anti-radiation missile. The missile is 13 ft 8 in (4.17 m) long and weighs 796 lb (361 kg) at launch, of which 145 lb (66 kg) is a high-explosive blast/frag warhead. Range is up to 50 miles (80 km) for a high-altitude launch and the missile reaches Mach 2.9 during the fly-out. The latest versions feature much improved guidance systems to avoid potential fratricide and collateral damage, although the future of a GPS-aided version is uncertain.

Boeing F/A-18E Super Hornet
VFA-14 'Tophatters'
CVW-11, USS *Nimitz*
Operation Iraqi Freedom, 2003

Freshly converted to the Super Hornet from the Tomcat, VFA-14 embarked on *Nimitz* alongside VFA-41. With Operation Iraqi Freedom in full swing, the carrier headed for the war zone, arriving in April 2003 in time for Air Wing Eleven to see action during the last weeks of the military campaign. The carrier and its air wing remained on-station to provide air cover for US troops as they began the daunting task of bringing security to Iraq after the fall of Saddam Hussein.

Intakes
The intakes are of an RCS-reducing diamond shape, although there is insufficient room in the fuselage to allow them to snake up and in to the engine face to any great extent. Instead, there is a radar blocker in front of the engine.

AGM-154 JSOW
This weapon is a glide bomb guided by GPS/INS and fitted with pop-out wings to increase its stand-off range. The baseline AGM-154A version is a munitions dispenser, and carries 145 BLU-97 bomblets. It is 13 ft 5 in (4.1 m) long and weighs 1,067 lb (484 kg). As it nears the target the AGM-154A is placed automatically into a shallow dive over the target and, at the correct point, the payload covers are blown off and the sub-munitions ejected by an inflatable bladder. Each bomblet weighs 3.3 lb (1.5 kg), and contains a 10 oz (287 g) shaped-charge warhead. The bomblets have a retarding parachute and an extending nose tube. The latter is used to detonate the warhead at the optimum distance above the target.

LEX
The leading-edge extensions are multi-ribbed structures which attach to the fuselage. The forward tip of the LEX is strengthened to provide a boarding step. As well as mounting forward-hemisphere countermeasures antennas, the LEXs also provide capacity for some of the EW black boxes and ancillary equipment, including the liquid cooling system.

Loadout
This Super Hornet carries a typical defence suppression loadout, comprising two AGM-88 HARM anti-radar missiles and a pair of AGM-154 JSOWs. The armament is completed by two AIM-120 AMRAAMs and two AIM-9 Sidewinders for self defence, plus the internal M61 Vulcan cannon.

Specifications – Super Hornet vs. Hornet

	F/A-18E	F/A-18C
Dimensions		
Wing span	44 ft 8½ in (13.62 m)	40 ft 5 in (12.32 m)
Wing span (folded)	30 ft 7¼ in (9.33 m)	27 ft 6 in (8.38 m)
Length	60 ft 3½ in (18.38 m)	56 ft 0 in (17.07 m)
Height	16 ft 0 in (4.88 m)	15 ft 3½ in (4.66 m)
Wing area	500 sq ft (46.45 m²)	400 sq ft (37.16 m²)
Weights		
Empty	30,500 lb (13835 kg)	29,619 lb (13435 kg)
Max. take-off	66,000 lb (29938 kg)	51,900 lb (23542 kg)
Carrier landing	42,900 lb (19459 kg)	33,000 lb (14969 kg)
Stores bringback	9,000 lb (4082 kg)	5,500 lb (2495 kg)
Internal fuel	14,460 lb (6559 kg)	10,860 lb (4926 kg)
External fuel	c. 16,290 lb (7390 kg)	c. 6,720 lb (3048 kg)
Performance		
Maximum speed	Mach 1.8	Mach 1.8
Approach speed	143.5 mph (231 km/h)	154 mph (248 km/h)
Service ceiling	50,000 ft (15240 m)	50,000 ft (15240 m)
Radius, attack	c. 760 miles (1220 km)	c. 540 miles (870 km)
CAP endurance at 230 miles (370 km) from carrier	1.8 hours	1 hour
Powerplant		
Type	2 x F414-GE-400	2 x F404-GE-402
Afterburning thrust	22,000 lb (97.9 kN)	17,775 lb (79.1 kN)

Right: This VFA-41 F/A-18F is seen on 1 April, the day it arrived on Lincoln after deploying forward from Nimitz. During their sojourn on Lincoln the four extra Super Hornets were attached to VFA-115. In the foreground is a GBU-16 Paveway II bomb, one of the weapons employed by the Super Hornets during OIF.

Below: F/A-18Cs refuel from a KC-135R during OIF as the VFA-41 CAG-bird looks on. The Super Hornet is configured as a tanker with two wing tanks, which appears to be a standard loadout for the two-seat F/A-18F. The F/A-18E single-seater routinely operates with four wing tanks.

Below: Nimitz deck crew conduct a FOD sweep during OIF operations on 17 April. Most of the Hornets in this view are Supers, with a cluster of VFA-14's F/A-18Es round the fantail. The four Super Hornets deployed to Lincoln returned to Nimitz on 6 April after the carrier entered the Persian Gulf. Air Wing Eleven flew combat missions up to and after the stated end of the combat phase on 1 May.

and air-to-ground modes as its APG-65 predecessor but offers a 10-fold increase in processing capabilities and greater memory; it is also easier to maintain and is more reliable. The APG-73, which was introduced in May 1994, started as a joint US-Canadian effort to improve the APG-65's electronic counter-countermeasures (ECCM) system. It uses the same antenna and transmitter as the APG-65, but incorporates all new electronics.

Later versions of the radar, used primarily in the F/A-18D, incorporated a high-resolution synthetic aperture radar (SAR) for mapping during reconnaissance missions, autonomous targeting for JSOW and JDAM weapons, and the ability to track up to 24 targets, prioritising the top eight threats. The APG-73 uses colour to distinguish enemy aircraft from friendlies and unknown aircraft, and also displays target information. One feature shows the number of degrees the target must manoeuvre in order to evade a fired missile. An azimuth track capability was added in 1998 which allows differentiation of aircraft stacked on top of one another.

AESA for Block II

Beginning in 2007, the Super Hornet will incorporate the next-generation agile-beam APG-79 Active Electronically Scanned Array (AESA) radar built by Raytheon as part of the aircraft's planned Block II upgrade programme. According to the Navy, the APG-79 represents "a revolutionary leap" in capability and provides the Super Hornet with a state-of-the-art radar. Indeed, Boeing AESA Program Manager Don Thole said, "AESA is the key component of the Super Hornet that gives us the capabilities we sought." Thole continued, "This represents the first time in over 25 years where a brand new radar technology has been introduced." APG-79 builds on and improves the AESA technology featured in certain Alaska-based F-15C squadrons. APG-79's AESA features a new open architecture that incorporates the ability to expand software systems. It also uses a new fibre-channel interface that permits faster distribution of information.

According to Navy officials, the radar uses a search-while-track system that significantly improves the track quality of multiple targets with "little or no degradation of the search capability of the radar". For operators, one of the principle benefits is target updating, which means that crews receive information more quickly on their target's actions. With traditional radars, operators have to wait while targeting information is updated between radar sweeps. Boeing's Don Thole says, "You essentially have single target tracking imagery with a multi-target tracking capability." Moreover, it searches while it tracks the target on a need-to-know basis. Once a target is located, the radar automatically and periodically looks back to keep track of

combined interrogator transmitter, decoupled cockpits for enhanced flexibility, multi-function information distribution system, and further enhancements to the planned integrated defensive electronic countermeasures system. Each of these systems plays a key role in the overall Super Hornet road map. Until such systems are fielded, however, the Super Hornet will not fully realise either its potential or the operational capabilities with which it was envisaged.

The radar – APG-73 and APG-79 AESA

A key feature of the E/F is its radar. Baseline Super Hornets feature the APG-73 radar installed in late model F/A-18C/Ds (Lot XVI and beyond) and retrofitted into early model F/A-18C/Ds. The APG-73 features the same air-to-air the target, at a much higher level of fidelity and frequency than mechanical models.

NAVAIR APG-79 Program Manager Commander Dave Dunaway said, in a 2002 interview, "The radar will change the way we do business. We are currently limited by the radar's ability to detect air-to-air targets at range. In other words, we have to wait and let the radar catch up before we can shoot the missile. With the AESA, we'll be able to shoot the missile even before the target comes within the missile's range. The APG-79 has been designed to enable the aircrew to detect and process the target well before it enters the maximum range of the Super Hornet's air-to-air missiles, allowing missile launch at maximum range."

Air-to-ground resolution and range are vastly increased, with estimates of three times the detection range for large targets and two times the detection range of current systems for smaller targets. The APG-79 also presents higher-resolution SAR maps. "The aircrew can see minute runway details on the map and can identify aircraft." The APG-79 can also scan air-to-air and air-to-ground nearly simultaneously, which gives a huge advantage in multiple target attack capability and is part of the reason why the radar is touted as revolutionary. With the APG-79, a pilot can still maintain a track on a ground target while simultaneously detecting, locking and attacking an air threat. Other benefits derive from combining AESA-generated information with that from other sensors to give a clearer picture of the target.

From an airframe perspective, two modifications were required to incorporate the APG-79. First, pursuant to ECP 6038R1, the forward fuselage has been extended to accommodate the slightly larger frame. These changes began with Lot 26 aircraft now under production and are intended to allow an easy retrofit once the AESA comes on line. Moreover, the new forward section features 40 per cent fewer parts and 51 per cent fewer fasteners, and can be built in 31 per cent less time than the prior -E/F fuselage section. The second modification involved a more powerful cooling system upgraded by Northrop Grumman to help maintain a constant temperature for the APG-79. The system provides 16 kW of liquid cooling capacity, with room for additional capability. Boeing says that AESA uses all but 1 kW of this additional cooling power, but notes that designers believe that they have considered all aspects and possibilities.

Boeing's Don Thole stated that cooling is essential to the radar and is a key to its reliability. "Keeping the radar cool, and the ability to hold the temperature constant, are key to the unit's reliability." Thole also noted that in terms of reliability, the APG-79 is "phenomenal". Test results are currently showing a five-fold decrease in mean time between failure rates. Part of the reliability comes from the fact that the radar utilises fewer parts; another factor is the lack of a traditional radar dish. Estimates are that the AESA will not need array maintenance for 10 to 20 years.

Three aircraft are ultimately designated for AESA test flights. The first flight of an AESA-equipped Lot 21 F/A-18E took place on 30 July 2003 at China Lake, during which work was performed on real beam mapping. A total of 18 flights has already been made, the tests focusing on various radar modes and SAR and real beam maps. A production-equivalent -E and -F are scheduled to join the test programme in 2004.

The AESA system is currently under full-scale development and should begin LRIP incorporation in 2005, followed by introduction into the fleet -E/Fs from 2007. Eight units have been approved for LRIP I, with 12 units scheduled for LRIP II and 22 units for LRIP III. TECHEVAL is now scheduled for February 2005, followed by OPEVAL in February 2006. APG-79 units will be installed in production aircraft beginning with Lot 30 in 2006, and IOC is scheduled for 2007. The first AESA-equipped squadron is scheduled for deployment in September 2007. Eventually, some 400 F/A-18E/F and EA-18G aircraft will be fitted with the APG-79, including approximately 135 retrofits of post-

Lot 26 aircraft. F/A-18E/Fs prior to that Lot cannot be modified for AESA due to the absence of fuselage modifications associated with ECP 6038R1.

Weapons

Another advantage of the Super Hornet is its weapons carriage capability. Not only can the E/F carry vastly more tonnage than the C/D it replaces, it can carry a more robust and flexible assortment of weapons, including the long-range and highly-accurate 'J'-series weapons such as JDAM, AGM-154 JSOW and AGM-158 JASSM. Although the Super Hornet can carry more air-to-air ordnance (namely AIM-9 Sidewinders and AIM-120 AMRAAMs) than its predecessor models, the real advantage comes in the air-to-ground arena. Currently, the Super Hornet can carry various combinations of the JSOW, AGM-84 Harpoon, GBU-10/-12/-16, Mks 82 and 83 iron bombs, GBU-29/-30/-31 JDAM, AGM-65 Maverick and AGM-88 HARM. The 2,000-lb (907-kg) GBU-24 Paveway III LGB is at present awaiting clearance.

According to crews, the added stations, combined with the increased range and bring-back, make the Super

In the aftermath of the main fighting, US warplanes kept up a constant patrol over Iraq to root out pockets of resistance and to provide on-call air support should ground forces come under attack. Armed with GBU-12 LGBs, this VFA-41 F/A-18F is patrolling over Baghdad International Airport.

After nearly 10 months at sea on a cruise which was extended to cover operations throughout the combat phase of Iraqi Freedom, VFA-115 returned to Lemoore on 1 May 2003. Its aircraft wore impressive tallies of mission marks (left) recording the type of ordnance dropped, in this instance a mix of JDAMs, LGBs, unguided bombs and a single JSOW. In November 2002 Lt Eric 'Popeye' Doyle had shared with Lt John Turner the distinction of dropping the Super Hornet's first bombs in anger.

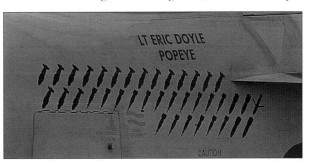

Hornet a very lethal aircraft. A section of Super Hornets can now handle virtually any threat that materialises – be it long-range air-to-air, surface-to-air or precision strike – while at the same time providing the flexibility to hit targets of opportunity as needed. Moreover, with the new AESA radar, and the better targeting offered by the ATFLIR, the Super Hornet can take full advantage of stand-off weapons.

Weapon stations

As noted in the introductory comments about the Super Hornet, one of the benefits of larger and stronger wings is the addition of two new hardpoints, stations 2 and 10. Rated at 2,150 lb (975 kg) each, these new pylons are capable of carrying air-to-air and air-to-ground weapons. The additional stores greatly increase the Super Hornet's lethality and mission flexibility, permitting a more effective precision strike with a self-escort/self-protect capability. In the air-to-air role, the Super Hornet can carry as many as 12 AIM-120s and two AIM-9s, plus a centreline fuel tank. In the strike role, a Super Hornet can launch with three fuel tanks and still have enough open stations left to carry a warload of two HARMS, a JDAM, two Sidewinders and a laser-guided bomb (LGB).

JHMCS

One of the major systems upgrades from the EMD and baseline E/F is the addition of the revolutionary Joint Helmet-Mounted Cueing System. A shared effort between Boeing and Visions Systems International, JHMCS uses a magnetic head tracker to synchronise the pilot's head movements such that a crew member can train the aircraft's radar, air-to-air weaponry, infra-red sensors and air-to-ground weaponry merely by pointing the helmet at the target and pressing a button on the control stick. The technology also exists for interleaving SHARP imagery, although Boeing has not been asked to adopt this ability. JHMCS represents a joint-service, multi-aircraft system that will be incorporated into the F-15C, F-16 and the F/A-18C/D/E/F. Currently, four squadrons (two F-15C and two Super Hornet) operate the system. A modified F-16 is currently being evaluated at Ogden ALC (Hill AFB), and JHMCS is expected to become operational on F-16s in the next 12 to 18 months.

Mike Reitz, Boeing's Program Manager for the JHMCS, says, "A critical application of JHMCS is when it is mated with the new Raytheon high off-boresight AIM-9X Sidewinder." The AIM-9X allows engagements of targets at greater than 90° off boresight, which, according to Reitz, means that "crews can now attack almost any targets that can be seen". He says that AIM-9X/JHMCS "eliminates the need to manoeuvre the shooter aircraft into the effective seeker arch of the missile, which makes the Super Hornet even more lethal". Reitz adds that JHMCS means "if the pilot can see it, he can kill it".

JHMCS also offers aircrews the ability to view critical aircraft data on a helmet-mounted visor display so that they no longer must look back into the cockpit during critical engagements. Located on the right visor, this monocular mini-HUD allows users to view information on airspeed, altitude and target range without ever unlocking their view of the enemy aircraft. Target acquisition is obtained by directing a small + (plus sign) on the visor onto the target. Early tests found that this system presented some limitations, in that the helmet and seat configuration prevented the pilot from looking up or behind the aircraft. Thus, two additional indicators are found at the top of the visor, left

VFA-102 'DIAMONDBACKS'

VF-102 (callsign DIAMONDBACK) converted from F-4Js to F-14s in 1981, and participated in Desert Storm. On the squadron's last Tomcat cruise it flew combat missions in F-14Bs over Afghanistan from the deck of USS *Theodore Roosevelt* (CVN 71). Returning in spring 2002, the squadron moved to Lemoore to begin conversion to the F/A-18F. In November 2003 VFA-102 departed for its new home at NAS Atsugi in Japan for assignment to CVW-5 ('NF' tailcode) and the carrier USS *Kitty Hawk* (CV 63). All squadron aircraft wear the badge of a diamondback rattlesnake coiled around the globe on the fin, and CAG/CO/XO aircraft wear the squadron's multi-diamond nose stripe. The tailcode is in Japanese-style script to signify the squadron's new assignment.

These images were recorded during VFA-102's CarQuals aboard USS John C. Stennis (CVN 74) in August 2003. The squadron converted to the Super Hornet alone, rather than as half of an E/F pair, and later deployed to Atsugi (CVW-5) as a direct replacement for VF-154. It will be joined in time by an F/A-18E squadron, although none of Air Wing Five's current F/A-18C units is yet slated to convert to the 'Rhino'.

and right, which give the pilot an additional 30° field of view. Once a target is designated, the JHMCS remembers its location, thereby allowing a crew member to look away and then return to the target using a small arrow that gets shorter as the pilot's view moves towards the target.

The system was originally intended only for pilots, but the Navy is now planning to provide the unit to weapons systems officers (WSOs) as well, which will enable independent targeting and tasking for crew members: for example, a pilot would be able to prosecute an air-to-air threat while the WSO executed a ground attack. Boeing's Mike Reitz says that the dual-cockpit capability is also important for talking crew members onto targets. "With both crew members fitted with the JHMCS, the WSO can locate a target, then visually direct the pilot to that target almost instantaneously. Once a crew member designates the target, a special symbol appears on the other crew member's visor that allows him or her to look to what the other is seeing. This significantly enhances crew co-ordination." Currently, crews have to 'talk' one another on to a target, which often wastes valuable time.

JHMCS completed OPEVAL in mid-2002 and is now fitted to F/A-18E/Fs in VFA-14 and -41. It may also be with VFA-102, as that squadron has taken VFA-41's aircraft to Atsugi, Japan. According to Boeing and Navy officials, the JHMCS is slated to be retrofitted into some F/A-18C/D models beginning in 2006. According to Mike Reitz, one of the upgrades being pursued for the JHMCS is a panoramic night-vision goggle capability. Currently, pilots use their

standard JHMCS visor during air operations but don NVGs at night or at dusk, especially around the carrier. The new visor would incorporate an NVG capability with a panoramic field of view.

SHARP

Raytheon's SHAred Reconnaissance Pod (SHARP) system joined the fleet with VFA-41's deployment aboard USS *Nimitz* (CVN 68) as the Navy's new tactical reconnaissance pod. SHARP will eventually replace the TARPS (Tactical Air Reconnaissance Pod System) unit currently used by F-14s

Below: One of VFA-102's F/A-18Fs lands at Atsugi on 13 November 2003 after its ferry flight from Lemoore. The 'Diamondbacks' have replaced VF-154's Tomcats in Air Wing Five, which is permanently based in Japan. VF-154 had returned to the US at the end of September to commence its conversion to the F/A-18F.

VX-31 'DUST DEVILS'

Weapons R&D work has been undertaken at China Lake for many years, originally organised under the Naval Weapons Center. On 1 January 1992 a streamlining of the US Navy's test organisations resulted in the creation of the Naval Air Warfare Center Weapons Division, which controlled the weapons test activities at its headquarters at China Lake (handled by the newly created Naval Weapons Test Squadron China Lake – NWTSCL 'Dust Devils') and Point Mugu (NWTSPM 'Bloodhounds'). On 1 May 2002 Naval Air Systems Command introduced another change, with five of its squadrons acquiring 'VX' (Air Test and Evaluation Squadron – AIRTEVRON) designations. NWTSCL became VX-31, retaining its nickname and 'Dust Devil' badge.

Above: Part of Naval Air Systems Command (NAVAIR), VX-31 undertakes developmental testing on weapons and aircraft systems, and as well as the F/A-18E (illustrated) and F, it operates the F/A-18A/C/D, AV-8B, AH-1W, HH-1N and T-39D. Once development work has been completed by VX-31, the new equipment is then allocated to VX-9 for operational evaluation.

Right: An F/A-18F from VX-31 taxis in at China Lake after a test mission. Most of the units aircraft are 'orange-wired' – that is, they are configured to accept a variety of test and recording equipment. China Lake offers extensive ranges of over 1.1 million acres (445170 hectares) for the testing of air-to-ground weapons, in near-perfect year-round flying conditions. Air-to-air tests are conducted over the Pacific.

This particular F/A-18E was the fourth production aircraft, and was assigned to the NWTSCL 'Dust Devils' and painted in full-colour markings. Here it is seen testing a rocket pod, with cameras mounted on test installations under triple ejector racks to record weapons separation.

The system was approved for LRIP in 2002 and the first two pods (of 10) were received on 2 April 2003 during a ceremony at Raytheon's Technical Services Company facility in Indianapolis. Captain Charles Wright of CVW-11 aboard USS *Nimitz* commented on the pods' use during work-ups, noting that "the pictures are great". Four pods were deployed with VFA-41 aboard *Nimitz* and are reported to have provided excellent images.

ATFLIR

Hornet operations during the 1991 Gulf War demonstrated that the F/A-18 needed an autonomous laser designation system if it was to take the lead in the Navy's strike mission. At that time, Hornets carried only the ASQ-173 (which allowed tracking but not designation) and had to rely on other aircraft, such as A-6Es, for laser target designation. The answer came in the AAS-38A, but only limited numbers were then available and served only with the Marine Corps F/A-18D squadron, VMFA(AW)-121. Subsequently, all F/A-18Cs were equipped with the improved AAS-38B, which added a self-tracking capability to the unit's designator.

The Super Hornet uses a much-improved third-generation system known as Advanced Tactical FLIR. Made by Raytheon Corporation, the ATFLIR includes integrated FLIR, IR and laser spot trackers, and a laser designator which allows target identification and tracking in virtually all environments. Tests and fleet usage have demonstrated a four-fold improvement in performance over current Navy FLIRs, allowing greater stand-off distances for weapons employment. Designated the ASQ-228, ATFLIR uses 680 x 480-element mid-wave staring focal plane technology and offers a field of view of either 0.7°, 2.8° or 6.0°. It also features a continuous auto-boresight alignment capability that enables first-pass kills. The ATFLIR's targeting range will be augmented by new radar modes for the APG-79, which will give a high-resolution synthetic aperture radar ground imaging capability that is "fantastic", says Boeing's Paul Summers.

According to Navy officials, the real benefit of ATFLIR is its extended range, which allows maximum use of current and planned weapons systems such as the GBU-24 LGB and JDAM. ATFLIR is also more reliable than earlier models, due in part to the fact that it has about two-thirds fewer components, none of which is considered a high-failure item. Mean time between failures is over 300 hours. ATFLIR completed OPEVAL in 2003 and is now operationally deployed with VFAs-14, -41 and -115. Captain Gaddis noted, "One of the signs that the ATFLIR OPEVAL was going well was that the squadron testing the system turned in almost half of its allotted ordnance unexpended." Gaddis added, "The system was performing so well, and was so reliable, that the test and evaluation crews were giving spare parts to VFA-41 to use operationally with their

and provides day and night capability, with day stand-off ranges out to 45 nm (83 km). According to Rear Admiral James Godwin III, Program Executive Officer for Tactical Aircraft, the pod represents a "quantum leap in capabilities" for the F/A-18 fleet. The pod, which is approximately the size of a 330-US gal (1259-litre) tank, mounts on the centre-line station of F/A-18C/D/E/F aircraft using a standard 30-in (76-cm) attachment, and features a Mil-Std 1760 interface. SHARP was designed with a rotating mid-section to enhance visual coverage and to protect the camera window.

VX-23 'SALTY DOGS'

From 1945 the Naval Air Test Center at Patuxent River has been the principal US Navy test base. On 1 January 1992 the NATC became the Naval Air Warfare Center Aircraft Division (NAWC-AD), and its test operations were further divided into four squadrons covering strike/fighter, ASW, rotary-wing and test pilot training (USNTPS). On 1 May 2002 the three test squadrons at 'Pax' were given AIRTEVRON designations. The Naval Strike Aircraft Test Squadron (NSATS), to which various Hornet/Super Hornet models have been assigned, was rechristened VX-23. NSATS/VX-23 aircraft wear an 'SD' tailcode, standing for 'Strike Directorate'. The initials gave rise to the 'Salty Dogs' nickname.

pods." A total of 574 ATFLIRs is planned and will be compatible with -C/D models, as well. The pod, which measures about 72 in (1.83 m) and weighs approximately 400 lb (181 kg), mounts on the Super Hornet's left fuselage station, which means that additional stores may be carried on the wings.

MIDS-LVT

The F/A-18E/F is the lead aircraft platform for the new Multi-functional Information Distribution System – Low Volume Terminal (MIDS-LVT), a system designed to provide near-real time situational awareness for aircrews by integrating data from multiple information sources. MIDS provides an advanced, high-capacity, jam-resistant, digital communications link facilitating near real-time exchange of voice and data information. MIDS also allows the exchange of target information among multiple platforms using a network, such that a strike fighter with expended ordnance could pass targeting information to another shooter miles away. MIDS also provides Super Hornet crews with an overall integrated air picture that identifies friend and foe and displays velocities and headings. This obviously increases crew and section efficiency, as target pass-off times are significantly shortened.

Part of the Block II upgrade path, the system incorporates tactical air navigation functionality (replacing the ARC-118 TACAN system), which allows it also to serve as a navigational aid. Testing of the MIDS system commenced in 2002 and it completed OPEVAL later that autumn, going to sea with VFAs-14 and -41 during their Persian Gulf deployments in 2003. During OPEVAL, MIDS performed outstandingly and resulted in no 'blue-on-blue' engagements between aircraft using MIDS in 866 flight hours. Crews using the system have praised the substantial enhancement of situational awareness, saying it is superior to that provided by the TIDS/Link-16 aboard the F-14.

Joining the fleet

As the EMD and OPEVAL continued, plans commenced at NAS Lemoore, California, for the Super Hornet fleet readiness squadron, VFA-122. A former A-7 FRS, the 'Flying

Below: Bedecked in photo-calibration marks, a VX-23 F/A-18E takes the wire at Patuxent River. The squadron regularly uses the TC-7 catapult and Mk 7 arresting gear which equips Runway 14/32 at the base, enabling the unit to test carrier suitability of new aircraft or equipment in a tightly controlled environment before it goes to sea. The runways are also fitted with the same visual landing aids as found on carriers, and an Automatic Carrier Landing System (ACLS).

Eagles' were officially reactivated on 1 October 1998 and stood up ceremonially on 15 January 1999, under the command of Commander Mark I. Fox; the FRS immediately began to establish the parameters for transitioning instructors, and later crews, to the new aircraft. To help smooth the overall transition, the Navy activated a Fleet Introduction Team at NAS Lemoore under the initial leadership of Commander Phil Tomkins, with its first order of business being the refurbishing of hangars and ready rooms necessary for the reactivation of VFA-122 in 1998.

VFA-122 – the Super Hornet FRS

VFA-122 still stands as the sole Super Hornet FRS, and is responsible for creating the Super Hornet training syllabus and for developing the tactics needed to employ the Super Hornet in accordance with its capabilities. The squadron began training future instructor pilots and WSOs in 1999 and received its first students in June 2000; new classes began every six weeks thereafter. With instructor pilot (IP), instructor WSO (I-WSO), and syllabus work completed, VFA-122 officially opened for business in June 2001, when

four newly-winged pilots destined for VFA-115 arrived at VFA-122. The remainder of the squadron followed after completing its CVW-14 deployment in January 2001.

The Super Hornet FRS currently has 35 IPs and 10 I-WSOs. Approximately 485 enlisted maintenance personnel oversee the squadron's 37 jets and train future squadron maintenance personnel. Of VFA-122's allotment, 11 are single-seat Es and 26 are two-seat Fs. Eight of the latter are configured as twin-stick models to assist pilot training. To train new aircrews, VFA-122 uses its own aircraft plus those destined for new squadrons, which explains why many visitors to Lemoore see aircraft that appear to be squadron aircraft flown on 'Flying Eagle' sorties. These 'borrowed' aircraft are then released to new squadrons as soon as the unit is certified 'safe to fly'. So far, VFAs-115 (F/A-18E), -41 (F/A-18F), -14 (F/A-18E), -102 (F/A-18F), -2 (F/A-18F), and -137 (F/A-18E) have been certified and have joined the fleet. Former Tomcat squadrons VFAs-2, -14, -41 and -154 have permanently relocated to the Pacific Hornet base at NAS Lemoore; in November 2003, VFA-102 left Lemoore and replaced VF-154 in Atsugi, Japan.

VFA-2 'BOUNTY HUNTERS'

VF-2 (callsign BULLET) was established as the US Navy's second fleet Tomcat squadron in October 1972. During its long association with the F-14 it saw combat over Iraq (Desert Storm and Southern Watch). The last Tomcat cruise was in F-14Ds with CVW-2 aboard *Constellation* (CV 64). In early 2003 the unit transitioned to the F/A-18F – still assigned to CVW-2 ('NE' tailcode) but now for service aboard USS *Abraham Lincoln* (CVN 72), replacing CVW-14. The unit's aircraft retain the nose 'Langley stripe' – albeit in shades of grey on regular squadron machines – and a further representation is on the fin (including two stars to represent the squadron number) with a skull superimposed.

To minimise the effect on fleet operations, an effective plan was developed to transition squadrons to the -E/F between deployments as part of their normal work-up cycle. Using this system, as detailed below, full introduction of the -E/F can be accomplished within four years. Most instructional work is performed at NAS Lemoore, although weapons training detachments are made to Key West, Florida, and El Centro, California, as well as detachments to various fleet carriers as available for carrier qualifications. Most detachments consist of five or six aircraft and last about five days.

Like most other fleet readiness squadrons, VFA-122 operates a multi-tracked syllabus to train new Super Hornet crews. CAT 1 courses are tailored to students fresh from the training command and typically last about eight months. This syllabus has 10 phases, including familiarisation, formation flight, all-weather intercepts, section radar attack, basic fighter manoeuvres, fighter weapons, low-altitude tactical training, strike, strike fighter and carrier qualifications. The latter incorporates 10 day traps, six night traps, two day touch-and-goes and another two at night, as well as night-time refuelling missions. CAT 2 courses apply to former Tomcat and Hornet pilots. Some differences also exist for crews intended for the single and two-seat models. CAT 3 students are essentially Hornet pilots requalifying in the Super Hornet, and CAT 4 is for experienced F/A-18C

pilots who are destined for the test pilot billet at either Patuxent River or China Lake.

Planned conversion schedule

Deliveries of new Super Hornets continue daily. Single-seat -E models largely replace older F/A-18C squadrons and two F-14 squadrons; two-place -Fs are replacing the remaining F-14 squadrons. As of mid-2003, sources indicate the following transition dates for 2003 through 2007:

Year	Squadron	Current aircraft	Super Hornet version
2003	VF-154	F-14A	F/A-18F
2004	VFA-22	F/A-18C	F/A-18F
	VF-154	F-14A	F/A-18F
2005	VFA-81	F/A-18C	F/A-18E
	VF-32	F-14B	F/A-18F
	VF-103	F-14B	F/A-18F
2006	VF-213	F-14D	F/A-18F
	VFA-86	F/A-18C	F/A-18E
	VF-211	F-14A	F/A-18F
2007	VF-11	F-14B	F/A-18E
	VF-143	F-14B	F/A-18E
	VF-31	F-14D	F/A-18F
	VFA-105	F/A-18C	F/A-18E
	VFA-146	F/A-18C	F/A-18E

Below left: VX-9 at China Lake continues to provide a vital bridge between the dedicated test units (VX-23 and VX-31) and the front line. Among its recent accomplishments was the evaluation of the JHMCS system at sea, confirming its suitability for use by embarked squadrons.

Below: On 5 September 2003 Boeing delivered the first Lot 26 Super Hornet with a redesigned forward fuselage. This has fewer parts, is cheaper to produce, and has a larger frame to allow it to take the APG-79 AESA radar.

Much talk still surrounds the proposal to base a Super Hornet FRS on the East Coast. In 2002, the Navy conducted a feasibility study into locating the FRS at NAS Oceana, Virginia Beach. The two alternatives considered call either for basing six Super Hornet fleet squadrons and the FRS at Oceana, and locating four E/F squadrons at MCAS Cherry Point, North Carolina, or putting eight fleet squadrons and the FRS at Oceana (120 aircraft) and two squadrons at Cherry Point (24 aircraft). In September 2003, the Navy recommended the latter course and also the construction of a smaller outlying field at Washington County, North Carolina.

First blood

VFA-115 not only held the honour of the Super Hornet's first operational deployment, but also holds the honour of being the first Super Hornet squadron to see combat. VFA-115 initially flew missions over Afghanistan in support of Operation Enduring Freedom, but did not expend any ordnance. According to Lieutenant Stephen Walborn, a pilot with VFA-115, "The missions over Afghanistan were primarily of a 'show-the-flag' nature, but we were ready with ordnance to go where we were needed." Walborn said that the Super Hornets were typically armed with precision-guided munitions for these flights. "We tried to plan our flights around our bring-back capability, which is greater than that of the -C model, to ensure that we could recover what we left with." Walborn added, "[missions] essentially were planned around not dropping our ordnance." Many of the Afghanistan missions, Walborn noted, "were five to six hours long and involved tanking".

The 'Eagles' flew 214 combat missions during Operations Enduring Freedom and Southern Watch (the latter beginning in November 2002) and expended 22 JDAMs on a total of 14 targets during Southern Watch. VFA-115's Super Hornets also flew missions in support of Iraqi Freedom, beginning with sorties launched at the start of the war on 20 March 2003. Walborn said that the Iraqi Freedom missions were different from those flown during either Enduring Freedom or Southern Watch. "At this point we were planning to drop, so we didn't have to worry about bring-back."

Many of the Iraqi Freedom missions were flown with mixed loads of laser-guided precision bombs and GPS-guided JDAMs. Walborn: "The goal was to keep ourselves as flexible as possible. We had to be able to hit either a fixed or moving target, so we had to carry ordnance for both missions." Of course, the Super Hornets kept a basic armament for air-to-air contingencies, although none developed. The 'Eagles' flew 5,400 hours and made 2,463 arrested landings. Many of the sorties were made deep into Iraqi territory and certainly farther than its older C brethren flew. Although the Super Hornet squadron flew fewer overall combat missions than the C squadrons, it carried more ordnance, farther.

One of the most significant contributions by VFA-115 came in its tanking role. For these missions, the Es were launched in the so-called 'five wet' configuration, with four 480-US gal (1817-litre) tanks and one aerial refuelling store, plus a basic complement of air-to-air missiles. Pilots found the Super Hornet well suited to the tanking mission. "Except for tanking in bad weather, the Super Hornet handled the task well. We would essentially fly a slot position and hold while the aircraft manoeuvred onto the basket," Walborn explained. "One of the benefits of having the Super Hornet in the tanking role is its radar, something the S-3B people don't have. The radar helps with situational awareness and helps us better locate and guide our aircraft to us. It also helps us deconflict multiple aircraft that are heading in to refuel."

In a fully-configured load-out, the -E/F can give nearly twice the fuel of the S-3B. Equipped with four external tanks and a centreline A/A42R-1 aerial refuelling store, the Super Hornet can carry a total of 29,000 lb (13154 kg) of fuel. Lieutenant Walborn stated that typical operations saw a single Super Hornet "dragging a section in-country, tanking, then returning to the ship to refuel and meet the section en route back to the carrier". During the war most long-range tanking missions were flown by Super Hornets, while Vikings handled the task over the Gulf and overhead. "The Super Hornet let us send tanking assets into Iraq, which was something that we could not do with the S-3B. And that is primarily because of the range, and the Super Hornet's ability to self-protect." VFA-115 concluded its deployment on 1 May 2003, in a ceremony featuring President George W. Bush, which marked the end of major hostilities in Iraq. The squadron dropped more than 380,000 lb (172368 kg) of ordnance during Iraqi Freedom and received the Navy's Unit Commendation.

VFA-115's Super Hornets were a combination of early Lot models and were not equipped with MIDS, JHMCS or ATFLIR. Although the latter system was available in limited numbers – four LRIP ATFLIRs were sent to sea with CVW-14 – the squadron preferred to use the existing AAS-38B NiteHawk because of reliability problems in the early LRIP ATFLIR pods. According to one pilot, "It was essentially a trade-off between a vastly superior picture and reliability issues. We chose the degraded imagery as a price for ensuring that the instrument worked when we needed it." Walborn said that at one point four aircraft from the

Nimitz air wing (two each from VFA-14 and VFA-41) flew over to *Abraham Lincoln* in advance of the *Nimitz*'s arrival in the Persian Gulf to fly combat missions, and offered 'Eagles' crews a glimpse of their newer ATFLIRs and MIDS capabilities. "The ATFLIR images we were seeing were incredible compared to the NiteHawk and we were told that the reliability issues on the full-rate production models were minimal." VFA-115 is now fully equipped with new ATFLIRs, and Lieutenant Walborn indicated that the squadron's full-rate production pods are "wonderful" and are significantly improved in terms of reliability.

From a performance standpoint, Walborn praised the Super Hornet: "The aircraft is amazing and has performed as advertised." According to Walborn, the aircraft handles excellently around the boat, although he added that he initially found it challenging because the aircraft "can easily be overpowered on ball". Walborn believes that the new systems planned for the later Block aircraft, such as MIDS and the JHMCS, will greatly enhance the aircraft's overall situational awareness and lethality. "With JHMCS, one big advantage comes in the air-to-ground role. We waste a lot of time looking for targets or talking other aircraft onto a target. With JHMCS and MIDS, we can pass the information we have directly to other crews, resulting in a much faster weapons-on-target time." VFA-115 will deploy with MIDS and JHMCS in mid-2004.

EA-18G – replacement for the EA-6B

As early as the mid-1990s it had become apparent that a replacement would be needed for the EA-6B Prowler, which had been flying since the mid-1960s. Not only were

Prowler airframes ageing, but even more hours were being accumulated as the aircraft assumed the jammer mission of the retired USAF EF-111 Raven. Moreover, operational demands from the numerous overseas commitments, such as Iraq's 'No-fly' Zones, Bosnia and Kosovo, began to take their toll; some Prowlers were showing fatigue stress on their wings, which limited their flight envelope.

While the Navy considered its options, Boeing (then McDonnell Douglas) began a government-funded six-month study of an electronic warfare version of the Super Hornet, referred to as the Command and Control Warfare (C²W) variant. Following that initial study, Boeing continued concept development using its own funds. The initial concept called for incorporation of a single multi-band jamming pod to replace the Prowler's five ALQ-99 pods

VFA-137's CAG-bird rests at Lemoore during the squadron's conversion training period in 2003. It will deploy alongside VFA-2 in 2004. Current US Navy plans call for each air wing to have four Hornet squadrons: two with Cs, one with Es and one with Fs. In the next decade the F/A-18C is scheduled to be replaced by the Lockheed Martin F-35C Joint Strike Fighter.

VFA-137 'KESTRELS'

Strike Fighter Squadron 137 was established as a new unit on 1 July 1985 to fly the F/A-18A Hornet, subsequently upgrading to the F/A-18C. Second of the F/A-18C squadrons to begin conversion to the Super Hornet, VFA-137 began its transition to the F/A-18E in 2003, and will partner VFA-2 in CVW-2 aboard *Abraham Lincoln*. Its badge comprises a stylised falcon's head superimposed on three aircraft pulling contrails.

Following VFA-137, the next two squadrons to convert will be VF-154 'Black Knights', which flew its F-14As back from Atsugi in September 2003 and stood up at Lemoore on 1 October, and VFA-22 'Fighting Redcocks' (F/A-18C).

the -F. In fact, all -F models, beginning with Lot 30 aircraft, will be structurally provisioned to handle -G equipment, adding approximately 55 to 60 lb (25 to 27 kg) in structural changes. This production set-up will allow additional -F models to be converted to -G models if needed. However, the Navy has decided that once a Super Hornet has been converted to an EA-18G, it will not revert back to an F/A-18F configuration.

Boeing has conducted five flight tests since November 2001 using a modified -F (EMD F1) and hosted over 500 Prowler aircrews in its St Louis cockpit simulator. According to Paul Summers, Boeing's Program Manager for the EA-18G, the five flights "have systematically expanded the envelope with ALQ-99 pods, as well as tested for noise and vibration". Summers noted that the flight programme has achieved a maximum altitude of 30,020 ft (9150 m) and speeds of Mach 0.9. For these flights, an -F was configured with three instrument-loaded ALQ-99 pods and two 480-US gal (1817-litre) tanks. Summers says that the tests "produced very promising results and confirmed that we could do what we were saying with the aircraft". Boeing has also conducted extensive wind-tunnel tests and verified the Super Hornet's electromagnetic compatibility with fully-radiating ALQ-99 pods using anechoic chamber tests. Summers told *International Air Power Review*, "We tested the -F with fully radiating pods to make sure that the jamming did not interfere with the aircraft's electronics and flight systems, and the -F passed all tests."

'Growler' production

Production of 90 EA-18Gs is planned at a cost of approximately $US57 million per copy. This number is largely due to the fact that the Navy will be withdrawing from the Air Force EW mission beginning in 2010, and the fact that the Marines have yet to make their decision on a Prowler follow-on for their four electronic warfare squadrons. According to the Navy, the Marines should decide sometime in 2005-06 whether to pursue the EA-18G or an EW variant of the F-35. The Navy plans 10 squadrons of EA-18Gs, one for each of the carrier air wings and one FRS, although it has not yet decided how many EA-18Gs will outfit each squadron. The current number being considered is five per squadron. At this time, no EA-18Gs are planned for the Naval Air Reserve.

Boeing anticipates approval of funds late this year for entering the System Development and Demonstration phase in 2004 and for additional aircraft for the test programme. According to Paul Summers, four EMD E/F aircraft will be converted for air testing, plus two test production articles built as EA-18Gs – EA-1 and EA-2 – will join the test programme in FY08. Four additional production models will be added to the programme and will join the fleet following OPEVAL, which is scheduled for 2006; the EA-18G should achieve IOC in 2009. Low-rate initial production will commence in FY09 with 12 units, followed by 18 in FY10. Full-rate production will begin in FY11 with 22 aircraft, followed by 20 and 14 aircraft in succeeding years. These figures may be altered if the Marine Corps decides to adopt the EA-18G.

When production commences, the Block I EA-18G will be very similar to the -F, with MIDS, JHMCS and TAMMAC (Tactical Aircraft Moving Map Capability), and independent, missionised cockpits. The latter will enable independent pilot/ECMO sensor and weapons operations. F/A-18E/F/G front cockpits will be identical, and the aft cockpit will be common between the -F and -G with the exception that the -G will possess a master radiate switch. Early production models, although equipped to handle the AESA, will be fitted with the APG-73 radar and then retrofitted with the APG-79. AESA will bring even more capabilities to the -G and may be used to enhance the aircraft's long-range passive sensor and jamming capabilities. It will also allow integration with other onboard sensors and the ALQ-218 precision receiver system to enhance precision targeting.

Boeing fit-tested ALQ-99 pods on the first EMD F/A-18F at an early stage (below, with HARM and notional wingtip ALQ-218 pods), and in November 2001 flew the aircraft in an EA-18G configuration (above). Northrop Gruman is handling the integration of the EW suite, which is based on the EA-6B's ICAP-III system. As well as the ALQ-99 pods, a key component is the ALQ-218 receiver suite, while the MIDS/Link 16 will be enhanced with additional functions. While HARM is currently the baseline anti-radar weapon, the AARGM (Advanced Anti-Radiation Guided Missile) is being considered for delivery as part of the initial EA-18G system.

and relied on a crew of two, rather than four. The programme's $US2 billion cost quickly became an issue, largely due to the research and development associated with the new pod. As a result, the Navy asked Boeing to refocus its efforts on incorporation of the proposed ICAP-III technologies then planned for the Prowler. The resulting restructuring reduced overall programme costs by almost 60 per cent.

The initial C²W variant replaced the wingtip Sidewinders with wingtip multi-band receivers and added several low-band electronic surveillance antennas and SATCOM, and built on proposed F/A-18F technology such as MIDS and AESA. The aircraft later became known as the EA-18G 'Growler', a nickname that is not official; a competition is underway among the EA-6B community to select an official name for the EA-18G.

Following an extensive Advanced Electronic Attack Analysis of Alternatives that began in 2001, the Navy selected the EA-18G as the Prowler replacement in December 2002. Boeing serves as the prime contractor and Northrop Gruman acts as the principal subcontractor, responsible for integrating the electronic warfare suite. The EA-18G is a Block II F/A-18F, modified to accommodate the new features of the G, and retains all mission features of

The EA-18G will be 90 per cent common with -F models, retaining the full -F capability and its planned room for growth. Most of the changes will be related to software specific to the -G mission. The fully-equipped -G will weigh 1,300 lb (590 kg) more than the -F, but will not carry a gun. Boeing says that some consideration may eventually be given to a trade-off between -F capabilities and new growth room for the -G. The Navy is currently funding studies to evaluate both a single and dual multi-band pod system, which, if adopted, could free up an additional store for air-to-ground ordnance, making the EA-18G even more lethal.

One of the advantages of the EA-18G over the EA-6B is its ability to deliver a range of offensive weapons in addition to its EW and EA roles. Initial production EA-18Gs, referred to as Block I models, will carry HARMs to combat air-to-surface targets and AIM-120 AMRAAMs to thwart air threats. Follow-on store loadings will allow the Block II and III -Gs (currently not funded) to carry JSOW and JASSM, and may incorporate IDECM. Another benefit offered by the EA-18G is its ability to fly nearly identical profiles with the strike packages. Moreover, the commonality with other Super Hornet airframes in the carrier air wing should provide savings in maintenance costs.

Planned growth paths

A Block upgrade has been in the E/F roadmap from the programme's beginning, capitalising on the inherent growth space of the E/F. The Block I upgrade began in late 2001 and added new DMV-179 single-board mission computers to replace the AYK-14s, which had exhausted their memory, and the PMC-642 fibre cable network interface module. The new computers rely on COTS (commercial off-the-shelf) technology and provide significantly greater processing power and more memory, and use C ++ open architecture, thereby allowing easy upgrades as new technology evolves. Block I also saw the addition of a more advanced EW suite, additional weapons, advanced mission displays and JHMCS.

The second major upgrade, called Block II, is currently underway at Boeing, commencing with Lot 26 production. Block II replaces the two MFDs carried over from the -C/D models with an advanced display, and adds the advanced aft crew station with its larger, 8 x 10-in (20.3 x 25.4-cm) colour display and additional cockpit hand controllers. It also has provision for growth into AESA, and additional network-centric technology. Block II aircraft also incorporate MIDS technology and are equipped with ATFLIR. Using the added processing power of the new Block I computers, so-called 'smart' displays as used in the Block I models were replaced with 'dumb' displays that receive their data from the mission computers via a broadband high-speed databus.

Integration of the IDECM and decoupled cockpits is essential, as is placing priority on clearing all of the planned stores configurations. The decoupled cockpits, also called independent crew stations, allow F/A-18F crews to perform air-to-air and air-to-ground missions simultaneously. Scheduled for introduction in 2004, the decoupled system will enable crews independently to guide and control various weapons and onboard sensors. Modifications to the APG-73 will also follow (until AESA is delivered), incorporating RUG II SAR modes for generating highly-accurate ground maps. These modes are now only available on the F/A-18D used by the Marine Corps.

Block II provides the basis for further network-centric development (the referenced Block II+) and for the EA-18G. Boeing Chief Engineer Jim Young described the programme's goal as necking down to a few common platforms, thereby enhancing the ability to maintain the fleet at a realistic price. Super Hornets eventually will be fielded in three significant configurations: Block I, Block II and Block II-based EA-18G.

Brad Elward

With a smart new paint scheme, F/A-18F-1 conducted more EA-18G trials in 2002. Current Navy planning calls for 56 EA-18Gs to be purchased between FY06 and FY09 under the second multi-year procurement contract (MY2), and a further 34 under MY3. From Lot 30 all F/A-18Fs will be built as 'F-plus' aircraft, with the structural modifications necessary to turn them into EA-18Gs. This comes with a structural weight penalty of just 55 lb (25 kg). To cover a perceived shortfall in EW cover, it is possible that some Fs may be configured as interim EW platforms.

Top left: In 2002 F/A-18F-1 was given schemes representative of fleet EW squadrons. The green scheme (top) is of VAQ-209 'Star Warriors', while the red scheme is that of the Prowler FRS, VAQ-129 'Vikings'.

With a successful service entry and combat debut behind it, the Super Hornet has shaken off many of the criticisms which dogged the type's early years.

Boeing
F/A-18 Hornet

Early F/A-18s were criticised for their poor performance, but today the F/A-18C/D is a sophisticated and capable fighting machine, with a combat record to prove it. That the Hornet has not only survived in the fleet, but prospered to become a great combat aircraft much in demand, is a tribute to the designers and engineers who have worked hard to get the best out of the airframe.

Top: The F-4 Phantom II and A-7 Corsair II were hard acts to follow, yet the Hornet which replaced them is now viewed as a worthy successor in both the fighter and attack roles. Such were the performance problems with the first generation of Hornets that it took some time to reach that point. Today the F/A-18 is the fleet's 'bread-and-butter' warplane, able to to handle a variety of roles with consummate ease, by day or night. Among these is defence suppression, for which it carries the AGM-88 HARM radar-killing missile.

Above right: An F/A-18 from VFA-151 punches through the sound barrier at low level, the vapour clouds graphically illustrating the shock waves that are formed at transonic speed.

The scene is a top-secret meeting of McDonnell Douglas executives, some time in 1974. The senior man has the floor. "We are going to monopolise the Navy tactical aircraft business. In 20 years, we'll have the only Navy fighter in production, and in 30 years there will be carriers going to sea without a single fighter or attack aircraft that doesn't say 'McAir' on the side. This is the plan.

"We're not going to design our own aircraft. We'll modify somebody else's design, and when they try to sell the original version for export, we'll beat them.

"Our design won't work very well when it enters service, and we'll keep having to change it and fix it. Eventually, the Navy will pay for a complete redesign and use our aircraft to replace the F-14 and A-6, even though it won't go as fast as an F-14 or carry as much as far as an A-6."

It is a fair guess that no such meeting ever happened and that no such outrageous plan was ever concocted. However, as the historical record will show, that is exactly what happened in the case of the Boeing/McDonnell Douglas F/A-18.

While the end of the Cold War has played a part in reversing the Hornet's fortunes, McDonnell Douglas Aerospace (MDA) – which, from 4 August 1997 has operated under the Boeing name following a merger – has made an important contribution through steady development and refinement of the design, mostly during production of the F/A-18C and its two-seat equivalent, the F/A-18D. It is primarily with these aircraft – the bridge between the frankly disappointing F/A-18A/B and the almost entirely new F/A-18E/F – that this article is concerned.

Hornet history

The F/A-18 design has its roots in 1966, at Northrop's advanced projects office in Hawthorne, not far from Los Angeles airport. The leader of the design team, Lee Begin, had been responsible for the F-5 fighter. With the latter established in production, Northrop was looking at ideas for a follow-on fighter which would eventually replace the F-5 and other widely used fighters of the same vintage. As in the case of the F-5, Northrop had the international market very much in mind.

The first designs resembled a scaled-up, high-wing F-5, with two engines and the same thin, minimally swept wing with leading-edge manoeuvring flaps. The design evolved between 1966 and 1969 in the light of market surveys and combat lessons from Vietnam. Begin's goal was to develop a relatively small fighter which could easily out-turn older, large-winged subsonic aircraft like the MiG-17, while retaining supersonic speed and the ability to carry large external weapons loads. The new fighter's wing span and aspect ratio increased. The design thrust/weight ratio approached 1:1 at combat weights. Leading-edge root extensions (LERXes) appeared and grew steadily larger and more complex with each iteration of the design. The LERXes affected the airflow over the tail, so the single vertical tail was replaced by twin canted surfaces.

Together with Northrop president Tom Jones, Begin believed that the Pentagon's main fighter competitions of the late 1960s would lead to large and costly aircraft which most countries could not afford. Northrop was never a front-runner in the contest to develop the USAF's F-4 replacement, won by McDonnell Douglas's F-15. By 1971, however, Begin's new fighter, the P-530, was far enough advanced to be shown in the form of a full-scale mock-up at the Paris air show. Northrop named it Cobra, because of its hood-like LERXes. The company's plan was to develop the Cobra in collaboration with one or more European partners, as a replacement for ageing F-104s and Mirages.

F-17 versus F-16 for LWF

Northrop fell victim to its own success in promoting the idea of the lighter, more agile fighter. A group of analysts, engineers and Air Force pilots, nicknamed the 'Fighter Mafia', managed to attract the attention of budget-conscious, innovative civilian leaders at the Pentagon. The US Air Force was still unconvinced of the value of a smaller fighter, but was persuaded to sponsor a programme under which two designs would be built and flown as prototypes. This was enough to bring other competitors into the ring – most significantly, General Dynamics, which was awarded a contract to build two YF-16 Lightweight Fighter (LWF) prototypes in April 1972. Northrop, to no one's surprise, was the other winner, with a Cobra derivative known as the YF-17.

By the time the prototypes flew, the stakes had been raised dramatically. The Department of Defense, facing post-Vietnam budget cuts, directed the Air Force to buy 650 new fighters based on the winning LWF design, and four NATO nations looking for an F-104 replacement (Belgium, Holland, Norway and Denmark) agreed to buy their aircraft as a single package. In the absence of a credible European alternative, it appeared most likely that the winner of the USAF contest would scoop the European market too.

Most observers agreed that the bomber-builders of Fort

Worth stood little chance against Northrop, with its extensive light-fighter experience and years of work on the P-530, so it was all the more surprising when the YF-16 out-pointed its rival in tests and won the USAF contest.

The US Navy takes a different route

The competition was not quite winner-takes-all, however. Congress had directed the US Navy to use a version of one of the LWF designs to meet its requirement for a new fighter/attack aircraft, formerly known as VFAX but now identified as the Navy Air Combat Fighter (NACF). The Navy's requirement was stiffer than the USAF's: for instance, it called for the ability to carry AIM-7 medium-range air-to-air missiles, and the radar specification was tougher, calling for a larger antenna than would fit in the YF-16 or YF-17. Both factors tended to make the NACF into a larger aircraft than the USAF design. Either aircraft would need a new engine: the fact that the F-16 had the same engine as the F-15 was an advantage in the USAF contest but was of no help in NACF. It was also clear from the outset that the Navy preferred a twin-engined aircraft.

The Navy insisted that the NACF prime contractor be a company with experience in carrier fighters. GD teamed with a Texas neighbour, Vought, while Northrop joined forces with McDonnell Douglas. Of the two prime contractors, only McDonnell Douglas had recent supersonic fighter experience; the company had lately worked with Hughes on the sophisticated radar for the F-15.

McDonnell Douglas and Northrop were announced as winners in May 1975, and the first F/A-18 flew in November 1978. It was a new aircraft, sharing only its general layout with the YF-17. Compared with its predecessor, it was larger and more powerful, incorporating the stronger structure and

An F/A-18C Hornet assigned to VFA-113 launches off the bow of USS John C. Stennis (CVN 74) during cold-weather operations in 2004 in the Gulf of Alaska.

The Walleye family of glide bombs is built around the basic Mk 83 (Walleye I) and Mk 84 (Walleye II) bombs, to which are added control fins and a guidance system. At the nose of the bomb is a TV camera, which relays the scene ahead, via a tail-mounted datalink, to the controlling aircraft. Using an onboard TV display the Walleye is flown to its target by means of a joystick controller. Only Walleye II remains in the US Navy and US Marine Corps inventory. The longer-range ER/DL versions are fitted with extended wings to improve their gliding performance. This Naval Strike Warfare Center F/A-18 is carrying a basic AGM-62 Walleye II (which is always only carried on the outboard stations 1 or 5) along with the associated AWW-9 datalink pod on the centreline (station 3).

ground up to accept pods for electro-optical navigation and targeting aids, and the AIM-7 medium-range air-to-air missile, neither of which could be carried on the F-16. McDonnell Douglas touted the new fighter as a true multi-role type, as opposed to the simpler F-16A.

Canada and Australia, both with large fleets of older supersonic fighters, were persuaded by these arguments and selected the F-18A over the F-16 before the new fighter had finished its flight tests. One of the F/A-18's rivals was Northrop's land-based F-18L, similar in size to the F/A-18 but with an almost completely redesigned structure. Unfortunately for Northrop, the export customers found that the lower risks of the F/A-18A, already in full-scale development for the US Navy, outweighed the higher performance promised by Northrop.

Advantages of the F/A-18

Canada, with its large expanses of Arctic terrain, and Australia, with its overwater interception mission and the need to overfly the Australian interior (known to pilots as the GAFA, or the Great Australian ****-All), assigned some value to the F-18's twin engines. In fact, the new fighter's General Electric F404 was proving to be trouble-free, in sharp contrast to the F-16's F100 engine.

The F/A-18's new-technology cockpit was also widely acclaimed, and its radar and weapons integration drew no criticism. This was just as well, because other important attributes of the new aircraft were drawing sharp criticism.

During development, the F/A-18 underwent some major changes. Dog-teeth disappeared from the wing and stabiliser leading edges. The wing itself was reinforced and the lateral controls were revised, because the long, thin wing proved insufficiently stiff – leading to a severe short-fall in roll rate. Long slots in the LERXes were sealed along most of their length, to reduce drag.

Even these measures, however, barely touched the basic problem. The F/A-18 was failing, by a large measure, to meet its warload and radius specifications. Both of the aircraft which it was supposed to replace (the F-4 and A-7) could carry larger loads over a greater distance. Weight and drag increases also meant that the F/A-18 was limited in its 'bring-back' capability. With normal fuel reserves, the new fighter could not land aboard a carrier at an acceptable approach speed with more than a minimal ordnance load.

In 1982, Navy test squadron VX-5 recommended that the F/A-18 programme be suspended until some way of alleviating the range shortfall could be found. Among other measures, McDonnell Douglas proposed a thicker wing and an enlarged dorsal spine, which would have improved the aircraft's range at the expense of transonic acceleration and speed.

The Navy, however, rejected these suggestions and over-rode VX-5's recommendations. By that time, the service had other priorities, including the development of modernised versions of the A-6 and F-14 and the definition of a long-range, stealthy bomber to carry the war to the Soviet navy's land bases. All these aircraft were expensive, and would not be built soon, or in large quantities – but the Navy's carrier fleet was expanding, and ageing F-4s and A-7s, dating back to the Vietnam War, had to be replaced. Cancelling or delaying the F/A-18 would leave the Navy short of modern aircraft, so the Navy decided to put the aircraft into production without attempting to fix the range problem.

The end of the F/A-18A

The F/A-18A garnered a total of three export customers – Canada, Australia and Spain. They were in a rather better situation than the US Navy, because the limitations on the Hornet's range and bring-back capability could be alleviated when it was operated from land bases. Canada, for instance, developed a 480-US gal (1800-litre) external tank to supplement the 330-US gal (1250-litre) tanks used by the US Navy. The US Navy did not adopt them because the

Above: On a mission over Bosnia this VMFA(AW)-224 F/A-18D drops a flare – on this occasion more for display than defence. NATO pilots quickly learned that chaff, flares and jamming were essential to their survival in the dangerous Bosnian skies.

Right: VAQ-34 were 'electronic aggressors' who flew sorties against the fleet and ground targets rather than individual aircraft. Here, one of the 'Flashbacks' F/A-18Bs taxis out with an AGM-88 HARM acquisition round.

Below: HARM launch by a USMC F/A-18D. A Hornet can carry a maximum of three AGM-88s for a SEAD mission.

landing gear required for carrier operations.

In many respects, the F/A-18 was technologically more advanced than the F-16A. Its fly-by-wire flight control system used digital rather than analog processors. It used more composite materials (in the wing skins, for example). It had a multi-mode radar, and a cockpit which used cathode-ray tube (CRT) displays in place of conventional dial-and-pointer instruments. It was designed from the

larger tank would not fit on the centreline. Nevertheless, the F/A-18's problems, combined with the arrival on the scene of the F-16C/D, ushered in a long sales drought.

Pilots were – as always – enthusiastic about the F/A-18A/B when it entered service in 1983. However, historical fact tells a different story. Some 410 of this initial version were built until production switched to the F/A-18C/D in 1987. By 1995, the Navy had retired most of the A/B models from carrier-based service, the shortest first-line career of any modern fighter. Apart from a small top-up batch of aircraft delivered to Spain from Navy stocks in 1995, there are no plans to offer these aircraft for export, or to upgrade them – unlike the older and more austere F-16A/B.

The fact was that VX-5 had been right. The F/A-18A/B was a somewhat inadequate aircraft which validated the adage "Jack of all trades, master of none" in its full and not altogether complimentary sense. It took a series of upgrades to produce a Hornet variant which could be called the master of most of its many missions. This process started with the first F/A-18C/D, delivered from September 1987. Basically designed to accommodate new technologies and weapons, the first F/A-18C/Ds have formed the basis for a series of Hornets whose exterior resemblance to the original A/B is entirely deceptive.

Airframe development

The F/A-18C/D airframe is not very different from that of the A/B, and has not changed significantly since it entered production in 1987. The reason was not so much that the original design was perfect, as that it had run into a hard limit on its growth.

The F/A-18 had been designed for an approach speed of 125 kt (231 km/h), but development problems increased this to 134 kt (250 km/h) on a standard day – a respectable figure for a land-based fighter, but on the high side for a carrier-based aircraft. This in turn set a cap on the F/A-18's maximum landing weight. The problem was complicated by the requirements of carrier operations. In bad weather or at night, a pilot may miss the wires once, twice or even more, making a full-afterburner take-off and climb to regain flying speed from a few hundred feet of deck. Because of this, the Navy requires large fuel reserves at the point where the aircraft makes its first landing attempt: for the F/A-18, up to 3,000 lb (1360 kg) in the daytime and 4,000 lb (1815 kg) at night.

The difference between the maximum landing weight and the fighter's empty weight, minus the fuel reserve, is the 'bring-back': the ordnance load with which the fighter can land aboard the carrier. Bring-back was not much of a concern until the 1970s and 1980s. Air-to-air missiles were relatively light in weight, while Mk 80 series bombs were 'cheaper than hamburger' (these days, about a dollar a pound) and it mattered little if they had to be jettisoned into the sea before landing. Heavy precision-guided weapons were another matter. Even the carrier's magazines could not store enough of these bulky and expensive weapons for them to be loaded on to an aircraft in the knowledge that they will have to be dropped if the target cannot be hit.

Unseen limits

On a typical day, a Lot 19 F/A-18C in an interdiction configuration (with an AAS-38 pod attached) approaches the carrier at 145 kt (270 km/h) with a maximum payload of 5,500 lb (2495 kg), including its fuel reserves. With night-time reserves, the fighter cannot bring AGM-84E SLAM or AGM-88 HARM missiles aboard the carrier. The

The Hornet has always acquitted itself well in ACM training. Until the mid-1990s, the aircraft was only cleared to a 7.5-g limit – significantly less than the 9-g limit of the F-16 and other rivals. The first F/A-18C 9-g clearance was received in 1996 after FCS and minor airframe changes were made.

Top: Seen aboard USS Theodore Roosevelt in July 1995, this HARM-armed F/A-18C of VMFA-312 was one of those involved in Operation Deliberate Force the following month. Roosevelt had embarked three Hornet squadrons (including one Marine unit) and only a single F-14 squadron for its Adriatic 'combat' cruise. When it was replaced on station by the USS America, in early September, this air wing make-up was retained.

Above: A second VMFA-312 Hornet aboard Roosevelt carries a single AGM-88, 500-lb GBU-12 Paveway II, Sidewinders and a lot of extra fuel. The smaller LGBs were of value in Bosnia where it was critical to avoid all and any collateral damage.

F/A-18D is in an even tighter situation, with a second crew member and ejection seat, plus a heavier canopy. (It is worth noting that the Marine Corps, operating from land bases, make more use of the F/A-18D in the interdiction role than the Navy.)

Bring-back weight is a difficult limit to circumvent. Most fighters, after they enter service, follow the same development path: take-off and landing weights and engine thrust are all steadily increased. At the same time, the empty weight also increases, because new equipment is added and the more powerful engines are heavier, but the rise in empty weight is more than offset by the greater take-off and landing weight and the extra thrust, so the aircraft is still as fast and manoeuvrable as ever. The F-16 is typical, gaining 20 per cent in thrust and weight during development.

The F/A-18 could not follow this path because any increase in empty weight reduced the already limited bring-back weight. Major airframe changes have, therefore, been avoided. Apart from some antennas, the only visible modification to be made during the F/A-18's service career was the addition of a pair of strakes or 'billboards' above the LERX. At angles of attack above 45°, the strakes help to break up the vortices generated by the LERX, which otherwise cause buffeting around the vertical tails. This is uncomfortable and hard on the structure. The strakes have been retrofitted to most F/A-18s.

Hornet stealth measures

One significant change, however, is very far from visible. It is conventional wisdom, and correct, to state that a conventional fighter cannot be modified into a stealthy aircraft. This is not to say that stealth technology cannot be usefully applied to a conventional design.

An all-out stealth aircraft is designed for an extremely low radar cross-section (RCS) over a wide band of radar frequencies, and with a near-equal RCS from any direction. The goal is to delay detection as long as possible. But a smaller reduction in RCS, aimed at a narrower bandwidth and concentrated on the most sensitive aspects – typically, head-on – will also yield some tactical advantages. In a beyond-visual-range missile engagement, it reduces the range at which a hostile fighter can detect and track the aircraft, giving the reduced-RCS fighter the first look and first shot. It gives surface-to-air missile systems less warning time and reduces the range at which their radars can 'burn through' defensive jamming (that is, the range at which the natural return energy from the target exceeds the power of the jammer).

'Glass Hornet'

Stealth programmes in the late 1970s and early 1980s spurred the development of new types of radar-absorbent material (RAM) which were lighter, more durable and more effective than their predecessors, along with analytical tools and test facilities which took some of the trial and error out of designing or modifying an aircraft for low RCS. As a result, the USAF and US Navy both initiated programmes to reduce the RCS of their most widely used fighters. The USAF's low-RCS programme for the F-16 was known as Have Glass, and the equivalent F/A-18 configuration has been referred to as a 'Glass Hornet'.

Left: A VFA-37 F/A-18C departs USS Eisenhower *in February 1995. VFA-37 'Bulls' (previously VA-37) transitioned to the Hornet, from the A-7E, on 13 December 1990.*

The F/A-18 modification package designed by the Navy and McDonnell Douglas, and first incorporated in the Lot 12 night-attack aircraft, have not been described in detail. However, they are almost certainly similar to those used on the F-16. Glass Hornets can be identified by a gold-tinted canopy, coated with a thin layer of indium-tin-oxide (ITO). This makes the canopy reflect radar signals, which may seem a strange way of making an aircraft stealthy. From the most critical aspects, though, the canopy reflects radar signals away from the transmitter, and it has a much lower RCS than the many reflective objects (such as the seat headrests and HUD frame) inside the cockpit.

Another key area is the flat bulkhead behind the radar antenna. The radome itself is transparent at radio frequencies, so the radar bulkhead and the antenna drive can generate some strong reflections. A plastic RAM panel mounted in front of the bulkhead suppresses some of these echoes.

The engines and engine inlets are also strong radar reflec-tors. Paint-type RAM, consisting of carbonyl iron particles in a polymer binder, is probably applied to the inlet lips and to the interior of the duct, helping to absorb signals which bounce off the face of the engine. Other 'hot spots' are also treated.

The change was not free from penalties. The later F/A-18s carry almost 250 lb (113 kg) of RAM, further reducing their bring-back load. Also, the carbonyl iron is subject to corrosion in the saltwater-laden carrier environment. This did not affect the 'lossy' RCS-suppressing characteristics of the material, but did require frequent corrective maintenance. A corrosion-resistant RAM has been developed for the F/A-18E/F, and it is likely that this has also been applied to the F/A-18C/D.

Some more recent airframe improvements use technology drawn from other programmes. For the F-15E, McDonnell Douglas used thinner, more flexible polyurethane fuel bladders in the fuselage tanks, replacing the Nitrol rubber

Below: USS America *ended its last cruise in early 1996 on patrol in the Adriatic, before returning to the USA.* America *had CVW-1 (Carrier Air Wing 1) onboard, which included the Hornets of VFA-82, VFA-86 (as seen here) and VMFA-312. It, too, followed the emerging pattern of deploying just a single F-14 unit (VF-102).*

McDonnell Douglas also designed 600-US gal (2270-litre) underwing tanks for the F/A-18. This allows the Hornet to carry as much fuel in two identical tanks as it could previously carry in three dissimilar tanks (two 480-US gal/1800-litre tanks under the wings and one 330-US gal/1250-litre tank on the centreline) but with lower drag and the centreline station free. Originally offered to Israel, these tanks were tested in early 1996.

Navy Hornets have a maximum load limit of 7.5 g. Although Navy operators would argue that the difference between this limit and the F-16's 9 g boundary is not tactically significant, it has been used as a selling point by Lockheed Martin. McDonnell Douglas accordingly launched a programme of analysis and flight tests to ensure that the F/A-18 could be flown to 9 g at typical air-to-air combat weights without compromising the longevity of the airframe. The aircraft which were delivered to Switzerland were the first to feature flight control system (FCS) software which permits 9 g loadings, and the aircraft ordered by Thailand (but eventually taken up by the US Navy) also incorporate this option.

Engine development

Although the airframe has changed relatively little, some significant improvements have been made to the Hornet's engine. One of the features which made the new generation of agile fighters possible in the 1970s was the development of fighter engines which offered a much higher thrust/weight ratio than their predecessors. This in turn contributed to the high thrust/weight ratio of the aircraft itself, allowing a fighter with the large wing required for manoeuvrability to accelerate quickly at transonic and supersonic speeds.

The first engine in this class, the Pratt & Whitney F100, was not initially an unqualified success, suffering from stall problems which took several years to fix across the fleet. Against this background, the performance of the General Electric F404 stood out like a good deed in a naughty world. The engine was relatively free of handling limits from the outset. By 1988, the basic F404-GE-400 engine had accu-

material used earlier. The new tanks are not only easier to install (they have to be pushed into the completed fuselage through an access panel, unfolded and fitted with internal plumbing) but, because they are more flexible and less subject to cracking, they can be installed without some of the foam padding which had to be used with the older tanks. These tanks are used in the F/A-18E/F, and on F/A-18C/Ds from 1998.

Also, for land-based export Hornets, McDonnell Douglas has obtained approval for a smaller ullage allowance: that is, space left empty at the top of the tank to reduce the risk of spilled fuel. Together with the new tanks, the result is a 500-lb (227-kg) increase in the internal fuel capacity, a 5 per cent improvement.

mulated 700,000 flight hours, and reliability and maintainability statistics were good: 1.8 shop visits, from all causes, every 1,000 flight hours; less than one inflight shutdown in every 6,500 hours of engine operation (so that a pilot could well spend his entire career on F-18s and never have a shutdown); and 0.8 man-hours of maintenance per engine flight hour. All these numbers were a fraction of those for the larger F100. The F404 low-pressure system (fan and turbine) was scaled up for GE's F110, which was adopted as an alternative to the F100 in the F-16.

Some problems did surface as the F404 fleet approached the million-hour mark. The afterburner nozzle outer flaps suffered from premature joint wear, caused in part by the aerodynamics of the F/A-18 boat-tail and linked to the LERX-induced vibration of the vertical tails. An improved design was incorporated, based on the F110 nozzle. Some incidents in which the afterburner liner buckled in high-Mach, low-altitude flight were recorded in 1988, and the afterburner was strengthened to avoid a repetition of the problem.

F404 fire risk

The most serious problem cropped up in 1987, when fires broke out in a number of high-time engines. The fires broke through the outer bypass duct into the airframe, causing the loss of several aircraft. Failures in the front end of the compressor, caused by vibration, foreign object damage (FOD) or maintenance errors, produced debris which jammed in the tight clearances between the aft compressor blade tips and the compressor casing. This eroded the wear coating on the casing, and allowed the titanium blades, debris and case to rub together. Under these circumstances, titanium will burn away merrily.

Although this particular problem was solved by redesigning the blades in the front of the compressor, it was clear that titanium fires could still result from FOD or different types of damage. The first step was to develop a fire-resistant Viton rubber coating for the inner wall of the outer bypass duct, which was retrofitted across the fleet. Later F404 engines have a compressor case made of M152 steel

alloy, which eliminates the risk of titanium fires. Because the steel case is heavier than the original titanium component, these engines also have a lighter bypass duct made of carbon-fibre composite material. The duct uses a new high-temperature polymer matrix material called PMR-15. With the steel case and composite duct, the engine weighs almost exactly the same as the original all-titanium F404. The engine has since performed well, sustaining its reliability and maintainability through the 2 million- and 3 million-hour marks.

One area in which the original F404 has been outperformed by the F100 is in its ability to be upgraded. The F404 control system was designed to maintain the engine's handling characteristics and reliability throughout its service life. As the engine ages, the control system automatically

Top: The tiny 'blue bombs' (Mk 76 25-lb practice bombs) seem out of place on the TERs of these VMFA-314 aircraft. Despite its small size, the Mk 76 accurately replicates the ballistic characteristics of a 500-lb Mk 82 bomb.

Above: VFA-37 Hornets are seen aboard USS John F. Kennedy. The Kennedy returned to the fleet in September 1995 after a SLEP in the Philadelphia naval yard.

Right: A VFA-83 F/A-18C lands at NAS Dallas in 1994, with empty TERs (triple ejector racks). Despite its prowess as a fighter, the accent on US Hornet operations is very definitely on the 'A' rather than the 'F', and the aircraft are firmly committed to the light attack role.

Below: Snuggling under a tanker, a group of VFA-15 'Valions' F/A-18Cs poses for the camera. Note the black walk panels that extend along the LERXes. These Hornets are all Lot 14 night-attack aircraft.

opens the exhaust nozzle wider at given throttle settings. This maintains a constant fan speed and turbine exhaust temperature, but results in a gradual loss in thrust. Unlike Pratt & Whitney's F100-PW-220E, there is no cost-effective upgrade kit available to restore the lost power. This is why the Spanish air force acquired new engines for the ex-USN F-18s which it placed in service in 1995.

A Pratt & Whitney F404?

One major change in the F404 programme was proposed in 1988, when the Navy was planning to produce or modify more than 300 Grumman A-6Fs with F404-GE-100D non-afterburning engines. The Navy planned to qualify Pratt & Whitney to produce the F404, and to split production between the two companies, as a way of reducing cost. The move displeased GE, which saw it as a way of rewarding its competitor for GE's own efforts. The plan was dropped in 1989 after the A-6F was cancelled.

"Develop or perish" is a watchword in the engine business. In the late 1960s, GE Aircraft Engines had developed the 'building block' approach to engine development. Instead of meeting each requirement with a completely new engine, GE planned to develop families of engines around common cores, and to work on technology which could be applied to a variety of engine types.

From 1983, GE worked on a series of demonstrator engines based on the F404, which was used to test new fans, compressors and cores, combustors, turbines and augmentors. Most of these were funded by the Pentagon's Joint Technology Demonstrator Engine (JTDE) programme.

The first uprated version of the engine to enter full-scale development was the F404/RM12 for Saab's JAS 39 Gripen. This 18,000-lb (80.07-kN) thrust engine had a higher-airflow fan than the basic F404-GE-400, material changes to allow the engine to run at higher temperatures, and a more efficient augmentor.

The Enhanced Performance Engine

Much of the same technology was transferred to a follow-on powerplant for the F/A-18C/D, the F404-GE-402 Enhanced Performance Engine (EPE), which was originally developed to meet the Swiss air force's performance requirements and went on to become the standard engine from 1992. The EPE delivers about 10 per cent more static, sea-level thrust than the basic GE-400 engine, but, as in the case of the improved versions of the F100 and F110, static thrust is only part of the story. Jet engines are usually limited by their maximum operating temperature in the 'lower left-hand corner' of the envelope – that is, at high speeds and low to medium altitudes. Under these circumstances, the EPE can provide up to 20 per cent more thrust than the earlier engine, sharply improving acceleration, time to climb, and speed with a heavy weapon load.

The EPE uses the same basic fan design as the GE-400, because the original version was limited by temperature, rather than airflow, in the most important parts of the envelope, and because using the RM12 fan would have required more flight testing. Improved materials include single-crystal alloys in both turbine stages and higher-temperature alloys in the compressor.

With the EPE, the F/A-18 has up to 18 per cent more specific excess power at Mach 0.9 and 10,000 ft (3048 m). Transonic acceleration (from Mach 0.8 to Mach 1.6 at 35,000 ft/10668 m) is 27 per cent better. A typical runway-launched interception profile, from brake release to Mach 1.4 at 50,000 ft (15240 m), takes 31 per cent less time because it is dependent on achieving the greatest possible acceleration at low altitude.

Kuwait and Switzerland were the first customers for the new engine; the US Navy committed to it later, after deciding that the EPE's higher performance outweighed the slight loss of commonality with the earlier engine.

The EPE is expected to handle the F/A-18C/D's thrust requirements for the remainder of the type's career. Most of GE's current engineering work on the F404 is aimed at improving the engine's durability and reducing its manufacturing and ownership costs.

Avionics

If the airframe looks the same, and the engine has been improved but not redesigned, why do its operators think of the F/A-18C/D as a new aircraft? Most of the answer lies in the avionics.

The original F/A-18 full-scale development programme was accomplished with 11 aircraft. Remarkably, a decade and a half later, there are more F/A-18s engaged in flight tests at Patuxent River and China Lake than there were then: as many as 20 Hornets are assigned full-time to flight tests, not including the new F/A-18E/F.

This appropriately badged F/A-18 of VMFA-122 'Crusaders' is carrying live Mk 82 bombs on a weapons training sortie. On the Hornet's starboard 'shoulder' station can be seen a Lockheed Martin ASQ-173 LST/SCAM (Laser Spot Tracker/Strike CAMera). ASQ-173 can target weapons on the launch aircraft's HUD, using laser designation from another source (on the ground or in the air) – but only during daylight. It also houses a strike camera for bomb damage assessment. ASQ-173 is often carried in favour of the AN/AAS-50 navigation FLIR. When fitted, the larger AN/AAS-38 NITE Hawk FLIR and laser designator is always carried to port.

A Lemoore-based F/A-18C from VFA-137 'Kestrels' is seen with a single GBU-16 Paveway II. GBU-16 is based around the 1,000-lb Mk 83 GP bomb, mated with a set of (second-generation) guidance fins and seeker head. The US Navy has only recently begun to use the more advanced Paveway III system. Interestingly, during Operation Desert Storm US Navy aircraft dropped more British-designed Paveway II LGBs than US-designed ones. The British bombs (1,000-lb CPU-123s, developed by Portsmouth Aviation) reportedly had greater penetration capability against hardened targets.

Above: During FWIT 95 (Fighter Weapons Instructor Training) F/A-18s of VFA-105 were deployed to snow-covered Leeuwarden AFB, in the Netherlands, to exercise alongside other NATO forces.

Partners and rivals – the F/A-18 has competed against the F-16 (right) for many competitions, the Fort Worth product being more successful in export sales. The F-14 (below) is now fast disappearing from carrier decks, its place taken by the 'legacy' Hornet's bigger, younger brother.

Some of these aircraft are assigned to the development of new weapons. Because it can carry such a wide range of stores, most Navy weapon development offices pick the Hornet as their initial test aircraft. Most of the test fleet, however, are engaged in developing improvements to the F/A-18 itself.

The F/A-18 was the first true 'digital aircraft'. Many aspects of the Hornet – what the pilot sees on the cockpit displays, how the aircraft and its systems respond to stick and switch inputs, and how the onboard sensors work – are influenced if not actually determined by software, either in the aircraft's main mission computer or in processors built into the other avionics subsystems. Because of this, the F/A-18's capability has grown steadily and substantially through apparently minor hardware upgrades, combined with regular updates to the mission software – a new package is released to the operator about once every two years.

Core mission computer

The core of the avionics system is the Control Data International AYK-14 mission computer. This has been the standard Navy airborne computer throughout the 1980s; however, while the newest AYK-14s share some external interfaces with older units, the circuit boards inside have been largely revised. The first version fitted to the F/A-18, the XN-5, was replaced in service by the XN-6. All F/A-18C/Ds had the XN-8 version, with 2 million words of memory. This was retrofitted to Lot 8 and Lot 9 A/B models. The latest version is the XN-10. Its capacity is expected to be adequate to cope with the demands into the first decade of the 21st Century.

By today's standards, the AYK-14 is not a high performer. It is rugged and reliable – and unlike the case in the commercial world, the development of airborne military computer systems is paced by the rate at which software can be designed, thoroughly tested and introduced fleet-wide. Also, a restrained rate of advance in computing capacity means that, by the time a new software package is released, most of the aircraft in the fleet can use it.

The most important change in mission software to be released in the last few years is called multi-sensor integra-

tion (MSI). Introduced with the night-attack versions of the Hornet, MSI is intended to keep the crew's workload at a reasonable level despite the addition of new sensors and new weapons. With MSI, the computer receives inputs from different sensors, correlates them and displays them so that one target appears on the pilot's display.

In the air-to-air mode, for example, MSI matches a target detected by radar with the same target's signature on the targeting FLIR. The radar provides range and velocity information, which the FLIR cannot supply; but the FLIR provides more accurate elevation and bearing data and is better at resolving several closely spaced targets. MSI can select the best data from both sensors and display it to the pilot. Alternatively, the system can be put into a passive, 'quiet' mode in which targets are located with FLIR and the radar is used in bursts for ranging.

MSI can be used in air-to-ground operations as well. If the radar warning receiver (RWR) detects an emitter, it will provide accurate bearing information but only a rough estimate of range, based on signal strength. MSI can automatically point the radar at the target area in its high-resolution mode and locate it.

The first software package to incorporate MSI reached the fleet in October 1991, and the third MSI release entered service in the mid-1990s. One area which saw improvements is the suppression of enemy air defences (SEAD)

mission, where the HARM seeker, radar and RWR are integrated to locate threats and display them to the crew.

The F/A-18A/B cockpit set a pattern for a generation. Its multi-function displays ringed by bezel switches, the up-front control beneath the head-up display, and the hands-on-throttle-and-stick (HOTAS) controls have all been widely emulated. It has also lasted very well. The only major change came with the Lot 12 night-attack variant, in which the monochrome displays were replaced by Kaiser Kroma displays. These combine a monochrome CRT with a three-colour liquid-crystal display (LCD) 'shutter' over the screen, allowing them to display colour stroke information. Lot 12 also saw the introduction of a Honeywell digital map, based on an optical disk reader, which replaces the former film-based map. The new display is easier to read and more flexible – tactical information can be overlaid on it – and changing maps is much easier.

Helmet-mounted sight technology

Another new feature for the cockpit is the Joint Helmet-Mounted Cueing System (JHMCS), a helmet-mounted display under development for all three US fast-jet operators. The F/A-18 is the first Navy aircraft to be fitted with the JHMCS, which attaches to a pilot's standard helmet and can be used to designate airborne and ground targets for the fighter's weapon control system. It meets stringent specifi-

A VFA-94 'Mighty Shrikes' F/A-18C is pictured in the empty skies over Nevada. The US has learned hard lessons about 'blue-on-blue' kills in less friendly environments. In the late 1990s an improved IFF system underwent tests at the Naval Air Warfare Weapons Division, China Lake, on an F/A-18D. The new AN/APX-111 or Combined Interrogator Transponder (CIT) is fitted to 500 US Navy and Marine Corps Hornets, allowing their crews to survey airspace up to 100 miles (160 km) from their aircraft. The CIT provides identification, azimuth and range information on all targets in that zone.

The F/A-18 has become a popular mount for the US Navy's adversary squadrons. While the Navy has steadily cut back its aggressor training units (to the horror of many) those that survive operate mostly early-model Hornets in a variety of vivid colour schemes. This VFC-12 MiG-29 'lookalike' is one of those which replaced the squadron's former mount, the A-4F/M, at its East Coast base of NAS Oceana.

cations for symbol brightness and quality, head-tracking accuracy, ejection safety, wearability and supportability – issues which have hampered the deployment of helmet-mounted displays in the past. A three-year engineering and manufacturing development programme started in 1997.

The F/A-18 has flown with other helmet-mounted displays, because McDonnell Douglas/Boeing in general, and the company's resident cockpit guru Gene Adam in particular, have been strong advocates of what Adam calls "the HUD on your head" since the early 1980s. The aircraft has been used to test several of the Kaiser Agile Eye HMD prototypes. In 1993, while the F/A-18 was in competition for an Israeli air force order, McDonnell Douglas signed an agreement with Elbit to market the Israeli company's DASH (Display And Sight Helmet). DASH has been flown by US Navy pilots, and was also demonstrated in flight evaluations for the Israeli and Singaporean air forces. Early in 1996, it was used by the Navy in tests of Hughes and Raytheon off-boresight missile seekers at China Lake. The current JHMCS is produced jointly by Kaiser and Elbit.

Other elements of the basic avionics system have seen changes during production. The digital flight control system has been continuously upgraded, sometimes to improve the aircraft's handling qualities but usually in order to handle new weapons configurations. In the early 1990s, the DFCS computers were modified with larger programmable memory modules to make the update process easier. Industry mergers have created a remarkable situation for the DFCS. The General Electric division which originally developed the system was acquired in 1990 by Martin-Marietta, which in turn merged with Lockheed in 1995. As a result, the most critical avionics system on the F/A-18 is now produced by Lockheed Martin.

All-new inertial nav

The original Litton mechanical-gyro ASN-130 inertial navigation system (INS) was replaced with a lower-maintenance Litton ASN-39 ring-laser-gyro (RLG) INS in aircraft delivered from 1991. Aircraft handed over since September 1995 have also had a P-Code Global Positioning System (GPS) receiver, and this was subsequently retrofitted to all F/A-18s in service. The next step was the introduction of an integrated GPS/INS, which offers better accuracy and integrity than either system alone. The GPS corrects the long-term drift in the INS, while the INS can detect GPS errors caused by poor satellite signals. A Litton GPS/INS started tests in a King Air in early 1996 before being

installed on an F/A-18.

The new navigation devices are a very good match for low-cost 'semi-precise' GPS/inertial weapons such as JSOW and JDAM and – in the air-to-ground role – for a helmet-mounted display. If a pilot sees a target on the ground, he needs only to look at it – that is, point his helmet 'pipper' at it – to designate it. The weapons system can compute the target's exact location from the aircraft's attitude and direction (INS), its exact position relative to the ground and the elevation of the target and the boresight of the HMD. The data can then be used for an over-the-shoulder attack with JDAM or JSOW, without overflying the target or even being within line-of-sight of it.

Connected to the core avionics – the computer, displays and navigation equipment – are two main groups of 'peripherals', which are sensors that help find targets and defensive avionics which defeat threats. These, too, have been steadily improved since the Hornet entered service.

The world's best fighter radar

As in the case of any fighter, the Hornet's most important and expensive sensor is its radar. The GM-Hughes Electronics (now Raytheon) APG-65 radar fitted to the F/A-18A/B was an effective and flexible system for its day, drawing on much of the technology that had been developed for the F-15's APG-63. During the 1980s, the radar was progressively modified with more memory and faster processors, but by the end of the decade its growth potential had been fully realised. Later Hughes/Raytheon radars, such as the APG-70 fitted to later F-15s, had demonstrated new technologies and components which could be incorporated at low risk into an improved radar for the F/A-18.

The new radar, designated APG-73, was flown on an F/A-18 in April 1992, and deliveries started in May 1994, to VFA-146 and VFA-147 at NAS Lemoore, California. All subsequent F/A-18s, including export versions for Finland, Switzerland and Malaysia, have the APG-73, and the Navy retrofitted all Block 12 and later aircraft – that is, all the night-attack variants – with the new radar. (The APG-65 radars removed from these aircraft were fitted to USMC Harriers as they were remanufactured into the AV-8B Plus configuration.)

The basic APG-73 uses the same antenna and travelling-wave-tube (TWT) transmitter as the APG-65, but the rest of the hardware is new. The receiver/exciter unit is more sophisticated and provides much faster analog-to-digital conversion, allowing the radar to cut the incoming signal

into smaller fragments and thereby achieve better range resolution. The radar data processor replaces two units in the older radar (the signal processor and the data processor); signal processing speed is increased almost tenfold, and both functions can use much more memory. The third new unit is the power supply, which uses new solid-state techniques to provide much more reliable power conversion. Power supply reliability has been the bane of the radar designer's life for many years, but the new APG-73 unit ran for 2,500 hours on tests with only one failure.

All the new electronic units comprise racks that accommodate 5 x 9-in (12.7 x 22.9-cm) modules. These electronic units snap into the racks, which provide them with power, cooling and connections to the other modules and to the radar. Built-in test modules isolate any fault to an individual module, which can be changed quickly without removing the rack from the aircraft. Future hardware upgrades can be carried out in the same way.

The APG-73 offers higher resolution in its air-to-ground mapping and bombing modes ("My grandmother could win Gunsmoke with the APG-73," is one comment) and is better at discriminating between closely spaced airborne targets

for raid assessment. Air-to-air detection and tracking ranges are up between 7 and 20 per cent. One of the biggest single benefits is a wider receiver bandwidth which allows it to use more advanced electronic counter-countermeasures (ECCM) techniques to defeat jamming and confuse an adversary's radar warning receiver.

Phase 2 reconnaissance capability

The current APG-73, though, is the first of three phases in radar development. The main change in Phase 2 is the addition of a high-resolution synthetic aperture radar (SAR) mode in the radar. SAR is a radar technique which uses the movement of the aircraft between pulses to emulate the resolution of a very large antenna. On the F/A-18, SAR has been a problem because the inertial navigation system, which is needed to measure the movement of the aircraft, is in the middle of the fuselage. In flight, the body flexes between the nose and mid-section, introducing errors into the antenna pointing accuracy and thereby limiting the resolution that SAR can achieve. The Phase 2 radar incorporates a small Honeywell RLG inertial measurement unit to overcome this problem. It was fitted first to the USMC's recon-

On a sortie from MCAS Yuma, a Marines F/A-18C rolls in on a target with a live load of four 500-lb Mk 82 'slicks' and a pair of Zuni rocket pods. In Operation Desert Storm the US Marines used their F/A-18Ds as Fast FACs, and these tactics have been further refined over Bosnia. WP (white phosphorous) rockets have long been used as target markers by FACs, but conventional HE-tipped rockets work equally well. They can damage a target rather than warn it that it is about to come under attack. They are effective target markers, too – just look for the black smoke.

93

When it first appeared, the cockpit of the basic F/A-18A (above right) was the most advanced fighter cockpit in service, dominated by three monochrome CRT displays and featuring comprehensive HOTAS controls to allow head-up operation. The front cockpit of the F/A-18D (above) is little changed, and the rear cockpit of the all-weather F/A-18D (below) is similarly equipped. The next generation of fighter cockpits dispense with analog instruments on the main panel altogether, using small LCDs or CRTs as back-ups, and with full-colour display symbology.

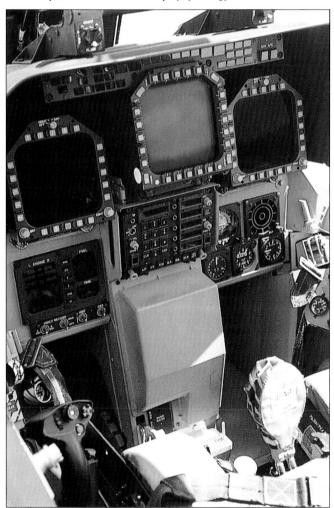

Boeing F/A-18D Night-Attack Hornet

1 Glass-fibre radome, hinged to starboard
2 Planar radar array radar scanner
3 Scanner tracking mechanism
4 Cannon port and gun gas purging intakes
5 Radar module withdrawal rails
6 Hughes AN/APG-73 radar equipment module
7 Formation lighting strip
8 Forward radar warning antennas
9 UHF/IFF antenna
10 Pitot head, port and starboard
11 Incidence transmitter
12 Canopy emergency release
13 Ammunition drum, 570 rounds
14 M61A1 Vulcan 20-mm rotary cannon
15 Retractable inflight-refuelling probe
16 Single piece wrap-round windscreen
17 Pilot's Kaiser AN/AVQ-28 raster HUD

24 Catapult strop link
25 Twin nosewheels, forward-retracting
26 Retractable boarding ladder
27 Nosewheel hydraulic jack
28 Nosewheel leg-mounted deck signalling and taxi lights
29 Forward avionics equipment bays, port and starboard
30 Engine throttle levers
31 Pilot's Martin-Baker SJU-6/A ejection seat
32 Rear cockpit rudder pedals (dual flight control system interchangeable with radar and weapons controllers)

18 Instrument panel with multi-function colour CRT displays
19 Control column
20 Rudder pedals
21 Ammunition loading chute
22 Ground power socket
23 Nose undercarriage wheel bay

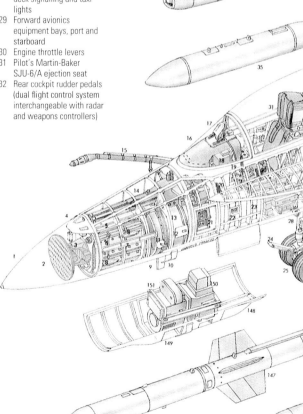

33 Rear instrument console with multi-function CRT displays
34 Single-piece upward-opening cockpit canopy
35 AWW-7/9 datalink pod for Walleye missile, fuselage centreline pylon-mounted
36 AGM-62 Walleye II ER/DL air-to-surface missile, starboard outboard pylon only
37 Naval flight officer's helmet with GEC-Marconi Avionics 'Cats Eyes' night-vision goggles
38 Naval flight officer's SJU-5/A ejection seat
39 Sidestick radar and weapons controllers, replacing dual flight control system
40 Liquid oxygen converter
41 Ventral radar warning antenna
42 Rear avionics equipment bays, port and starboard
43 Cockpit rear pressure bulkhead

44 Canopy actuator
45 Starboard navigation light
46 Tailfin aerodynamic load-alleviating strake
47 Upper radar warning antennas
48 Forward fuselage bag-type fuel cell
49 Radar/avionics equipment liquid cooling units
50 Fuselage centreline pylon
51 Boundary layer splitter plate
52 Port navigation light
53 Fixed-geometry engine air intake
54 Cooling air spill louvres
55 Cabin air conditioning system equipment
56 Leading-edge flap drive motor
57 Boundary layer spill duct
58 Air conditioning system heat exchanger exhaust
59 Centre fuselage fuel cells

60 Wing panel root attachment joints
61 Central Garrett GTC36-200 auxiliary power unit (APU)
62 Airframe-mounted engine accessory equipment gearbox, port and starboard
63 Engine bleed air ducting to conditioning system
64 Fuel tank bay access panels
65 Upper UHF/IFF/datalink antenna
66 Starboard wingroot joint
67 Starboard wing integral fuel tank
68 Stores pylons
69 Mk 83 1,000-lb LDGP bomb
70 Leading-edge flap
71 Starboard secondary navigation light
72 Wingtip missile launch rail
73 AIM-9L Sidewinder air-to-air missile
74 Outer wing panel, folded position
75 Drooping aileron
76 Aileron hydraulic actuator
77 Wing-fold hydraulic rotary actuator
78 Drooping flap vane
79 Starboard slotted flap, operates as flaperon at low speeds
80 Flap hydraulic actuator
81 Hydraulic reservoirs

82 Reinforced fin-root attachment joint
83 Multi-spar fin structure
84 Fuel jettison pipe
85 Graphite/epoxy tail unit skin panels with glass-fibre tip fairings
86 Tail position light
87 AN/ALR-67 receiving antenna
88 AN/ALQ-165 low-band transmitting antenna
89 Fuel jettison
90 Starboard all-moving tailplane
91 Starboard rudder
92 Radar warning system power amplifier
93 Rudder hydraulic actuator
94 Airbrake panel, open
95 Airbrake hydraulic jack
96 Fin formation lighting strip
97 Fuel venting air intake
98 Anti-collision beacon, port and starboard
99 Port rudder

100 Port AN/ALQ-165 antenna
101 AN-ALQ-67 receiving antenna
102 AN/ALQ-165 high-band transmitting antenna
103 Variable-area afterburner nozzles
104 Nozzle actuators
105 Afterburner duct
106 Port all-moving tailplane
107 Tailplane bonded honeycomb core structure
108 Deck arrester hook
109 Tailplane pivot mounting
110 Tailplane hydraulic actuator
111 Full-authority digital engine controller (FADEC)
112 General Electric F404-GE-400 afterburning turbofan engine
113 Rear fuselage formation lighting strip
114 Engine fuel control units
115 Fuselage side mounted AIM-7 Sparrow air-to-air missile
116 Port slotted flap
117 Control surface bonded honeycomb core structure
118 Wing-fold rotary hydraulic actuator and hinge joint

126 Port wing stores pylons
127 Pylon mounting hardpoints
128 Multi-spar wing panel structure
129 Port wing integral fuel tank
130 Leading-edge flap shaft driven rotary actuator
131 Port mainwheel
132 Levered suspension main undercarriage leg strut
133 Shock absorber strut
134 Ventral AN/ALE-39 chaff/flare launcher
135 330-US gal external fuel tank
136 Strike camera housing
137 AN/ASQ-173 laser spot tracker/strike camera (LST/SCAM) pod
138 Fuselage starboard side LST/SCAM pylon adaptor
139 Port side FLIR pod adaptor
140 AN/AAS-38 forward-looking infra-red (FLIR) pod
141 CBU-89/89B 'Gator' sub-munition dispenser
142 GBU-12 D/B Paveway II 500-lb laser-guided bomb
143 LAU-10A Zuni four-round rocket launcher
144 5-in FFAR
145 AGM-88 HARM air-to-surface anti-radar missile
146 AGM-65A Maverick air-to-surface anti-armour missile

119 Port aileron hydraulic actuator
120 Port drooping aileron
121 Wingtip AIM-9L Sidewinder air-to-air missile
122 Port leading-edge flap
123 Mk 82SE 'Snakeye' 500-lb retarded bomb
124 Mk 82 500-lb LDGP bombs
125 Twin stores carrier

147 AGM-84 SLAM air-to-surface missile
148 Advanced tactical airborne reconnaissance system (ATARS) unit, interchangeable with gun pack/ammunition magazine (F/A-18D(RC))
149 Sensor viewing apertures
150 Infra-red linescanner
151 Low- and/or medium-altitude electro-optical scanner

On patrol over Bosnia, a Marine Corps F/A-18D refuels from a drogue-equipped KC-135 of the 434th Wing. In many ways the Marines reinvented the Hornet, realising that the two-crew F/A-18D plus the Hornet's new nav/attack suite would make a useful replacement for its A-6Es. Thus the F/A-18D became far more than a conversion trainer. Deliveries of Night Attack F/A-18Ds began to the Marine Corps (VMFA(AW)-121) in April 1990.

Above opposite: USMC plans called for the establishment of six F/A-18D squadrons. All of them have three ATARS-capable F/A-18D(RC)s with RUG-2 radar, which replace a reconnaissance capability the Corps has been lacking since its last RF-4B Phantoms were retired. These VMFA(AW)-224 F/A-18Ds, carrying a mix of Mk 83s and AGM-88s, show just how valuable the Hornet is to the Marines in providing maximum air support for troops on the ground.

naissance-capable F/A-18D(RC) in 1997, and became standard from 1999.

The APG-73 Phase 3 radar has an active array, which is a physically fixed antenna comprising hundreds of transmit/receive modules. Advantages include virtually instantaneous mode changes and beam steering, and the elimination of components, such as the gimbal drives and transmitter, which can render the radar inoperative with a single failure. An active array can also be shaped so that it adds very little to the aircraft's total radar cross-section. Phase 3 will not appear on the F/A-18C/D, instead being developed as the APG-79 for the F/A-18E/F Super Hornet.

One of the features of the F/A-18 which has distinguished it from its competitors is that it has always been offered with infra-red navigation and targeting systems, which are attached to the body-side Sparrow/AMRAAM mounts. The first systems to be offered were the Hughes AAR-50 Thermal Imaging Navigation System (TINS), a wide-angle forward-looking infra-red (FLIR) imager which was designed to project an IR picture on the pilot's HUD, and the Ford Aerospace AAS-38 NITE Hawk (Navigation IR Targeting Equipment) FLIR, a steerable sensor which could track a target on the ground automatically as the aircraft moved. Ford, which became a division of Loral in 1990, delivered more than 300 AAS-38 pods to the USN and USMC by 1992, and they were used on more than 10,000 sorties in the Gulf War.

NITE Hawk, Laser Hornet

From 1992, the F/A-18 acquired the ability to designate targets for laser-guided bombs, as NITE Hawk production shifted to the AAS-38A FLIR-LTD/R (Laser Target Designator/Ranger). The new pods were issued to VFA-37 and VFA-105 and went to sea aboard *Kennedy* in October 1992, and were widely used by USN and USMC squadrons, including those operating over Bosnia. With the new pod, the F/A-18 can deliver LGBs without the help of a laser-carrying forward air controller on the ground. Once the target has been acquired on the FLIR and the autotracker has locked on, the bomb is released and guided automatically as long as the aircraft does not manoeuvre outside the FLIR gimbal limits or exceed the system's range. The LTD/R

also provides more precise range and velocity information for the delivery of unguided weapons.

The latest NITE Hawk version, the AAS-38B, has a new Texas Instruments signal processor and a laser spot tracker (LST). The latter makes it possible for the F/A-18 crew to quickly acquire a target which has been illuminated by another Hornet, an EA-6B Prowler (these aircraft carry designators but no LGBs) or a FAC on the ground. The faster processor improves performance in a number of ways. The autotracker works better and can be set either to track the entire scene or the centroid of a target. In the air-to-air mode, the new version can search the sky ahead of the aircraft much more quickly, giving the F/A-18 a true passive track-while-scan capability.

The next step in FLIR capability is provided by the Raytheon ASQ-228 Advanced Tactical FLIR, or ATFLIR. This incorporates third-generation FLIR technology, along with laser and IR spot-trackers and a laser designator, and provides a considerable step up in capability. At present it is being fielded on the Super Hornet only, but may make its way into the 'legacy' Hornet fleet at a later date.

The AAR-50 TINS remains in use, but is normally carried only when conditions such as a high overcast preclude the use of night-vision goggles (NVGs). NVGs give the pilot all-round night vision, and the operators prefer to use one of the side stations for an AMRAAM or Sparrow

Reliable IFF

Another important sensor (which is often overlooked) is the Identification Friend or Foe, (IFF) system. Kuwait was the first customer to replace the standard APX-100 with the Hazeltine APX-113 Combined Interrogator Transponder (CIT). Identifiable by the row of five short blade antennas above the fighter's nose, the APX-113 features electronic beam steering which allows it to determine the range, bearing and elevation of any aircraft which 'squawk' when interrogated by the Hornet. In early 1995, it was selected as the standard transponder for US Navy and Marine Corps Hornets. It was fitted to all Hornets after mid-1997 and was retrofitted to as many as 500 aircraft.

The F/A-18's digital core can also be connected to other sensors for specialised missions. The most important

programme of this kind is the US Navy/Marine Corps F/A-18D(RC) – reconnaissance-capable – variant, which entered USMC service at the end of the 1990s.

The reconnaissance version has had a long and sometimes difficult history. Early in the programme's history, McDonnell Douglas demonstrated that the Hornet's nose gun bay could accommodate a reconnaissance pallet, with flat camera windows in a fairing that would replace the access door. Technology and inter-service politics, however, delayed the programme.

The Marines' RF-4Bs, and the Navy's TARPS (Tactical Air Reconnaissance Pod System) pod which is carried on the F-14, used film-based cameras. By the mid-1980s, the development of electro-optical cameras, which have an array of charge-coupled devices (CCDs) in place of film, had reached a point where their image quality matched that of 127-mm reconnaissance film. This eliminated the cumbersome task of developing film in the field or on board ship.

The ATARS saga

At the same time, there was an active debate over the role of unmanned air vehicles (UAVs) for tactical reconnaissance. Some high-level Pentagon planners favoured the UAV, but the operators were reluctant to give up their manned reconnaissance aircraft until UAVs were proven to work. The final result was a programme called Advanced Tactical Air Reconnaissance System (ATARS). Control Data Corporation was awarded a contract to develop ATARS in May 1988. It was a single EO reconnaissance system which was planned to fit in the F/A-18's nose, in a pod on the F-16, and in Teledyne Ryan's AQM-145 Medium Range UAV, in two versions: an air-launched variant for the Navy and a ground-launched version for the USAF.

The following seven years were eventful but did not, unfortunately, result in much progress. Technical problems with the system's video recorder and other components delayed the programme. Control Data transferred the ATARS contract to Martin-Marietta in 1990. The USAF cancelled its version of the AQM-145, which (in 1994) was dropped by the Navy as well. In July 1993, the Air Force terminated the ATARS programme, stating that manned tactical reconnaissance was no longer a necessary mission.

Experience in Bosnia and Somalia revived interest in tactical reconnaissance. High-altitude stand-off platforms can be rendered useless by overcast or terrain, may not equal the resolution of a short-range image unless the weather is perfect, and may not be available when a theatre commander needs them.

The Navy continued to test ATARS after the USAF withdrew, and restarted the programme in June 1994 with McDonnell Douglas as the prime contractor (the third in the programme's life) and Loral – which provides the sensors – as a lead subcontractor. Flight tests restarted in April 1995. Navy plans covered the acquisition of an initial batch of 31 ATARS systems, to be fitted to USMC F/A-18Ds. The systems are distributed among the VMFA(AW) squadrons, three to each unit with others used for tests and as spares. The modified aircraft is designated F/A-18D(RC) and retains full combat capability apart from the gun, which has to be removed to make way for the ATARS system, which is mounted in the lower forward fuselage behind the radar.

The F/A-18B remains essentially a training aircraft. Forty aircraft were acquired for the US Navy and Marines, and this example is seen wearing the markings of VFA-106 'Gladiators', which was established as the East Coast Hornet FRS in April 1984. The unit is actually assigned a mix of F/A-18A/B/C/Ds, and in March 2005 is due to receive its first Super Hornets.

ATARS includes a low-altitude electro-optical (EO) sensor, a medium-altitude EO sensor and an infra-red lines-can imager, all produced by Loral. The low-altitude sensor covers a 140° arc below the aircraft and is normally used at 3,000 ft (914 m) above ground level or lower. The medium-altitude sensor can gather high-resolution imagery at altitudes of 25,000 ft (7620 m), up to 5 miles (8 km) from the target, taking the aircraft out of range of AAA and small SAMs, while the IR linescan provides high-resolution imagery at night.

Managing the suite

Computing Devices International's UK division provides the reconnaissance management system (RMS), which is based on the system developed for the RAF's Tornado reconnaissance variants. The RMS interfaces with the aircraft systems to activate the sensors automatically, according to the mission plan, and to scan and stabilise the sensor images. It processes imagery into a common recording format in real time, and compresses the data to match the data rates achievable by the Schlumberger digital recorder and the datalink. Random-access memory (RAM) in the RMS allows the pilot or backseater to rotate, 'zoom' and mark the recorded imagery on his multi-function display. Selected images can be datalinked to a station on an aircraft or a ship. Using a high-rate X-band datalink carried in a pod, combined with software enhancements, real-time imagery can be transmitted to ground stations.

The F/A-18D(RC) was the first Hornet to have the APG-73 Phase 2 radar with a high-resolution SAR mode, as noted above. This gives it the ability to gather imagery at long stand-off ranges (up to 70 nm/130 km) in bad weather, with a resolution in the 1-m (3-ft 3-in) range. ATARS entered evaluation in November 1998, and was first fielded in 1999.

While sensors such as radar and EO devices help find and locate targets, another group of avionics systems is used to

its smaller rival, the F-16, was that the Hornet carried an internal active jamming system. This was the Sanders (later, Lockheed Sanders) ALQ-126B, an improved version of a standard Navy system that was also used on the A-6 and F-14. Even when the F/A-18 entered service, however, the ALQ-126 was becoming less capable in the face of improved Soviet radars. It remains useful against older radars, many of which are still in service worldwide, and is still used on the F/A-18. Not every F/A-18 carries an active jammer at all times; typically, the systems are installed when a squadron is preparing for a cruise away from the US. Australian, Spanish and Canadian F/A-18s are fitted with the ALQ-126B, and Spanish and Canadian aircraft also use the Northrop ALQ-162.

ASPJ problems

The planned replacement for the ALQ-126 ran into a dense thicket of problems. The ITT/Westinghouse ALQ-165 Advanced Self-Protection Jammer (ASPJ) was conceived in the early 1980s as an improved internal jammer for the F/A-18, F-16, F-14 and A-6. The highly automated, software-controlled system incorporates many state-of-the-art electronic technologies, including microwave monolithic integrated circuits, application-specific integrated circuits and gate arrays. Like many other jammer programmes, it ran into serious technical problems, compounded by political troubles, and development ran years behind schedule. The USAF withdrew from the programme in 1990. At the end of 1992, the Navy terminated the ASPJ low-rate initial production programme because of the system's failure to meet all the test requirements imposed by the Department of Defense.

Some of the ASPJ's supporters within the Marine and Navy aviation communities continued to maintain that the ASPJ worked well enough to justify its production, and that the DoD had set unrealistically high performance standards that no onboard jammer could meet. Their views were clearly shared by the air forces of Finland and Switzerland, which both ordered the ALQ-165 for their Hornets after the US Navy had cancelled it – possibly the only instance in which a major system has been successfully sold for export

detect and defeat threats to the aircraft. Like other systems on the F/A-18, the defensive electronic countermeasures (DECM) suite is in a constant process of evolution, driven by technology, the changing threat and changing doctrine.

One of the original distinctions between the F/A-18 and

Another Hornet on patrol over Bosnia meets the tanker – which could be US, British or French. This aircraft also carries a single Mk 82 bomb, along with an AGM-65 on the outboard station one. Just visible over the nose is a GBU-16 LGB. With its NITE Hawk targeting FLIR on station four (the port 'shoulder' pylon), this Hornet should have beeen capable of finding and destroying virtually any target in Bosnia's rolling terrain.

ters on the nose, vertical tails and mid-body. The next step is the ALR-67(V)3, produced by GM-Hughes, which uses the same antennas but features a more advanced receiver. Its more powerful processor is better able to handle dense clusters of targets, particularly if they can frequency-hop, and it is better at detecting and tracking pulse-Doppler and monopulse radars. The ALR-67(V)3 entered production with the FY 1997 batch, and is also employed in the follow-on Super Hornet.

One change in DECM philosophy in recent years has been a revived recognition of the importance of expendable countermeasures. The original F/A-18 was fitted with two 30-tube Tracor ALE-39 dispenser 'buckets'. Starting with Finland's aircraft and 1996 Navy deliveries, however, the aircraft has four of the improved ALE-47 dispensers for a total of 120 launch tubes. These decoys include chaff, flares and the Texas Instruments GEN-X, an active radar decoy that repeats the signal from a radar that is trying to guide a missile on to the F-18.

New weapons

Going hand in hand with the development of new avionics to detect targets and threats is the deployment of new weapons to negate them. Boeing has long claimed that the F/A-18 is unrivalled in the variety of weapons which it is designed and cleared to carry. "We can launch anything in the inventory – black, white or grey," F/A-18 vice president Michael Sears has remarked. A wide choice of weapons is the key to the F/A-18's versatility, lethality and survivability, as it takes on an ever larger spectrum of missions.

Like the rest of the US fighter force, the Navy's F/A-18s have converted from the AIM-7 Sparrow medium-range air-to-air missile – a much refined version of a weapon designed in the 1950s – to the Raytheon (previously GM-Hughes Missile Systems Company) AIM-120 Advanced Medium-Range Air-to-Air Missile (AMRAAM), known to US pilots as the 'Slammer'.

AMRAAM is a large step forward from the AIM-7. The older missile uses semi-active radar homing (SARH), with a seeker that homes on to radar signals transmitted by the launch aircraft. The shooter must continuously illuminate the target from launch to impact. Consequently, the shooter's manoeuvres are limited by the need to keep the target within the gimbal limits of the radar; the shooter is blind to other targets when the missile is in flight; and the continuous radar beam is a beacon for hostile detectors, and an unambiguous warning to the target.

AMRAAM is an active radar homing (ARH) missile with its own radar. It also has an inertial navigation system and a datalink. Immediately before launch, the fighter's fire control system predicts where the missile will intercept the target and loads that information into the missile's memory via the MIL-STD-1760 interface in the pylon. The missile

after the prime customer has scrapped it. (Finland took delivery of its first system in November 1995.)

Relearning old lessons in Bosnia

On 2 June 1995, a USAF F-16 was shot down over Bosnia by an SA-6 radar-guided missile. Marine aviators flying F/A-18s in the theatre requested better ECM equipment. A Navy depot in Indiana held 96 ASPJ systems which had been delivered before the programme was cancelled, and some of these were rapidly fitted in 12 USMC F/A-18Ds and 12 USN F/A-18Cs. The system provides a much better detection capability against the SA-6 than the older ALQ-126B.

So far, the Navy does not plan to buy more ALQ-165s, although that option exists. Some of its components are being used in the Integrated DECM (IDECM) system for the F/A-18E/F, the B-1B and the F-15E.

The other basic element of the original DECM system was the Litton ALR-67(V)1 radar warning receiver (RWR). From 1990, this was replaced by the same company's ALR-67(V)2: these aircraft are distinguished by additional antenna blis-

flies out towards that point. The fighter's radar continues to track the target, and as the target's track and velocity change, it computes a new intercept point and transmits it to the missile. At a certain (classified) distance from the target, the AMRAAM automatically activates its own radar and locks on to the target.

The advantages are clear. The shooter's radar is free to search and track other targets throughout the engagement. In theory, the shooter's ability to launch and guide multiple missiles against multiple targets is limited only by the tracking ability of the radar, and once AMRAAM has locked on the attacker is free to manoeuvre at will.

The AMRAAM is also faster (Mach 4) and lighter than the AIM-7. One brochure photo shows an F/A-18 bristling with no fewer than 10 'Slammers', although the real-world probability of such a load-out must be close to zero. However, the lower weight does have important practical applications, because it allows the F/A-18 to carry paired AMRAAMs in place of a single AIM-7 on its underwing pylons.

After a long development period, AMRAAM entered service in 1992. Those who predicted an outcome similar to the mediocre performance of early AIM-7s in Vietnam have been confounded. The 'Slammer' has proven reliable and lethal. During 1993, USAF F-16Cs shot down two Iraqi fighters with AMRAAMs during Southern Watch operations over Iraq. In September 1993, AMRAAM was declared operational on the F/A-18C/D aboard USS *Theodore Roosevelt*.

The major production version is the AIM-120B, with an electronically reprogrammable signal processor which can be loaded with new software in the field to meet changing ECM threats. The AIM-120C clipped-wing AMRAAM, designed to fit the F-22A's belly weapon bays, became standard from Lot 9 (ordered in FY95, delivered from 1997) and

is essentially identical in performance to the original version.

BVR missile threats, today and tomorrow

Phase 3, a more radical development, acquired more importance as the Western fighter community has appreciated the potential of the Vympel R-77 (AA-12 'Adder') MRAAM, unveiled in 1992, and the Chinese SD-10/PL-12 weapon, which has been developed in co-operation with Russia and draws on R-77 technology. Bigger than AMRAAM, the R-77 has greater energy at maximum range and is harder to evade. The USAF had set better energy-at-

Top: A NITE Hawk-equipped F/A-18D totes a load of five 1,000-lb Mk 83 bombs, all live and ready to release.

Above: A second aircraft delivers its last pair of Mk 83s over the range. Note the empty VERs and the remaining load of eight Zunis.

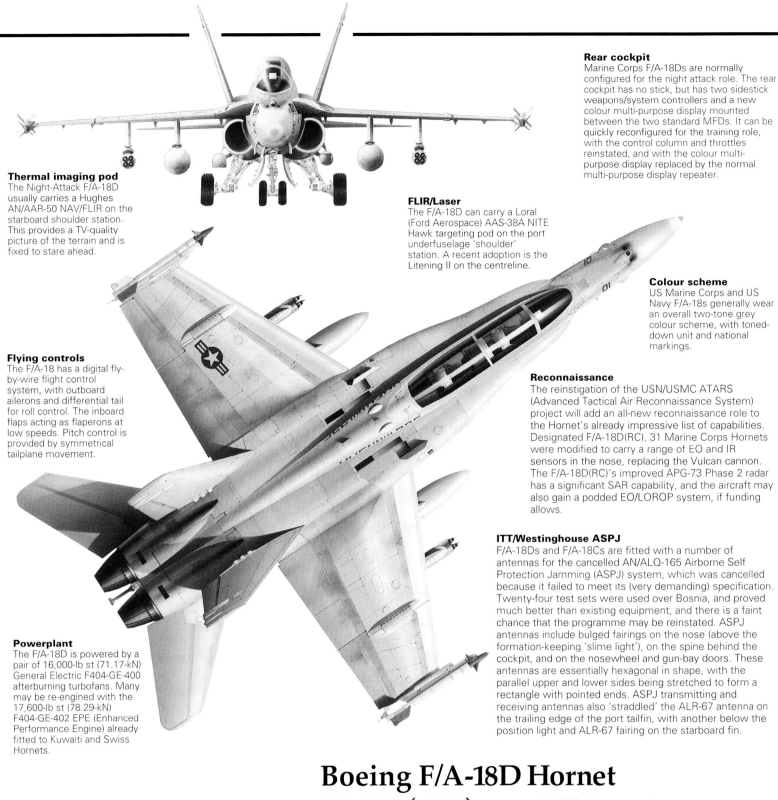

Thermal imaging pod
The Night-Attack F/A-18D usually carries a Hughes AN/AAR-50 NAV/FLIR on the starboard shoulder station. This provides a TV-quality picture of the terrain and is fixed to stare ahead.

Rear cockpit
Marine Corps F/A-18Ds are normally configured for the night attack role. The rear cockpit has no stick, but has two sidestick weapons/system controllers and a new colour multi-purpose display mounted between the two standard MFDs. It can be quickly reconfigured for the training role, with the control column and throttles reinstated, and with the colour multi-purpose display replaced by the normal multi-purpose display repeater.

FLIR/Laser
The F/A-18D can carry a Loral (Ford Aerospace) AAS-38A NITE Hawk targeting pod on the port underfuselage 'shoulder' station. A recent adoption is the Litening II on the centreline.

Colour scheme
US Marine Corps and US Navy F/A-18s generally wear an overall two-tone grey colour scheme, with toned-down unit and national markings.

Flying controls
The F/A-18 has a digital fly-by-wire flight control system, with outboard ailerons and differential tail for roll control. The inboard flaps acting as flaperons at low speeds. Pitch control is provided by symmetrical tailplane movement.

Reconnaissance
The reinstigation of the USN/USMC ATARS (Advanced Tactical Air Reconnaissance System) project will add an all-new reconnaissance role to the Hornet's already impressive list of capabilities. Designated F/A-18D(RC), 31 Marine Corps Hornets were modified to carry a range of EO and IR sensors in the nose, replacing the Vulcan cannon. The F/A-18D(RC)'s improved APG-73 Phase 2 radar has a significant SAR capability, and the aircraft may also gain a podded EO/LOROP system, if funding allows.

ITT/Westinghouse ASPJ
F/A-18Ds and F/A-18Cs are fitted with a number of antennas for the cancelled AN/ALQ-165 Airborne Self Protection Jamming (ASPJ) system, which was cancelled because it failed to meet its (very demanding) specification. Twenty-four test sets were used over Bosnia, and proved much better than existing equipment, and there is a faint chance that the programme may be reinstated. ASPJ antennas include bulged fairings on the nose (above the formation-keeping 'slime light'), on the spine behind the cockpit, and on the nosewheel and gun-bay doors. These antennas are essentially hexagonal in shape, with the parallel upper and lower sides being stretched to form a rectangle with pointed ends. ASPJ transmitting and receiving antennas also 'straddled' the ALR-67 antenna on the trailing edge of the port tailfin, with another below the position light and ALR-67 fairing on the starboard fin.

Powerplant
The F/A-18D is powered by a pair of 16,000-lb st (71.17-kN) General Electric F404-GE-400 afterburning turbofans. Many may be re-engined with the 17,600-lb st (78.29-kN) F404-GE-402 EPE (Enhanced Performance Engine) already fitted to Kuwaiti and Swiss Hornets.

Boeing F/A-18D Hornet VMFA(AW)-225 'Vikings' US Marine Corps

The two-seat Night-Attack F/A-18D has replaced the A-6 Intruder, OA-4M Skyhawk and RF-4C Phantom in the US Marine Corps all-weather attack squadrons, fulfilling secondary Fast FAC and reconnaissance roles. VMFA(AW)-225 was the third of six USMC squadrons to receive two-seat Night Attack Hornets, taking delivery of its first aircraft during July 1991. VMFA(AW)-121 had been the first unit, re-equipping in May 1990.

The AGM-62 Walleye II ER/DL (seen here on a USMC F/A-18D) is an unpowered glide bomb which employs an imaging infra-red seeker, like that fitted to the AGM-65 Maverick and AGM-84E SLAM. Use of the AWW-9 datalink pod (usually carried by an accompanying designator aircraft) allows lock-on after launch. The guidance pod and weapon can be carried by two separate aircraft.

Above and left: The AGM-84E Stand-off Land Attack Missile (SLAM) was derived from the AGM-84 Harpoon anti-ship missile to meet a US Navy requirement for a versatile stand-off weapon. The missile has a lengthened airframe and employs imaging infra-red homing instead of the Harpoon's active radar seeker. The missile was combat-proven during Operation Desert Storm, although it was still undergoing operational evaluation. An extended-range AGM-84H SLAM-ER with pop-out wings is now also fielded.

Among the laser-guided bombs carried by US Navy and Marine Corps Hornets is the GBU-16, effectively a 1,000-lb Mk 83 bomb with a long-winged Texas Instruments Paveway II guidance kit attached. The F/A-18 regularly carries laser-guided versions of the 500-lb Mk 82 and the 2,000-lb Mk 84 bombs, too, with Paveway II guidance kits.

Above and below: The AN/ASQ-173 LST/SCAM is a laser spot tracker similar to the Pave Penny pod fitted to USAF A-10s, although it also incorporates a strike camera. The starboard station can carry a Hughes AAR-50 NAVFLIR pod.

The Hornet's original APG-65 radar was once regarded as the best fighter radar in the world, and forms the basis of the APG-73 fitted to current production Hornets. The improved radar incorporates a new data processor, a new receiver module, and a new power supply system giving much improved performance and reliability with no increase in weight. The retrofit of existing F/A-18s with APG-73 has allowed US Marine Corps Harrier II Pluses to be fitted with surplus APG-65 radars.

AIM-120D is being developed for service entry in about 2008, improvements in the missile's propulsion and aiming system providing greater range lethality. It will also introduce a two-way datalink so that the weapon's own active radar can provide information back to the launch aircraft. The Super Hornet is slated to be the first Navy recipient of the AIM-120D. Meanwhile, a longer-term development of a new missile is being studied, based on ramjet-powered designs which first surfaced in the 1990s during AAAM work.

New short-range missiles

Short-range AAMs are another area where Russian technology has given the West a shock. The highly agile, vectored-thrust Vympel R-73 (AA-11 'Archer') was for a while considered to be the best SRAAM in the world, by a large margin, and left the US playing catch-up. Meanwhile, the Navy's proposed AIM-9R, with an imaging daylight seeker, was cancelled in 1992 due to cost and a lack of USAF interest.

To provide a new weapon for the US forces, Hughes and Raytheon competed to develop the AIM-9X, through a demonstration/validation programme. The AIM-9X combines the AIM-9's motor, warhead and safe-arm device with a new guidance and control system and control surfaces. It is more agile than the AIM-9 and has a seeker which can acquire targets at up to 90° off the missile's boresight. As developed, the AIM-9X is not as ambitious a programme as was once envisaged, and further development of short-range missiles continues. Other weapon systems are available for export Hornets: for instance, Australia has adopted the MBDA ASRAAM to replace the Sidewinder on its F/A-18s.

Air-to-surface stores

The F/A-18 also carries a wide range of air-to-surface ordnance. As a non-stealthy aircraft, stand-off weapons are important to its survival; also, the limited space for ordnance available on the carrier places a heavy premium on precision-guided weapons which can kill the target with a single shot, rather than large numbers of unguided weapons with a smaller kill probability.

The F/A-18A/B was fitted with the NACES (Navy Aircrew Common Ejection Seat) seat. When the ejection sequence is initiated the seat is blown from the aircraft by a gas cartridge. Canopy breakers fitted to the seat smash through the transparency. Once clear, the main rocket under the seat bucket fires to ensure separation from the aircraft. A Martin-Baker SJU-5/6 zero/zero seat was substituted in the F/A-18C/D.

range as the main goal of Phase 3 as long ago as the mid-1980s.

Although the Phase 3 AMRAAM was not specifically designed as a long-range weapon, it has a greater reach than the existing AIM-120C. To some extent, it would have filled the gap left as the F-14 is retired, along with the long-range AIM-54 Phoenix missile. At the time that the Navy terminated production of the F-14D, in 1989, the Navy was pursuing development of the Advanced Air-to-Air Missile (AAAM), which would not only have replaced the AIM-54 aboard the F-14 but which would have been compatible with the F-18 and A-12. Two teams were given AAAM study contracts: Hughes and Raytheon, with a ramjet-powered missile using a dual-mode seeker, and General Dynamics and Westinghouse, who offered a radical tube-launched missile using a pulsed rocket motor. The entire programme was cancelled in 1992, partly because the break-up of the Soviet Union had greatly reduced any near-term threat from long-range bombers with supersonic missiles.

Since the need for greater-energy missiles has been resuscitated, the US is pursuing a two-track approach. Firstly, the

One of the Hornet's most effective air-to-surface weapons is Boeing's own AGM-84E Stand-off Land Attack Missile (SLAM). This was originally developed as an interim weapon, pending the arrival of the then-classified Northrop AGM-137 Tri-Service Stand-off Attack Missile (TSSAM). TSSAM was a stealthy, highly accurate missile which, in its Navy version, was to carry a 1,000-lb (454-kg) penetrating warhead 115 miles (185 km) from its launch point. When development started in 1986, TSSAM was expected to enter service in 1990. As the programme slipped behind schedule, however, the Navy accepted McDonnell Douglas' proposal for a land-attack derivative of the AGM-84D Harpoon anti-ship missile (also carried by the F-18).

The SLAM programme started in 1989 and the missile was used operationally in Desert Storm, when an A-6 fired two missiles at an Iraqi hydroelectric plant. The rapid development was possible because the missile used off-the-shelf components. Instead of the Harpoon's radar seeker, SLAM has the imaging infra-red seeker from the AGM-65D Maverick, an integrated inertial/Global Positioning System navigation unit and the datalink from the Walleye glide bomb. The missile flies autonomously until it is in the vicinity of the target, when the seeker and datalink are automatically activated and transmit an image of the target to either the launch aircraft or a 'buddy' director aircraft. The operator verifies the target, selects an aimpoint and locks the seeker. SLAM is one of the most accurate missiles in existence, with a circular error probability (CEP) in single figures of feet.

Despite frantic efforts by its manufacturer, TSSAM did not recover from its problems and it was cancelled in December 1994. The Navy had already decided to cut back on its orders, and had funded development of the AGM-84H SLAM-ER (Expanded Response). This version has larger wings which increase the missile's range by 50 to 100 per cent depending on the flight profile, the Harris/Magnavox Improved Data Link which has greater range and better jamming resistance, a better warhead, and a revised nose which reduces drag and radar cross-section. The first combat use of AGM-84H came in December 1999, when a Marine F/A-18C from VMFA-251 launched one during Operation Desert Fox.

The F-18 also carries a shorter-range stand-off weapon in the shape of the Texas Instruments AGM-154 Joint Stand-off Weapon (JSOW). Originally known as the Advanced Interdiction Weapon System (AIWS), it was conceived by the Navy as a low-cost modular weapon which could replace a range of dissimilar systems including the Mk 20 Rockeye and CBU-59 cluster bombs plus the Walleye, AGM-123 Skipper and older GBU-series laser-guided bombs. Vought and TI were awarded demonstration contracts in 1991. In the following year, the USAF joined the programme, the name was changed to JSOW and TI was selected as prime contractor. The first guided drop was made in late 1994.

JSOW has been called 'a smart truck'. The nose section contains the guidance system. The mid-body is a 'strong-back' which carries a pair of high-aspect-ratio folding wings and the payload, with a fairing around it. The flight control system is located in the tail. The long wings give the missile a range of 15 miles (25 km) from a high-level launch, even without power.

VMFAT-101 'Sharpshooters' is the Marine Corps' primary F/A-18 FRS squadron for training Hornet aircrew. The squadron had long been equipped with Phantoms before transitioning to the Hornet. The aircraft nearest the camera has a typical training load of Mk 76 'blue bombs'.

VMFA(AW)-242 are the 'Batmen' from El Toro. The Batman identity is most apt for their night-attack mission. Crews train with FLIR and NVGs for precision attacks in all weathers.

Above: Even with empty bomb racks the Hornet is a threat, for it still has a 20-mm M61A1 Vulcan cannon. The gun, ammunition drum and feed system is mounted as a single unit on a pallet in the nose. The barrel is elevated by 2° to improve target tracking. The ammunition drum carries 578 rounds and the gun can fire up to 6,000 rpm. The ammunition is shielded from EMP to prevent premature detonation.

Right: The F/A-18 design service life, as far as the US Navy is concerned, is 6,000 flight hours. This would include 5,000 cycles with 2,000 catapult launches and arrested landings alone. Finnish evaluators estimated that, without the rigours of carrier operations, their Hornets may be good for up to 15,000 hours.

Opposite page: F/A-18s with the EPE powerplant can climb to 40,000 ft (12192 m) in 2.3 minutes at maximum thrust, while carrying two AIM-9s, two AIM-7s and a full tank of 20-mm ammunition. The EPE also reduces the maximum-thrust take-off roll by 10 per cent. The Hornet can be airborne within 1,700 ft (518 m) of runway, at the full fighter configuration weight of 37,000 lb (16798 kg).

The initial version of JSOW – the AGM-154A – uses GPS/INS guidance and carries BLU-97 Combined Effects Munition (CEM) warheads which are effective against air defence systems, non-armoured vehicles and parked aircraft. A later version (AGM-154C) has a BLU-111 hard-target warhead and precision guidance, and will replace the Navy's LGBs and Mavericks. As well as conventional attacks, the JSOW has proven its worth as a defence suppression weapon, with precision attacks against known-position air defence radars.

Another new bomb family is used on the F/A-18: the Boeing GBU-31/32 Joint Direct Attack Munition (JDAM).

McDonnell Douglas was selected to develop this weapon in September 1995, and it became operational in 1997. In its basic form, JDAM is a simple iron bomb with the addition of a tail section containing an INS/GPS guidance system and a standard 1760A interface. As in any bomb attack, the launch aircraft's weapon control system computes the bomb's trajectory and guides the pilot to the release point. With JDAM, the computer also loads the predicted trajectory into the bomb's guidance system, allowing it to cancel out errors caused by turbulence around the aircraft or by changes in wind velocity. The JDAM guidance system is inexpensive (around $18,000 per weapon) and requires no action by the launch aircraft after release, and has a CEP of 33-49 ft (10-15 m). The GBU-31 variant uses a 2,000-lb (907-kg) warhead – either conventional or penetrating, while the GBU-32 uses a 1,000-lb (454-kg) bomb.

JDAM accuracy is determined to a great extent by the accuracy of the data provided by the launch platform, so the advent of a SAR mode on the APG-73 radar led to a significant improvement in all-weather bombing accuracy. Hornets first dropped JDAMs in anger in 2000, when aircraft from VFA-82 and VMFA-251 dropped the weapon during Operation Southern Watch operations over Iraq.

Vital HARM capability

As the F/A-18 continued to expand its suppression of enemy air defences (SEAD) role, it became the Navy's main user of the Texas Instruments AGM-88 High-speed Anti-Radiation Missile (HARM). In the 1990s, the US Navy and USAF updated their HARM inventories with the AGM-88C Block IV, which has a more sensitive seeker, a better processor and more onboard memory, and can be updated with new software. This variant has not been released for export, and overseas customers are taking delivery of earlier versions from US stocks.

The HARM seeker can be active while the missile is on the pylon, and is a significant source of information on threats and targets in a SEAD mission. What it cannot do is determine the range to the target. Until recently, the only platform which could launch HARM in a 'range-known' mode, which gives the missile its greatest possible range and shortest time of flight, was a dedicated SEAD aircraft such as the F-4G Wild Weasel. This has now been retired, and the USAF SEAD mission is performed by the F-16 fitted with the Texas Instruments ASQ-213 HARM Targeting System (HTS). This small pod contains a passive antenna and a compact processor. Using data from the aircraft's navigation system, it detects and identifies emitters and, using triangulation, locates them. The HTS was tested on the F/A-18C/D at China Lake in early 1996.

Tactical Air-Launched Decoys

Another important but little-discussed F/A-18 store is not necessarily a weapon: the Brunswick Defense ALD-141 Tactical Air Launched Decoy (TALD). Based on the Israeli Samson, this 400-lb (180-kg) glider was used to protect Navy and Marine attack aircraft in the 1991 Gulf War, and more than 4,000 were on order by mid-1991. In the Gulf, as many as 20 TALDs were launched in salvos by the lead aircraft in a strike package, which would then turn home.

The TALDs were pre-programmed to fly a simulated attack profile, saturating target defences and forcing enemy search and tracking radars to activate, thus increasing friendly anti-radiation missile kill probabilities. Other TALDs were modified to mask the real strike force by deploying chaff. It has been followed by Improved TALD (I-TALD) which has a small Teledyne CAE312 turbojet engine (developed for the cancelled Tacit Rainbow anti-radar missile) and can simulate a wider variety of attack profiles. The turbojet gives I-TALD a range of up to 120 nm (222 km) when launched from 20,000 ft (6096 m), compared to TALD's range of only 68 nm (126 km) when launched from 35,000 ft (10668 m). I-TALD can be launched from heights as low as 500 ft (152 m) and at speeds of up to Mach 0.9. The first airborne launch, from an F-4 over Point Mugu, occurred in October 1995, and fit tests with the F/A-18 began in November from NAS Patuxent River.

USN/USMC operations

While McDonnell Douglas has incorporated these innovations into the Hornet, its primary users have responded by making the F/A-18 the single most important fighter in the US Navy's history.

In June 1995, the F/A-18 recorded its 2 millionth flight hour with the US Navy and Marine Corps. By that time, non-

US Hornets had flown about half a million hours and the worldwide F/A-18 community was adding hours at a rate of 230,000 per year. Over 1,270 aircraft had been delivered.

The F/A-18 has also proven itself to be the most reliable, lowest-maintenance and safest tactical aircraft in Navy/Marine Corps service. The Hornet flies an average of 1.8 hours between failures, compared with 0.5 hours for the F-14 and A-6E. It requires 17.3 maintenance man-hours per flight hour, compared with 46.5 hours for the F-14 and 44.4 hours for the A-6E. In the first 1.5 million flight hours in service, the Navy and Marines lost 67 Hornets in accidents, compared with 124 F-14s and 102 A-6s.

Thoroughly modern Hornet

Of course, the F/A-18 certainly should be better than either the A-6 or the F-14 in all respects. The A-6E and the F-14A – which dominates the F-14 statistics – have avionics and engines which reflect the technology of the 1960s. The re-engined, digital F-14D and A-6F Intruder II would have been more directly comparable to the F/A-18, but the former was built only in small numbers and the latter was cancelled outright. As for safety, the F-14 has suffered from an engine that was never designed for its mission, and the A-6 started its career in the early 1960s, when it was not

unknown for a squadron to lose seven out of 40 aircraft in a month to accidents – culture, training and technology have played parts in reducing accident rates.

From the operator's viewpoint, the fact that such comparisons may be loaded in favour of the F/A-18 matters less than the fact that the Hornet is so much more friendly to its pilots and maintainers than the other aircraft in the fleet. Another significant figure is that the Hornet's 2 million-hour mark was reached after 12 years in service – an even faster accumulation of hours than the F-4 during the Vietnam era. This reflects the fact that F/A-18s generate sorties at a higher rate than other Navy tactical aircraft.

The F/A-18 has other useful attributes. Its advanced cockpit and (in later versions) MSI make it a relatively easy aircraft to fly. Engines and aerodynamics are well suited for deck landing – Hornet squadrons regularly score highest in boarding rates.

Maintainability and safety statistics also translate into hard cash. Maintenance is expensive in personnel, training and parts. The Navy/Marine Corps F/A-18 losses in the type's first 10 years of service cost well over $2 billion to replace, an amount that represents half the cost of a new carrier. The result is that the F/A-18's life-cycle cost compares very favourably with older aircraft.

Reliability is an extremely important attribute for a carrier-based aircraft. A carrier's ability to put firepower on target depends not only on the range and warload of its aircraft, but also on their reliability. An aircraft that suffers a failure and cannot be launched cannot be quickly taxied off to one side and replaced, and neither can the carrier afford to launch many spare aircraft – but, given the statistics, the likelihood that one or more F-14s in a strike package will abort for technical reasons is relatively high. On the carrier, diagnostic, repair and test facilities are limited, so reliability problems will rapidly have an impact on the rate at which the carrier can sustain operations: after a surge of sorties, the maintenance crews may need time to deal with a back-log of problems. Fewer problems also mean that the carrier does not need to carry as many replacement parts.

Finite assets

Similarly, multi-mission capability has a special value aboard a carrier. The carrier air group goes to the war with the assets with which it left its home port. During a three-month cruise in 1993, the USS *Theodore Roosevelt* took part in two contingency operations in different regions. Its three F/A-18 squadrons first took part in combat air patrol (CAP) missions in support of C-130s which were air-dropping food and medicine around Sarajevo, then switched to longer CAP missions as part of Operation Deny Flight. Using their FLIR systems, they could also monitor helicopter traffic, which was exempted at the time from the UN's 'no-fly' ban.

Later, the carrier moved to the Red Sea, and the Hornets flew missions in support of Operation Southern Watch. In this case, there was a potential threat from Iraqi ground forces, and the Hornets carried air-to-ground munitions and (in some cases) the latest FLIR pods with laser designation and ranging capability.

While an air wing dominated by one-mission aircraft – air-combat F-14s and A-6 strike aircraft – could have covered the same missions, it would have been difficult to maintain the same sortie rates because fewer aircraft would have been available. In the case of Southern Watch, attack aircraft carrying air-to-ground weapons would probably have needed a fighter CAP to protect them from unexpected attacks, so more sorties would have been needed to perform the same basic task.

Multi-role capability is the most important new capability that the Hornet brought to the Navy. In turn, the most

Carrier operations are still the Hornet's raison d'être. Night operations from an almost invisible deck call for a complete faith in the deck crew. Any landing, day or night, is down to the pilot and the LSO to get a good trap, on the right wire, first time.

An F/A-18C flies alongside the prototype Super Hornet, clearly showing the size differential which gives the Super much better range/load performance. Development of the 'legacy' or 'Baby' Hornet slowed down with the F/A-18E/F nearing production, but the older aircraft will play a valuable role for at least another decade.

This is the USMC F/A-18D used for ATARS (Advanced Tactical Airborne Reconnaissance System) trials. ATARS was originally a joint USN/USAF project but has had a disjointed history. Initiated in 1982, the system first flew in 1984 yet the programme was cancelled in 1993, when the USAF withdrew. In 1994 the Navy reactivated the project with McDonnell Douglas as prime contractor (the third in ATARS's history). ATARS has been adopted by the USMC for fitment to a few of its F/A-18Ds. The system became operational in early 1999, VMFA(AW)-332 receiving the ATARS in time to deploy with it to Taszar in Hungary during Operation Allied Force. The US Navy has opted for the SHARP pod to provide a reconnaissance capability for its F/A-18E/F Super Hornets.

"an unbelievable improvement in warfighting capability." The same assessment was made from a different angle when the US Navy sold a batch of F/A-18A/Bs to Spain: a McDonnell Douglas official said that the A/B "no longer fits in the Navy's warfighting plans."

One F/A-18 pilot describes the F/A-18A/B as "a basic day/visual bomber with some superb close-in manoeuvring capabilities," capable of defeating almost any adversary except a well-flown F-16 in a dogfight. As for bombing, "we got good hits in the day, but our night/all-weather capabilities were austere. The FLIR in the A model basically got you day accuracy with bad eyesight."

The same pilot describes the early C/Ds as "nothing to brag about. The only difference we could see was the IFEI (integrated fuel/engine instrument display)." The real change came with the Lot 12 night-attack variants, he felt. The LTD/R upgrade to the FLIR pod "changed everything – night and day – since we can now drop a range of precision weapons. The AMRAAM made us super-competitive in the beyond-visual-range arena, and software upgrades all along have made the airplane more capable, but rapidly used up existing memory."

Hornet replaces the A-6F

It was a combination of all these factors which persuaded the Navy and Marine Corps to increase their dependence on the F/A-18 – in addition to budget cutbacks. Total US defence spending peaked in 1985 and started a slow decline thereafter, squeezing the Navy's ambitious modernisation programme. One of the first programmes to be affected was the Grumman A-6F Intruder II, intended as a replacement for USMC A-6s, which was cancelled in 1988. This also meant an end to production of the A-6, so the Navy and Marines would be short of aircraft within a few years. The Navy therefore elected to replace Marine A-6s with F/A-18Ds. Then, in 1989, planned production of the F-14D Super Tomcat was curtailed to 54 aircraft – again, increasing the service's need for the F/A-18 to fill the gap until a new aircraft would be available.

The F/A-18 does not equal the warload/range performance of either the A-6 or the F-14, but – for the time being – the Navy was willing to live with the Hornet's perfor-

important feature of the F/A-18C/D was that it was a much better multi-role aircraft than the A/B. In fact, many operators (together, apparently, with the export market) believe that the most important step in F/A-18 development was the advent of the night-attack Lot 12 version, ordered in FY87 and delivered from late 1989. Commander William Gortney, who commanded one of the F/A-18C/D squadrons on the *Roosevelt* cruise, has described the night-attack version as "almost a different airplane" compared with the A/B, and

mance rather than trying to change it. The Hornet's greater reliability and its ability to defend itself (reducing the need for escort and CAP sorties) both tend to offset its lesser warload, by enabling the carrier to put more bomb-carrying aircraft on target. The Navy has changed its tactics, stressing the use of HARM-carrying escorts and EA-6B Prowlers to suppress enemy air defences and allowing the Hornets to stay at medium altitude for a longer segment of the ingress and egress route, improving their range. (The Hornet's ability to defend itself against fighters is important in this case, as well.)

Littoral warrior

The collapse of the Soviet Union encouraged the Navy to concentrate more resources on the F/A-18, at the same time as declining defence budgets led the service to cancel modest improvements to the A-6 and reject proposals for modernised F-14s. The Soviet Union's missile-carrying bombers, submarines and even its Ekranoplans had presented the most serious long-range threat to the Navy's carriers. As it became clear that the threat was a thing of the past, and would not recover for decades, the Navy defined a new strategy of 'littoral operations', concentrating on the Navy's role in support of conflict within a few hundred miles of a sea coast. Compared with the blue-water strategies of the Cold War, it called for carriers to operate much closer to land. Again, this made the F/A-18's range less of an issue.

The process was furthered by the cancellation of the A-12, and the continuing decline of defence budgets pushed the Navy more towards the F/A-18. Modest upgrades to the F-14 and A-6 were cancelled, and F/A-18 production plans were extended to avoid any gap between the last F/A-18C/D and the first F/A-18E/F.

Hornet shortage

Boeing's St Louis plant delivered the 1,479th and last Hornet in September 2000. Of the total, 1,048 were for the US Navy and Marine Corps. The final deliveries were four F/A-18Cs and four F/A-18Ds for the Marine Corps which had originally been ordered by Thailand before that country's economy collapsed in the late 1990s. The extra aircraft were indeed welcome.

A post-Cold War reduction in force levels but with increased operational commitments combined with the gradual retirement of the F-14 force and the slow build-up of the F/A-18E/F Super Hornet force to place an enormous burden on the F/A-18C/D fleet, which was under the strength required to fully meet its requirements. To partially relieve that burden a modification programme was introduced to raise obsolescent F/A-18As to a combat capability level approaching that of the newer C/Ds.

Under Engineering Change Proposal (ECP) 583, F/A-18As serving with both the US Navy and Marine Corps have been given APG-73 radars, GPS and Link 16 datalink. The weapons capability has been expanded to include AIM-120, JDAM and AGM-154 JSOW. The resulting aircraft is known as the F/A-18A+ (or jokingly as the F/A-18C-), and it entered service with US Naval Reserve units VFAs-201, -203 and -204, and with Marine squadrons VMFAs-115, 122 and -312.

The latter units are assigned to US Navy carrier air wings, along with a number of USMC F/A-18C squadrons. This is another symptom of the 'Hornet shortage' and resulted from a formal agreement reached between the two air arms in

the mid-1990s for the USMC to provide four Hornet squadrons for the Navy's air wings. For some time the USMC squadrons involved were VMFAs-251, -312, -314 and -323, but the introduction of the F/A-18A+ has added VMFAs-115 and -122 to the list of USMC units with a carrier commitment.

Hornets in action

Since the end of the 1991 Gulf War, the Hornet has been back in action in three major theatres: the Balkans, Afghanistan and Iraq. These have not only involved carrier operations, but also land-based operations by Marine Corps aircraft.

As noted earlier, the Hornet's first major involvement over the Balkans was covering the Sarajevo air bridge in 1992, after which the United Nations imposed a 'No-fly' zone in April 1993 under Operation Deny Flight. Carrier-based Hornets from the Adriatic helped police the zone, often refuelling from drogue-equipped KC-135s from the USAF. The first carrier to be involved in Deny Flight was *Theodore Roosevelt*, carrying the Hornets of VFAs-15 and -87, and VMFA-312. As well as CAPs, the Hornets also flew anti-surface maritime patrols, armed with Mavericks, LGBs and Walleyes.

With the skies over Bosnia firmly under UN control, the next step was to provide protection for ground forces. On 20 July 1993 eight F/A-18Ds from VMFA(AW)-533 deployed to Aviano AB in Italy, which became the focus for fighter operations over the Balkans. At the time, they represented the latest standard of Hornet – APG-73 radar, F404-GE-402 engines, laser designators and (from the summer of 1995) ALQ-165 ASPJ EW systems. These aircraft, like USAF F-15Es, operated with a pilot in the front seat and a weapon system operator (WSO) in the back seat. The pilot flies the aircraft and stays head-out, while the WSO operates the radar and FLIR.

A typical load-out for these missions was a mixed bag of weapons: two AIM-9s, one AIM-7 or AIM-120, two 500-lb (227-kg) GBU-12 LGBs, a 500-lb (227-kg) unguided bomb and a FLIR/LTD-R pod. WSOs in the Bosnia operations also

10,000

JETS FOR FREEDOM

MCDONNELL DOUGLAS

carried digital cameras with zoom lenses for near-real-time reconnaissance.

'Flex' missions

In a single mission, a pair of F/A-18Ds might 'flex' among several missions. Using their radars, they would ensure that there were no aircraft violating the UN's Deny Flight 'No-fly' restrictions. They were available to provide close air support (CAS) for UN forces on the ground, as requested by a ground forward air controller. They could also act as FACs for other aircraft, locating ground targets and talking incoming strike aircraft on to the target. Helicopters could be tracked and identified on the FLIR, and their landing sites could be photographed.

Balkan missions by Navy and Marine Hornets increased in intensity during 1993 and early 1994, resulting in bombs being dropped for the first time by VMFA-251 Hornets flying from Aviano on 11 April, in support of British SAS troops at Gorazde who were coming under fire while supporting food airdrop efforts into the beleaguered town. Although fusing problems meant that two of the three bombs dropped did not explode, the bomb/gun attack was considered a success, with several armoured vehicles crippled. On 21 November 1994 six F/A-18Ds from VMFA(AW)-332 led

the raid on the Serb-Krajina airfield at Udbina. They fired Mavericks and HARMs against air defences, destroying at least one SA-6 SAM system.

Until the summer of 1995 air actions over Bosnia were sporadic and restrained. However, the mortar attack on Sarajevo which killed 37 civilians was the final straw for NATO, which let slip the leash on its tactical aircraft in Operation Deliberate Force, which began on 29 August 1995. Hornets again led the raids, charged with crippling the air defence system which the Serbs had established in Bosnia. Under the codename Dead-Eye Southeast, the initial force comprised US Navy EA-6Bs and F/A-18Cs flying from *Roosevelt*, and USMC F/A-18Ds. Using LGBs and HARMs, the force dealt a devastating blow to the air defence network, making operations much easier for the strike packages which followed. Hornets were involved throughout the campaign, which ended on 13 September, flying from Aviano with VMFA(AW)-533 and from the carrier with VFA-15, VFA-87 and VMFA-312.

Marine F/A-18Ds flew more than 100 strike missions during Operation Deliberate Force, which was credited with persuading the Serbs to return to the bargaining table. Many of these operations were SEAD missions, mainly using GBU-16 1,000-lb (454-kg) LGBs. The smaller GBU-12s were

For a US Navy pilot, the single-seat, high-performance and deadly Hornet must be one of the most prized positions in today's Navy. Allied with the two-seater's increasing sophistication as an attack aircraft, and the promise of the F/A-18E/F, the Hornet can justifiably claim to be one of the most versatile, and capable, combat aircraft in the world.

Carrying a HARM under its wing, a Hornet launches into the sunset. From the time of its combat debut over Libya in 1986, the Hornet has been involved in virtually every US combat action – large or small.

used where targets were located close to centres of population and the risk of collateral damage was higher.

Weather often prevented the successful use of LGBs from safe altitudes during daytime missions. As a result, more than half the missions were flown at night, when darkness concealed the fighters from ground fire and it was safe to fly at lower altitudes, under the weather. Eventually, the Hornets hit most of their designated targets.

These missions were significant in many ways. In particular, the two-crew aircraft with its fully integrated sensors was shown to be able to perform a very useful mission with what would, in earlier times, be considered a very small weapon load. In fact, unloading multiple 2,000-lb (907-kg) bombs may be positively undesirable in an operation short of war, where hitting the wrong target is worse than missing the right one.

Operation Allied Force

Deliberate Force effectively ended the conflict in Bosnia, but tensions remained high in the Balkans for the remainder of the decade. By early 1999 the international focus was firmly on the Serbian province of Kosovo, where Serb army

and special police units were fighting against Kosovan separatists. NATO imposed an ultimatum for Serbia to withdraw its forces from the province and, when that was ignored, launched an all-out air campaign called Allied Force. As befitted its place as the primary US Navy/Marine Corps attack platform, the Hornet was heavily involved. It also went to war over Serbia and Kosovo with export customers Canada and Spain.

Since the end of the Bosnian war the US Navy no longer maintained a permanent carrier presence in the Adriatic, and the Marines had recalled their Hornets from Aviano. At the start of the Allied Force campaign on 24 March 1999, there were no US Hornets involved. However, by the 26th of the month, USS *Theodore Roosevelt* – easily the 'fightingest' of the 'Nimitz' boats – was preparing to leave Norfolk with Air Wing Eight aboard, including the 24 F/A-18Cs of VFA-15 and VFA-87. Originally slated to continue on to the Persian Gulf, the carrier was directed to the Adriatic instead when it arrived in the Mediterranean on 3 April. It arrived on-station on 5 April, beginning combat operations immediately. The HARM-carrying F/A-18s were particularly welcome in bolstering NATO's SEAD forces, although the Hornets were also used for attack duties (with Mk 80 series bombs, Mavericks, LGBs and JSOW) and CAPs (with up to four AIM-120 AMRAAMs and two AIM-9 Sidewinders).

On 21 April the Pentagon announced that USS *Enterprise*, returning from an operational cruise in the Persian Gulf, would have its deployment extended for operations over Kosovo. Two days later this was rescinded, and it returned home, taking the F/A-18Cs of VFA-37, VFA-105 and VMFA-312 with it.

As the conflict deepened and commander General Wesley Clark requested growing numbers of aircraft, in late April NATO officials visited Hungary to assess a number of potential bases from which attacks could be mounted across the border into Serbia. On 5 May Hungary announced that 24 F/A-18Ds would be based at Taszar air base, despite domestic public opposition to this move. The aircraft, from VMFA(AW)s-332 and -533, departed for the war zone on 20 May, the first arriving on the 22nd. VMFA(AW)-332 deployed its ATARS aircraft. The first mission from Taszar was flown on 28 May – the 66th day of the campaign, the two-seat Hornets being mainly used at night for precision attacks. An agreement signed on 9 June ended Allied Force, with the withdrawal of Serbian forces from the province beginning on the following day.

Enduring Freedom

Long before the dust had settled from the terrorist atrocities committed in the US on 11 September 2001, the fingers were pointing at Osama bin Laden and his al-Qaeda

network, which trained its operatives and prepared for actions in Afghanistan, under the patronage of the Taliban regime. Planning began almost immediately for a campaign which would, it was hoped, eradicate the leadership, organistation and training facilities of al-Qaeda, with the secondary aim of removing the Taliban from power. Operation Enduring Freedom was launched on the night of 7 October 2001 with an aerial assault against the few strategic air defence/command and control targets that existed, in concert with Tomahawk cruise missiles launched by US ships and UK submarines.

Operations in Afghanistan – even more so than in Allied Force – were defined by some unusual factors. Firstly, the US was not 'at war' with the Afghan people, just its leadership and the terrorists it harboured. Secondly, the nature of Afghanistan's military meant that there was virtually no threat in the 'old world' meaning, and consequently very few large, fixed strategic targets. Instead, targets would consist primarily of fleeting vehicles, small groups of irregular fighters, individual buildings, cave entrances and the like. For this war precision and timeliness would be everything, and the Hornet – with its excellent avionics and its ability to drop LGBs and JDAMs – was perfectly equipped for the task.

During the course of the fighting phase of Enduring Freedom, five US Navy aircraft-carriers were involved, although not simultaneously. Launching strike aircraft (mainly F-14s) on the first night of the war were USS *Enterprise* and USS *Carl Vinson*. The first three days of the campaign involved the destruction of the air defences, after which there was a lull. Major raids began again on 13 October, by which time RAF tankers were available to

F/A-18Cs from VFA-87 (foreground) and VFA-15 carry live GBU-12 laser-guided bombs. This weapon was very important in both Afghan and Iraqi campaigns. Its 500-lb (227-kg) warhead has a relatively small blast 'footprint', reducing the dangers of collateral damage, and it has a reputation for high accuracy. Furthermore, several can be brought back aboard the carrier as part of the Hornet's meagre 'bring-back' quota, whereas only one JDAM can be brought back safely.

Left: Based at NAS Oceana, VFA-106 'Gladiators' is the East Coast Hornet training squadron. US Navy two-seaters do not deploy regularly aboard carriers as part of an air wing, but they are used by the two training units during carrier qualifications campaigns when a vessel is available.

Below: The F/A-18A has been used widely by US Navy adversary units, most aircraft being painted up to resemble 'enemy' fighters. Based at NAS Fallon in Nevada, NSAWC has a number of Hornets at its disposal.

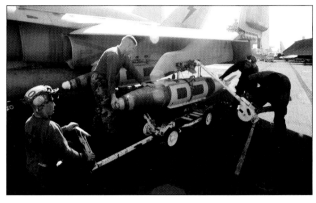

Ordnancemen aboard Theodore Roosevelt load GBU-32 JDAMs on to the wing pylons of a VMFA-251 Hornet during Operation Enduring Freedom in October 2001.

support US Navy aircraft, especially the Hornets. On 17 October *Theodore Roosevelt* arrived (with 36 F/A-18Cs from VFA-82, VFA-86 and VMFA-251), the veteran of Desert Storm and Allied Force, among others, adding another important campaign to its *curriculum vitae.* 'TR' had arrived to relieve *Enterprise,* but all three carriers launched aircraft for a few days before the 'Big E' withdrew from the Arabian Sea. *Roosevelt's* air wing largely conducted night operations, while *Carl Vinson* worked the day shift. Further F/A-18s were deployed to the theatre when USS *Kitty Hawk* arrived from the Pacific. It only carried a partial air wing, but did embark the F/A-18Cs of VFA-195.

Hornets over Afghanistan

Operations were conducted at a high rate over Afghanistan until 16 December, when the Tora Bora mountain range was finally 'cleared' of Taliban control. Hornets were used to drop many GBU-12 and GBU-16 laser-guided bombs, often working in concert with F-14 Tomcats which provided laser designation. As the only Navy aircraft capable at the time of dropping JDAM, this weapon also figured prominently. JDAMs were employed mainly during the opening phase of the air campaign against fixed targets, but as the Taliban forces went on the run, the accent focused on LGB operations. By the end of the campaign the 500-lb (227-kg) GBU-12 was the main weapon as its smaller warhead was more suited to the kind of low-collateral damage missions being flown. Virtually all Hornet missions began with a pre-mission refuelling from S-3B Vikings before the aircraft headed inland. Further refuellings were carried out, usually from RAF VC10 and TriStar tankers, while the Hornets waited for targets. Most missions were in the order of four to six hours, but some reached nine hours duration.

When the US Marines established a land base at Dolangi airfield (Camp Rhino) in late November (Operation Swift Freedom), F-14s and F/A-18s provided a protective close air support umbrella. In mid-December USS *John C. Stennis* arrived with VFA-146, VFA-147 and VMFA-314, just in time to fly combat missions during the last days of the campaign.

Above: The squadron commander's aircraft from VFA-82 catches the wire on its return to Roosevelt after a fruitless mission over Afghanistan on 5 November. The photo illustrates the ability of the Hornet to trap safely with GBU-12s still carried.

Right: This VFA-195 F/A-18C is also trapping with a GBU-12, this time on Kitty Hawk on 21 November. This carrier was home-ported at Atsugi in Japan, and was dispatched to the Afghan theatre with a partial air wing aboard plus extra helicopters for Special Forces support.

Following the swearing-in of Hamid Karzai as leader of the interim government on 22 December, operations continued against Taliban/al-Qaeda fighters wherever they were found, requiring the ongoing deployment of tactical fighters to the region that continues today. Manas in Kyrgyzstan was established as a major base for aircraft policing Afghanistan: among the aircraft deployed have been USMC F/A-18Ds, initially by VMFA(AW)-121. In early March 2002, US Navy F/A-18s were among the aircraft used during Operation Anaconda, a major effort to root out and destroy a sizeable al-Qaeda force in the Shah-i-Kot valley.

Hornets over Iraq

In the wake of the Desert Storm operation, protective zones were established over northern and southern Iraq. During December 1992/January 1993 the Iraqis mounted a series of challenges to these zones. One immediate result was the diversion of USS *Kitty Hawk*, with the F/A-18Cs of VFAs-27 and -97 aboard, from operations off Somalia (Operation Restore Hope) to the Persian Gulf in late December. When a retaliatory strike was launched by US and UK warplanes on 13 January 1993 against Iraqi air defence sites, included in the strike package were six F/A-18Cs, and the covering force included two more Hornets. Weapons used were Mk 82 bombs and AGM-88 HARMs. On 18 January there was a follow-up raid. The raids heralded a decade of sporadic but increasing action against Iraq that would culminate in the final attack in 2003.

Throughout Operation Southern Watch – the policing of the southern zone – Hornets flying from carriers had occasionally engaged Iraqi ground targets. These actions were as a result of reactions to aggression. In December 1998, however, the US/UK force turned on Iraq in the Desert Fox pre-emptive strike against air defence and other military targets as a result of continued frustration over the lack of co-operation by Iraq with UN weapons inspectors. A month earlier an even larger raid, known as Desert Viper, had been planned and almost executed, although it was called off with aircraft in the air and en route to their targets.

Nevertheless, the three-day Desert Fox campaign kicked off on 16 December 1998. In the interests of achieving maximum surprise, it was initially an all-Navy affair, as to use USAF or RAF aircraft based in the theatre would have alerted the Iraqi defences as to the possibility of a raid. TLAM cruise missiles and carrier strike aircraft from USS *Enterprise* carried out the first night's raids. The F/A-18Cs of VFA-37, VFA-105 and VMFA-312 were involved. As well as attack missions with 2,000-lb GBU-24 Paveway III laser-guided bombs, the Hornets provided SEAD support with

AGM-88 HARMs, and launched ADM-141 TALDs to confuse the Iraqi defences. On 17 December Lieutenant Carol Watts of VFA-37 became the first US female pilot to undertake combat operations. On the third and last night the Hornets from USS *Carl Vinson* were also involved.

Operation Iraqi Freedom

After more than a decade of frustration, President Bush and his 'coalition of the willing' took decisive action against Iraq on the morning of 20 March 2003, when Operation Iraqi Freedom was launched with an opportunistic 'decapitation' strike by a pair of F-117s. The main air campaign got under way that evening. As part of the forces assembled for the operation, the US Navy had five carriers and their Hornets available. In the Persian Gulf were USS *Kitty Hawk* (VFA-27, VFA-192 and VFA-197), USS *Constellation* (VFA-137, VFA-151 and VMFA-323) and USS *Abraham*

Bathed in the evening sunlight, VFA-94's 'CAG-bird' heads for Afghanistan after refuelling, clutching JDAMs under its wings. The date was 4 November and the aircraft already has 20 mission marks adorning the nose. The 'Mighty Shrikes' formed part of Air Wing Eleven aboard Carl Vinson.

Above: Now fully integrated into the Navy's carrier air wings, Marine Hornet squadrons have seen much action in recent years while flying from carrier decks. For the Afghan war VMFA-251 was aboard Theodore Roosevelt. This aircraft launches with a typical late-war loadout, comprising three fuel tanks for maximum endurance over the assigned engagement zone, and two GBU-12 LGBs with which to hit small and often fleeting targets.

Left: A VFA-195 aircraft launches from Kitty Hawk. *By the latter part of the war the total absence of any air threat allowed Hornets to leave even Sidewinders behind.*

Iraqi Freedom Hornets: above a VMFA-115 F/A-18A+ refuels from a KC-135 over Turkey during a mission to northern Iraq, while above right is a variety of weapons laid out on the hangar deck of Lincoln, including JDAMs, HARMs and TALD decoys. Below is the commander's aircraft from VFA-25, about to launch from Lincoln, while at bottom a VFA-27 aircraft launches from Kitty Hawk with two GBU-12s.

Lincoln (VFA-25 and VFA-113, plus the Super Hornets of VFA-115). Sailing in the eastern Mediterranean were USS *Theodore Roosevelt* (VFA-15, VFA-87 and VFA-201) and USS *Harry S. Truman* (VFA-37, VFA-105 and VMFA-115). 'TR' – back for yet another war – was unique in embarking a US Naval Reserve unit (VFA-201 with F/A-18A+) on a combat cruise for the first time in many years. The Marines established a large Hornet force at Ahmed al Jaber AB in Kuwait, comprising F/A-18Cs from VMFA-121, VMFA-232 and VMFA-251, and F/A-18Ds from VMFA(AW)-225 and VMFA(AW)-533. The Royal Australian Air Force also sent F/A-18s to Al Udeid in Qatar. The total Hornet force for OIF numbered around 250 aircraft.

For the Hornet force the war began with aircraft launched from 'Connie' against targets near Basra, ahead of the main

offensive. As coalition troops crossed the border into Iraq, the main campaign got under way, with Hornets attacking fixed targets as well as supporting friendly troops. F/A-18s from both the Navy and Marine Corps supported British forces advancing on Basra. Marine Hornets were involved in the fierce fighting encountered by Task Force Tarawa around an-Nasiriyah. JDAMs were widely used, especially the GBU-32 1,000-lb (454-kg) version. On the third day the two carriers sailing in the Mediterranean joined in the battle, having received permission from the Turkish government to overfly Turkey on their way to targets in northern Iraq. These missions were long affairs, requiring multiple refuellings. Sortie generation rate was hampered by the lack of sufficient USAF tankers to support these missions.

On 25 March VFA-151 F/A-18Cs from 'Connie' made minor history when they designated a target for an S-3B firing a laser-guided AGM-65E Maverick, the first use of the Viking against a land target. The next day Hornets from *Roosevelt* covered the paradrop of 1,000 troops to establish a base at Bashur-Harir airfield in the Kurdish area of northern Iraq. Two days later, Navy Hornets were involved in the action at Karbala, in which US Army Apaches took a heavy mauling from the stiff local resistance. After fierce fighting, the US Army's 3rd Infantry broke through the 'Karbala Gap' on 2 April, supported by Hornets and other CAS types. During the fighting that night, tragedy struck *Kitty Hawk*'s Air Wing Five when a VFA-195 F/A-18C was shot down by

a SAM.

It was initially thought that an Iraqi missile was responsible, although it later transpired that a US Army Patriot PAC-3 battery had 'probably' shot down the Hornet while attempting to engage Iraqi tactical missiles. The pilot, Lt Nathan White, was initially reported to have ejected and a search effort was undertaken. However, it was later reported that he had been killed in the shoot-down.

On 6 April USS *Nimitz* arrived on station to add its muscle to the war effort. Its Air Wing Eleven included the F/A-18As of VFA-97 and F/A-18Cs of VFA-94, in addition to two Super Hornet squadrons (VFA-14 and VFA-41). This cruise was significant as it marked the first and only time all four US Navy combat versions of the F/A-18 (A, C, E and F) would fly together in one air wing, and the last cruise for the unmodified F/A-18A.

On 9 April Baghdad fell, and attentions turned to Tikrit. Hornets were very active in supporting the Marine Task Force Tripoli which took the town after fierce fighting. On 14 April *Abraham Lincoln* headed for home after nine months at sea, and *Constellation* – on its final cruise – and *Kitty Hawk* followed soon after. Yet there was still plenty of work to be done as US aircraft maintained a permanent umbrella over ground forces attempting to restore order in a confused and anarchic country.

Throughout the conflict the Hornets had performed well, despite being hampered by a lack of tanker assets. Initial assessments based on incomplete data suggested an 87.3 per cent mission-capable rate for the F/A-18C and 79.6 per cent for the F/A-18A. The Hornet was used on a wide variety of tasks, including precision strikes against fixed targets (mostly with JDAMs) and combat air patrols (armed with four AIM-120s and two AIM-9s). As the strategic air campaign diminished and the ground forces encountered more severe resistance, the emphasis turned to the close air support mission, Hornets primarily using a mixture of LGBs, JDAMs and Mavericks. They worked closely with forward air controllers, loitering in 'kill box' areas for targets to emerge.

To the future

In the first decade of the 21st century the US Navy is working towards an all-Hornet carrier air wing, comprising two squadrons of Super Hornets (one each of F/A-18E and F/A-18F) and two of 'Baby' Hornets (F/A-18C or F/A-18A+).

The service is well advanced in its plans to replace the F-14 Tomcat with the Super Hornet, and the all-Hornet Navy should be a reality by 2008. The first-generation aircraft are due to serve well into the next decade, when they are slated for replacement by the Lockheed Martin F-35C Joint Strike Fighter. The Marine Corps will retain their 'legacy' Hornet force until the F-35B is fielded.

Between the US Department of Defense and export customers, deliveries and commitments for the F/A-18 family now top 2,000, and production will continue until at least 2013. It is not a bad record for an aircraft which was almost cancelled before it entered service.

Bill Sweetman; additional material by David Donald

Above: Hornets maintained their near-blanket cover of Iraq throughout the hours of darkness. This VFA-15 jet prepares to launch from Roosevelt.

Above left: Flying from Truman, VMFA-115 flew its missions over northern Iraq after transiting through Turkish airspace. Here an aircraft releases a GBU-32 JDAM.

Above: Naval Reserve units had been absent from combat operations for many years, but returned during Iraqi Freedom in the shape of VFA-201 'Hunters', which flew F/A-18A+s from the deck of Roosevelt. Here one of the squadron's aircraft is prepared for a mission on 7 April, while JDAMs and LGBs await loading in the foreground.

Left: VFA-105's 'boss-bird' launches from Truman for a CAP mission during Iraqi Freedom, with two AIM-120 AMRAAMs on the inner port wing pylon. The nose legend reads 'Give 'em Hell' while the squadron's nickname is on the drop tanks.

F/A-18 Hornet operators

United States Navy

As of mid-2004, the US Navy operated a total of 22 active-duty Fleet squadrons equipped with the F/A-18C. The last active-duty F/A-18A unit, VFA-97, converted to the F/A-18C in early 2004. Augmented by four Marine Corps squadrons, the fleet is distributed amongst the Navy's 10 carrier air wings, each of which deploys with two or three F/A-18C squadrons aboard. The Navy's Hornet community is administered by Strike Fighter Wings serving the Atlantic and Pacific Fleets, shore-based at NAS Oceana (previously at Cecil Field) and NAS Lemoore, respectively. The Strike Fighter Wings also parent F/A-18E units, and each has a Fleet Readiness Squadron equipped with the F/A-18A/B/C/D. The Lemoore wing also has the F/A-18E/F FRS. Further augmentation of the fleet units is provided by two Naval Reserve squadrons from Air Wing 20, which retain the F/A-18A, albeit in upgraded A+ form.

Second-line units comprise various test and evaluation agencies which operate small numbers of aircraft for testing new systems for both the first-generation Hornet and the Super Hornet. F/A-18Bs are also on the strength of the USN Test Pilot School. F/A-18As and Bs are the equipment of the Naval Flight Demonstration Squadron, better known as the 'Blue Angels'. Finally, the F/A-18 forms the backbone of the Navy's dissimilar air combat training programme, equipping a single active-duty unit at Fallon (NSAWC, serving alongside F-16s) and a Reservist-manned unit at Oceana which provides adversaries for the Atlantic Fleet fighter/strike fighter units. In 2004 the latter unit was augmented by aircraft from the disbanded Naval Reserve unit VFA-203.

Designation	Nickname	Homeport	Code	Aircraft
Strike Fighter Squadrons (VFA)				
VFA-15	Valions	NAS Oceana	AJ	F/A-18C
VFA-22	Fighting Redcocks	NAS Oceana	NH	F/A-18C (to E)
VFA-25	Fist of the Fleet	NAS Lemoore	NK	F/A-18C
VFA-27	Chargers	NAF Atsugi	NF	F/A-18C (to E)
VFA-34	Blue Blasters	NAS Oceana	AA	F/A-18C
VFA-37	Bulls	NAS Oceana	AC	F/A-18C
VFA-81	Sunliners	NAS Oceana	AA	F/A-18C (to E)
VFA-82	Marauders	MCAS Beaufort	AB	F/A-18C
VFA-83	Rampagers	NAS Oceana	AA	F/A-18C
VFA-86	Sidewinders	MCAS Beaufort	AB	F/A-18C
VFA-87	Golden Warriors	NAS Oceana	AJ	F/A-18C
VFA-94	Mighty Shrikes	NAS Lemoore	NH	F/A-18C
VFA-97	Warhawks	NAS Lemoore	NH	F/A-18C
VFA-105	Gunslingers	NAS Oceana	AC	F/A-18C (to E)
VFA-106#	Gladiators	NAS Oceana	AD	F/A-18A/B/C/D
VFA-113	Stingers	NAS Lemoore	NK	F/A-18C
VFA-125#	Rough Riders	NAS Lemoore	NJ	F/A-18A/B/C/D
VFA-131	Wildcats	NAS Oceana	AG	F/A-18C
VFA-136	Knighthawks	NAS Oceana	AG	F/A-18C
VFA-146	Blue Diamonds	NAS Lemoore	NG	F/A-18C (to E)
VFA-147	Argonauts	NAS Lemoore	NG	F/A-18C
VFA-151	Vigilantes	NAS Lemoore	NE	F/A-18C
VFA-192	World Famous Golden Dragons	NAF Atsugi	NF	F/A-18C
VFA-195	Dambusters	NAF Atsugi	NF	F/A-18C
VFA-201*	Hunters	NAS Ft Worth	AF	F/A-18A+
VFA-204*	River Rattlers	NAS New Orleans	AF	F/A-18A+

Fighter Composite Squadron (VFC)
VFC-12*	Fighting Omars	NAS Oceana	AF	F/A-18A/A+/B

Miscellaneous operators
VX-9	Evaluators	NAWS China Lake	XE	F/A-18A/B/C/D
NSAWC		NAS Fallon		F/A-18A/B
NFDS	Blue Angels	NAS Pensacola	BA	F/A-18A/B
VX-23	Salty Dogs	NAS Patuxent River	SD	NF/A-18A/C/D
VX-31	Dust Devils	NAWS China Lake		NF/A-18A/B/C
USN Test Pilot School		NAS Patuxent River	TPS	F/A-18B

* = Reserve squadron
\# = Fleet Readiness Squadron

Disestablished US Navy F/A-18 operators
VAQ-34	Electric Horsemen	NAS Lemoore	GD	F/A-18A/B
VF-45	Blackbirds	NAS Key West	AD	F/A-18A
VFA-127	Desert Bogies	NAS Fallon	NJ	F/A-18A/B
VFA-132	Privateers	NAS Cecil Field	AE	F/A-18A
VFA-161	Chargers	NAS Lemoore	NN	F/A-18A
VFA-203*	Blue Dolphins	NAS Cecil Field	AF	F/A-18A+
VFA-303*	Goldenhawks	NAS Lemoore	ND	F/A-18A
VFA-305*	Lobos	NAS Point Mugu	ND	F/A-18A
VX-4	Evaluators	NAWS Point Mugu	XF	F/A-18A/C/D
VX-5	Vampires	NAWS China Lake	XE	F/A-18A/B/C/D
NWEF Albuquerque		Kirtland AFB		F/A-18A

VFA-115 'Eagles' and VFA-137 'Kestrels' have converted to the F/A-18E Super Hornet, and are scheduled to be followed by VFA-22 and VFA-27 (2004), with VFA-81 (2005), VFA-105 (2007) and VFA-146 (2007) also slated for the Super Hornet. The East Coast FRS (VFA-106) will receive Super Hornets from March 2005. The F/A-18C is due to serve until replaced by the F-35C Joint Strike Fighter from around 2013.

Above: The best-known of the Navy's Hornets are the F/A-18As of the 'Blue Angels' display team.

Right: This F/A-18C Hornet is assigned to VFA-105. It is preparing to land aboard USS Harry S. Truman during Exercise Summer Pulse 2004.

Above: VFA-25's CAG-bird wears a full-colour 'Fist of the Fleet' badge on the fin, with the letters 'CAG' superimposed on the multi-coloured fin-stripe.

Above: The Naval Fighter Weapons School – Top Gun' – relocated from Miramar to Fallon, and became part of NSAWC. Here one of the unit's F/A-18Bs is seen at the Nevada base, complete with eye-catching black scheme. NSAWC flies F/A-18s alongside F-16s.

Left: VFA-151 'Vigilantes' flies with Air Wing Two, reassigned from Constellation to Abraham Lincoln in 2004.

United States Marine Corps

In mid-2004 the USMC active-duty Hornet force comprised four squadrons on the East Coast at Beaufort (Marine Air Group 31, part of the 2nd Marine Aircraft Wing), which are transitioning from A to C models and three (all F/A-18C) on the West Coast, the latter having moved to Miramar from El Toro. The Miramar Hornet squadrons form part of Marine Air Group 11 within the 3rd Marine Aircraft Wing. A Miramar-parented unit is forward-based at Iwakuni in Japan with MAG-12 (1st MAW). The active-duty USMC F/A-18C community maintains a commitment to supply four squadrons to the Navy's carrier air wings, and these aircraft usually wear the tailcode of the air wing to which they are allocated, rather than their individual unit tailcode.

The Marine Forces Reserve parents the 4th Marine Aircraft Wing, which has four squadrons flying the older F/A-18A. They are based at Fort Worth (MAG-41), Atlanta (MAG-42), Miramar (MAG-46) and Washington/Andrews AFB (MAG-49). The single Marine Corps training unit is based at Miramar, and has examples of all four versions (A,B, C and D) in its inventory.

The six active-duty squadrons which fly the F/A-18D two-seater in the night attack role are divided between the two principal Hornet bases, serving with MAG-11 at Miramar and MAG-31 at Beaufort. One F/A-18D squadron is forward-deployed to MAG-12 at Iwakuni on a rotational basis

Designation	Nickname	Base	Code	Aircraft
Marine Fighter Attack Squadrons (VMFA)				
VMFA-112*	Cowboys	NAS Fort Worth	MA	F/A-18A
VMFA-115	Silver Eagles	MCAS Beaufort	VE	F/A-18A+
VMFA-122	Crusaders	MCAS Beaufort	DC	F/A-18A+
VMFA-134*	Smokes	MCAS Miramar	MF	F/A-18A
VMFA-142*	Flying Gators	NAS Atlanta	MB	F/A-18A
VMFA-212	Lancers	MCAS Iwakuni	WD	F/A-18C
VMFA-232	Red Devils	MCAS Miramar	WT	F/A-18C
VMFA-251	Thunderbolts	MCAS Beaufort	DW	F/A-18C
VMFA-312	Checkerboards	MCAS Beaufort	DR	F/A-18A+
VMFA-314	Black Knights	MCAS Miramar	VW	F/A-18C
VMFA-321*	Hell's Angels	NAF Washington	MG	F/A-18A/B
VMFA-323	Death Rattlers	MCAS Miramar	WS	F/A-18C

VMFA(AW)-533 is one of six squadrons to have adopted the two-place F/A-18D for night-attack duties, replacing the A-6E in this role. Here an aircraft prepares to launch rockets over the Yuma training range.

Marine All-Weather Fighter Attack Squadrons (VMFA(AW))				
VMFA(AW)-121	Green Knights	MCAS Miramar	VK	F/A-18D
VMFA(AW)-224	Bengals	MCAS Beaufort	WK	F/A-18D
VMFA(AW)-225	Vikings	MCAS Miramar	CE	F/A-18D
VMFA(AW)-242	Batmen	MCAS Miramar	DT	F/A-18D
VMFA(AW)-332	Polka Dots	MCAS Beaufort	EA	F/A-18D
VMFA(AW)-533	Hawks	MCAS Beaufort	ED	F/A-18D

Marine Fighter Attack Training Squadron (VMFAT)				
VMFAT-101#	Sharpshooters	MCAS Miramar	SH	F/A-18A/B/C/D,

* = Reserve squadron
 # = Fleet Readiness Squadron

Deactivated USMC F/A-18 operators				
VMFA-235	Death Angels	NAS Miramar	DB	F/A-18C
VMFA-333	Shamrocks	MCAS Beaufort	DN	F/A-18A
VMFA-451	Warlords	MCAS Beaufort	VM	F/A-18A
VMFA-531	Grey Ghosts	MCAS El Toro	EC	F/A-18A

Left: *Refuelling support for the Marines Hornet force is provided by the KC-130 Hercules.*

Above: *VMFAT-101 trains both USN and USMC crews, hence the 'Navy' titles on this aircraft.*

Carrier assignments
as of 2004

CVW-1, 'AB', *Enterprise*, Lant
(VMFA-251, VFA-82, VFA-86)
CVW-2, 'NE', *Abraham Lincoln*, Pac
(VMFA-323, VFA-151)
CVW-3, 'AC', *Harry S. Truman*, Lant
(VMFA-312, VFA-37)
CVW-5, 'NF', *Kitty Hawk*, Pac
(VFA-27, VFA-192, VFA-195)
CVW-7, 'AG', *Washington*, Lant
(VFA-136, VFA-131)
CVW-8, 'AJ', *Roosevelt*, Lant
(VFA-105, VFA-15, VFA-87)
CVW-9, 'NG', *Carl Vinson*, Pac
(VMFA-314, VFA-146, VFA-147)
CVW-11, 'NH', *Nimitz*, Pac
(VFA-97, VFA-94)
CVW-14, 'NK', *John Stennis*, Pac
(VFA-113, VFA-25)
CVW-17, 'AA', *Kennedy*, Lant
(VFA-34, VFA-83, VFA-81)

Right: In 2003 VFA-137 gave up its F/A-18Cs (illustrated) for the single-seat F/A-18E Super Hornet.

Northrop Grumman
EA-6B
Prowler

Until the EA-18G enters service, the EA-6B is the only true SEAD platform available to the US armed forces. Following the retirement of its Air Force counterpart (the EF-111A) – the result of a deliberate and controversial policy of 'jointness' – Navy and Marine Prowlers have assumed a unique position as the United States' only combined active/passive anti-SAM and anti-radar aircraft. With the growth of SAM and radar technology, many have argued that US warfighting capabilities in this area should be expanded, not contracted. These voices are met by the perennial question of how to balance ever-shrinking defence budgets while countering the known threat.

In a figurative way, if not literally, the Prowler is the final product of the 'Grumman Iron Works', the dynasty that created the US Navy's great carrier warplanes for six decades. Located in eastern Long Island, the Naval Industrial Reserve Facility at Calverton (the Grumman Calverton facility or 'Iron Works') served as the final assembly point for the EA-6B. Plants 6 and 7 dominated the landscape. The ¼ mile-long Plant 6 served as the final production line, with Plant 7 serving as the operational hangar facility during flight test and sell-off. Today the great name and traditions of Grumman have been subsumed into the larger Northrop Grumman corporate body and the 'Iron Works' has been shut down – a victim of massive cutbacks in the defence manufacturing base in the US, and worldwide. Grumman no longer builds aircraft, but continues to support its aircraft in US military service while retaining its status as an important aerospace defence contractor.

The EA-6 has always lived in the shadow of the A-6 Intruder, which is rightly seen as one of the best attack aircraft ever built. However, the close of 1996 saw the end of the A-6 Intruder's 31-year combat career with the US Navy. The Intruder was deemed to be too expensive to operate in a Navy forced to cut back its front-line types and one whose deep-strike mission had become less important in a post-Cold War world. So, as 1996 slid into 1997, the last Atlantic and Pacific Fleet A-6 squadrons made their final cruises before retirement. The sense of loss that came with the end of the A-6's career was only heightened by the sight of surplus airframes being poured into the Atlantic Ocean, off the Florida coast, to form an artificial reef.

Yet, as the A-6's star waned that of the EA-6B ascended. The same budget stringencies that ended the Intruder's career pushed the EA-6B onto centre stage. Since it entered service in 1971 (as an EKA-3B Skywarrior replacement), the Prowler has jammed and confused

SAM-related radar and communications. Later it gained the capability to attack and destroy those same emitters with the HARM missile. Now the Prowler has become the only US combat aircraft with this capability and the world's premier active/passive SEAD (suppression of enemy air defences) platform.

The Prowler has undergone many changes (the addition of HARM capability was just one), but operations from the early 1990s – beginning in Bosnia, through Kosovo and Afghanistan, to Iraq – marked a number of milestones. For the first time, the Prowler was the sole jamming aircraft in the theatre, and its missions were truly 'joint', an integrated effort by the US armed services such as had been attempted in Desert Storm but not achieved. More than ever, the aircraft has become a showpiece for 'jointness' – operations carried out by different branches of the armed forces working together under a single command. The competition rather than co-operation of US service branches in Vietnam and in the 1980 hostage rescue attempt in Iran prompted Congress to enact the Goldwater-Nichols Law of 1986, which mandated 'jointness' and makes it indispensable to US strategy. The creation of US Navy joint-service 'expeditionary' Prowler squadrons is controversial, however, and many wonder if the Air Force was right to retire its F-4Gs and EF-111As.

During the Gulf War, most SEAD was provided by individual services for their own strike forces. Overall SEAD assets in the Gulf region included 102 Air Force aircraft with dedicated roles (F-4G, EF-111A), and 39 dedicated Navy aircraft (EA-6B), plus 308 ARM-capable Navy and Marine aircraft (A-7E, A-6E, F/A-18).

Above left: The key to the EA-6B's success as a jamming system – and one of the reasons it survived and the EF-111A did not – is its four-man crew. Having three dedicated ECMOs, plus a pilot, allows a far greater division of duties between the crew than in other comparable aircraft. This 'lessening' of the workload allows everyone to do a better job once in action.

Above: The USMC's Prowler force has now stabilised at four squadrons, all of which were formerly components of a single unit, VMAQ-2. These aircraft are from VMAQ-1 'Banshees', which formed in July 1992.

Right: Seen here landing aboard USS Carl Vinson (CVN 70) is VAQ-139's brightly painted CAG bird. This EA-6B was one of the participants in the COMPTUEX '95 exercise, held in December of that year.

Although Joint Forces Air Commander (JFAC) General Charles Horner's Air Tasking Order orchestrated the complex operations, in practice they were hardly 'joint': most Air Force strikes were covered by Air Force SEAD and all Navy/Marine strikes were covered by Navy/Marine SEAD. The Navy and Marine Corps also provided most of the support for coalition air forces, which had no SEAD capability. Sixty per cent of Desert Storm SEAD sorties were flown by Navy and Marine Corps aircraft.

The Prowler's electronic warfare mission has evolved over the years. To the theatre commander, the EA-6B ranks as a 'high value asset' in both of its primary jobs. The first of these is electronic support measures (ESM): the gathering of intelligence on SAM sites, radar and C³ (command, control and communications) locations. The Prowler flies this mission 'buttoned up', with its jammers off, collecting electromagnetic emanations but putting out as few as possi-

ble. The intelligence it gathers is often employed by theatre analysts in conjunction with the 'take' by other platforms like the RC-135 Rivet Joint and EP-3 Aries II. The Prowler's second and most important job is SEAD: the neutralisation, denigration or destruction of radar/missile

threats with jamming ('passive' SEAD) and/or HARMs ('lethal' SEAD). SEAD includes the added duty of jamming/denigrating communications, and in recent times the Prowler has also been involved in psychological warfare operations (psyops).

Left: This view over the wings of a VAQ-131 Prowler clearly shows the two wing fences fitted to the EA-6B (the EA-6A had three). Also visible is the wing-folding mechanism and the paired hinges for the wingtip speed brakes.

Below: VAQ-131 'Lancers' has been an established squadron since September 1950 and an EW unit since 1968. The squadron routinely deploys as part of Carrier Air Wing 2.

The EA-6B's electronic warfare (EW) mission is part of what the Pentagon calls Command & Control Warfare (C²W). In this context, the EA-6B is not just a Navy weapon but is the US joint services' primary tool in suppressing and defeating an enemy's air defence network, opening a way for joint operations to interdict far behind battle lines. During a major conflict, the theatre commander and officers at the national command level develop a C²W plan that encompasses five components – operational security, military deception, psychological operations, electronic warfare and physical destruction. The goal, as written in the policy document, is to "influence, degrade or destroy adversary C² capability while protecting friendly C² capabilities." To the EA-6B crew, this means neutralising an enemy's air defences.

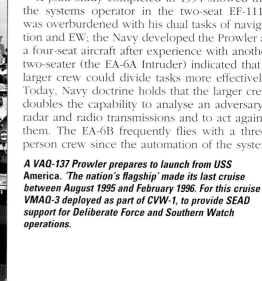

EA-6B versus EF-111A

For some time the EA-6B has been the only EW aircraft able to jam, deceive, disrupt, and shoot. The US Air Force retired the McDonnell F-4G Advanced Wild Weasel in 1994 and the EF-111A Raven, or 'Spark Vark,' followed suit in 1998. The EA-6B and EF-111A use similar capabilities to jam radar signals, since both employ variants of the ALQ-99 tactical jamming system (TJS). The Raven, however, was never modernised and remained equivalent to the

ICAP EA-6B of the early 1980s, while today's upgraded ICAP II Block 89 EA-6B has a newer TJS suite and is effective over a greater frequency range, making it more a threat to recent Russian-bloc SAM radars. The EF-111A never had a communications jamming mission like the Prowler, and lacked the USQ-113 communications jammer that gives current Prowlers their capability to foul VHF and UHF communications. Ravens could have been

upgraded for the lethal SEAD role with missiles, but they never were, and remained unarmed.

The EF-111A had greater range and was faster, enabling it to keep up more easily with a fast-moving strike package. The US joint services elected to surrender these advantages in exchange for the EA-6B's ability to operate from carriers, employ HARM missiles and degrade communications. In fact, the EA-6B is fast enough to keep up with most strike packages, particularly en route when acting as 'shooters'. Loaded with ordnance, the F/A-18 and F-16 seldom exceed 520 kt (596 mph; 960 km/h) except in the delivery phase, where the Prowler would not participate (it would be just another target for short-range air defences if in that close). Prowlers are faster and accelerate much better than the A-6E Intruder. Range is less, however, since the J52-P408 burns more fuel than the P-6 or P-8 in the A-6.

A joint study completed in 1994 showed that the systems operator in the two-seat EF-111A was overburdened with his dual tasks of navigation and EW; the Navy developed the Prowler as a four-seat aircraft after experience with another two-seater (the EA-6A Intruder) indicated that a larger crew could divide tasks more effectively. Today, Navy doctrine holds that the larger crew doubles the capability to analyse an adversary's radar and radio transmissions and to act against them. The EA-6B frequently flies with a three-person crew since the automation of the system

A VAQ-137 Prowler prepares to launch from USS America. 'The nation's flagship' made its last cruise between August 1995 and February 1996. For this cruise VMAQ-3 deployed as part of CVW-1, to provide SEAD support for Deliberate Force and Southern Watch operations.

really requires only a pilot and two ECMOs. Individual air wing tactics and squadron tactical memoranda require the fourth person, and another set of eyeballs can be valuable – but a crimp on manpower may make it reasonable to leave the relatively marginal fourth crew member on the ship planning the next sortie rather than bagging flight time if the operational tempo is high. Still, a three-person crew retains the advantage over the EF-111A.

The US Air Force retains a lethal SEAD capability with its Lockheed Martin F-16C/D Block 50D Fighting Falcon, equipped with the Texas Instruments AN/ASQ-213 HARM targeting system (HTS). The HTS F-16 is fast enough to escort a strike package and can fire HARMs to suppress radars. HTS raises the 'shooter' aircraft from the ranks of those which fire HARM in only a 'range unknown' mode (F/A-18 Hornet, non-HTS F-16) to those which give the missile at least some bearing information plus range, firing in the 'range known' mode – but the 'bearing' provided by the F-16 is approximate at best.

The HTS F-16 has less reach and accuracy than the Prowler and has no capability to jam or disrupt emissions; its role is also an intensive tasking for a single pilot. To the commander in the combat zone, the HTS F-16 is a part-time EW asset which will escort strike packages when the Prowler cannot, but will also be used as a traditional air-to-ground fighter-bomber much of the time.

Today's EA-6B ICAP II Block 89A Prowler bristles with electronic equipment from nose to

tail. The Prowler carries jamming gear externally and receiving equipment internally. Four wing stations and one centreline station can carry AN/ALQ-99F TJS pods, although fewer are usually employed: a typical configuration is three jammer pods on stations 1, 3, and 5, with external tanks on inboard pylons 2 and 4.

Jamming systems

Two high-powered noise jammers and a tracking receiver are found in each TJS pod, electrical power for which is provided by an external turbine generator on the front, which spins in the slipstream. A forward antenna for self-protection by the deception jamming suite protrudes from the base of the air-refuelling probe in front of the windshield. (The EA-6B's refuelling probe is canted to the right at 12° for better pilot visibility, unlike that of the A-6 Intruder.) A fibreglass-coated fin-cap encloses the principal array of system integration receivers, which detect hostile transmissions and relay data to the central computer.

In international use, letters of the alphabet (A through J) are used to define specific radio frequency ranges. EA-6B crews have their own terminology for the wavelengths of the spectrum, however. In American military usage, band numbers 1 through 9 are used to define radio frequency ranges – but the exact definitions remain classified. On the EA-6B, the fin-top receivers cover bands 4-9 while bulged fairings

EA-6B Prowler variants

Prototypes

First flew on 25 May 1968. Five prototypes flight tested, most with partial or no EW suite.

Standard

The initial model, now known as the 'standard'; identified in Grumman documents as **BASCAP (BASic CAPability)**. First production delivery July 1971. Twenty-three aircraft built.

EXCAP (EXpanded CAPability)

Version for the late 1970s. Twenty-five aircraft upgraded to this standard. Standard and EXCAP had jammers operated by ECMO-1 and -2 on the right side while ECMO-3 ran ALQ-92 communications jammer.

ICAP (Improved CAPability)

Retroactively called **ICAP I** (or **ICAP-1**). Multi-band exciter (MBE). Forty-three aircraft upgraded to this standard. ICAP put all TJS controls in back with ECMO-2 and -3, freeing ECMO-1 for navigation only.

ICAP II (or ICAP-2)

Retroactively named **ICAP II Block 82**. Provided additional jamming capabilities. First flight 24 June 1980. All surviving aircraft upgraded. First production aircraft delivered 3 January 1984. ICAP II introduced a new generic pod with a universal exciter (replacing MBE) which covered frequency bands 1 through 9, allowed mixing of transmitter bands within a pod, and provided new modes of operation and software control modulations. The new system was designated AN/ALQ-99F. Each pod is capable of jamming in two frequency bands simultaneously. Since the 1980s, the 'base' on which Prowler improvements were contemplated. Introduced advanced AN/AYK-14(V) Standard Navy Airborne Computer, known to Prowler crews as the 'Yuck 14'. ICAP II employs the AN/ASN-130 navigation system and the AN/ASN-123 tactical display. ICAP II aircraft can be linked together via TACAN datalinks enabling EA-6Bs to work together in a co-operative effort against an adversary. Introduced Carrier Airborne Inertial Navigation System (CAINS). Subvariants of ICAP II include **Block 82** (70 aircraft), **Block 86** (14 plus 56 aircraft, no longer in service), and **Block 89** (43 aircraft).

ICAP II Block 82

Retroactive name of surviving ICAP II aircraft. Recognition feature: vertical VHF/UHF antennas. No antenna under chin. Two verticals on turtleback. The version used by all USMC squadrons. Introduced AGM-88A/C. First HARM-capable aircraft delivered 21 January 1986. Seventy aircraft, including 15 former EXCAP aircraft. Last one sent for Block 89A conversion in early 2004.

ADVCAP (ADVanced CAPability)

Also called **Block 91**. Three prototypes tested. Would have introduced Receiver Processor Group (RPG) for the TJS, dual AYK-14, XN-8 VHSIC computers, AN/ALQ-149 communications countermeasure system, third ECMO suite in right front seat, AN/ARN-118 TACAN, two additional external AN/ALE-41 chaff dispensers or two internal ALE-39 chaff and flare boxes, GPS, and disc-based onboard loader/recorder. Activation of two additional pylon stations outboard the wing folds. J52-P-409 turbojets. Vehicle enhancements for improved aerodynamics inclusive of the development of a Navy Standard Automatic Flight Control System (SAFCS). A subvariant identical to ADVCAP but without newer jamming sub-system was approved for export.

ICAP II Block 86

First EA-6B given the 'Block' title, determined by the fiscal year it was ordered. Compared to predecessor ICAP II (retroactively called Block 82), Block 86 – in use until January 1997 – has new radios (ARC-182 VHF/UHF, KY-58, ARC-199 HF/KY-75), enhanced signal processing (CIU/E), integration of the ALQ-126 of the self-protection system B variant and a digital fuel quantity system. Other front cockpit improvements. ALQ-99 receiver system slightly modified with 'parallel encoders' to increase signal processing capability. Fourteen upgraded aircraft. Fifty-six new airframes were delivered to Block 86 standard. All survivors upgraded to Block 89 by 1997.

ICAP II Block 89

Recognition feature: one swept-back antenna on chin and two or three on turtleback. Main changes: 'safety of flight' items, such as halon fire extinguishers for the engine bays and fire-hardened control rods and cables. One aircraft new-built to this standard (BuNo. 164403, 170th and last EA-6B built) delivered to NATC Patuxent River, Maryland in September 1991. Forty-three aircraft were modified to Block 89 standard.

ICAP II Block 89A

Funded in FY 1998 (beginning 1 October 1997). Minor changes, principally an electronic flight instrumentation system (EFIS). Improved cockpit instrumentation; Litton embedded GPS/INS missionised integration. First two airframes identified for conversion to Block 89A were a 'validation' (val) aircraft and a 'verification' (ver) aircraft, with the pair becoming 'valver' aircraft. Modifications done by NADEP Jacksonville, Florida, with deliveries beginning in 1998.

ICAP III

Upgraded version with ALQ-218 receiver system and new software allowing reactive jamming of selected (frequency-agile) radars. Also integrated communications jammer and other improvements. Two aircraft converted as demonstrators, followed by approval for 10 low-rate production conversions. Further procurement undefined.

SPECIFICATION

Grumman EA-6B Prowler

Type: four-seat tactical jammer and electronic warfare aircraft
Powerplant: two Pratt & Whitney J52-P-408/408A turbojet engines each rated at 11,200 lb (49.82 kN) thrust
Performance: never-exceed speed 710 kt (815 mph; 1311 km/h); maximum speed 541 kt (621 mph; 999 km/h); cruising speed 418 kt (480 mph; 772 km/h); service ceiling 37,600 ft (11460 m); ferry range (with five drop tanks) 1,747 nm (2,009 miles; 3233 km); approach speed 122 kt (140 mph; 225 km/h); minimum landing speed 122 kt 140 mph; 225 km/h); minimum landing distance 2,185 ft (665 m)
Weights: empty 32,574 lb (14775 kg); internal fuel 15,574 lb (7064 kg); external fuel 10,025 lb (4547 kg); ferry configuration 60,045 lb (27235 kg); maximum take-off gross weight 61,043 lb (27688 kg); maximum 'bringback weight' (carrier landing) 45,500 lb (20638 kg)
Dimensions: span 53 ft 0 in (16.15 m); span (folded) 25 ft 10 in (7.87 m); aspect ratio 5.31; length 59 ft 10 in (18.24 m); wheel base 17 ft 2 in (5.23 m); height 16 ft 3 in (4.95 m); wing area 528.90 sq m (49.13 m²)

on the side of the fin cover bands 1-3. On the trailing edge of the fin-top 'football' is the 'beer-can' fairing for the aft-facing ALQ-126 DECM system. The Prowler's search and navigation radar is the Norden APS-130, a downgraded version of the Grumman A-6E Intruder's APQ-156, with attack functions deleted. The radar provides accurate ground mapping. The APS-130, which is considered almost unbreakable, replaced the original APQ-129, which provided a better picture but was plagued by serious 'down' rates.

AN/ALQ-99

Early Prowlers, including those of the Vietnam era, faced significant limits because each AN/ALQ-99 pod had to be dedicated to a predetermined band. Thus, there were low band (1-2) pods, band 7 pods, and so on. This made life difficult for maintainers and meant that, once launched on a mission, a Prowler could be employed only against SAM missile radars on predetermined wavelengths, and was useless against an unanticipated threat. Early Prowlers were unarmed, although missile armament was always a conceptual feature on the aircraft.

The ALQ-99F jamming system is made up of the receivers, central processing computer, and up to five (normally three) pods. They can operate in full auto (detection and automatic assignment of jamming power) and manual (ECM operators manually search the spectrum and assign jamming) modes.

The wing of the Prowler, with its four carrying stations (the total becomes five when a centreline station is counted), looks identical to that of the A-6 Intruder and has similar dimensions, but has a different internal structure. The keel centre-section area was designed as a renewable resource rather than a permanent fit. Changing out a wing centre-section requires so little effort that it can be done in just hours at the depot level. The Prowler wing spans the same 53 ft (16.15 m) as the Intruder, but its internal structure is quite different. These differences are intended to make the wings sturdier than those of the Intruder because of the 'bring-back weight' of external pods carried by the Prowler. The Navy operations manual, NATOPS, allows a Prowler 'bringback weight' of 45,500 lb (20640 kg), or some 9,500 lb (4310 kg) heavier than that allowed for the Intruder.

The EA-6B is powered by two Pratt & Whitney J52-P-408 or -408A turbojet engines rated at 11,200 lb (49.82 kN) thrust at take-off and 9,300 lb (41.37 kN) in normal flight. The original EA-6B powerplant was the A-6A's J52-P-8 engine, modified to P-408 standard beginning in 1973 with the addition of variable inlet guide vanes, allowing an increase in thrust.

The Prowler can carry up to four ALE-41 external, pod-mounted chaff dispensers. They are widely disliked, assumed to conflict with EW functions, and are virtually never used.

The 170 Prowlers manufactured at Calverton have been repeatedly improved with upgrades to existing aircraft and manufacture of new variants. The Block 89 aircraft introduced 'safety of flight' improvements such as fire-proof control rods and improved fire extinguishers. Some have new wing centre-sections. Block 89A standard, which was delivered to the Navy from 13 January 1999, introduced GPS and an EFIS cock-

Above: VMAQ-3 'Moondogs' now uses an 'MD' tailcode (reflecting the squadron name) instead of the original 'AB' codes seen here.

Right: All of the aircraft in this quartet of EA-6Bs carry an identical load-out of two fuel tanks, a single ALQ-99F jamming pod and HARM missile. This is clearly a training load-out. Any operational mission would be flown with at least two pods, and three would be the norm – particularly if tanker support was available.

pit. Block 89A enhanced the interoperability features of the Prowler. By 2004 the Navy aimed to have an all-Block 89A fleet, having upgraded its earlier Block 82 and 86 aircraft to the current standard, which includes AYK-14 processor and USQ-113 communication jammer.

The Prowler's fuselage is borrowed from the A-6 Intruder and lengthened by 54 in (137 cm) to accommodate four crew positions. The crew consists of one pilot (front left seat) who is a naval aviator and is always in charge of flying the aircraft (although any crew member may be a mission commander), and three electronic countermeasures officers located as ECMO 1 (front right), ECMO 2 (rear right) and ECMO 3 (rear left). The crew sits in pairs beneath two separate clamshell canopies which are pneumatically actuated and open to 35°. All four occupy roomy cockpits and are strapped into Martin-Baker GRUEA-7 zero-zero ejection seats. The two officers in the rear seats face an instrument panel that rises well above head level: they have visibility to the side but not forward.

Prowler crew roles

ECMO 1 is the navigator and handles communication. He can hear what the back-seaters do but has no oscilloscope to follow the action, and usually provides an extra set of eyes for the pilot, not just outside the aircraft but in performing instrument scans. Obviously, communication is vital to the success of a combat sortie or a military campaign. Typically, ECMO 1 monitors two communications nets. 'Net 1' consists of AWACS (Airborne Warning and Communications System) aircraft, escort fighters, and any other friendly assets committed to the air-to-air situation. 'Net 2', or the EWC&R (electronic warfare communications and reporting) net, comprises the EC-130 command, other EW aircraft, Joint Stars, and (in the Bosnian example) CAOC – NATO's Combined Air Operations Center, at Vicenza, in Italy. ECMO 1 is thus kept very busy flying, navigating and communicating; although not otherwise part of the SEAD mission, he has a key role in the employment of HARM.

ECMO 2 and 3 are the warfighters who detect a signal and designate a potential target. ECMO 1, who has the HARM control panel, sends the target 'packet' to the missile; this provides the pilot with steering cues (vertical and horizontal needles) on his attitude reference gyro, which is otherwise used during carrier landings. When the aircraft is in the launch window the pilot gets a cue that he can shoot, and pulls a trigger located on his stick handle.

VX-9 was established in 1994 as the USN's principal operational test and evaluation unit, combining the former VX-4 and VX-5. This 'Evaluators' Block 89A Prowler is seen arriving at its Point Mugu home, demonstrating the efficacy of the EA-6B's tail skid.

Left: Eve of Destruction *is a Desert Storm veteran serving with VAQ-141. The Prowler can carry 30-round AN/ALE-29A or AN/ALE-39 chaff/flare dispensers in the aft extendible (avionics) equipment platform, or 'birdcage'. The AN/ALE-39 differs from its forebear by having the capability to also deploy expendable active countermeasures (jammers).*

Right: VAQ-133 'Wizards' inherited the mantle of an earlier Navy unit of the same name, when it was re-established as the first joint expeditionary EW unit in April 1996.

Below: The EA-6B and F-14 are the last survivors of Grumman's great naval combat aircraft dynasty. Both have had to adopt new roles in order to survive budget cuts.

The naval flight officers (NFOs) who fill the ECMO jobs rotate from one seat to another. The squadron is likely to arrange a rotation in which an ECMO returns to the same seat every third flight. This is a drawback for new ECMOs who spend every third flight as ECMO 1, where they acquire relatively little useful experience.

Introduction of HARM as an operational Prowler weapon in 1986 was the biggest single change in the history of the EA-6B, transforming it from a passive weapon like the EF-111A into a 'shooter'. The current HARM version is the Block IV model of the TI (Texas Instruments) AGM-88C1 HARM, replacing the Block I and II versions employed during Operation Desert Storm. In the early 1990s, the US Navy explored a second source competition anticipating an AGM-88C2 low-cost HARM seeker built by Loral Ford (at the time) which would have been in magazines along with TI-built missiles. The proposed C2 passed all tests, but never went into production. TI kept lowering the cost so the issue became moot. In the world of HARM, block numbers designate hardware, software and CLC changes (the missile's serial for proper configuration management).

HARM employs a broadband anti-radar homing seeker and a computer-controlled seeker and autopilot. The 13-ft 8-in (4.17-m) missile weighs 800 lb (360 kg), reaches Mach 2.0 and employs its passive radiation homing capability to deliver a fragmentation warhead to targets up to 50 miles (80 km) away. The three modes of the HARM, Block II/IV are Pre-Briefed (PB), Range-Unknown (RU), and Range-Known (RK), the last being the most accurate. The modes give different ranges, flight profiles, time of flight, acquisition angles, and target specificity.

HARM can be carried on four of the Prowler's five attachment points: the centreline point is not used because of potential damage to the fuselage in a launch. Published reports of a dual HARM launcher enabling two missiles to be hung from a single point are in error.

Since ECMO 1 has the master arm switch as part of the HCP (HARM control panel) at his right knee and the pilot has the trigger on his stick, the HARM is, as one crewman describes it, "fired by a committee." Any one of the three ECMOs can designate the missile, assign the target, feed data, and tell the HARM what targets

to pursue. In a well-orchestrated attack, the back-seaters locate and designate the target, ECMO 1 throws the master arm switch (making the pilot's trigger 'hot') when prompted on the intercom, and the pilot shoots. The missile launch involves a tremendous amount of noise and smoke, readily obvious to all crew members.

HARM is regarded as a success story, a military system that arrived on time and worked right. Every shooter in a carrier air wing uses the same Block IV AGM-88C1 version (only training rounds retain the earlier AGM-88A designation), although interfaces and operations methods for each aircraft are different. The F/A-18 (and previously the A-7 and A-6) use the weapon as a sensor and process the data through a pre-programmed command launch computer (which is reconfigurable if new threats emerge), which programmes the HARM for a specific set of threats and particular flight profile. The EA-6B, however, uses its ALQ-99 system as the sensor, and then programmes the HARM for post-launch performance much like the F-4G did (first with the APR-38 and later APR-47 systems). By developing the system for both types of capability in order to be compatible with the Air Force Weasels, the Navy has a much more flexible system which adapted well to the EA-6B's capabilities.

The Prowler has an excellent safety record (0.5 mishaps per 100,000 flying hours), but for all its capabilities remains a challenge to technicians and maintainers. A mechanic claims the Prowler is known below decks as 'The Bridge Club' (a reference to its four-member crew) and remarks that keeping the EA-6B in operation involves "all the headaches of keeping all these systems working properly, a David and Goliath kind of task. There are also the weekly, monthly, etc. inspections where we have to take off a bunch of panels to look for stress cracks and corrosion." Taking a bath is also a challenge: "Washing this beast is a definite task to be reckoned with."

The Prowler's adoption of HARM (from the 13th production ICAP II aircraft, and then retrospectively) transformed the aircraft into a truly versatile combat aircraft. Early fears that the missile's own autonomous seeker might be jammed by ALQ-99 proved groundless.

First deployment with HARM by the EA-6B was made by squadron VAQ-140 'Patriots' aboard USS *John F. Kennedy* (CV 67) in 1988. The carrier had the 'all-Grumman air wing' tried by the Navy for a time, equipped with F-14 Tomcats and A-6 Intruders but only an *ad hoc* detachment of the Vought A-7E Corsairs which were then the service's only other HARM shooters. The Prowler detachment thus provided a capability not found elsewhere on the ship.

HARM in combat

The Prowler first used HARM missiles in combat during Operation Desert Storm. There, mission planners equipped the Prowler for the SEAD combat mission by making typical trade-offs: all five hardpoints can accommodate ALQ-99 pods or fuel, while four of the five can be used for HARMs. Thus, the EA-6B could carry five ECM pods for an exceedingly short-range sortie against a complex air defence threat.

Typically, the EA-6B Prowler is loaded with three ALQ-99F pods and two external tanks of fuel. Much depends on circumstance. For example, during the Gulf War, carrier aircraft operating from the Red Sea had easy access to plenty of Air Force tankers for frequent refuellings, so carried two HARMs, three ECM pods, and no external fuel. In contrast, Prowler crews flying from the Persian Gulf had less access to aerial refuelling, so carried three pods, one drop tank, and one HARM. In current operations, mission

planning is driven almost exclusively by the availability of tankers for the strike force and its accompanying Prowlers; with its dedicated KA-6D Intruder tankers now retired, the Navy is dependent on the S-3B Viking with its buddy store (or, increasingly, buddy-equipped F/A-18 Super Hornets) and Air Force refuellers.

Inter-service differences over SEAD were never more evident than in Desert Storm. As one naval aviator describes it, "The USAF planned to employ HARM to clear specific targets in specific

nside the Prowler

he pilot's cockpit in today's EA-6B is ominated by the APS-130 screen. Above it re the primary flight instruments. Canopy ettison and hook controls are above and to he right. To the left of the radar are the ngine RPM/TGT, oil and hydraulic ndicators. Radar controls, emergency witches and throttles are on the left onsole. Radio, wingfold, and auxiliary ontrols are on the centre panel.

ECMO 1 also has an APS-130 display. Above it is the ALQ-92 display (removed). To the left of these screens (in a vertical stack) are the station select (jettison), nav/TACAN and ECM dispenser controls. ALQ-92 frequency controls and the chaff programmer are located to the right of the main panel. ALE-41 controls, radio/ICS switches, KY-28 and interior light switches are all on the side console.

The ECMO 3 station (behind the pilot) has environmental and radio/ICS controls on the left (side) console. Above them are the bearing/distance/heading controls and indicator panels plus TJS receiver controls for the ALQ-99F system. The main instrument panel has the large digital display indicator (DDI) screen at its centre, with signal activity lights above, video display and DDI controls below.

ECMO 2/3 stations are largely identical. Both share a central instrument panel containing a UHF frequency/channel indicator, Mach/ airspeed indicator, cabin pressure indicator, altimeter, eject warning light, canopy controls, TJS master controls and access to the onboard computer. Below these, on the central console, are TJS pod power and digital recorder controls.

EA-6B Prowler units

VAQ-128 'Fighting Phoenix'

A squadron with this designation (carrying on the traditions of A-6 Intruder Fleet Replenishment Squadron VA-128 'Golden Intruders') became the fourth Prowler joint expeditionary squadron in 1997. It was based at Whidbey Island, Washington, but was deactivated on 7 May 2004.

VAQ-129 'Vikings'

Callsign EAGLE. Began as VAH-10 operating the A-3, and was established 1 May 1970. Created by the redesignation of VAH-10, also the 'Vikings', which had three EKA-3B detachments at the time of the designation change. Acquired current designation on 1 September 1970. Began operating A-6As in 1970, and EA-6Bs in 1972. Acts as the FRS for the EA-6B type. In continuous existence as a Prowler unit.

VAQ-130 'Zappers'

Callsign ZAPPER, formerly ROBINSON. Established as VW-13 on 1 September 1959, operating the Martin P4M-1Q Mercator. Redesignated as VAQ-130 on 1 October 1968 to become the first EA-6B operator. Operated EKA-3B until 1970. During Desert Storm, was commended for its operations against Iraqi targets. Saw action in Iraqi Freedom, 2003. Currently operates EA-6B ICAP II Block 89, authorised strength of five. Assigned to CVW-3 aboard *Harry S. Truman*.

VAQ-131 'Lancers'

Callsign SKYBOLT. Established and called to active duty as VP-931 on 3 September 1950; redesignated as VP-57 on 4 February 1953; became VAH-4 on 3 July 1956 and VAQ-131 on 1 November 1968. Had combat experience in Vietnam, Grenada, Lebanon, Desert Storm and Iraqi Freedom. Assigned to CVW-2 on *Abraham Lincoln*.

VAQ-132 'Scorpions'

Callsign SWAMP FOX. Began life as VAH-2 on 1 November 1955, equipped with EA-3. Picked up current designation on 1 November 1968. Was the first EA-6B squadron to deploy, in 1972. The squadron saw combat in Vietnam, Desert Storm and Allied Force. Currently allocated to CVW-17 aboard *John F. Kennedy*.

VAQ-133 'Wizards'

Callsign MAGIC. Established on 1 April 1996 as one of the new Prowler expeditionary squadrons to support USAF electronic combat needs. Retains nickname and traditions of an earlier Navy squadron with same designation, disestablished in 1992. Neither squadron bearing this designation has been in combat. VAQ-133's authorised strength is five EA-6B ICAP II Block 82 aircraft, although six side numbers are set aside for its use (630-635). When it began operations, the squadron had three aircraft. Deployed to Iwakuni, Japan in January 1997.

VAQ-134 'Garudas'

Callsign GARUDA. Established 17 June 1969. In continuous existence. Expeditionary squadron. Retained 'NL' tailcode now used as expeditionary tailcode for 'Prowlers' (formerly CVW-15 on *Vinson*). Saw action during US withdrawal from Vietnam in 1975, and over Serbia/Kosovo in 1999.

VAQ-135 'Black Ravens'

Callsign BLACK RAVEN. Established 15 May 1969. In continuous existence as a Prowler squadron. Saw action in Operations El Dorado Canyon against Libya (1986) and Praying Mantis against Iran (1988). Made two HARM shots in Iraq after Desert Storm. Subsequently saw combat in Afghanistan (2001) and Iraq (2003). Currently allocated to CVW-11 aboard *Nimitz*.

VAQ-136 'Gauntlets'

Callsign IRONCLAW. This was the first Prowler squadron which had not previously flown the 'Whale' (Douglas EKA-3 Skywarrior). Participated in Operation Desert Storm. Overseas since 1980 in Japan. Home-ported with CVW-5 (*Kitty Hawk*) at Yokosuka, Japan, with shore base at Atsugi. Participated in Operation Iraqi Freedom

VAQ-137 'Rooks'

Callsign ROOK. Was re-established for Navy operations in the 1990s. The earlier squadron with the same name and designation saw action in Lebanon, against Libya (Prairie Fire), Desert Storm. 'New' VAQ-137 saw service in Enduring Freedom. Now assigned to *Enterprise*'s CVW-1.

VAQ-138 'Yellowjackets'

Callsign RAMPAGE. Established on 27 February 1976, and in continuous existence since then. Saw action in Serbia/Kosovo and Afghanistan. Now assigned to CVW-9 (*Carl Vinson*).

VAQ-139 'Cougars'

Callsign GHOSTWALKER. Established 1 July 1983. Deployed during Operation Desert Shield, but did not see combat. Flew during Operation Iraqi Freedom and is now assigned to CVW-14 aboard *John C. Stennis*.

VAQ-140 'Patriots'

Callsign STINGER. Established 1 October 1985. In continuous existence as a Prowler squadron. Deployed during Operation Desert Shield, but did not see combat. Flew during Operation Allied Force. Now allocated to CVW-7 aboard *George Washington*.

VAQ-141 'Shadowhawks'

Callsign DESPERADO. Covered rescue of USAF pilot Scott O'Grady in Bosnia 8 June 1995. In 1996, shore-based at Aviano. Saw action in Desert Storm, Deliberate Force (Bosnia), Allied Force, Enduring Freedom and Iraqi Freedom. Assigned to CVW-8 aboard *Theodore Roosevelt*.

VAQ-142 'Gray Wolves'

Was a short-lived Prowler squadron that made one cruise before evolving into VAQ-35. The squadron stood up again on 4 April 1997 as the third expeditionary unit.

VAQ-209 'Star Warriors'

Naval Air Reserve squadron, established 1 October 1977, at NAF Washington (Andrews AFB, Maryland). The squadron's insignia is a likeness of *Star Wars'* Darth Vader. Deployed to Bosnia during 1995 and also saw action during Operation Allied Force.

VMAQ-1 'Banshees'

Callsign BANSHEE; 'CB' tailcode. Saw action in Bosnia, Kosovo and Iraq.

VMAQ-2 'Death Jesters'

Ex-'Playboys', callsign EASY. Participated in El Dorado Canyon (1986). Fought in Desert Storm (1991) and over Serbia/Kosovo. Dropped former nickname 'Playboys' after members alleged to be in Tailhook scandal (1991). 'Panthers' nickname adopted for a while.

VMAQ-3 'Moon Dogs'

Callsign DOG, 'AB' tailcode, changed to 'MD'. Participated in combat in Bosnia.

VMAQ-4 'Seahawks'

Callsign HAWK, 'RM' tailcode. Established Whidbey, activated in 1991 during Desert Storm and transitioned to Prowlers. Moved to Cherry Point as a regular Marine unit in September 1992.

VX-5 'Vampires'

'XE' tailcode. Established 18 June 1957, was a key US Navy operational test and evaluation squadron, located at NWTC China Lake, California. Its mission was to test and evaluate Navy weapons and weapons systems. The squadron flew most Navy aircraft including the EA-6B. VX-4 at Point Mugu and VX-5 at China Lake, both in California, were disestablished on 29 April 1994 and merged the following day into VX-9.

VX-9 det. 'Evaluators'

Established on 30 April 1994 at Point Mugu from the former VX-5, combined with VX-4. The squadron had at least one EA-6B Prowler on charge until 1995.

VAQ-209's aircraft proudly wear a badge depicting Star Wars' Darth Vader. A Navy Reserve unit based at NAF Washington, DC (Andrews AFB), VAQ-209 holds the distinction of landing the first Prowler on USS John C. Stennis (CVN 74), during 1996. The unit has deployed aircraft to combat zones to augment active-duty squadrons, notably for action in the Balkans theatre.

corridors to and from targets. The Navy figured you should kill whatever threat is emitting (although, in fact, Navy SEAD was passive until HARM came along). The Desert Storm experience showed that both tactics have their place, and the genius was having both capabilities inherent in the HARM design." Experts killed plans in the early 1980s for different variants of the HARM missiles tailored to Navy tactics and Air Force tactics.

During Desert Storm, in addition to employing EA-6Bs, the Navy dedicated a number of sorties each day to SEAD as the primary mission using A-7, F/A-18 and A-6 aircraft typically loaded with two HARMs in addition to other ordnance (Rockeye, AIM-9, AIM-7 and 20-mm). A-7s in particular proved to be valuable HARM shooters for long-range strikes near Baghdad for which other aircraft carried strike ordnance. Once the SEAD portion of the mission was completed, or if other missions emerged as priorities, the assets could be used in other ways (for rescue combat air patrol, armed reconnaissance or CAS).

With the retirement of the F-4G Advanced Wild Weasel, the USAF developed the F-16 HTS pylon mounted in the HARM launcher. This was necessary because the F-16 did not have room for a command launch computer to support the onboard processing that was done in A-7, A-6 and F/A-18 Navy HARM implementation schemes. The EA-6B uses the ALQ-99F system to programme HARM much like the F-4G implementation with the APR-38 and subsequent systems. Upgraded F-16 HTS provides limited bearing information using HARM's direction-finding capability. If the threat emitter is within HARM range, its bearing is all the missile needs. With that information it will then know the direction to turn, acquire the designated threat signal and make its own range calculations. In terms of maximising engagement range, this is not the optimum way to 'fly' HARM, since the missile uses energy and wastes some time in the boost phase to determine where it is going, but it is an effective way to work with a limited launch platform.

Prowler combat mission

Not blessed with excessive fuel capacity, the Prowler carries 15,400 lb (6990 kg) of JP fuel internally and about 2,000 lb (910 kg) in each external tank. The US Navy has transitioned from JP-5 and JP-8 fuel. Typically, the Prowler launches with full fuel capacity (except on a

The Prowler and the electronic spectrum

The Prowler's ALQ-99 system was originally designed to counter 1960s- and 1970s-era Soviet ground-based and naval radars, which operated largely in the 1-10 Ghz range. They included 'Yo-Yo' (SA-1), 'Fan Song' (SA-2), 'Flat Face' (SA-3, operating at <1 Ghz), 'Long Track'/'Pat Hand' (SA-4), 'Square Pair' (SA-5), 'Long Track'/'Thin Skin'/'Straight Flush' (SA-6) and 'Land Roll' (SA-8) ground-based SAM acquisition radars, and their naval equivalents – 'Peel Group' (SA-N-1), 'Fan Song' (SA-N-2), 'Head Light' (SA-N-3), and 'Pop Group' (SA-N-4). Many other radar systems were also well within the Prowler's reach, which extends to at least 20 Ghz (20,000 Mhz). The Prowler can effectively operate within today's A to J band (from 0-20,000 Mhz/HF to SHF transmissions). These bands cover the same wavelengths as the old I, G, P, L, S, C&S, C&X, X, and K (partially) bands which they replaced. Little has been publicly released about the EA-6B's detection and jamming capability against the entirely new generations of Russian SAM systems that have been developed for the Russian armed forces and sold to customers world-wide.

Prowler wing

The EA-6B's wing is a cantilever, all-metal structure, stressed to 5.5*g*. The wings have a sweepback of 25° at quarter-chord, but the root leading edges are swept back more sharply than this and incorporate stall warning strips. They induce exaggerated airflow noise and vibration, to warn of impending stalls at high angles of attack.

Nose gear

The EA-6B is equipped with nosewheel steering which becomes active once the arrester hook is deployed. The steering is controlled by the rudder pedals and will allow turns of up to 60°.

Crew safety

The Prowler is equipped with four Martin-Baker GRUEA-7 ejection seats, which fire through the canopy. The seats can be used at ground level and at speeds upwards of 80 kt (92 km/h; 57 mph) IAS.

EA-6B ICAP II (Block 89) Prowler

This aircraft was one of those attached to VAQ-134 'Garudas' when the unit sailed aboard the USS *Ranger* (CV 61), before that ship was decommissioned on 10 July 1993. VAQ-134 is now a joint expeditionary Prowler unit, and the *Ranger* is held in reserve at Bremerton, Washington.

ALQ-99F pods

It is not uncommon for the frequency coverage of the Prowler's onboard jammers to be duplicated by the external pods. This increases the aircraft's mission flexibility but also allows the Prowler's onboard systems to be cooled (turned off), and reduces the overall drain on the Prowler's own electrical system. Each pod has its own independent 27-kVA ram air turbine (RAT). The RATs can be spun up at airspeeds in excess of 100 kt, but will not provide enough power for both of the pods' transmitters until the aircraft reaches 220 kt IAS. The penalty for this is a one per cent reduction in range (for each operating RAT) due to the resultant parasitic drag.

The 'football'

The bulged fibreglass fin-tip fairing for the Prowler's ALQ-99F system has long been known as the 'football'. The TJS receivers in the 'football' covered frequency bands distinct from those covered by other onboard antennas – such as the twin blister antennas below the 'football' on either side of the fin.

External stores

The Prowler is designed to carry up to five AN/ALQ-99 jamming pods on its four wingtip and single centreline station. It can also carry a maximum of four AGM-88 HARMs. Beyond this, the only other external stores cleared for EA-6B carriage are standard twin-finned Aero 1D fuel tanks, AN/ALE-41 chaff pods (two can be carried on a single pylon) and CNU-188/A baggage pods.

Prowler tanker

In the late 1970s Grumman proposed a KA-6H tanker based on the EA-6B. The space provided by the 'football' and ECMO 2/3 stations allowed 45 per cent more off-loadable fuel to be crammed in compared to the existing KA-6D tanker. The project was cancelled in 1979.

Above: Part of the Block 86 upgrade to the EA-6B removed the 15° off-boresight restriction that had previously hampered the Prowler as a HARM shooter. Prowlers can now fire HARMs at any target, without changing course. It also allowed EA-6B crews to reprogramme the missiles in flight for new threat signals. By 1996 all Block 86 aircraft had been upgraded to Block 89 standard.

Left and below: From a shore base at Aviano AFB, in north-eastern Italy, USN and USMC Prowlers became instrumental in the NATO air campaign over Bosnia. The aircraft seen here, armed and ready, are from VAQ-130 (left) and VMAQ-3.

car-qual training sortie or a short-cycle maintenance flight), refuels from a tanker, and accompanies a strike force 600 miles (965 km) to cross into an opponent's territory. Mission commander aboard the aircraft often is not the pilot but one of the ECMOs (as explained earlier, the senior ECMO is not necessarily the occupant of the ECMO 1 crew position). At low altitude, the EA-6B has no difficulty maintaining a cruising speed of around 500 kt (575 mph; 925 km/h), which is similar to the speed at which an F/A-18E/F Super Hornet fully laden with bombs can conveniently cruise. As one ECMO describes it, "At low altitude [10,000 ft/6096 m], the EA-6B can stay with just about any bomb dropper, and I have run Jaguars, Tornados, F-16s, F-14s and F/A-18s out of gas down real low, maintaining 500 kt indicated. The problem is, since the EA carries its external stores home with it, they usually can run away on the way home." When it entered service, the Prowler needed only to keep up with A-6s and A-7s, and "chasing pointy-nosed bomb-droppers at high altitude was never a design requirement."

ADVCAP – aborted programme

No longer part of the Navy's planning is the advanced Prowler version known as ADVCAP or Block 91, launched in 1983, flown in prototype form for the first time on 29 October 1990 and planned for production in the early 1990s. As well as new systems, it was also planned to have new engines. Under the Vehicle Enhancement Program (VEP), further improvements were

planned to the aerodynamics, a prototype flying on 15 June 1992. Among other things, ADVCAP would have increased the Prowler's carrying stations from five to seven. Every Prowler ever built has two additional wing stations (called station A and B, outside the wing fold) but no pylons were ever hung from them. Three Block 91 prototypes were built.

This costly 'Cadillac of Prowler variants' was once the 'Great White Hope' of the fleet but today is, much like generous defence spending, merely a memory of other times. When ICAP III emerged in the 21st century, it was a 'poor man's substitute' for the version that might have been.

Action in Bosnia

The Prowler played a central role in the nearly 1,000-day Operation Deny Flight, conducted from 12 April 1993 to 20 December 1995 in Bosnia-Herzegovina. Following the 8 June 1995 rescue of a US Air Force F-16C pilot shot down (on 2 June) by a SAM in Bosnia, in early August 1995, four NATO aircraft attacked two Serbian surface-to-air missile radar sites, in Croatia, using HARMs. Two US Navy EA-6Bs (they usually operated in pairs in Bosnia) and two F/A-18Cs struck sites near Knin and Udbina in self-defence after the aircraft were targeted by SAM-associated radars. During the subsequent brief period of strike operations against the

Bosnian Serbs (codenamed Operation Deliberate Force), Navy Prowlers fired 13 HARMs; at best, only one of the HARMs was a kill, confirmed ironically not by US intelligence but by a Bosnian Serb officer interviewed on the Cable News Network.

This flurry of fighting, when naval aviators made logbook entries in green ink (signifying combat), is recalled by an ECMO in these words: "VAQ-141 had deployed with Carrier Air Wing Eight aboard the USS *Theodore Roosevelt* (CVN 71) with an 'augment' of two aircraft from reserve squadron VAQ-209. Once in the Adriatic, they were constantly tasked for operations 'over the beach'. Whenever the 'TR' went into port, 141 was off-loaded to Aviano where they worked with the USAF and USMC units based there. It's important to note that the EA-6Bs were the only portion of CVW-8 that NATO commanders wouldn't allow out of the area. While the rest of CVW-8 was in port on liberty in Haifa or Rhodes, VAQ-141 was in Aviano flying peace-keeping missions. In addition, VAQ-130 deployed to Aviano directly from Whidbey for Deliberate Force and joined 141 to make up a 10-aircraft squadron under 141 control."

Another ECMO, Lieutenant Commander Tom Burke of VAQ-209, remembers that, "we would fly with jammers off, waiting for the SA-6, which was the main threat [the 3M9 Kub SAM, NATO name 'Gainful', is a self-propelled mobile system]. Upon picking up signals, depending on the rules of engagement, we could fire. When the raids started, the ROE were relaxed. The raids were 'joint', with the Air Force and NATO allies, and required air-to-air refuelling. We took off from Aviano, flew down over the Adriatic, and caught the tankers, which could be British TriStars, Spanish C-130s or US Air Force KC-135s. Then we would go 'in country', fly around for an hour and a half, go out, refuel, and pop back in. We flew with two drop tanks, two pods, and one HARM."

These Navy Prowlers were replaced by two Marine Corps units. One of these, VMAQ-1, fired HARMs during Bosnia operations. After that the Marine Corps held the Aviano commitment while Navy squadrons remained on carriers in the area. On 3 February 1998 tragedy struck the Aviano detachment when a VMAQ-2 aircraft assigned the 31st Air Expeditionary Wing on a low-level training mission severed the lines supporting a cable car at the Italian ski resort of Cavalese on 3 February 1998, plunging the car to the mountainside and killing its 20 occupants. The collision with the cable damaged the fin and wing leading edge of the Prowler. A year later, Prowlers would play a key part in the NATO Allied Force action against Serbia.

EA-6B operations

The Marine Corps' EA-6B force is located at MCAS Cherry Point near Havelock, North Carolina. The US Navy's entire EA-6B force (except reserve squadron VAQ-209) is garrisoned at Whidbey Island, in the Puget Sound near Seattle, Washington. VAQ-209 is at Andrews AFB near Washington, DC. Whidbey is made up of two bases – Ault Field on the wind-ward (western) side in a portion called Clover Valley, and the Seaplane Base on the leeward side (east) of the island. The town of Oak Harbor is in between. The Seaplane Base is still used for base housing and Navy Exchange (the converted PBY hangar), and is also the home for 'Dolly', the EW signal simulator the EA-6Bs use while airborne.

'Detachments' of Prowlers are described going aboard a carrier as part of the ship's air wing, but routine procedure is for an entire squadron of four or five EA-6Bs to go to sea for a cruise, typically lasting four to six months. Deployment to 'concrete' locations – such as Iwakuni, Japan, to support the US commitment in Korea – are usually for six months. From 1996 to 2002 USMC Prowler squadrons did not have a carrier commitment, but this was reinstated following an agreement between the Navy and Corps for the latter to provide additional units to the fleet. In the reciprocal of this agreement, Navy Prowlers also support the US Marine Corps Unit Deployment Program. In 2002 VAQ-133 became the first Navy Prowler unit to deploy in support of the USMC's forward-deployed air group at Iwakuni.

When planning for a mission, commanders and EA-6B crews know that they have the flexi-bility afforded by an aircraft that is both a shooter and a jammer, replacing other aircraft such as the F-4G and EF-111A which are either

Prowlers over Bosnia

The Grumman EA-6B Prowler made its combat debut in the Bosnian theatre of operations in November 1994 after Serb forces besieging the Bihac pocket activated their integrated air defence network containing scores of V-75 Dvina (SA-2 'Guideline') and 3M9 Kub (SA-6 'Gainful') SAM batteries. For months the Serbs had been building up their air defences to stop Bosnian and Croat resupply aircraft getting into the pocket, claiming an Antonov An-32 shot down on 1 August. By mid-November NATO's 5th Allied Tactical Air Force (5 ATAF) was gearing up to mount strikes against the Serb air base at Udbina inside Croatia, to deter the Serb air force conducting air strikes against Bihac in contravention of the United Nations' 'No-Fly Zone'.

VMAQ-4 'Seahawks' was ordered to deploy to NAS Sigonella, Sicily, on 19 November 1994 to provide 5 ATAF with specialised SEAD capability. Refuelling by USAF KC-10A tankers, the Marine Prowlers made an 11-hour non-stop transatlantic ferry flight from their home at Cherry Point, NC on 21 November, just prior to a major NATO air strike against Udbina. Within hours of being on the ground the squadron's six aircraft began flying operational sorties over Bosnia. NATO air commanders were becoming increasingly concerned about the Serb SAM threat to their aircraft, and the firing of two SA-2s against Royal Navy Sea Harriers flying near Bihac on 22 November forced them to change tactics.

On the morning of 23 November 1994, 5 ATAF launched a major strike package to protect eight British, Dutch and French reconnaissance aircraft that were to pin-point the location of the SAMs around Bihac. Flying 'shot gun' on the Jaguars, Mirages and F-16s was a SEAD package centred around the VMAQ-4 Prowlers, which were armed with AGM-88s. This package was put together very quickly as events unfolded, with the Prowlers being diverted from another mission, to the USAF base at Aviano, to receive briefings from senior NATO commanders.

As the package skirted the southeast edge of the Bihac pocket, a Serb SA-2 battery at Otoka illuminated the aircraft with its fire control radar, so the Prowlers fired two HARMs. Minutes later another SAM site came on line at Dvor, and another HARM was fired at it. The Prowler crews, using information from RC-135 'Rivet Joint' aircraft and previous photo-missions, had a good idea of the SAM positions and

manoeuvred themselves carefully to get the best shots at the radars guiding the hostile missiles. Serb missile crews were highly skilled at using long-range surveillance radars when given notice of NATO air patrols, and tended only to switch on radars for very short periods to prevent them being targeted by HARMs. The results of the first HARM strikes were decidedly mixed, so NATO and UN commanders agreed that a further combined armed reconnaissance package was authorised for later in the afternoon. F-15Es led the package, dropping two LGBs on the Otoka site and destroying SA-2 launchers. To protect the Strike Eagles, Prowlers fired three more HARMs when the SA-2s' and SA-6s' radars came up.

The VMAQ-4 Prowlers stayed in Italy for two months to support continued NATO air operations over Bosnia, flying 220 combat missions. The squadron was based mainly at Sigonella but regularly detached aircraft to Aviano to be closer to the action.

With the return of a US Navy aircraft-carrier to the Adriatic at the end of January 1995, VAQ-130 'Zappers' took over duty as 5 ATAF's specialist SEAD unit. At times when the USS *Eisenhower* was away from the Adriatic, VAQ-130 would disembark five aircraft to Aviano to provide SEAD coverage over Bosnia for up to 10 days at a time.

In May 1995 the USS *Theodore Roosevelt* arrived in-theatre and its embarked Prowlers, from the active-duty VAQ-141 'Shadowhawks' augmented by reservists from VAQ-209 'Star Warriors', assumed 5 ATAF's SEAD role. Prowlers and other HARM-armed aircraft now had to be present in Bosnian airspace to 'open the SEAD window' before other allied aircraft could follow them into the area of operations.

The *Roosevelt*'s Prowlers remained on patrol over Bosnia for the next six months, with detachments being sent to Aviano when the carrier was not in the Adriatic. On 8 June they provided SEAD support for the rescue of downed USAF pilot Captain Scott O'Grady from northwest Bosnia. As the rescue force was passing over the Serb-held Krajina region of Croatia, it was illuminated by SAM radars; VAQ-141/209 Prowlers detected the radars but NATO commanders refused to give authorisation for them to engage because the Serbs were then holding hostage hundreds of UN peacekeepers. Prowlers had not been in the air at the time the hapless USAF pilot

was shot down. Early in July the Prowlers were called to protect NATO fighters deep in Bosnian airspace as they flew close air support for UN troops trapped in the Srebrenica enclave. On 7 August two EA-6Bs and two F/A-18Cs from the *Roosevelt* took part in a HARM attack on Serb SAM radars at Knin, in the Krajina, after they were called to provide air protection for UN troops caught in the Croatian Operation Storm offensive.

By August 1995 the UN and NATO had finally lost patience with the Bosnian Serbs' policy of attacking so-called 'safe areas', and plans were formed for an air campaign to punish further provocation. First, the Serbs' integrated air defence system had to be neutralised. US Navy officers from VAQ-141 'Shadowhawks' and -209 'Star Warriors', plus other SEAD specialists on the USS *Theodore Roosevelt*, developed a plan to accomplish this, under the codename Dead Eye.

NATO was given the go-ahead to launch Operation Deliberate Force after 38 civilians were killed in a mortar attack in Sarajevo on 28 August. 5 ATAF had to be ready to attack in the early hours of 30 August. The first strike package, codenamed Dead Eye South East, was made up of EA-6Bs and F/A-18Cs from the *Roosevelt*, supported by F-16Cs equipped with the HARM Targeting System (HTS) and armed with AGM-88s. Its task was to take out the Serb air defences around Sarajevo, which it did with great determination, firing HARMs to put early warning radars out of action and dropping LGBs on the Serb SA-6 battery deployed near the Bosnian capital.

As the bombing offensive unfolded, 5 ATAF took no chances in case the Serbs covertly moved any of their mobile SA-6s to threaten NATO aircraft, so a SEAD package had to be in the air to 'open the SEAD window' before strike aircraft were allowed to go 'feet wet' over Bosnia. SEAD packages were built up from pairs of HARM shooters and jamming aircraft. Prowlers were teamed in pairs with other EA-6Bs, Hornets and HTS-equipped F-16s. They would enter Bosnian airspace and fly in racetrack patterns to protect the strike aircraft as they made their bombing runs. If Prowlers were not in the air then the strike aircraft entered holding patterns outside Bosnia until the SEAD aircraft were ready to lead the way. USAF EF-111A and EC-130H 'Compass Call' jamming aircraft closely co-ordinated their operations with the Prowlers to ensure maximum SEAD protection for NATO aircraft.

On 5 September 5 ATAF expanded its operations to hit at the Serb IADS targets in northwest Bosnia, striking first with stand-off missile to neutralise key air defence sites. Again the Prowlers from the *Roosevelt* were in the forefront of the offensive, using HARMs against early warning radars.

SEAD coverage continued around the clock through Operation Deliberate Force, with Prowlers being in the air almost continuously. The brunt of this effort fell on the six EA-6Bs of VAQ-141 and those from the reserve unit VAQ-209, with aircraft split between the *Roosevelt* and ashore at Aviano in northern Italy. By 5 September the intensity of SEAD operations meant two more aircraft from VAQ-130 'Zappers' were deployed to Aviano to help in the non-stop effort to defeat the Serb SAMs. During 10-12 September the *Roosevelt* handed over to the USS *America* and its embarked Prowlers from VMAQ-4 'Seahawks'. Additional support was provided by four more EA-6Bs of VMAQ-1 'Screaming Banshees', which relieved the Prowlers at Aviano towards the end of September.

During Deliberate Force a total of 56 HARMs was fired, with 10 being launched from VAQ-141's Prowlers alone. The squadron was airborne for 603 hours during 137 combat sorties in Deliberate Force.

In the weeks after Operation Deliberate Force, 5 ATAF maintained the intensity of its air activity over Bosnia to protect UN peacekeepers and keep the pressure on the Serbs. In an attempt to turn back the Croat and Bosnian offensive towards Banja Luka, the Bosnian Serb air force took to the air in early October, so NATO fighters began patrols to stop them breaching the UN 'No-Fly Zone'. Prowlers had to accompany the fighter sweeps into the SAM-infested areas of northwest Bosnia. On 4 October VMAQ-1 Prowlers were illuminated three times by Serb SAM radars, and on each occasion they launched a HARM.

During September and October 1995, the US Navy and Marine Corps Prowlers maintained a high level of SEAD protection in the face of the Serb IADS, and not a single NATO aircraft was shot down by a radar-guided SAM. The only aircraft lost during Operation Deliberate Force was the victim of a heat-seeking SAM at low level. In the words of VMAQ-4 executive officer, Major 'Muddy' Waters, "We were a success – no one was shot down on our watch." **Tim Ripley**

Above: This VMAQ-1 EA-6B refuels from a USAF KC-10A before attacking Serbian SAM sites on 4 October 1996.

Below: This VF-141 Prowler is being armed in preparation for the Operation Deliberate Force strikes in August 1995.

Above: This VAQ-132 'Scorpions' EA-6B (attached to CVW-17 onboard the USS Enterprise) is seen on a jamming sortie over the Adriatic. The aircraft is carrying an operational load of three ALQ-99F pods plus two 300-US gal (1136-litre) Aero 1D external fuel tanks. The EA-6B already has a useable internal fuel load of 2,268 US gal (8585 litres).

Right: VAQ-137 is dubbed the 'Rooks', and the unit's badge comprises a stylised North American Indian bird.

shooters or jammers. This is consistent with the Pentagon's overall plan to shift from one-mission aircraft to multi-mission aircraft. The F/A-18E/F Super Hornet replacing the F-14A/B/D is another example of this emphasis.

To the theatre commander (as well as in Navy doctrine), the dual-role, shooter-jammer EA-6B Prowler represents a dramatic change that began with the installation of HARM in 1986. Until then, Air Force SEAD doctrine was to 'prosecute to destruction' (F-4G with HARM missile) whereas Navy doctrine was to 'prosecute to suppression' (EA-6B without HARM). The Air Force method was to use a SEAD aircraft to clear a pathway for the strike package by destroying air defence radars in a selected corridor, whereas the Navy approach was to jam everything in the region. Now that the Navy EA-6B Prowler seeks not merely to disrupt and denigrate, but also to destroy, it becomes a more versatile weapon, a more 'joint' asset, and a prime candidate for the joint Navy-Air Force squadrons taking shape today.

The Prowler mission

The job assigned to the EA-6B is determined by the JFAC's operations staff when making up the daily Air Tasking Order (ATO). Fortunately, the Navy has improved the 'jointness' of its communications which hampered delivery of the ATO during the Gulf War. When the ATO is received at the airfield or carrier, mission planners slot the EA-6B into a take-off time and position based on the competing priorities of the other strike aircraft (the Air Force always preferred to use the EF-111A in pairs, but the EA-6B frequently operates as a one-ship element). At the tactical level, ECMOs make use of a computer system, the PRB Associates AN/TSQ-142 Tactical EA-6B Mission Support (TEAMS) System, to create the electronic order

The EA-6B does not have fuselage airbrakes (only the EA-6A had them). Instead, it uses wingtip airbrakes which deploy to 120°. The individual panels are approximately 2 ft x 4 ft (0.6 m x 1.2 m) – giving a total braking area of 32 sq ft (2.97 m²).

of battle. Each squadron has a TEAMS machine made up of two consoles, which aircrew (almost always ECMOs) use to plan their mission. The TEAMS develops information on navigation track, fuel consumption, jamming and HARM plans. The entire mission is dropped to a tape drive, which is loaded into the aircraft from the back seat. The results can then be manually adjusted or overridden during flight. The system was introduced concurrent with ICAP II and is now in its third version as it keeps up with airframe developments. Prior to its introduction, ECMOs were required to manually enter all mission data by keypad, a long, laborious process which is little missed. The aircraft also has a recorder system that records the actual mission for debriefing purposes.

Navy-Air Force operations

Pivotal to the ongoing future of the Prowler was an agreement (technically a memorandum of agreement, or MOA) between the Air Force and Navy. Under the terms of the MOA, the Navy is tasked to establish five 'expeditionary' EA-6B Prowler squadrons to provide 'joint' electronic combat support for Department of Defense land-based units following the retirement of the US Air Force EF-111A. The expeditionary squadrons are ready to deploy to land bases or operational carriers, whenever directed.

Rear Admiral Dennis V. McGinn, the Navy's Director of Air Warfare, described the agreement in testimony before the US Congress's Subcommittee on Airland Forces on 15 March 1996, as part of the service's Aircraft

Procurement, Navy (APN) plan. "Our nation's tactical jamming asset, the EA-6B, remains the premier tactical electronic warfare platform in the world. Projected to be in inventory until 2015, ICAP II (Block 89A) will require an upgrade planned to begin in 1998. Based on the Lower Cost Alternative to ADVCAP Study, planned modifications will address aircraft structure and supportability, as well as enhanced warfighting capabilities, including a receiver upgrade. Beginning this year [1996], the EA-6B will assume the role of stand-off jammer for the Air Force, as well as for the Navy and Marine Corps, totally replacing the EF-111A by the end of FY 1998."

As conceived, the plan called for 'concrete' squadrons with no seagoing capability that would have operated solely from shore bases – meaning Iwakuni, Japan, where the commit-ment has traditionally but not always been handled by the Marines, and Aviano, Italy, from where flying operations over the Balkans were mounted. Once the joint squadrons were up and running, the Prowler was expected to take over land-based EF-111A commitments to the US European Command at Incirlik, Turkey, and to the US Central Command, which had recently moved to Al Kharj ('Al's Garage'), Saudi Arabia. The agreement to keep the joint Prowler squadrons land-based did not last long, however. Although it received much from the deal – the Air Force transferred $500 million in electronic warfare funds that it otherwise would have spent on the EF-111A – the Navy reneged on the plan to keep the joint units land-based.

The plan created personnel problems for the Navy since it meant that a new naval aviator in an EA-6B squadron would be treated differently than the equivalent person in another squadron: junior officers receiving first-tour orders to a 'concrete' squadron would have to wait for a second tour with a CV squadron to gain fleet experience. The deal met the Air Force's needs but not the Navy's, so the Navy proposed an addendum that these squadrons must always be able to deploy on short notice wherever needed (including a boat). Therefore, USAF pilots in these squadrons would be required to maintain carrier quals.

On 1 July 1996, a three-man, all-Air Force crew headed by pilot Lieutenant Colonel Ronald Rivard landed an EA-6B Prowler on USS *Constellation* (CV 64) in the Pacific. This first all-Air Force achievement came just after the first USAF flyers graduated from EA-6B training the previous month. Rivard had been a Navy pilot for seven years and had logged more than 100 carrier landings in Vikings 15 years previously.

While the training for Air Force Prowler crews progressed, operational problems remained as the two services merged separate practices. For example, compared with the Air Force, Navy squadrons do not practise rapid deployments as often, do not deploy with extensive spare parts packages and support equipment on extended deployments, and use different chemical warfare gear. To iron out these differences, the two existing joint-service squadrons flew in Red Flag exercises at Nellis AFB, Nevada, in an operational readiness inspection at Shaw AFB, SC, in a composite wing exercise at Mountain Home

Tanking with drogue-equipped USAF aircraft, such as this KC-135R, has become routine for Prowler crews. They have also had to adapt to a new era of completely integrated operations.

Air AFB in Idaho, in NATO air operations over Bosnia, and in support of UN air operations over southern Iraq.

Prowler at war

Along with its deckmates, the EA-6B has had a very busy time since the end of the 1991 Gulf War. As the only jamming platform, the force was spreadly thinly between three major operational tasks: Operation Southern Watch in southern Iraq (carrier-based), Northern Watch in northern Iraq (based at Incirlik, Turkey) and in the Balkans (flying from either carriers in the Adriatic or from Aviano). In December 1998 Prowlers from USS *Enterprise* (VAQ-130) were involved in Operation Desert Fox, a three-day air campaign against Iraqi targets. *Carl Vinson*'s EA-6Bs joined in on the final day. As usual, the small force was severely over-taxed, having to accompany most of the strike packages most of the way to the target.

When NATO attacked Serbia in March 1999 under Operation Allied Force, it was clear that the EA-6B would have a major part to play. Serbia's air defence network was large and well integrated, and was manned by experienced and highly regarded personnel. The centre for Prowler operations was Aviano AB in Italy, which by 20 April housed no fewer than 25 EA-6Bs, drawn from VMAQs-1, -2 and -4, and VAQs-132, -134, -138 and -140. The Naval Reserve unit VAQ-209 also provided two aircraft. In early April USS *Theodore Roosevelt* arrived in the Adriatic for war operations, bringing the EA-6Bs of VAQ-141 with it. At Aviano the EA-6Bs worked closely with other EW assets, such as the F-16CJ SEAD platforms and EC-130H Compass Call communications jammers.

Operations over Serbia and Kosovo were extremely intense, Prowlers accompanying virtually all strike packages, including F-117 'Stealth Fighter' operations. Standard loadout

The EA-6B's immediate future is secure, and there are now more deployed squadrons than at any time in the aircraft's history. However, as the only US jamming asset and with the number and intensity of operational taskings of recent years, the community has been stretched to near-breaking point.

was three TJS pods, one HARM and one fuel tank. On the fourth night of the war an F-117 was shot down by a Neva-M (SA-3) missile, and in the ensuing inquest the lack of EA-6B jamming coverage at the time was flagged as a factor. Another factor was that the F-117 had followed the same route as in previous nights, a fact that had not escaped the Yugoslav defences which were expecting it.

The intensity of operations in Allied Force provoked a fierce debate after the war over the need for more SEAD forces, particularly jammers. It also raised the question of the Prowler's speed – some USAF pilots reported that the EA-6B could not keep up with the strike packages, which in turn meant they were operating from greater distances than would normally be desirable. In the F-117 incident, for example, the EA-6B was reportedly too far away for its jammers to affect the SA-3 system.

War on terror

Two years later, the Prowler was back at war again, this time over Afghanistan in Operation Enduring Freedom, the US-led response to the 11 September attacks. For the first few days the EA-6Bs flew on routine SEAD operations, firing a handful of HARMs in the process, but with the paltry Afghan air defence system eradicated and the Taliban forces largely on the run, the Prowlers switched to a new mission – communications intelligence and jamming.

In this role the aircraft used their USQ-113 systems to jam various Taliban communications, including – it was reported – mobile phones. The Prowlers worked hand-in-hand with EC-130H Compass Call aircraft as well as the Navy's EP-3E Aries II Sigint platforms which were operating from Bahrain.

However, when the US and UK attacked Iraq in March 2003 in Operation Iraqi Freedom, the Prowlers were again facing a full air defence network, and returned to their primary SEAD role, although they were also used in an unspecified psychological warfare role as well, operating in concert with EC-130E psywar aircraft and EC-130Hs.

In order to assault the Iraqi air defence system a sizeable force of Prowlers was gathered, based on three carriers in the Persian Gulf (*Abraham Lincoln*/VAQ-139, *Kitty Hawk*/VAQ-136 and *Constellation*/VAQ-131), two in the eastern Mediterranean (*Theodore Roosevelt*/VAQ-141 and *Harry S. Truman*/VAQ-130) and at Prince Sultan Air Base (Riyadh) in Saudi Arabia (VMAQ-1 and others). The Marine Prowlers operated as part of the Air Force-led 363rd Air Expeditionary Wing.

In the last few days of the war the air wing from USS *Nimitz* (VAQ-135) also joined the fray. A total of 35 EA-6Bs was deployed for Operation Iraqi Freedom. Prowlers were also based at Incirlik in Turkey as part of the Northern Watch deployment, but they played no direct part in OIF.

EA-6Bs supported all the main strike packages, and were probably airborne for the pre-emptive decapitation raid flown by F-117s which started the war. One raid for which their work was acknoweldged was another decapitation attempt on 7 April, when a B-1B dropped four JDAMs into a residential area of Baghdad after reports that Saddam Hussein was to attend a meeting in a restaurant. Prowlers remained on watch after the fighting subsided, although the threat of radar-guided SAMs had largely been replaced by shoulder-launched IR-guided weapons and rocket-propelled grenades.

Hook down, an EA-6B from VAQ-137 'Rooks' flies past its 'homeplate' (Theodore Roosevelt) *on 4 December 2001, at the tail end of the combat phase of Operation Enduring Freedom. During this campaign the Prowler was mainly used in a communications jamming role.*

ICAP III – the final Prowler?

Following the cancellation of ADVCAP, the need to maintain the Prowler's continued improvement remained. Currently, the Prowler is being upgraded to a new ICAP III configuration, which will almost certainly be the last major upgrade applied to the aircraft and should see it through to the end of its career.

Northrop Grumman received a $200 million development contract in early 1998 for a major systems update. The contract called for the conversion of two prototypes, the first of which undertook a 1-hour 45-minute maiden flight from St Augustine on 16 November 2001.

ICAP III – sometimes known as 'ADVCAP Lite' – has most of the advanced receiver capability of the cancelled ADVCAP, but at a fraction of the weight. It therefore does not require the extensive and expensive airframe and engine modifications that were planned for the Block 91/ADVCAP.

Answering new threats posed by the 'double-digit' SAM systems (SA-10, SA-11, SA-12 and SA-17), ICAP III covers a variety of major enhancements, including a sophisticated new receiver system (LR-700, later designated ALQ-218) and software which allows the jamming system to react to the radars it is targeting. The frequency of the jamming transmissions is changed as fast as that of the frequency-agile radars. The system is effectively turned into a selectively reactive one, rather than a pre-emptive one. It can provide much higher jamming power on a specific frequency rather than 'blanket' coverage of a much wider band, in which the radar is exposed to much less jamming energy.

Other improvements include an integrated communications jamming system in place of the Block 89A's stand-alone BAE Systems USQ-113, new colour displays and controls, and Link 16 datalink capability. The latter would provide the Prowler with increased connectivity with other platforms, allowing it to receive information from offboard sources while feeding its own information into the wider net. However, while ICAP III is being built initially with the Link 16 hardware, the software has yet to be defined. Further advances include a move to full digital operation of the ALQ-218 system, which would allow the system to identify specific emitters, and the addition of an enhanced emitter location technique known as phased-circle location. It is hoped that these upgrades could be introduced about two years after ICAP III enters service.

In April 2002 the first ICAP III aircraft began systems testing with NAWC-AD at NAS Patuxent River, Maryland, both in the air and on the ground in an anechoic chamber. It later went to NAS Point Mugu and NAWS China Lake for tests of the new ALQ-218 receiver system, including flights over the Nellis ranges and their arrays of threat radars. Following a 29-flight technical evaluation in early 2003, the ICAP III was approved in mid-2003 for low-rate initial production (LRIP), 10 conversions being covered by a $91.8 million contract. The first upgraded aircraft was delivered in 2004, and initial operational capability is planned for March 2005, although how many aircraft are upgraded has yet to be defined, and may be linked to the rate of delivery of the Prowler's successor – the EA-18G. A five-month Opeval, handled by VX-9 at NAWS China Lake, began in April 2004. If successful, an Opeval pass will lead to full-rate production authorisation.

In the interim, in 2002 the Navy ran a series of trials with Prowlers featuring a modified Improved Data Modem (IDM) and new small, lap-top computers. Provided with an improved battlespace management capability, the Prowler crews demonstrated the ability to receive targeting data from an EP-3 or RC-135 and relay it (and Prowler-generated information) to HARM-carrying F/A-18 fighters. In the standard Block 89A the EA-6B crew can only communicate with F/A-18s by voice.

The future

Looking beyond the Prowler, whose career seems assured to around 2015, McDonnell Douglas (now Boeing) and Northrop Grumman announced on 7 August 1995 that they agreed to jointly develop a derivative of the F/A-18E/F Super Hornet as an EW aircraft. The variant, called the F/A-18 C²W (Command and Control Warfare) version, is to be the replacement for the EA-6B. Most scenarios for EA-6B missions tie up fighters used as HVUCAP (high value unit combat air patrol), and the F/A-18 C²W offers the advantage of being able to protect itself against opposing fighters. The F/A-18 C²W, now designated EA-18G and known as the 'Growler', further aids planners by allowing them to utilise similar flight profiles, increasing fuel efficiency. Automation will enable the EA-18G to do the Prowler's job with only two crew members, although the EW system is based on that of the EA-6B ICAP III.

Only the Navy is scheduled to get the EA-18G, while the USMC is prepared to keep its Prowlers flying to around 2015, 'cherry-picking' the best airframes from its own fleet and those discarded by the Navy. The Marines are looking to keep around 30 aircraft flying: five for each of its four squadrons plus others for training and attrition reserve. USMC Prowler crews currently train with the Navy, so the syllabus would have to be transferred to Marines control. A more modern engine is high on the 'wish-list' for the Prowler fleet, as is the next-generation AARGM anti-radiation missile as a replacement for HARM. Both are under study, but no decision has been taken at the time of writing. AARGM is due to enter service around the same time as the EA-18G, and would most likely not be fielded on Navy Prowlers. However, due to their extended service, USMC EA-6Bs may carry the weapon. To eventually replace the Prowler, the USMC is looking to an EW version of the Lockheed Martin JSF, possibly based on the US Navy's F-35C model rather than the STOVL F-35B. The USAF is studying a stand-off jamming version of the B-52 Stratofortress, as well as JSF or F/A-22 derivatives.

In the meantime, the EA-6B fleet has been worked harder than ever, with a high rate of operational commitments. A GAO report at the end of 2002 highlighted the problems facing the community: spares and personnel were being

Two views show the two 'prototype' ICAP III conversions on the ramp at China Lake, California, during Techeval by VX-9. The new ALQ-218 receiver system allows the EA-6B to 'focus' its jamming power selectively against individual radars, making it far more effective.

As it has been in several conflicts, the use of the Prowler was fundamental to the success of allied warplanes in the attacks on Iraq in 2003. The Prowler is tasked with supporting virtually all strike packages – even those in which stealth aircraft such as the F-117 are involved. However, their use in such missions has to be carefully planned as they may alert defences as to the F-117's approach. Left is VAQ-135's CAG-bird returning to Nimitz after an Iraqi Freedom mission in April 2003, while below crews from the same unit prepare to launch. Note the sand-coloured flying suits.

stripped from non-deployed units, while only 91 of the required 104 EA-6Bs were available. There were serious proposals to reopen production to bolster the current fleet of around 120 aircraft, but with the EA-18G scheduled to enter service in 2009 it was considered possible to eke out the service lives of the current Prowler fleet until that time.

The task of prolonging the fleet will not be easy: in 2003 the Navy was forced to ground 19 Prowlers and issue a new contract for wing centre-section kits, of which 60 had been delivered and fitted by October 2003. Replacement outer wing panels are also being built, the first to be delivered in July 2005. However, the wing replacement process has proceeded at a slower pace than required to maintain the EA-6B force at the necessary level. Another measure which will help alleviate the looming 'Prowler gap' is the provision of an interim EW capability by fitting F/A-18Fs with some of the ICAP III equipment, but not the full suite envisaged for the EA-18G. All F/A-18Fs from 2003 are being built with the wiring necessary for easy conversion to 'EA' standard.

Another upgrade under study for the Prowler is the fitment of a digital flight control system in the form of the BAE Systems ASW-59A, a version of the ASW-59 used successfully in the F-14 Tomcat. Contracts have been let for ground tests systems, with options for flight tests systems to be delivered in October 2004.

Although the men and women of Prowler squadrons love their aircraft and would not trade it, most acknowledge that today's EA-6B – and tomorrow's – is necessarily a compromise. The EA-6B is not as good a HARM shooter as the F-4G and in some circumstances not as good a jammer as the EF-111A, but it continues to perform both jobs when neither of the others do. The US Air Force became a partner in EA-6B operations for the wrong reason – to achieve cost saving – by retiring the EF-111A Raven, and the US Navy got into the lethal, missile-shooting SEAD business very late in the game. The EA-6B does an excellent job, but it is also important because it is now the only game in town.

Robert F. Dorr;
additional material by David Donald

Above: During Iraqi Freedom the Marine Corps Prowlers operated from Prince Sultan AB at Riyadh. This VMAQ-1 aircraft sits out a thunderstorm as lightning crackles above the desert base.

Left: VAQ-136 was aboard USS Kitty Hawk (CV 63) in the Persian Gulf for Operation Iraqi Freedom. The blades of the ram-air generators on the TJS pods are feathered when not in use to reduce drag.

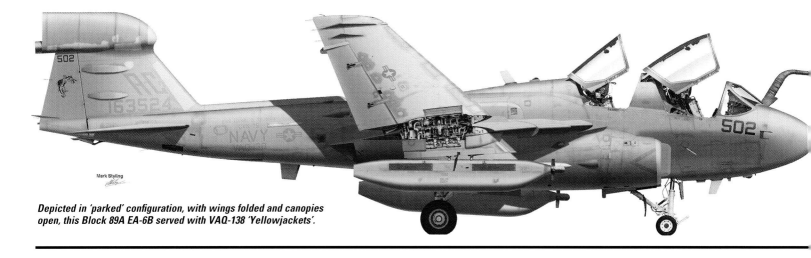

Depicted in 'parked' configuration, with wings folded and canopies open, this Block 89A EA-6B served with VAQ-138 'Yellowjackets'.

Northrop Grumman EA-6B Prowler ICAP II/Block 89

1 Fixed flight refuelling probe, offset 12° to starboard
2 AN/ALQ-126 DECM (defensive electronic countermeasures) spiral antenna
3 Cockpit front pressure bulkhead
4 Upward-hinging glass-fibre radome
5 AN/APS-130 search radar scanner
6 Scanner mounting and tracking mechanism
7 ILS antennas
8 Anti-collision beacon
9 Lower IFF antenna
10 Radar equipment bay
11 Pitot head, port and starboard
12 Forward cockpit pressure floor
13 Rudder pedals
14 Control column
15 Instrument panel shroud
16 Refuelling probe spotlight
17 Windscreen rain dispersal air duct
18 Stand-by compass
19 Windscreen panels
20 Forward cockpit canopy
21 Electronic countermeasures officer No 1's (ECMO-1) GRUEA-7 ejection seat
22 Canopy hydraulic jack
23 Circuit breaker panel
24 Ejection seat face blind firing handle
25 Pilot's GRUEA-7 ejection seat
26 Approach indexer
27 Centre control console
28 Engine throttle levers
29 Port side console panel
30 Fold-out boarding step
31 Nose undercarriage hydraulic retraction jack
32 Nosewheel leg pivot mounting
33 Lower VHF antenna
34 Nosewheel leg door
35 Door-mounted taxiing light
36 Deck approach lights
37 Hydraulic nosewheel steering unit
38 Catapult strop link
39 Twin nosewheels, aft-retracting
40 Drag link/breaker strut
41 Port engine air intake
42 Boundary layer splitter plate
43 Nitrogen bottle, emergency undercarriage lowering
44 Rear cockpit fixed footrests
45 Handgrip
46 ECMO's instrument consoles
47 Canopy hinge point
48 Fixed centre arch
49 Starboard AN/ALQ-99F jamming pod
50 Rear cockpit canopy

51 ECMO-2's GRUEA-7 ejection seat
52 Rear canopy hydraulic jack
53 ECMO-3's GRUEA-7 ejection seat
54 Cockpit rear pressure bulkhead
55 Rear side console panel
56 Radar slew control handle
57 Boarding steps
58 Incidence transmitter
59 Intake duct framing
60 Temperature probe
61 External emergency canopy release
62 Fold-out boarding ladder
63 Ground test panel
64 Generator cooling air intake
65 Engine accessory equipment gearbox
66 Pratt & Whitney J52-P-408/408A engine
67 Electrical system equipment
68 Stair warning strip
69 Hydraulic reservoir
70 Extended chord leading-edge glove section
71 Leading-edge slat drive shaft from central motor
72 Port mainwheel bay
73 Equipment cooling air spill duct
74 Avionics equipment bay, flight control system, port and starboard
75 Control rod linkages
76 Upper anti-collision beacon
77 Upper VHF No. 1 antenna
78 Starboard inboard wing segment integral fuel tank, total usable internal capacity 2,268 US gal (8588 litres; 1,889 Imp gal)
79 Inboard wing fence
80 Fuel system piping
81 Starboard wing fold joint
82 Leading-edge slat drive shaft and screw jack actuators
83 Starboard two-segment leading-edge slat
84 Slat guide rails
85 Outboard integral fuel tank
86 Outboard wing fence
87 Starboard navigation light
88 Wing tip electro-luminescent formation light
89 Split trailing-edge airbrake, open
90 Fuel jettison
91 Starboard two-segment single-slotted trailing-edge flap, extended
92 Flap guide rail and carriage telescopic fairings
93 Two-segment roll-control spoiler/lift dumper
94 Flap guide rails
95 Screw jack actuators
96 Spoiler hydraulic actuator
97 UHF/TACAN antenna

98 Fuselage fuel tank access panel
99 Lateral control actuator
100 Fuel tank vent and supply ducting
101 Fuselage upper longeron
102 Centre fuselage bag-type fuel tank
103 Wing centre-section integral fuel tank
104 Centre-section carry-through spar box
105 Flap and slat control runs
106 Central flap drive motor and gearbox
107 Emergency ram-air turbine, extended
108 Fuel system recuperator
109 Aluminium honeycomb dorsal access panels
110 ADF antenna
111 Fuselage rear bag-type fuel tank
112 Curved (S-shaped) engine exhaust duct
113 Liquid oxygen converters (3)
114 External cable duct
115 Close-pitched fuselage frame structure
116 Dual VHF No. 2 antennas
117 Environmental control system ram air intake
118 Fuel system venting intake
119 Wing folded position
120 HF antenna
121 Aft fuselage frame and stringer structure
122 Fin spar root attachment joint

123 Starboard all-moving tailplane
124 Tailplane hydraulic actuator
125 Aluminium honeycomb fin skin panels
126 Tactical jamming system (TJS) band 2/3 receiving antenna
127 Four-spar fin torsion box structure
128 TJS band 1 receiving antenna
129 Compass remote transmitter
130 Glass-fibre fin tip pod 'football' fairing
131 Forward band 4-9 TJS receiving antennas
132 Forward oblique band 4-9 antennas, port and starboard
133 Band 4-9 receivers
134 Aft oblique band 4-9 antennas, port and starboard
135 Aft band 4-9 antenna fairing
136 Aft AN/ALQ-126 DECM antenna
137 Rudder
138 Aluminium honeycomb core rudder structure
139 Fixed vane
140 Tail navigation light
141 AN/ALQ-126 transmitting antenna
142 Fuel vent

143 Rudder hydraulic actuator
144 Trailing-edge aluminium honeycomb core structure
145 Two-spar tailplane torsion box structure
146 Port all-moving tailplane
147 Tailplane pivot mounting
148 Tailplane hinge control arm
149 Tailplane sealing plate
150 AN/ALQ-126 transmitters and receivers

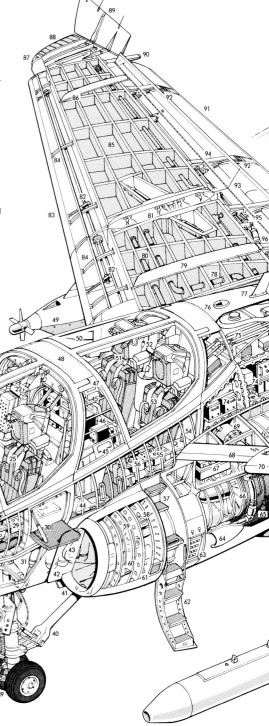

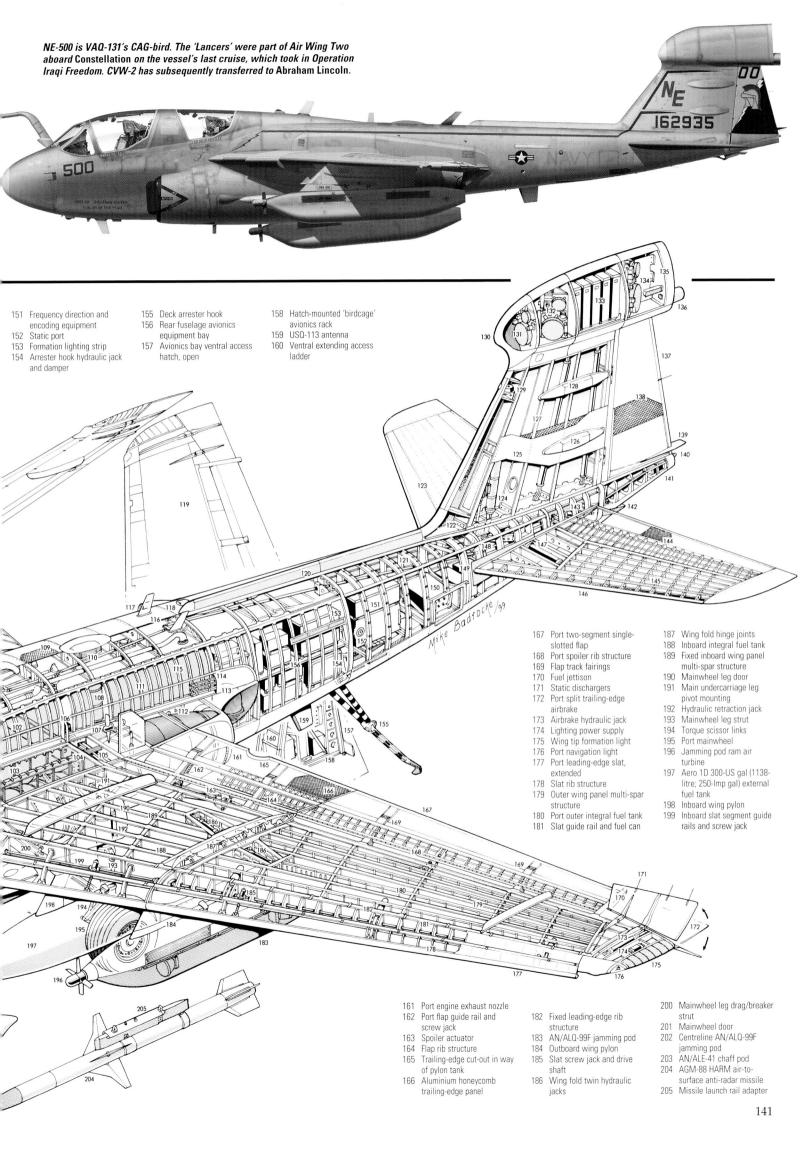

NE-500 is VAQ-131's CAG-bird. The 'Lancers' were part of Air Wing Two aboard Constellation on the vessel's last cruise, which took in Operation Iraqi Freedom. CVW-2 has subsequently transferred to Abraham Lincoln.

151 Frequency direction and encoding equipment
152 Static port
153 Formation lighting strip
154 Arrester hook hydraulic jack and damper
155 Deck arrester hook
156 Rear fuselage avionics equipment bay
157 Avionics bay ventral access hatch, open
158 Hatch-mounted 'birdcage' avionics rack
159 USQ-113 antenna
160 Ventral extending access ladder

Mike Badrocke/99

167 Port two-segment single-slotted flap
168 Port spoiler rib structure
169 Flap track fairings
170 Fuel jettison
171 Static dischargers
172 Port split trailing-edge airbrake
173 Airbrake hydraulic jack
174 Lighting power supply
175 Wing tip formation light
176 Port navigation light
177 Port leading-edge slat, extended
178 Slat rib structure
179 Outer wing panel multi-spar structure
180 Port outer integral fuel tank
181 Slat guide rail and fuel can

187 Wing fold hinge joints
188 Inboard integral fuel tank
189 Fixed inboard wing panel multi-spar structure
190 Mainwheel leg door
191 Main undercarriage leg pivot mounting
192 Hydraulic retraction jack
193 Mainwheel leg strut
194 Torque scissor links
195 Port mainwheel
196 Jamming pod ram air turbine
197 Aero 1D 300-US gal (1138-litre; 250-Imp gal) external fuel tank
198 Inboard wing pylon
199 Inboard slat segment guide rails and screw jack

161 Port engine exhaust nozzle
162 Port flap guide rail and screw jack
163 Spoiler actuator
164 Flap rib structure
165 Trailing-edge cut-out in way of pylon tank
166 Aluminium honeycomb trailing-edge panel

182 Fixed leading-edge rib structure
183 AN/ALQ-99F jamming pod
184 Outboard wing pylon
185 Slat screw jack and drive shaft
186 Wing fold twin hydraulic jacks

200 Mainwheel leg drag/breaker strut
201 Mainwheel door
202 Centreline AN/ALQ-99F jamming pod
203 AN/ALE-41 chaff pod
204 AGM-88 HARM air-to-surface anti-radar missile
205 Missile launch rail adapter

E-2 Hawkeye

Left: The VAW-116 LSO calls instructions to one of his charges on its return to Constellation. His tunic reflects the nicknames for the E-2 ('Hummer') and the LSO ('Paddles'), the latter harking back to the days when LSOs used bats to transmit landing instructions.

When the Grumman G-173 Hawkeye first flew on 21 October 1960, there could have been few witnesses present who would have bet money on the aircraft still being in production over 40 years later. Since 1964 the Hawkeye has protected US Navy carrier battle groups and shepherded their aircraft, tasks which it still performs today and will do for many years yet. It has been used operationally in numerous conflicts, and has outlasted all of its contemporaries. It has seen deck companions come and go, but for 40 years its traditional haunt at the base of the carrier's island has never been seriously threatened by a replacement.

Grumman (now Northrop Grumman) has a long history of integrating airborne early warning systems into carrierborne aircraft, beginning with the TBF-3W Avenger with APS-20A radar, followed by the AF-2W Guardian (with APS-20E), WF/E-1B Tracer (with APS-82) and finally the W2F/E-2 Hawkeye, which in its initial versions featured the APS-96 radar. The Hawkeye's strange configuration was a result of dramatically conflicting requirements: aerodynamic efficiency for long range/endurance, the need to carry a very large radar in a position where it had a relatively unobstructed 360° view, low carrier approach speed, and the ability to fit onto carrier decks and lifts. Apart from the very similar unflown Yak-44 'Russian copy', the E-2 remains the only aircraft ever designed from the start for the AEW mission

As a result, the aircraft features high aspect ratio (9.27) wings with high-lift devices for long range and low approach speed, a dorsally mounted rotodome to house the radar, a pressurised cabin to house the operators, and efficient T56 turboprop engines. To fit the confines of the hangar deck, the rotodome could be lowered by around 2 ft (0.61 m) when not in use. The height restriction also dictated the use of four vertical fins as a means of providing sufficient keel area, and yaw authority during an asymmetric take-off, without the height exceeding that of the hangar roof; the E-2's height is a remarkable 5.58 m (18.31 ft). The slender wings were fitted with a folding system which hinged the wings back while rotating them through 90° so that they lie parallel to the fuselage. With wings folded, the E-2 has a span (across the propeller blades) of 10.68 m (35.04 ft), compared to 24.56 m (80.58 ft) with the wings spread. At 17.60 m (57.75 ft) long, the E-2 is only marginally longer than an F/A-18, and

Arguably the least glamorous of the aircraft on the US Navy's carrier decks, the E-2 nevertheless has a vital role to perform, one which is central to the carrier battle group's ability to project power on a global basis. No air wing operation could be conceived without the Hawkeye acting as airborne sentinel, watching for hostile action while directing friendly aircraft. In addition to its traditional blue-water defensive role, constant development has allowed the Hawkeye to adapt to other roles which have become increasingly important – littoral and overland operations and theatre missile defence.

Above: Representing the original Hawkeye design is W2F-1 (E-2A after 1962) BuNo. 148712, the fifth aircraft built and seen here testing the fuel dump system. Note the original rounded nose profile which distinguished the E-2A/B models from the E-2C.

Below: The propellers of this E-2C leave spiral vortices behind them as they bite into the moist air. The Hawkeye regularly launches ahead of the rest of the air wing, is aloft during the course of two launch/trap cycles, and then lands last after marshalling returning aircraft.

In service for over 30 years, and scheduled to serve for at least 20 more, the Hawkeye remains a vital part of the US Navy carrier air wing. Although the E-2 has changed little externally – highlighting the basic soundness of the original design – its systems have been aggressively updated throughout its career, a process which continues unabated in the 1990s. The result is an aircraft which is set to maintain its position at the forefront of AEW&C technology into the next century.

about 6 ft (1.8 m) wider in folded span.

Fully equipped for life on board a carrier, the Hawkeye was tailored for its role with a host of new features, which included an advanced autopilot for flying precise orbits, and an unusual rudder-only turn feature, which made good use of the widely-spaced fins and was employed to keep the radar level during orbits.

E-2As entered service with the Pacific Fleet's VAW-11, and in late 1965 undertook their first Southeast Asia combat cruise. In 1969 the first E-2B conversion was flown, representing a major improvement over the A by virtue of its Litton L-304 digital mission computer. This was swiftly followed by the E-2C, which was dubbed Hawkeye II, so wide-ranging were its improvements. All subsequent US Navy production aircraft have been designated E-2C, but the latest aircraft are very different from the aircraft which first entered service with VAW-123 in November 1973. Today, this initial batch is known as the Basic E-2C.

Basic 'Charlies' were readily identifiable by a lengthened, reprofiled nose housing antennas for the ALR-59 PDS (Passive Detection System)

and a large airscoop added aft of the flight deck, necessary to increase cooling for the new mission equipment. Uprated T56-A-425 engines were installed, with ASN-92 CAINS (Carrier Aircraft Inertial Navigation System) and ASN-50 heading and attitude reference system fitted for accurate overwater navigation. Mission system improvements included doubling the number of L-304 computers and the installation of the APS-120 radar. The new sensor included many features of the APS-111 tested on one E-2A in the late 1960s, the most important of which was the improvement to manual overland tracking by the employment of 'double-delay' technology, which analysed three successive returns from a target to isolate it from the background. The radar was augmented by an APX-72 or -76 IFF system, and was itself raised to APS-125 standard from 1976 with moving target Doppler filters which effectively provided automatic overland target tracking. Communications with the carrier battle group and other aircraft was handled by five UHF and two HF radios.

Basic E-2Cs were the mainstay of the fleet until 1980, when an improved version of the

Hawkeye started to enter service. When upgraded variants began to appear in a two-stage programme in the late 1980s (known as Group I and Group II), the 1980-standard Hawkeye was retrospectively christened the Group 0. This standard introduced four important features which significantly upgraded its operational effectiveness.

Reducing the sidelobes

Most importantly, the APS-125 radar was replaced by the APS-138 with a TRAC-A (Total Radiation Aperture Control – Antenna). The new antenna design largely rectified a major problem suffered by previous Hawkeyes – large sidelobes which rendered the radar considerably less effective against small targets, especially over land. The TRAC-A antenna allowed the APS-138 system to increase its detection range of small overland targets to around 120 nm (138 miles; 222 km). The more sharply focused beam made the APS-138 far less prone to enemy jamming.

Other elements of the Group 0 1980 upgrade included the replacement of the elderly ALR-59

A Group II Hawkeye from VAW-116 floats over Constellation's churning wake. The Hawkeye is relatively docile during the approach but its wide span makes alignment with the centreline crucial to avoid hitting obstacles to either side.

PDS with the ALR-73, which provided much greater angular accuracy for the passive detection of targets way beyond radar range, and the expansion of the computer memory to 16K. Communications were enhanced by the addition of ARC-182 Have Quick jam-resistant radio. Group 0 aircraft (although not then known as such) ruled the roost for most of the 1980s, and are still in limited service today, although plans to upgrade them to Group II standard were terminated as the cost of the modification (which included a full structural relifing for carrier service to at least 2020) were not far short of a new aircraft. Fifty-five aircraft were built to the Group 0 standard.

Although it is a relatively large aircraft, the Hawkeye is very manoeuvrable on deck. The angle of the nosewheel here gives some idea of the turning circle achievable.

In 1988 the first of 18 Group I aircraft appeared, and this type entered service with VAW-112 in August 1989. The Group I had new engine flight deck instruments and revised lighting, a cooling system with 12-ton (as opposed to 10-ton) capacity, an SCADC (standard central air data computer) and improved APS-139 radar. The radar was augmented by a vastly improved mission computer system which, although still based on the L-304, had high-speed processors that effectively quadrupled the number of tracks it could follow compared to the E-2C Group 0, which could handle 400.

For the pilots, however, the main difference was the installation of the T56-A-427 engines. Rated at 5,250 eshp (3916 ekW), the Dash 427 provided a significant power increase, combined with increased reliability and reduced fuel-burn. To make it more attractive to land-based operators, the Dash 427 incorporates a low-speed ground idle setting, which had hitherto been considered unnecessary as the E-2 had been designed only with carrier operations

in mind. Although the new engines had been flown in a Hawkeye as early as 1986, it was not until 17-19 December 1991 that they were given an impressive public outing when a Group I Hawkeye (BuNo. 163535) was used to set a series of 20 time-to-height, closed-circuit speed and altitude records.

Group II Hawkeye

Significant though the improvements introduced by Group I were, they merely provided a springboard for a far more advanced Hawkeye – the Group II. This entered service in June 1992 with VAW-113 and consists of both new-build aircraft and conversions from 16 Group I aircraft. Having initially equipped the Pacific Fleet with Group IIs (leaving the Atlantic Fleet with Group 0s), the US Navy progressed rapidly towards an all-Group II fleet. What follows is a detailed description of the Group II's systems.

At the heart of the E-2's mission avionics system is the L-304 computer processing system, also known as the OL-77/ASQ. It takes inputs from the radar, IFF, PDS and navigation systems, processes the data and presents it on the three main displays. The L-304 can also receive and output data into the communications suite. The mission can be pre-planned and loaded into the L-304 by the TAMPS (Tactical Aircraft Mission Planning System), and there is a recorder incorporated for subsequent analysis of the data input. The whole mission system has an IFPM (In-Flight Performance Monitoring) system for self-test, which operates every three to four seconds.

New to the Group II is the phenomenal Lockheed Martin APS-145 ARPS (Advanced Radar Processing System) with its fan beam antenna. The latter is the Randtron APA-171 antenna array/rotodome assembly, which incorporates the IFF system. The radar provides fully automated operation with continuous coverage from the surface to high altitude. It has a single operating mode that offers simultaneous detection/tracking for both surface (maritime) and airborne targets. The radar works in 10 channels, which are automatically monitored and selected for optimum performance (to avoid

The Schoolhouse

For much of the Hawkeye's career there were two training units: VAW-110 at Miramar ('NJ', below) for the West Coast and VAW-120 at Norfolk ('AD', right) for the East Coast. Today the latter is entrusted with all Hawkeye training, operating a sizeable number of aircraft. It also handles C-2 Greyhound training with a handful of aircraft using AD-63x Modex numbers.

interference) or to combat jamming, and incorporates an AMTI (airborne moving target indicator). A major advance is the triple-PRF operation, also known as blind-speed control, which cancels the clutter encountered at certain frequencies by earlier two-PRF radars and which caused gaps in the radar's coverage. Furthermore, the rotodome can operate at variable speeds between five and six rpm (previously operated at a fixed six) for greater options.

Environmental processing

Naturally, the radar incorporates advanced ECCM (electronic counter-countermeasures), and it has an advanced environmental processing operation. The latter breaks down the radar scan (or at least that part of the scan that grazes the surface) into around 4,000 processing cells, each 5.6° in angular width and typically 4 miles (6.43 km) in length. The system identifies the type of terrain that is contained within that cell (sea, flat terrain, rough terrain, etc.) and gates itself automatically to remove the ground clutter (high clutter from rough terrain, very low from a calm sea surface). Previously, this job had been done manually.

Height-finding of targets is accomplished by using DTOA (differential time of arrival) techniques rather than by an elevation scan. Each target gives two radar returns: one which reflects straight back to the E-2's radar and another which bounces down off the surface and then up to the radar. The position of the target is known accurately because of the radar plot, so, by measuring the time difference between the straight and reflected returns, it is a simple geometric exercise to compute the target's altitude.

Equally impressive is the new IFF system with Hazeltine OL-483/AP airborne interrogator. It operates co-directionally with the radar (as opposed to operating half a revolution behind as on the E-3), making it much easier to solve multi-path anomalies. It has an increased throughput compared to earlier IFF systems, enabling it to operate effectively in a difficult airborne environment with many targets. It has an overlapping 'degarbling' function to handle multiple targets with small range separations. As it is fully integrated with the mission computer, the IFF data is therefore fully integrated with traces from the other primary systems (radar and PDS), and the traces can be recorded for later

playback. It, too, has an IFPM function for self-test.

For passive detection the ALR-73 PDS remains unchanged from previous Hawkeyes. With antennas in the nose of the aircraft and in the outer endplate fins, the PDS offers 360° coverage, and operates simultaneously in four frequency bands. Up to 250 passive tracks can be followed. The PDS receives signals from a wide range of emitters, and analyses them to determine PRF (pulse repetition frequency), frequency, PW (pulse width), scan rate and modulation type. The PDS has a preloaded threat library which stores the individual intelligence 'I-files' of many known radar systems. The precise location of emitters can be computed using triangulation (that is, by measuring the bearing of the emitter from different positions along the Hawkeye's flight path).

As can be imagined, a huge amount of data from the radar, IFF and PDS has to be assimilated by the L-304 computer. In the Group II aircraft this has EHSP (Enhanced High-Speed Processing) which allows the computer to follow over 1,600 'live' tracks, that is those produced by the radar and IFF. In addition, the system can handle an additional 800-plus GRP (geo, remote, passive) tracks. Geo tracks correspond to fixed land points (such as airfields) while passive tracks are those generated by the PDS. Remote tracks are those received through datalinks and are generated by offboard sensor systems. The system can also handle over 20 simultaneous intercept solutions.

Secure voice and datalink

Communications are handled by a comprehensive suite which incorporates two HF radios for secure voice and Link-11 air-to-ground tactical data (ARQ-34), three VHF/UHF Have Quick secure voice radios and three UHF radios which handle the functions of secure voice transmission, communications relay, Link-4A air-to-air and Link-11 air-to-ground data transmission (ARC-150). Finally, the Group II Hawkeye introduces the Link-16 JTIDS (Joint Tactical Information Distribution System).

A crew of five operates the Hawkeye, comprising two pilots and three weapon systems operators. The pilots of the Group I/II

Deck crew clear the cat as a VAW-126 'Hummer' waits for launch. The blast deflector is raised, the nosewheel tow strut is attached to the catapult shuttle and the aircraft is moments from launch. The glazed panel on the underside of the nose protects the aircraft's twin landing lights and 'traffic light' landing indicator set.

Pacific Fleet Hawkeyes

VAW-112 was one of several Pacific Fleet Hawkeye squadrons established on 20 April 1967 from the various detachments of VAW-11.

VAW-115 is the Hawkeye squadron for CVW-5, forward-deployed in Japan with a shore base at Atsugi. Here a 'Sentinels' E-2C flies past Mount Fuji.

VAW-113 became the first Group II squadron, receiving its first aircraft in June 1992. In 1993 it undertook an evaluation cruise in Carl Vinson.

VAW-116 was one of several E-2 squadrons which operated during Desert Storm. Apart from VAW-115, the Pacific E-2s are shore-based at NB Ventura County (Point Mugu).

VAW-114 'Hormel Hawgs' was officially disbanded on 31 March 1995 along with the remainder of Air Wing Fifteen.

VAW-117 was a late-comer to the Pacific Fleet, not standing up until 1 July 1974. It is currently assigned to Air Wing Eleven on Nimitz.

aircraft welcome the extra power of the Dash 427 engines, which provide a cross-bleed start facility, better single-engine climb performance and, to the delight of Navy 'bean-counters', a 13 per cent reduction in fuel-burn. The ASN-92/ASN-50 navigation suite is retained from earlier aircraft, but the Group II aircraft also incorporate GPS (global positioning system). GPS data are displayed on joint JTIDS/GPS display units on both the flight deck and in the cabin.

The three systems operators occupy the main cabin, seated side-by-side facing to port. With the consoles installed, together with seats and the racks of electronic equipment, there is little spare room. In Hawkeye parlance the cabin is known as the CIC (Combat Information Center) and has three consoles. At the centre console sits the CICO (Combat Information Center Officer), who is the mission commander. Although the pilots are responsible for navigation and safety, it is the CICO who chooses the location, altitude and orientations of patrols to fulfil the tasking. The CICO is also responsible for assigning tasks to the operators sitting to

either side, and controlling the workshare in the CIC. Communications with command authorities at land bases or in the carrier's own CIC would largely fall to the CICO.

To the CICO's right sits the RO (Radar Operator), whose initial task is to turn the equipment on, usually before the aircraft has taken off. Traditionally it was the RO's job to monitor and adjust the equipment to maintain optimum performance of the system, but the high level of automation has largely removed this requirement. He/she now acts as an airborne controller, albeit junior to the other two operators.

On the CICO's left is the ACO (Air Control Officer). The initial task in this seat is to establish communications links with other air defence elements such as interceptors and the carrier's CIC. Again this is accomplished on deck or land. When 'on task', the ACO joins the RO and CICO in monitoring aircraft and controlling friendlies.

New displays

In Hawkeyes up to and including Group I, each WSO had a round monochrome main

display, but in the Group II this has been changed for an 11-in (27.94-cm) square screen with colour symbology, known as the EMDU (Enhanced Main Display Unit). This provides a graphic representation of the main computer's processed data. Each operator can choose which information is displayed to suit their particular tasks.

A base map is often displayed, showing coastlines, political borders and special areas (for instance, 'No-Fly Zones' or missile engagement zones). GRP tracks can be overlaid, showing the positions of airfields and radar sites. On top can then be overlaid the radar/IFF data, using different symbology for various types of vehicle. Simple geometric shapes are used to denote fighters, commercial aircraft, ships and the like. Using the IFF equipment allows each target symbol to be displayed in a colour according to its status (for instance, blue for friendly, orange for unknown and red for hostile). The use of colour greatly eases the rapid interpretation of the tactical display.

Each symbol is also annotated with course, speed and altitude. Using a lightpen, a

controller can 'hook' a specific target to a friendly fighter, and the computer will automatically work out an intercept vector. For suitably-equipped fighters (notably the F-14 Tomcat), a datalink transfers the local situation display and intercept information straight into the F-14's rear cockpit without the need for voice transmissions. A key feature of the new EMDU is its 'windows' approach. This allows information to be displayed in a small window on the main screen, and can also show magnified areas of the display for detailed analysis or control work. The main display remains behind the windows. Of course the main display itself can be changed in magnification, available range scales being 25, 75, 125, 200, 300, 400, 500 and 1,000 nm.

Each operator has a central EMDU which is flanked by software, display and range scale controls to the left, and alphanumeric data entry panels to the right. Above the EMDU is the upper main display which has video distribution and intensity controls. Below the EMDU is the ADU (Auxiliary Display Unit) which displays alphanumeric track information, system status and initialisation parameters for the avionics system. A software function select panel allows each WSO full access to the hundreds of options available.

Individual controls

At the central console, the CICO has main control of the voice communications suite, and his/her console is flanked with UHF/VHF radio controls, although any of the three operators can access the radios once they have been tuned to the correct frequencies. Further to the right are the controls for the radar and IFF, traditional responsibilities for the RO. To the left of the CICO's console are the HF and datalink controls, operated by the ACO. Included in them is the new MFCDU (Multi-Function Control Display Unit) which is the dual Link-16 JTIDS and GPS display mentioned previously. Another MFCDU is installed on the flight deck, and the pilots have the use of one of the three UHF/VHF radios carried. Each WSO console has individual lighting, clocks and ventilation, while instruments for basic aircraft information (heading, altitude, airspeed) are repeated above the CICO's console.

Easy access to all of the systems controls, including communications and intercom, makes crew co-ordination much easier than with a larger AEW system, while the system is fully automated to make good the lack of personnel. Although there exists a difference in experience between the three systems operators, there are no specialisations, and each can undertake all facets of system initialisation and operation.

Unlike that of the E-3 AWACS, the E-2C's system is fully operational at take-off, and the aircraft can be 'on task' as soon as it is airborne. In the defensive role the primary reason for having an AEW aircraft in the first place is to extend the radar horizon, so that low-flying (less than 100 ft/30 m) aircraft can be detected a long way from the carrier. Within three minutes of take-off the Hawkeye can reach 10,000 ft

Above: This view shows the CIC (Combat Information Center) of a Group II Hawkeye, showing the positions of, from left to right, the ACO, CICO and RO. Group II introduced a new display with EMDU square colour main screens. The smaller screen underneath is the ADU screen. Note that the ACO is using a lightpen, which is the main instrument for 'hooking' targets.

Right: A trailing wire antenna for the HF comms system is deployed from under the port rear fuselage, just outboard of the cut-out for the A-frame arrester hook.

(3048 m), from where the radar horizon is already 125 nm (143 miles; 231 km). After eight minutes it has reached 20,000 ft (6,097 m) with a horizon of around 180 nm (207 miles; 333 km), and after 18 minutes reaches its initial operational cruise height of 30,000 ft (9146 m), from where the horizon is 220 nm (253 miles; 407 km) away. A standard patrol can last for six hours, during which time the aircraft slowly climbs as it burns off fuel. A six-hour mission will 'reach the top' at about 37,000 ft (11280 m), by which time a second E-2 will be on station during continuous operations. A defensive patrol close to base could be extended to 10 hours with a single inflight refuelling, although at present the US Navy has only a trials aircraft fitted for receiving.

For offensive operations, or defensive patrols further from base/carrier, the E-2 has an unrefuelled time on station of 4 hours at 300 nm (345 miles; 555 km) from base or just over an hour at a 600-nm (690-mile; 1111-km) radius, these figures rising to 7½ hours and 4½ hours respectively with one refuelling. At extreme

from the US Customs Service) has ended due to high cost. Nevertheless, US Navy E-2s are still tasked with anti-smuggling missions as and when required. Surface surveillance can also be targeted against smuggling, and in a combat scenario it provides a useful warning against potential raids, especially by small coastal craft.

Interrupted production

Production of 139 E-2C Hawkeyes at the old Grumman plant at Calverton, New Jersey, came to an end in 1994 following budgetary cuts in FY 1992. Work continued, however, at the Fort Augustine plant in Florida, where retrofits from Group I to Group II were undertaken. The first of 16 aircraft was redelivered to the US Navy on 21 December 1995, and this work ended in 1997. All of these updated aircraft went to the Atlantic Fleet. By this time low-rate Group II production had been reinstated at Fort Augustine and the plant turned out around four aircraft per year. Engineering work is handled by Northrop Grumman's Electronic and Systems Integration Division at Bethpage, New York. The last Group II Hawkeye was delivered to the US Navy in mid-2001, before deliveries of the next-generation aircraft got under way.

Hawkeye at war

Following the end of Desert Storm in 1991, the E-2 – like the rest of the Navy – found itself increasingly embroiled in a bitter war in the Balkans, while at the same time maintaining a constant watch over the 'No-fly' zone in southern Iraq under Operation Southern Watch. In December 1992 the E-2Cs of VAW-116 aboard USS *Ranger* also covered Operation Restore Hope, the US landings in Somalia. For a few days after the landings an E-2 provided an advisory air traffic control service for aircraft landing at Mogadishu.

range a refuelled one-hour station can be undertaken at 1,000 nm (1,151 miles; 1852 km) radius. During maximum intensity operations the E-2 can be turned round and airborne again in under 15 minutes, including a crew change and refuelling.

Far-sighted radar

At its operating altitude the Group II Hawkeye has an impressive reach. As previously noted, low-flying fighter-size aircraft can be detected at more than 220 nm (253 miles; 407 km) distance (the effective horizon), while aircraft at altitude can be seen at about 300 nm (345 miles; 555 km). Low-flying cruise missiles show up at more than 120 nm (138 miles; 222 km), while helicopters can be tracked from about 100 nm (115 miles; 185 km) distance. In the simultaneous maritime surveillance role, detection range for small patrol boats is more than 125 nm (143 miles; 231 km). Altogether, the scan volume of the APS-145 encompasses six million cubic miles of airspace.

This capability can be put to effective use in a number of ways, many of which can be performed simultaneously. The primary role is defensive – providing early warning of approaching aircraft using radar, IFF and the PDS. The Hawkeye system can then be used to direct appropriate reactions, being able to vector interceptors accordingly. A datalink can be maintained with a ground/carrier-based command centre and a real-time picture can be presented to commanders.

On offensive operations the Hawkeye is used to provide AEW cover for the attack force, warning of hostile fighters and assigning targets to the fighter escort, and also providing airspace management to ensure deconfliction among friendly units. The PDS provides a useful Elint system to monitor hostile air defence radar activity and warn of its presence. The recovery of a large strike package can be a potentially dangerous time, and the Hawkeye will effectively manage the traffic entering the pattern to avoid mid-air accidents and to regulate the spacing as aircraft return to the carrier. Similarly, the Hawkeye is very valuable for vectoring tankers and receivers to smooth the refuelling process, and in a search and rescue operation can provide radar top cover.

In peacetime the Hawkeye has a valuable drug interdiction role, although its full-time use by the US Coast Guard in this role (taken over

Hawkeyes in the Atlantic Fleet

Like those of the Pacific Fleet, the Atlantic Fleet Hawkeye detachments (from parent squadron VAW-12) were raised to squadron status on 1 April 1967. VAW-121 was one of the initial tranche of three units which stood up on that date.

VAW-124 was established on 1 September 1967. Today it is part of CVW-8 in Roosevelt. The Atlantic Fleet Hawkeyes are shore-based at Chambers Field, Norfolk, Virginia.

VAW-122 'Steeljaws' was the unlucky Atlantic Fleet E-2 squadron when the fleet reduced from six to five air wings. It was assigned to CVW-6.

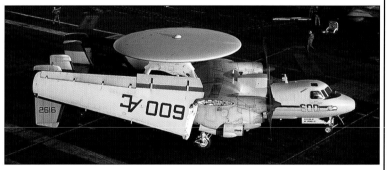

VAW-125, established on 1 October 1968, took a leading role in Desert Storm, when one of its aircraft directed two Hornets to shoot down two Iraqi F-7s.

VAW-123 aircraft feature a huge spiral marking on top of the rotodome. The unit was one of the initial three Atlantic units to stand up.

The last of the Atlantic Fleet E-2 units, VAW-126 was formed on 1 April 1969. This is the current incarnation of the squadron's 'Seahawk' nose marking.

Southern Watch involved a carrier being permanently on-station in the Persian Gulf to augment Saudi-based coalition aircraft. In January 1993 USS *Kitty Hawk* was the duty carrier, having been redirected from its earlier task of relieving *Ranger* off Somalia. It carried the 'Hormel Hawgs' of VAW-114. The Hawkeyes were used to control a series of raids against air defence targets – the first major attacks on Iraq since the end of the war. From that time, E-2s monitored the 'No-fly' zone and oversaw coalition operations, which involved sporadic attacks against Iraqi installations which threatened them.

As a fierce war flared up in Bosnia in early 1993, USS *Theodore Roosevelt* was sent to the Adriatic to help with UN operations. The air wing's first task was to cover US airdrops into eastern Bosnia. During the course of these operations the 'Bear Aces' of VAW-124 lost an E-2C, and its five crew, returning from a mission, although this was not down to enemy action. A 'No-fly' zone was established on 12 April 1993 as Operation Deny Flight, and *Roosevelt*'s Hawkeyes joined with French, USAF and NATO E-3s in establishing a 24-hour watch over Bosnia's skies.

Over the coming months operations intensified and incursions in the 'No-fly' zone increased – mostly by helicopters and small aircraft. Hawkeye crews were very busy monitoring the situation and controlling UN fighters. In September 1995 NATO conducted a major air campaign against the Bosnian Serb forces, known as Operation Deliberate Force. *Roosevelt*'s VAW-124 was involved, as was VAW-123 from USS *America*, which relieved 'TR' on 9 September. Deliberate Force effectively ended the war in Bosnia. *Roosevelt* was back in the Adriatic again in April 1999, lending the considerable weight of its air wing to Operation Allied Force, the NATO attack on Serbia which began in late March. VAW-124 was aboard with five E-2Cs.

11 September 2001

On this infamous day terrorists deliberately crashed airliners into the Pentagon and the twin towers of the World Trade Center, and a fourth crashed in Pennsylvania. Within minutes of the attacks NORAD embarked on a major operation to ground all civilian air traffic and to secure American airspace. E-2 Hawkeyes were involved alongside USAF E-3s in the major effort

to provide immediate radar coverage. In the days that followed US fighters established CAPs over and around key areas, such as military installations and cities, under Operation Noble Eagle. Shore-based E-2s, and those deployed aboard carriers sailing in home waters, were involved in AEW operations.

Going on the offensive against the terrorist organisation that lay behind the attacks, the US launched Operation Enduring Freedom on 7 October 2001. Hawkeyes were involved in the major air campaign which followed, flying from the decks of *Enterprise* and *Carl Vinson*, and later joined by aircraft from *Theodore Roosevelt*, *Kitty Hawk* and *John C. Stennis*. For the first few days the aircraft flew on typical AEW missions, but the complete absence of any air threat meant that for most of the war the Hawkeyes operated as 'airborne traffic cops', directing the flow of strike aircraft into and out of Afghanistan from orbits over Pakistan. They facilitated the carrier recovery process, and aided refuelling rendezvous.

Six Hawkeye squadrons were involved in Operation Iraqi Freedom in 2003. They were VAW-113 'Black Eagles' (*Abraham Lincoln*), VAW-115 'Liberty Bells' (*Kitty Hawk*), VAW-116

Left: A VAW-116 E-2 takes the No. 2 wire. All five Hawkeye squadrons of the Pacific Fleet are equipped with the Group II version, as was VAW-114 before its disbandment.

Below: The Roman 'II' on the nose identifies the lead aircraft of this pair as the first E-2C Group II (BuNo. 164108). This followed 100 Basic/Group 0 and 18 Group I aircraft (of which 16 were upgraded to Group II). Before E-2C production was shut down in 1994, 21 Group IIs were built for service with the Pacific Fleet. With manufacture reinstated at Fort Augustine, another 36 Group IIs were built, to bring the total of the latest variant to 73.

'Sun Kings' (Constellation), VAW-117 'Wallbangers' (Nimitz), VAW-124 'Bear Aces' (Theodore Roosevelt) and VAW-126 'Seahawks' (Harry S. Truman) for a total of 24 aircraft. VAW-117 took the Hawkeye 2000 to sea – and to war – for the first time on this cruise, although the aircraft were not able to fully use the new CEC equipment.

Hawkeye 2000

Capable though the Group II is, development has far from stopped on the aircraft, leading to the next generation E-2, known loosely in its early days as the Group II Plus, or Hawkeye 2000. Flying in some Group II aircraft is a new navigation system, CAINS 2, while a Standard AFCS (Automatic Flight Control System) has also been installed.

Far more important is the next logical step in Hawkeye evolution – the MCU (Mission Computer Upgrade). With Group II the Litton L-304 computer had reached saturation point, despite the integration of the latest in high-speed processors. To enable the E-2 to continue to develop its potential, a new computer was required. The unit chosen was the Raytheon Model 940, which is a modification of the Digital Equipment Corporation 2100 Model A500MP system and similar to that used in the E-8C J-STARS. This is a commercial computer, modi-fied for Navy use under the E²COTS (Extended Environment Commercial Off-The-Shelf) programme, which uses Ada language as opposed to the previous Assembly. The computer offers greater memory and faster processing compared to the L-304, and its open architecture offers large potential for improvement and expansion in the future.

The new computer is far more reliable than the earlier unit and, when it does shut down, is much quicker 're-booting'. The old system took around 20 minutes to get going again, whereas the new MCU is up and running in less than three minutes. Furthermore, the new computer is considerably lighter, and takes up a lot less precious room in the E-2's cramped cabin than the old equipment.

Accompanying the MCU are new work-stations produced by Lockheed Martin/APL. Dubbed ACIS (Advanced Control Indicator Set), the new displays have a 19-in (48-cm) square screen. Each ACIS is a single LRU (line-replace-able unit), as opposed to four LRUs with the old displays. The new systems allows the Hawkeye's mission profile to be pre-loaded, rather than be typed in by the operators. The system also has the memory to store worldwide maps, as opposed to data for a relatively small region.

ACIS and MCU first flew in a trials modifica-tion aircraft (BuNo. 164109) on 24 January 1997 and were evaluated at Patuxent River. MCU and ACIS were first fielded in the E-2Cs of VAW-117, which took the upgraded aircraft to war over Afghanistan in 2001, flying from Carl Vinson. New production E-2s incorporate the MCU/ACIS, while retrofit kits are being manu-factured for existing aircraft.

Naval Reserve

From 1970 until recently the US Naval Reserve manned two full air wings, each with an AEW component (E-2 from 1973). VAW-78 operated with the East Coast CVWR-20 while VAW-88 flew with the West Coast CVWR-30. Both used E-2Bs for some time after the E-2C became front-line equipment, although both received 'Charlies' in the 1980s. When the Reserve was cut back to just one air wing, the West Coast unit was deactivated, along with its constituent squadrons. Although this saw the demise of VAW-88, the Reserve then stood up a Hawkeye unit (VAW-77) at Atlanta. The squadron's E-2Cs are not assigned to carrier operations, but instead undertake anti-drug smuggling patrols, operating over the southern United States and the Caribbean. In this role the unit has replaced the Hawkeyes previously operated by the US Coast Guard.

VAW-78 'Fighting Escargots' is the USNR carrierborne AEW squadron, based at Norfolk.

The 'Cottonpickers' of VAW-88 were based at Miramar, and flew as part of Reserve Air Wing 30.

Above: Painted in high-visibility markings, this E-2C Group II is the flagship of the training unit, VAW-120. The squadron operates a mix of Groups 0, I and II, in addition to its C-2 Greyhounds.

Right: VAW-117's CAG-bird Group II Hawkeye leaps from the deck of Kitty Hawk. The extra power of the T56-A-427 engines and the extensive high-lift devices make the latest Hawkeye a sprightly performer around the deck, and greatly increase the single-engined safety margins.

An important facet of the Hawkeye 2000 is its increased capability in the TMD (Theatre Missile Defence) role, which has become increasingly important with the proliferation of 'Scud'-type weapons. Detection, tracking and classification of such missiles can be accomplished far more quickly with the new system, providing the opportunity for a realistic defence.

Sensor fusion

Another improvement developed for the Hawkeye 2000/Group II Plus is the incorporation of CEC (Co-operative Engagement Capability), the US Navy's multi-platform sensor fusion/communications system. This allows vessels to share sensor information about threats from a variety of platforms. Using a C-band datalink, CEC provides the same, expanded air picture to all nodes on the network. The E-2 becomes the airborne node of the CEC network, giving the fleet a far deeper field of vision. The CEC network also eliminates conflicting information for the same target. CEC automatically reconciles any conflicts to provide a single track for each target, easing the job of controllers. Incorporation of CEC requires the addition of a large ventral radome housing the electronically-scanned phased-array antenna of the USG-3 equipment. The antenna has a high power output to ensure that it is resistant to jamming.

As well as CEC, the Hawkeye 2000 aircraft also features fully integrated satellite communications antennas (some aircraft have a satcom installation already), denoted by a 'hat' antenna in the centre of the rotodome. The satcom systems offers secure dual-band voice transfer, with full datalink capability expected to be funded at a later date.

All the additional equipment requires a new cooling system to provide greater capacity. The Allied Signal vapour-cycle hardware provides

the opportunity to switch to an 'environmentally-friendly' non-freon coolant (R134a). Despite the considerable systems advances, the only aircraft enhancement is a new power-augmented stabilisation system which makes the aircraft easier to control.

On 11 April 1998 the first Hawkeye 2000 undertook its maiden flight at St Augustine, Florida. A total of 21 new-build aircraft was ordered (plus one for France), and 54 earlier aircraft are to be upgraded to the same standard. The $1.3 billion contract for the new-build aircraft was awarded in 1999, with the first scheduled for delivery in October 2001, followed by four in 2002 and five per year until the final delivery in July 2006. The first production system test aircraft (BuNo. 163849 – formerly a Group I aircraft) flew on 28 June 2001, while the first new-build machine flew in October.

Hawkeye 2000s first went to sea in late 2002 with VAW-117 'Wallbangers', based at NB Ventura County/Point Mugu and assigned to Air Wing Nine in *Nimitz*. In 2003 the Atlantic Fleet received its first aircraft at NAS Norfolk, where CVW-17's VAW-125 was the first recipient. The 'Tigertails' were the last active-duty squadron to

Specification
Northrop Grumman E-2C Hawkeye
Powerplant: two Allison T56-A-427 turboprops, each rated at 5,100 eshp (3803 ekW) and driving Hamilton Standard Type 54460-1 four-bladed constant-speed propellers
Dimensions: wingspan 80 ft 7 in (24.56 m); length 57 ft 9 in (17.60 m); height 18 ft 3¾ in (5.58 m); wing area 700 sq ft (65.03 m²); tailplane span 26 ft 2½ in (7.99 m); rotodome diameter 24 ft 0 in (7.32 m); wheel track 19 ft 5¾ in (5.93 m); wheelbase 23 ft 2 in (7.06 m)
Weights: empty 40,484 lb (18363 kg); maximum take-off 54,426 lb (24687 kg); maximum usable fuel 12,400 lb (5624 kg)
Performance: maximum speed 389 mph (626 km/h); maximum cruising speed 374 mph (602 km/h); carrier approach speed 119 mph (191 km/h); stalling speed 86 mph (138 km/h); minimum take-off run 1,850 ft (564 m); landing run 1,440 ft (440 m); service ceiling 37,000 ft (11275 m); ferry range 1,773 miles (2854 km)

use the Group 0 aircraft, and had performed well in Operation Iraqi Freedom. In 2004 Northrop Grumman was awarded a second multi-year contract covering a further three E-2C Hawkeye 2000s and five TE-2C dedicated trainer equivalents.

When the first Hawkeye 2000s were introduced into service, the CEC equipment merely

Two views show E-2Cs from VAW-123 manoeuvring on the deck of Theodore Roosevelt during Operation Enduring Freedom in 2001. During this campaign the Hawkeyes had little do in the way of airborne early warning, but were instrumental in deconflicting the flow of strike aircraft into and out of the theatre. Refuelling was also a big 'player' in the war – especially for the carrier's Hornets – and the E-2 crews ensured that all rendezvous procedures went smoothly.

acted as a relay between CEC-equipped surface vessels and beyond line-of-sight recipients. The Hawkeye's own radar tracks were not added into the CEC 'mix' as the software was not ready – a function of the *Nimitz* air wing being deployed earlier than originally scheduled. In the future, Navy commanders would like to see the full CEC capability being maintained over 24-hour operations. This would entail raising each Hawkeye squadron's complement from four to six.

In addition to the main elements of the Hawkeye 2000 upgrade, Northrop Grumman planned to add a passive IRST (infra-red search and track) sensor (considered and rejected some years ago). A development contract was awarded for this in 1996 and test hardware appeared in 1997. The IRST was podded, and mounted front and rear to provide 360° coverage. An upgrade to the Passive Detection System is also planned for Hawkeye 2000s, using the Lockheed Martin ALQ-217 ESM system in place of the current ALR-73. ALQ-217 is to be subsequently upgraded to provide specific emitter identification (SEI) data so that the aircraft can accurately 'fingerprint' any radar emissions it encounters.

In 1997 the US Navy fitted an E-2C at the NAWC-AD Patuxent River with an inflight-refuelling probe. It is mounted above the flight deck with pipes carrying the fuel around the forward fuselage back into the centre-section fuel tanks. At the time the adoption of probes fleet-wide was deemed an unnecessarily expensive move, but following the 2003 war in Iraq, in which Hawkeyes routinely flew to the limits of their endurance (around six hours), it is being seriously studied again.

Another improvement is the adoption of eight-bladed Hamilton Sundstrand NP2000 propellers offering improved performance and reliability, and reduced maintenance costs. Following a lengthy evaluation by VX-20 at Patuxent River, the new propeller was approved in 2003 for fitment to fleet aircraft from January 2004, the work being carried out by the Naval Air Logistics Center at NAS North Island as the aircraft go through depot-level maintenance. The Navy's contract covers 188 propellers plus options for another 54 to equip both its E-2 Hawkeye and C-2 Greyhound fleets.

In 2002 Northrop Grumman was instructed to conduct an 'alternate engine' study, examining the possibilities of replacing the Rolls-Royce

T56-A-427 currently fitted. Any new engine would have to fit the existing nacelle.

Advanced Hawkeye

Beyond Hawkeye 2000, Northrop Grumman is studying further enhancements under the Advanced Hawkeye (AHE) label, also knwon as the LEA (Littoral E-2 Aircraft). A radar modernisation programme is in place to continue the improvement of the radar's abilities. Key features of this are a solid-state transmitter, hi-dynamic range receivers, a new L-3 Communications ADS-18A phased-array antenna and the adoption of STAP (Space/Time Adaptive Processing) technology. The ADS-18A can still rotate mechanically, but also has electronic steering for greater flexibility. The radar can stop rotating and continue to scan electronically in one sector. The radar's detection range is roughly double that of the current APS-145, and it offers considerable improvements in reducing clutter in overland and littoral operations.

Another element of the Advanced Hawkeye is a 'tactical cockpit' with modern large MFD displays and a missionised co-pilot's position. The latter will make the co-pilot more involved with the surveillance tactics in addition to his/her normal flight duties. The cockpit will be GATM (Global Air Traffic Management)-compliant. Other improvements include updated mission computer, new IFF system, new generators and a new communications suite. The latter will allow the aircraft's systems to gather and fuse data from a wide variety of sources, in turn allowing the Hawkeye to become a key node in net-centric operations. It will be able to act as a forward air control platform and to ably conduct the theatre missile defence mission.

In early 2002 Northrop Grumman was awarded a $49 million contract for a Pre-Systems Development and Demonstration (Pre-SDD) phase covering the Hawkeye Radar Modernization Program (RMP). Testing of the radar got under way in the autumn of 2002, fitted into the rotodome of a Lockheed Martin

A dramatic shot captures the moment a VAW-115 Hawkeye is hurled into the air from Kitty Hawk's catapult on the first day of Operation Iraqi Freedom. Intervention by Iraqi aircraft remained a possibility, especially during the early days of the war, although the threat receded dramatically following early raids against Iraqi airfields.

Below: A feature of the Hawkeye 2000 are new ACIS displays for the three operators. These were first tested in 1997 and joined the fleet in 2001.

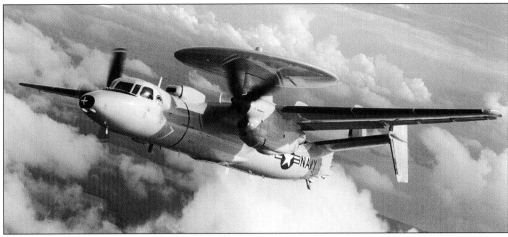

NC-130H Hercules operated by the US Navy's VX-20 test squadron at Patuxent River. The Hercules was not modified with any operator consoles, radar data instead being recorded for subsequent analysis on the ground.

On 4 August 2003 Northrop Grumman received the full SDD contract, for $1.9 billion, under the terms of which two AHE prototypes are to be produced. Current plans call for the prototype RMP/Advanced Hawkeye to be flown in 2007, with production aircraft following the year after. IOC is planned for 2011. Current plans envisage a total of at least 75 Advanced Hawkeyes being built from new, extending the E-2's production run into the 2020s.

With development of Advanced Hawkeye funded, the E-2's place on the US Navy's carrier decks through the medium term is assured. A notional replacement appeared in the form of the Common Support Aircraft (CSA) study, and other AEW schemes such as a radar-equipped version of the V-22 Osprey have been touted.

Seen outside the 'Force Test' (VX-20) hangar at Patuxent River, this Hawkeye tested the Hamilton Sundstrand NP2000 eight-bladed propeller, which is now being fitted fleet-wide.

However, none are presently under serious consideration and it will be many years before any successor could be developed and fielded.

For the moment, that day is probably more than 20 years away, and it is quite conceivable that Grumman's E-2 will notch up over 60 years of front-line service. From the outside it may well look the same, but the notional Hawkeye of 2025 will doubtless be as different in its capabilities compared to today's service machines as the latter are when compared with the first E-2As which joined the fleet in 1964.

David Donald

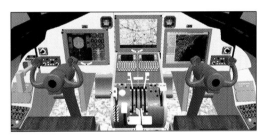

Above: Among the improvements planned for the Advanced Hawkeye is an all-new cockpit with large MFDs. The right-hand seat has a 'missionised' work-station showing similar displays to the three operator stations in the cabin, allowing the co-pilot to be more involved in mission execution.

Above: Having served as the MCU/ACIS testbed, this Hawkeye (BuNo. 164109) was used to test the optional inflight refuelling probe, mounted centrally above the flight deck.

Air Wing Two's Hawkeye unit is VAW-116 'Sun Kings'. It saw action against Iraq during Constellation's last cruise in 2003, and has since transferred to USS Abraham Lincoln.

Northrop Grumman E-2C Hawkeye Group II

1. Starboard wing, folded position
2. Upper double acting rudder segments
3. Starboard passive detection system (PDS) antennas
4. Lower rudder segments, light alloy structure
5. Static dischargers
6. Ventral fin segment, light alloy rib and stringer structure
7. Leading-edge pneumatic de-icing boots
8. Wing fold jury strut spigot
9. Aft PDS antennas
10. Fuel vent outlet
11. Fuel jettison
12. PDS receiver
13. Starboard elevator
14. Fin upper segments, glass-fibre structure
15. Anti-collision beacon
16. Inboard two-segment rudder, starboard only
17. Inboard rudder horn balance
18. Port elevator rib structure
19. Tail navigation light
20. Elevator hinge control links
21. Rudder cable control quadrant
22. Tailplane attachment joint
23. Elevator control quadrant and hydraulic actuator
24. Tailplane mounting fuselage double frame
25. Shock absorber strut
26. Retractable tail skid
27. Fuselage/tail assembly joint frame
28. Deck arrester hook
29. Fuselage tie-down fitting
30. Arrester hook damper
31. PDS receivers
32. Rear pressure dome
33. Hook port damper and retraction jack
34. Hook damper dashpots
35. Rudder cable control and artificial feel unit
36. Starboard fuselage-mounted trailing aerial reel and winch
37. Port tailplane rib structure
38. Port inboard plain fin, glassfibre structure
39. Port outboard two-segment rudder
40. Rudder hydraulic actuator (3)
41. Port wing fold jury strut
42. AN/APA-171 rotodome
43. Rotodome rotation, 5 rpm
44. Pivot mounting
45. Rotodome glass-fibre rib structure
46. UHF antenna array
47. Rotodome leading-edge de-icing boot
48. Rear support struts
49. Equipment cooling duct
50. Fuel jettison and vent lines
51. Ditching hatch
52. Cabin rear bulkhead
53. Doorway
54. Control runs
55. Chemical toilet
56. PDS power supply
57. Starboard Fowler-type flap rib structure
58. Flap outboard guide rail and screw jack
59. Aileron hydraulic actuator
60. Starboard drooping aileron
61. Aileron rib structure
62. Static dischargers
63. Drooping aileron/flap interconnecting torque shaft
64. Starboard navigation and strobe lights
65. Machined wing skin/stringer panel
66. Leading-edge de-icing boots
67. Three-spar wing torsion box structure
68. Hinged leading-edge ribs
69. Aileron cable control and operating link
70. Built-up wing ribs
71. Sloping rear spar
72. Wing fold hydraulic jack
73. Hydraulic spar locking pins
74. Wing fold skewed hinge axis
75. Cabin window panels
76. Portable oxygen bottle
77. Air control officer's seat
78. Combat information centre officer's seat
79. Control and display consoles
80. Radar operator's station
81. Hinged window blinds
82. All seats swivel to forward-facing for take-off and landing
83. Wing fold joint sloping rib
84. Engine exhaust bay venting air intake
85. Nacelle frame structure
86. Engine fire extinguisher bottle
87. Mainwheel leg pivot mounting
88. Tie-down shackle
89. Torque scissor links
90. Port mainwheel
91. Wheel swivelling link, stowed horizontally on retraction
92. Mainwheel doors
93. Drag/breaker strut
94. Hydraulic retraction jack
95. Nacelle inboard side pressure refuelling connection
96. Engine bay firewall
97. Air-cycle cooling air duct, cabin conditioning system
98. Ground operating blower
99. Air-cycle ducting
100. Wing spar attachment fuselage main bulkhead
101. Vapour-cycle cooling system, equipment cooling
102. Avionics equipment racks, port and starboard with high-speed processors
103. Wing root mounting rib
104. Wing spar/fuselage attachment joint
105. Radar waveguide
106. Central flap drive hydraulic motor
107. Wing panel centreline joint rib
108. Rotodome pylon front support struts
109. Pylon structure
110. Rotodome drive motor
111. Hydraulic lifting jack, rotodome lowered 22¼ in (56.5 cm) for hangarage
112. IFF co-axial feeders
113. IFF antenna array
114. Port Fowler-type flap
115. Flap guide rails and screw jacks
116. Wing fold hinge axis
117. Port wing fold hydraulic jack
118. Aileron hydraulic actuator
119. Port drooping aileron
120. Automatic hydraulic jury strut
121. Port navigation and strobe lights
122. Leading-edge de-icing boot
123. Port engine nacelle
124. Wing integral fuel tank, total system capacity, 7030 litres (1,546 Imp gal)
125. Overwing fuel filler
126. Antenna cable supports
127. Leading-edge control and cable runs
128. Vapour-cycle cooling system condenser
129. Exhaust duct with ground operating blower
130. AN/APS-145 radar equipment rack
131. Fuselage upper longeron
132. RF amplifier
133. Hydraulic system reservoir and flight system fitters
134. Cabin pressurisation valves
135. Port engine installation unit
136. Firewall adapter
137. Rolls-Royce (Allison) T56-A-427 turboshaft engine
138. Engine bearer struts
139. Engine accessory equipment gearbox
140. Intake duct with heat exchanger de-icing
141. Oil cooler
142. Oil cooler air intake
143. Engine air intake
144. Anti-vibration engine-gearbox mounting
145. Cowling nose ring
146. Propeller shaft
147. Propeller reduction gearbox
148. Generator
149. Engine oil tank
150. Fuselage external cable and pipe duct
151. Fuselage lower longeron
152. Close-pitched fuselage frame structure
153. Starboard side avionics equipment racks; AN/APS-145 radar, IFF and flight systems equipment
154. Vapour-cycle equipment cooling ducts
155. Radar duplexer
156. Port side avionics equipment racks; standard central air data computer (SCADC) and joint tactical information display system (JTIDS) equipment
157. Condenser air intake
158. Port nacelle access panels
159. Engine oil tank
160. Propeller reduction gearbox
161. Propeller hub pitch-change mechanism
162. Hamilton Standard four-bladed fully-feathering and reversible propeller
163. Propeller blade root cuff
164. Composite propeller blade with steel spar

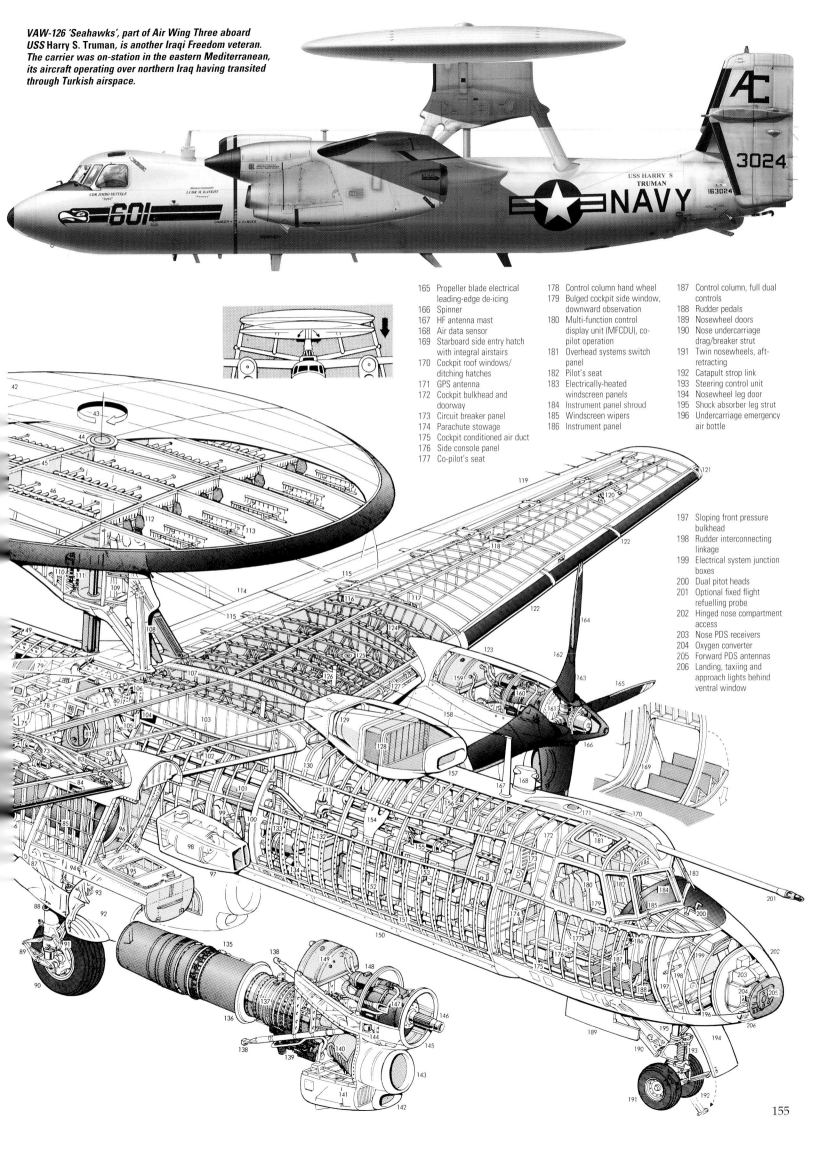

VAW-126 'Seahawks', part of Air Wing Three aboard USS Harry S. Truman, is another Iraqi Freedom veteran. The carrier was on-station in the eastern Mediterranean, its aircraft operating over northern Iraq having transited through Turkish airspace.

165 Propeller blade electrical leading-edge de-icing
166 Spinner
167 HF antenna mast
168 Air data sensor
169 Starboard side entry hatch with integral airstairs
170 Cockpit roof windows/ ditching hatches
171 GPS antenna
172 Cockpit bulkhead and doorway
173 Circuit breaker panel
174 Parachute stowage
175 Cockpit conditioned air duct
176 Side console panel
177 Co-pilot's seat

178 Control column hand wheel
179 Bulged cockpit side window, downward observation
180 Multi-function control display unit (MFCDU), co-pilot operation
181 Overhead systems switch panel
182 Pilot's seat
183 Electrically-heated windscreen panels
184 Instrument panel shroud
185 Windscreen wipers
186 Instrument panel

187 Control column, full dual controls
188 Rudder pedals
189 Nosewheel doors
190 Nose undercarriage drag/breaker strut
191 Twin nosewheels, aft-retracting
192 Catapult strop link
193 Steering control unit
194 Nosewheel leg door
195 Shock absorber leg strut
196 Undercarriage emergency air bottle

197 Sloping front pressure bulkhead
198 Rudder interconnecting linkage
199 Electrical system junction boxes
200 Dual pitot heads
201 Optional fixed flight refuelling probe
202 Hinged nose compartment access
203 Nose PDS receivers
204 Oxygen converter
205 Forward PDS antennas
206 Landing, taxiing and approach lights behind ventral window

Sikorsky
HH/MH/SH-60 Seahawk

Pitted against the Boeing Vertol BV-179, Sikorsky Aircraft's model S-70B was selected as the winner of the US Navy Light Airborne Multipurpose System (LAMPS) Mk III programme in September 1977. Developed from the US Army's UH-60A utility helicopter, the Seahawk was assigned the designation SH-60B. LAMPS Mk III was an integrated system comprising both airborne and ship-based equipment, and was very different from previous projects.

Uniquely, IBM Systems Integration Division had been named as the prime contractor for the LAMPS III programme in 1974, and was responsible for overall systems integration. (IBM Systems Integration Division – then known as IBM Federal Systems – was sold to Loral

Corporation in March 1994. Loral was subsequently acquired by Lockheed Martin in April 1996 and became Lockheed Martin Federal Systems. It is currently known as Lockheed Martin Systems Integration). Sikorsky Aircraft was assigned responsibility for the air vehicle, and served as the principal sub-contractor to IBM. Five YSH-60Bs were ordered and the initial example made its first flight from Sikorsky's Stratford, Connecticut, facility on 12 December 1979. The third aircraft, which was the first equipped with complete mission avionics, arrived at the Naval Air Test Center at NAS Patuxent River, Maryland, for testing in June 1980.

Rather than operating from aircraft-carriers, the SH-60B was designed as a force multiplier

operating from smaller aviation-capable ships, including guided-missile frigates, destroyers, guided-missile destroyers and guided-missile cruisers. LAMPS Mk III was intended to provide the ships with the ability to locate and engage targets beyond the horizon, complementing the earlier LAMPS Mk I system and its Kaman SH-2F Seasprite helicopters. Flown by a three-man crew, comprising a pilot, co-pilot/airborne tactical officer (ATO) and a sensor operator (SO), the aircraft was equipped for a variety of missions, including anti-submarine warfare (ASW) and anti-ship surveillance and targeting (ASST). Today these missions are referred to as Undersea Warfare (USW) and Surface Warfare (SUW). For search and rescue missions the aircraft was equipped with a rescue hoist, and a 6,000-lb (2722-kg) capacity cargo hook enabled it to carry out vertical replenishment (VERTREP) duties.

The first fleet readiness squadron (FRS) was established at NAS North Island, California, on 21 January 1983 and the Navy accepted the initial production aircraft the following month. Helicopter Antisubmarine Light Squadron Four One (HSL-41) received its first Seahawk on 28 September 1983 and the SH-60B's maiden deployment began in February 1985.

Left: A tiger-striped SH-60B assigned to the 'Battle Cats' of HSL-43 flies over the Hotel Del Coronado near its home station at NAS North Island.

Right: An HSL-42 SH-60B lifts off from the flight deck of USS Stephen W. Groves (FFG 29) while conducting counter narcotic operations in the Caribbean Sea in December 2003. The Seahawk is equipped with FLIR Contingency Kit (FCK) modifications, an AAS-44 FLIR being mounted on the starboard weapon pylon.

Left and right: From 1993 the SH-60B gained an impressive anti-ship capability for the SUW role in the form of the Kongsberg AGM-119B Penguin missile. The weapon is seen here being fired by an HSL-51 aircraft (left) and carried by a Seahawk from HSL-43 (right). Both SH-60Bs have received the AHP upgrade which added FLIR in the nose. Note how the missile's wings fold for carriage.

IBM/Sikorsky delivered 186 SH-60Bs to the Navy by the time production ended in 1996, and 148 remain in operational service. SH-60Bs currently serve with 10 operational and two fleet readiness squadrons (FRS), as well as a single naval reserve squadron. Depending upon operational commitments, each 'fleet' squadron operates 9-15 aircraft that are normally divided into two-aircraft detachments. With fewer ships to support, the reserve squadron operates just five SH-60Bs. The detachments generally deploy aboard aviation-capable ships assigned to carrier strike (CVSG) or surface strike groups (SSG), or are tasked individually.

While retaining much commonality with the UH-60A, the SH-60B differed significantly from the utility model. The UH-60A's General Electric T700-GE-700s engines were replaced by T700-GE-401 engines, each rated at 1,690-shp (1260-kW) for an additional 136-shp (101-kW). They were tailored for marine operations. Additionally, the SH-60B carried 592-US gal/3,848-lb (2241 litres/1745 kg) of fuel that increased the radius of action over the Blackhawk, and the UH-60's armoured seats were deleted. A redesigned main rotor system featured a rotor brake and an electrically operated folding system. The tail wheel was moved forward, and a folding tail was incorporated to reduce the Seahawk's footprint on smaller flight decks. The landing gear was also simplified due to a reduction in the landing sink rate from 42 ft (12.8 m) per second to just 12 ft (3.66 m)

per second. A recovery, assist, secure and traverse (RAST) system allowed the helicopters to be recovered in rough seas. Although later removed, an emergency flotation system was also incorporated.

The SH-60B's mission equipment included the Texas Instruments AN/APS-124 surface search radar, AN/ASQ-81 magnetic anomaly detector (MAD), Raytheon AN/ALQ-142 electronic support measures (ESM) and the IBM AN/UYS-1 acoustic processor. It also had provision for carrying 25 sonobuoys in pneumatic launchers on the port side of the aircraft. An onboard datalink allowed the sensor data to be transmitted back to the ship's LAMPS operator stations in 'real-time'.

Above: Crewmembers aboard USS Fletcher (DD 992) carry out maintenance on an HSL-45 SH-60B. The SH-60B has a towed ASQ-81 MAD 'bird'.

This SH-60F is assigned to the 'Night Dippers' of HS-5 and flies over the Mediterranean Sea in August 2002 during its embarkation aboard USS John F. Kennedy (CV 67) as part of Carrier Air Wing Seven CVW-7. Each carrier air wing normally has four or five SH-60Fs allocated for the inner zone USW mission.

Beginning in 1987, defensive systems were installed in a small number of aircraft and included Tracor AN/ALE-39 chaff/flare dispensers, Honeywell AN/AAR-47 missile plume detector and Sanders AN/ALQ-144 infra-red jamming systems. Provision for a single 7.62-mm M60 machine-gun was also incorporated. More powerful T700-GE-401C engines replaced the original -401 on new production aircraft in 1988. Whereas early aircraft featured two stores stations capable of carrying fuel, weapons or sensors, a third station was added on the 83rd and subsequent examples.

Offensive weapons initially included the Mk 46 torpedo, however, in June 1993 the first Block I Seahawks achieved initial operational capability (IOC) with the IR-guided AGM-119B Penguin anti-ship missile. The integration of the Penguin allowed the SH-60B to conduct anti-surface warfare (ASUW) missions. Initiated in 1989, the Block I programme also added an enhanced sonobuoy processing capability, GPS and the Mk 50 torpedo. A number of aircraft were also equipped with the so-called FLIR Contingency Kit (FCK), which installed an AN/AAS-44 FLIR/laser range designator on the starboard weapon pylon. The FCK also added a 0.50-in (12.7-mm) GAU-16/A machine-gun to replace the single M60.

Under the later Armed Helicopter Program (AHP), both Block 0 and Block I aircraft were equipped with the FLIR/Hellfire System (FHS), which installed the AN/AAS-44 turret on a new hardpoint on the aircraft's nose. The FHS provided the capability to fire and target four laser-guided AGM-114 Hellfire missiles. The GAU-16/A installation was also incorporated as part of the AHP, improving the aircraft's small arms capability.

Carrier version

Development of the S-70B-4 CV Inner Zone ASW helicopter began on 6 March 1985 when Sikorsky received a $50.9 million full-scale

Above: This HS-3 SH-60F is seen aboard Theodore Roosevelt *in May 2003. The carrier and Air Wing Eight were returning from a 3½-month deployment in support of Operation Iraqi Freedom.*

Below: SH-60Fs are tasked with utility missions in addition to the primary USW role. Here an HS-6 aircraft recovers Search and Rescue (SAR) swimmers to USS Nimitz *during a training sortie.*

development contract from the Navy. Referred to as the 'Ocean Hawk' by Sikorsky and designated SH-60F, the carrier-based variant shared the configuration of the earlier SH-60B, and YSH-60B BuNo. 161170 was modified to serve as a prototype.

A contract for seven helicopters was issued in January 1986 and the first SH-60F made its initial flight on 19 March 1987: it was accepted by the Navy on 30 June 1987. The SH-60F entered operational service with Helicopter Antisubmarine Squadron Ten (HS-10) at NAS North Island on 22 June 1989 and HS-2 became the first carrier-based fleet squadron to transition, accepting its first Seahawk on 27 March 1990. The squadron made its first operational deployment aboard USS Nimitz (CVN 68) in February 1991. The last of 10 deployable squadrons transitioned from the SH-3H in 1995. Although the Navy originally had a requirement for 175 SH-60Fs, only 82 were actually built by the time production ended in 1994, and 74 remain in service. Each of the fleet's 10 carrier-based HS squadrons operates four or five SH-60Fs, while a single reserve squadron has six examples.

Because the SH-60B and SH-60F were intended for different missions, the LAMPS III mission equipment and RAST system were deleted from the SH-60F. In their place the CV Helo was equipped with an integrated antisubmarine warfare system that comprised Allied Signal Oceanics AN/AQS-13F dipping sonar and six gravity-launched sonobuoy tubes. An additional weapon station added to the port side of the fuselage on an extended pylon allowed the SH-60F to carry two Mk 50 torpedoes and a 454-litre (120-US gal) auxiliary fuel tank, or three Mk 50 torpedoes simultaneously. A 105-US gal (397-litre) auxiliary fuel tank was carried internally, providing the aircraft with an endurance of over four hours. The cabin layout was revised, adding a fourth crew member, and maximum mission gross weight was increased to 21,800 lb (9888 kg).

Combat rescue

Developed in parallel with the US Coast Guard's HH-60J medium-range recovery (MRR) Jayhawk, the US Navy's HH-60H was tailored for combat search and rescue (CSAR) and special warfare support (SWS) missions. Intended as a replacement for the Bell HH-1K, then serving with the US Naval Reserve, the HH-60H was a derivative of the SH-60F. The initial requirement called for 18 examples and Sikorsky received a contract for the first five HH-60Hs in September 1986. The HH-60's first flight occurred at Stratford on 17 August 1988, and the Navy accepted its first HH-60H on 30 March 1989. Initial deliveries were made to Helicopter Combat Support Squadron (Special) Five (HCS-5) at NAS Point Mugu, California, on 8 July 1989 and the HH-60H achieved IOC on 30 April 1990.

In October 1990 the Navy announced plans to assign two HH-60H aircraft to each of its HS squadrons. Deliveries to fleet squadrons began in November 1990 when HS-2 accepted its first

example, which deployed alongside the SH-60F aboard USS *Nimitz* (CVN 68) in February 1991. By the time production ended in 1996, Sikorsky had delivered 42 HH-60Hs.

HH-60Hs are currently assigned to each of the fleet's 10 carrier-based HS squadrons, operating alongside SH-60Fs. The nominal assignment includes two or three HH-60Hs. The two reserve HCS units each operate a mix of four HH-60Hs and two SH-60Fs. Currently, 39 HH-60Hs are on the active inventory.

The HH-60H differed from the SH-60F in several aspects, besides the obvious deletion of ASW equipment. Although it retained the SH-60F's starboard side sliding door, a pair of sliding windows was installed on the port fuselage in place of an avionics bay. The internal auxiliary fuel tank was deleted but the helicopter retained the capability to carry fuel externally. Seating was provided for four crew, comprising a pilot, co-pilot, and two aircrewman. Powered by the T700-GE-401C, the aircraft was the first naval variant to be equipped with the UH-60's hover infrared suppression system (HIRSS). Whereas the aircraft was equipped with provisions for installing the SH-60B's RAST system; the equipment is typically not installed.

Defensive weapons included pairs of 7.62-mm M60 or M240 machine-guns. Cockpit

lighting and instrumentation was compatible with night vision goggles. Its electronic warning and countermeasures systems comprised the General Instruments AN/APR-39 radar warning receiver, Honeywell AN/AAR-47 missile plume detector, Sanders AN/ALQ-144 infra-red jammer and Hughes AN/AVR-2 laser warning receiver. AN/ALE-47 chaff/flare dispensers were incorporated later, along with the AN/ARS-6 personnel locator system. Its CSAR duties called for a mission radius of 250 nm (463 km) and the ability to recover four personnel. Alternatively, the aircraft was required to insert/recover an eight-man SEAL team at a range of 200 nm (371 km).

Initiated in 1996, the HH-60H Armed Helicopter Program provided the aircraft with the FLIR/Hellfire system (FHS) and either GAU-16/A machine-guns or 7.62-mm GAU-17/A Mini-guns. The latter was only installed on the aircraft assigned to reserve squadrons HCS-4 and HCS-5. Like the SH-60B installation, the extended portside pylon allowed an M299 launcher assembly to be installed on a BRU-14/A bomb rack. The M299 is capable of carrying up to four laser-guided AGM-114K Hellfire missiles.

Combat support

Seeking a replacement for the H-46 Sea Knight in April 1997, the Navy awarded Sikorsky a contract for a single YCH-60, constructed using UH-60L serial 96-26673, which was transferred from the Army. The hybrid was intended to demonstrate the Blackhawk's suitability as a VERTREP platform. First flown at Stratford on 6 October 1997, the YCH-60 conducted its first demonstrations at sea with a Navy combat stores ship on 19 November 1997. During three hours of testing the YCH-60 demonstrated its handling qualities and VERTREP capabilities, conducted deck landings and was hot-refuelled.

Ordered in 1998, the first production CH-60S made its maiden flight at Stratford on 27 January 2000. The second production example was delivered to the Navy Rotary Wing Test Squadron (NRWTS) at Patuxent River on 15 May 2000. In late 2000 the helicopter supported 40 hours of shipboard testing as part

When it is not providing rescue cover, the HH-60H can be used for transport duties. Here an HS-6 machine prepares to lift ordnance from the deck of Nimitz. *HH-60Hs are fitted with the HIRSS exhaust kit.*

HH/MH/SH-60 operators

Command/Operator	Location	Type	Tail Code
Chief of Naval Operations (CNO)			
Naval Strike and Air Warfare Center	NAS Fallon, NV	SH-60F, HH-60H	
Commander Naval Air Force Atlantic Fleet (COMNAVAIRLANT)			
HS-3 'Tridents'	NAS Jacksonville, FL	SH-60F, HH-60H	AJ
HS-5 'Night Dippers'	NAS Jacksonville, FL	SH-60F, HH-60H	AG
HS-7 'Shamrocks'	NAS Jacksonville, FL	SH-60F, HH-60H	AC
HS-11 'Dragonslayers'	NAS Jacksonville, FL	SH-60F, HH-60H	AB
HS-15 'Red Lions'	NAS Jacksonville, FL	SH-60F, HH-60H	AA
HSL-40 (FRS) 'Airwolves'	NS Mayport, FL	SH-60B	HK
HSL-42 'Proud Warriors'	NS Mayport, FL	SH-60B	HN
HSL-44 'Swamp Fox'	NS Mayport, FL	SH-60B	HP
HSL-46 'Grandmasters'	NS Mayport, FL	SH-60B	HQ
HSL-48 'Vipers'	NS Mayport, FL	SH-60B	HR
HC-6 'Chargers'	Chambers Field, NS Norfolk, VA	MH-60S	HW
HC-8 'Dragon Whales'	Chambers Field, NS Norfolk, VA	MH-60S	BR
Commander Naval Air Force Pacific Fleet (COMNAVAIRPAC)			
HS-2 'Golden Falcons'	NAS North Island, CA	SH-60F, HH-60H	NE
HS-4 'Black Knights'	NAS North Island, CA	SH-60F, HH-60H	NK
HS-6 'Indians'	NAS North Island, CA	SH-60F, HH-60H	NH
HS-8 'Eightballers'	NAS North Island, CA	SH-60F, HH-60H	NG
HS-10 (FRS) 'Warhawks'	NAS North Island, CA	SH-60F, HH-60H	RA
HS-14 'Chargers'	NAF Atsugi, Japan	SH-60F, HH-60H	NF
HSL-37 'Easy Riders'	MCAF Kaneohe Bay, HI	SH-60B	TH
HSL-41 (FRS) 'Seahawks'	NAS North Island, CA	SH-60B	TS
HSL-43 'Battle Cats'	NAS North Island, CA	SH-60B	TT
HSL-45 'Wolfpack'	NAS North Island, CA	SH-60B	TZ
HSL-47 'Sabrehawks'	NAS North Island, CA	SH-60B	TY
HSL-49 'Scorpions'	NAS North Island, CA	SH-60B	TX
HSL-51 'Warlords'	NAF Atsugi, Japan	SH-60B	TA
HC-3 'Packrats'	NAS North Island, CA	MH-60S	SA
HC-5 'Providers'	Andersen AFB, Guam	MH-60S	RB
HC-11 'Gunbearers'	NAS North Island, CA	MH-60S	VR
Commander Naval Air Systems Command (COMNAVAIRSYSCOM)			
HX-21 'Rotary Wing'	NAS Patuxent River, MD	NSH-60B, SH-60B/F, MH-60R/S	
USNTPS	NAS Patuxent River, MD	NSH-60B, YSH-60F	
Commander Operational Test & Evaluation Force (COMOPTEVFOR)			
VX-1 'Pioneers'	NAS Patuxent River, MD	SH-60B/F, MH-60R/S	JA
Commander Naval Air Force Reserve (COMNAVAIRFORES)			
HS-75 'Emerald Knights'	NAS Jacksonville, FL	SH-60F	NW
HSL-60 'Jaguars'	NS Mayport, FL	SH-60B	NW
HCS-4 ' Red Wolves'	Chambers Field, NS Norfolk, VA	SH-60F, HH-60H	NW
HCS-5 ' Firehawks'	NAS North Island, CA	SH-60F, HH-60H	NW

The primary tasks of the HH-60H are combat SAR and special forces support, and these roles are regularly practised. Above an HH-60H from HS-7 fast-ropes an explosive ordnance disposal team on to the deck of Harry S. Truman *during a training sortie, while below an HS-15 aircraft lands in the Croatian countryside during a CSAR exercise.*

of the navy's Development Testing (DT) programme.

The helicopter's designation was changed to MH-60S on 6 February 2001 in recognition of the multiple missions – including VERTREP, search and rescue (SAR), combat SAR and airborne mine countermeasures – that would be undertaken. The MH-60S subsequently underwent operational testing with Air Test and Evaluation Squadron One (VX-1) at Patuxent River between October 2001 and March 2002. It officially entered service on 8 February 2002, although Helicopter Combat Support Squadron Three (HC-3) at NAS North Island, California, had begun training aircrew in August 2001. The first operational examples were delivered to HC-5 at Andersen AFB, Guam, on 30 March 2002. The Navy had placed orders for 79 examples through 2004, and under current plans 271 will be ordered.

The MH-60S combines the UH-60L airframe with a number of features common to the Seahawk family. Besides the airframe it retains the utility model's landing gear, dual sliding cabin doors, gunner's windows, fuel system, hover infrared suppression system (HIRSS), wire strike system and provisions for the external stores support system (ESSS). Due to its ability to absorb higher sink rates the UH-60L tail wheel was retained, although the SH-60's doors – which contain jettisonable windows – replaced jettisonable cockpit doors.

A pair of MH-60S Knighthawks from HC-5 Det. 4 conducts a vertical replenishment between the USS Kiska *(T-AE 35) and USS* Kitty Hawk *(CV 63) in February 2003, during Iraqi Freedom operations. The MH-60S completely replaced the CH-46 in the combat support role in 2004, HC-11 'Gunbearers' at North Island being the last squadron to make the transition.*

Like all naval Hawks, it is powered by the T700-GE-401C engine, while the SH-60's automatic flight control system (AFCS), rotor brake, automatic folding main rotor, rapid folding tail pylon and horizontal stabiliser replaced the standard UH-60L components. Also equipping the 'Knighthawk' are windshield wash and fuel dump systems, rescue hoist, hover in flight refuelling system (HIFR) and main wheel tie downs. A newly designed cargo handling system featuring reversible floor panels was also incorporated. When reversed, each panel is equipped with rollers that assist the movement of cargo. The MH-60S features the H-60 common 'glass' cockpit. Developed by Lockheed Martin and shared with the MH-60R, it includes four 8 x 10-in (203 x 254-mm) full-colour, night vision device-compatible displays, a digital communications suite, common programmable keysets, a fully integrated GPS/INS, mass memory data storage and a rugged integrated mission computer.

Operated by a crew of four, the MH-60S can be equipped with up to 13 passenger seats and has a maximum payload capacity of 5,500 lb (2495-kg). Two 40 x 48 x 40-in (1 x 1.2 x 1-m) triwall pallets, weighing up to 4,733-lb (2147-kg), can be carried internally and the aircraft is capable of carrying cargo externally on a hook rated for 9,000-lb (4082-kg).

The initial Block 1 versions of the MH-60S are referred to as 'trucks', and are tasked with VERTREP, vertical on-board delivery (VOD) and SAR missions. The helicopter's duties will however, gradually be expanded, and effective with the 51st and subsequent example, a removable organic airborne mine countermeasures (OAMCM) capability was incorporated.

Flown for the first time in July 2003, the Block 2 aircraft feature a tow point in the lower fuselage, fittings for a removable operator console and a 400-US gal/2,600-lb (1514-litre/1179-kg) auxiliary internal fuel tank. A removable carriage, stream, tow and recovery system (CSTRS), built by Concurrent Technologies, is also incorporated on the port side fuselage. The OAMCM kit initially includes the Raytheon AN/AQS-20A sonar mine detection set, Northrop Grumman AN/AES-1 airborne laser mine detection system (ALMDS), and Edo's towed Organic Airborne & Surface Influence Sweep (OASIS) system.

Flight testing of the CSTRS and the ALMDS began on 12 April 2004 when the first captive-carry tests were conducted. The OAMCM derivative will achieve IOC in November 2005. A subsequent update will add the Northrop

The MH-60S Knighthawk first went to war during Operation Iraqi Freedom, embarked aboard several support ships alongside the last CH-46s operating in the role. The MH-60s were kept very busy shuttling supplies around the carrier groups. Here an HC-5 aircraft moves a fuel tank from Lincoln to Nimitz, while another slings bombs around the deck of Constellation.

Grumman Rapid Airborne Mine Clearance System (RAMICS), which utilises an aircraft-mounted 30-mm cannon to detonate floating or moored mines. The latter system will be deployed around 2007, along with the Raytheon Airborne Mine Neutralization System (AMNS). Both AMNS and the OASIS will be deployed from the CSTRS. The 81st and subsequent aircraft will be built to Block 3 standard, which will include all previous features along with the capability to operate as armed helicopters. Equipped with an infra-red sensor, crew-served weapons and precision-guided weapons, the Block 3 aircraft will be able to conduct SUW and CSAR missions, and support special operations forces. It is due to reach IOC in October 2006.

Multi-mission

Initially referred to as LAMPS Mk III Block II Upgrade, the SH-60R Multi-Mission Helicopter Upgrade (MMHU) entered the EMD phase during 1993. Combining the functions of the SH-60B and SH-60F in a single variant opti-

mised for offshore and littoral or inshore warfare, the programme was intended to improve the crew's ability to locate the enemy and prosecute the targets while conducting USW or SUW missions.

Sikorsky initially overhauled two SH-60Bs, comprising BuNos 162976 and 162977, in support of the EMD programme. Mission equipment was installed at the Lockheed Martin Federal Systems facility in Owego, and the first updated aircraft made its initial test flight under the designation YSH-60R on 22 December 1999. NSH-60B BuNo. 162337 was modified as an aerodynamic/structural test platform and also supported the flight test programme. The first YSH-60R was delivered to the NRWTS in May 2000 and the initial phase of Development Testing (DT) was carried out at Patuxent River between January 2000 and April 2001.

Training for the MH-60S fleet is conducted by HC-3 at North Island, California. This squadron also trained CH/HH/UH-46 crews until the training commitment for the Sea Knight ended in 2002. The Pacific Fleet has another HC unit at North Island, and one based on Guam.

Above: In its Block 2 form, the MH-60S will adopt the mine clearance role when the equipment has been cleared for use. This aircraft flew in April 2004 with the CSTRS heavy towing arm installed, from which was suspended a development AES-1 ALMDS pod.

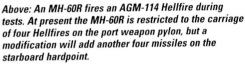

Left: NSH-60B BuNo. 162337, operated by HX-21 at NAS Patuxent River, prepares to land on the deck of USS Ronald Reagan (CVN 76) in September 2003. The Seahawk was used as an aerodynamic testbed for the airframe modifications associated with the MH-60R.

Above: An MH-60R fires an AGM-114 Hellfire during tests. At present the MH-60R is restricted to the carriage of four Hellfires on the port weapon pylon, but a modification will add another four missiles on the starboard hardpoint.

Seven additional SH-60Bs were completely remanufactured by Sikorsky as part of the first low-rate initial production (LRIP) batch. Modifications included a series of structural upgrades intended to extend their service lives, allowing them to remain in service through 2020. The airframes also underwent standard depot level maintenance (SDLM) and were equipped with the new H-60 common 'glass' cockpit. The first MH-60R test article made its initial flight at Stratford on 19 July 2001. Following Navy acceptance, the aircraft underwent additional testing in Stratford before being assigned to the NRWTS (redesignated as HX-21 on 1 May 2002). To better reflect its multimission capability, the aircraft was redesignated the MH-60R on 25 May 2001.

This view of one of the two NMH-60Rs highlights the asymmetric Hellfire carriage. The trials machines were initially designated YSH-60R, and were converted from SH-60Bs. Production MH-60Rs will be new-build airframes rather than conversions.

Due to the differences between the configurations, the YSH-60Rs were eventually redesignated as NMH-60Rs. Both of the NMH-60Rs are currently stored at Owego. The fourth MH-60R, and the first equipped with a fully operational weapon system, made its initial flight in Owego on 4 April 2002. VX-1 subsequently received the first of two MH-60Rs on 31 March 2003 and the squadron initiated operational testing phase IIA (OT IIA) during the summer of 2003. An Operational Evaluation (OPEVAL) is scheduled to begin in 2004.

Initially the Navy planned to convert 243 SH-60B/Fs to SH-60R configuration but the scope was eventually increased to include 273 conversions of SH-60B/F and HH-60H airframes. The programme was restructured in 2001 and the decision was made to procure new airframes. Sikorsky received a second LRIP contract covering six new-build MH-60Rs that will be delivered beginning in June 2005. The service plans to purchase 270 MH-60Rs and the

newest Seahawk model will reach initial operational capability in 2005.

Although the MH-60R shares a common cockpit and -401C engines with the MH-60S, it retains the SH-60 airframe configuration. Besides structural upgrades that provide a 20,000-hour service life, the aircraft features several minor changes over the earlier Seahawk airframes. Rated for a maximum take-off gross weight of 22,500 lb (10204 kg), the MH-60R landing gear has been extended 6 in (15.24 cm) in order to support the increased weight.

Like its predecessor, the MH-60R will be flown by a three-man crew comprising the pilot, co-pilot/ATO and tactical system operator (SO). It features a completely new mission avionics and weapon systems suite. The primary components of the upgrade comprise the Telephonics AN/APS-147 multi-mode radar (MMR) and the Raytheon AN/ASQ-22 airborne low frequency sonar (ALFS). The new multimode radar is equipped with Long Range Search (LRS), Target Designate (TD), Periscope Detect (PD) and Inverse Synthetic Aperture (ISAR) modes, as well as air-to-ground trackwhile-scan (TWS) and coastal mapping modes. Likewise, the ALFS provides expanded deep and shallow-water capabilities.

Although it retains the SH-60B's pneumatic sonobuoy system, the aircraft will not be equipped with a magnetic anomaly detector (MAD). It will, however, feature the new AN/ALQ-210 electronic support measures (ESM), designed by Lockheed Martin. The system will automatically interface with the MH-60R's defensive avionics suite to provide an integrated electronic surveillance, support and radar warning capability. The defensive avionics comprise AN/AVR-2 laser detectors, AN/APR-39A radar warning receiver, AN/ALQ-144 infrared countermeasures, AN/AAR-47 missile plume detectors and AN/ALE-47 chaff/flare dispensers. A Texas Instruments AN/AAS-44 forward looking infrared (FLIR) system, and AN/UYS-2A acoustic processor are also included. Its upgraded communications suite includes AN/ARC-210 radios, and satellite communication (SATCOM) capability. The MH-60R is capa-

ble of deploying Mk 46 and Mk 50 torpedoes, and laser-guided AGM-114 Hellfire missiles.

A Block I update programme, which has already been authorised, will equip the MH-60R with a starboard weapons pylon that will increase its Hellfire capacity to eight missiles. It will also add the Mk 54 antisubmarine torpedo and the updated AN/AAS-44A FLIR. Block I will also provide the MH-60R with a removable infrared suppression shroud similar to HIRSS, as well as the tactical common data link (TCDL). A new air-to-surface missile may also be incorporated.

CONOPS

As the MH-60S and MH-60R are deployed the Navy is undertaking a major restructuring of its rotary-wing organisation. This concept of operations (CONOPS) will see the total number of 'fleet' squadrons increased from 25 to 31 units. Beginning in March 2005 it will also cause the number of type wings to be reduced from six to just four, while the surviving wings will be renamed. The first squadrons will also be renamed in March 2005 when the HC squadrons are redesignated as Helicopter Sea Combat (HSC) squadrons. Under current plans the reorganisation will not be complete until 2015, when the last examples of the MH-60R are delivered.

Currently, each carrier air wing (CVW) deploys with a single HS squadron while surface combatants within the Carrier Strike Group (CVSG) are assigned small detachments from one or more HSL squadrons. Additionally, a logistic support ship attached to the CVSG carries a pair of VERTREP helicopters detached from an HC squadron. The current aircraft mix nominally includes four SH-60Fs, two

The USW role remains an important one for the Seahawk, especially since the withdrawal of the S-3 Viking from the mission in 1998. In the MH-60R update USW capabilities are retained and expanded, despite the deletion of the MAD 'bird', which is viewed as largely redundant in modern anti-submarine warfare. The aircraft retains its 25-tube sonobuoy launcher (above), while it has a new dunking sonar in the shape of the ASQ-22 (right, under test at AUTEC/Andros Island) and the latest Mk 54 torpedo.

HH-60Hs, six to eight SH-60Bs and two MH-60S helicopters for a total mix of 14-16 aircraft.

Under CONOPS the structure of the CVW will change dramatically, and the CVSG will be assigned a single Helicopter Maritime Strike Squadron (HSM) with 12 MH-60Rs. Four of these aircraft will operate from the carrier while the bulk will be detached aboard the surface combatants. An HSC squadron will divide its eight MH-60S multi-mission helicopters between the carrier and the logistic support ship, with the former operating six and the latter just two examples of the multi-mission helicopter.

Beginning in 2008, each CVSG will deploy with 18-20 helicopters and 10 HSC and 10 HSM squadrons will be dedicated to the Navy's 10 deployable CVWs. From 2012 six so-called 'expeditionary' HSC squadrons – evenly divided between the Atlantic and Pacific fleets – will detach two to four MH-60Ss with each amphibious group to provide SAR, CSAR and AMCM support. These squadrons will also

detach aircraft to deployed combat support vessels. Under the CONOPS, five so-called 'expeditionary' HSM squadrons will detach MH-60Rs aboard surface combatants that are tasked to deploy individually and those assigned to surface strike groups. Although each will operate 9-10 MH-60Rs, three squadrons will support the Pacific Fleet and two will be assigned to the Atlantic Fleet. A sixth squadron will be assigned to the Naval Reserve Force.

Eventually, 38 MH-60S Knighthawks will support SAR duties at 14 Naval Air Stations, replacing the Bell HH-1N and Sikorsky UH-3H. As an interim measure, redundant SH-60Fs will be assigned to these facilities from 2005. Five fleet readiness squadrons (FRS) currently support training, but as part of the CONOPS the FRS community will be reduced to four squadrons comprising individual HSC and HSM training units within both the Atlantic and Pacific Fleets.

Tom Kaminski

Lockheed Martin
S-3 Viking

Originally designed to serve as the carrier air wing's dedicated anti-submarine warfare platform, the S-3 became the air wing's most flexible asset in the 1990s, charged with a wide variety of tasks. By the time the anti-submarine mission was relinquished towards the end of the decade, the S-3 had evolved into a versatile multi-role platform, ideal for the US Navy's new-found littoral taskings. However, between 2004 and 2009 the service will retire its whole fleet, a victim of the budget-driven needs to reduce the number of types in the air wing.

Often overlooked, the S-3 Viking has been a vital part of the carrier air wing since its introduction to service in 1975 but, after 30 years of sterling service, it is being offered up by the US Navy as a sacrificial lamb to the budget managers. Along the way it has performed without complaint and with little fanfare, and taken a major role change in its stride.

The roots of the Viking go back to 1964, when the Navy began the search for a Grumman S-2 Tracker replacement under its VSX programme. The Tracker was an old airframe, and its sensors were not designed to counter the new breed of nuclear-powered Soviet submarines. Faster, quieter and deeper-diving than their predecessors, the new subs could remain submerged for days and cover vast expanses of ocean. Clearly a new generation of anti-submarine aircraft was needed.

Following an intense competition, Lockheed was declared the VSX winner on 1 August 1969, and was given a development contract that included two static test airframes and six (later raised to eight) flying prototypes. The first of these flew on 21 January 1972 at Palmdale, California.

Long loiter time and carrier operations were the prime drivers behind the new S-3 Viking's layout, resulting in an aircraft with moderately swept, high aspect ratio wings. The long wings meant that an unusual wing-fold arrangement was employed, with the wings being staggered when folded. The large tail gave good control authority across a wide speed range, but required folding (to port) so that the Viking could fit the carrier's hangars. Power was provided by a pair of podded General Electric TF34-GE-400 high bypass ratio turbofans for excellent fuel economy.

The Viking's crew consisted of a pilot, COTAC (co-pilot and tactical operator), TACCO (tactical co-ordinator in charge of the overall mission) and SENSO (sensor operator, primarily responsible for working the acoustic systems). At

Above and left: VS-21 was the first Pacific Fleet squadron to get the S-3B, completing its transition in April 1990 before deploying to Atsugi in Japan to join Air Wing Five. The squadron's Viking badge is particularly appropriate.

their command was a sophisticated anti-submarine/anti-surface sensor suite which comprised an acoustic system for use with a variety of sonobuoy types (up to 60 buoys could be carried), Texas Instruments APS-116 search radar, OR-89 FLIR in a retractable turret, ASQ-81 magnetic anomaly detector in a retractable tail boom, and ALR-47 electronic support measures (ESM). A comprehensive navigation and communications suite was installed. At the heart of the mission avionics was the Univac 1832 (AYK-10) General Purpose Digital Computer. A ventral bomb bay housed torpedoes, bombs, depth charges or mines, while wing pylons could mount drop tanks, unguided bombs or rockets, or air-launched decoys.

S-3As were first delivered to the Replacement Air Group (RAG, now known as the Fleet Readiness Squadron/FRS) at NAS North Island – VS-41 – in February 1974. VS-29 was the first operational unit to receive the S-3A in September. It deployed a small detachment aboard USS *John F. Kennedy* from July 1975, leading to a full squadron deployment in *Enterprise* for a WestPac cruise in 1976-77. Meanwhile, the Atlantic Fleet's VS-22 made the first full operational deployment in 1976, aboard *Saratoga*. By the end of 1977 all VS squadrons had converted to the Viking, and the last of 179 production aircraft was delivered in August 1978.

With the Viking the US Navy also completed a transformation of its sea-going anti-submarine forces, with Vikings flying their mission from within a multi-purpose air wing. Previously, Trackers had operated with specialist ASW wings aboard 'Essex'-class carriers. Initially, 10 S-3As were assigned to each squadron, although this was later reduced to eight (and in the recent past to six). While the SH-3 Sea King and battle group destroyers patrolled the 'inner zone', the Viking was assigned the 'outer zone' ASW defence role.

From 1976 three pre-production YS-3A aircraft and an early production machine were converted to US-3A status for COD (carrier on-board delivery) duties, with ASW equipment removed and cargo being carried in the weapons bay and underwing pods. Two further S-3As were converted to partial US-3A status and were designated S-3A(COD). One YS-3A was modified with a weapons bay-mounted hose/drogue unit as a KS-3A to demonstrate the Viking's suitability in the tanker role, although the Navy preferred to stay with the KA-6D and regular Vikings equipped with buddy refuelling pods.

'Bravo' Viking

By the early 1980s the S-3A's mission suite was becoming obsolete as the Soviet Union fielded increasingly quiet

The ES-3A Shadow recorded one of the shortest operational careers of any Navy aircraft. Its early demise was brought about by budgetary restraint, and robbed the carrier air wing of a dedicated Sigint-gathering capability, although EA-6Bs could perform some of the mission. This machine was assigned to VQ-5's detachment on Kitty Hawk.

In recent times the S-3 has performed arguably its most useful work as a tanker. Its flexibility in this role is enhanced by being able to receive fuel itself thanks to a retractable probe above the flight deck. As the Viking is retired, so the fleet will lose an important tanker asset, although both single- and two-seat Super Hornets can operate as tankers, carrying four large tanks under the wings and a 'buddy' pod on the centreline. What the Super Hornet tanker provides in extra speed when escorting strike aircraft, it loses in fuel offload capacity. In recent conflicts US Navy aircraft have become increasingly reliant on USAF and RAF tankers.

This S-3B of VS-24 'Scouts' is depicted as it appeared during a cruise with Air Wing Eight aboard USS John F. Kennedy.

Lockheed Martin S-3 Viking

For anti-submarine work the acoustic system was overhauled, with a UYS-1 Proteus Spectrum Analyzer Unit replacing the old OL-82 Acoustic Data Processor, and other new systems. More importantly, the S-3B was fitted with a Texas Instruments APS-137 radar. This development of the APS-116 had a slightly reduced range compared with the older unit, but introduced inverse synthetic aperture radar (ISAR) technology, allowing operators to identify vessel types and spot 'snorting' submarines with greater ease. The addition of the IBM ALR-76 ESM suite was another major enhancement, as the new system was far more accurate and sensitive than its predecessor. The ALR-76 gave the S-3B a meaningful Elint capability, while it could also be used in conjunction with the ISAR to verify identification of vessels. The installation of ALR-76 was accompanied by the fitment of ALE-39 chaff and flare dispensers, giving the S-3B a self-defence capability. Finally, the S-3B gained the ability to launch the AGM-84 Harpoon anti-ship missile, becoming the only aircraft in the fleet that could use all of the missile's advanced targeting features.

submarines. Under the Weapons System Improvement Program, launched in 1981, the Navy sought to radically overhaul the Viking's capabilities to meet the new challenge, and to improve its anti-surface capabilities and survivability. The result was the S-3B, which introduced a host of new equipment. Following prototype conversions of two S-3As to the new standard undertaken by Lockheed, the naval air depots at North Island and Cecil Field (the shore bases for the Viking fleet) accounted for 119 production S-3B upgrades.

Lockheed began its two trials conversions in 1983, and the first of them flew in its new guise on 13 September 1984. Following successful trials, production conversions began in 1987. VS-27 was established at NAS Cecil Field to become the dedicated FRS for the S-3B, receiving its first aircraft on 17 December 1987. VS-30 was the first front-line unit to get the 'Bravo', in July 1988, but it was VS-31 that was the first to deploy, in 1990. All squadrons had converted to the new variant by the end of 1994.

Left: An S-3B from VS-21 'Redtails' prepares to launch during combat operations from Kitty Hawk over Afghanistan in November 2001. The Viking is marshalled towards the catapult, its wings unfolding as it taxis. The tail will also be unfolded prior to launch.

Below: A deck crewman gets swiftly out of the way after attaching the nosewheel strut of a VS-21 Viking to the catapult shuttle. This scene was also recorded in November 2001 during Operation Enduring Freedom.

Desert Storm

It was the improved ESM suite and ISAR radar which allowed the S-3B to undertake many new roles when it went to war over Iraq in 1991. The ESM was especially useful in the weeks before the opening assault as the coalition compiled an electronic order of battle. When the air war began, the Viking's ESM provided warnings of Iraqi radars to strike packages, allowing them to alter their ingress/egress routes at the last minute to avoid the SAM/AAA sites. Another role in the early days of the war was the launching of TALDs (Tactical Air-Launched Decoys), which mimicked the characteristics of strike aircraft to saturate and confuse the Iraqi air defence system.

As the air campaign widened, S-3s were used in the Gulf region for armed surface reconnaissance, during the course of which the ISAR radar was used regularly to provide accurate identification of Iraqi coastal patrol boats. On 2 February VS-24 Vikings attacked a coastal AAA site with Mk 82 bombs, while on 24 February a VS-32 aircraft detected, identified and attacked a patrol boat. Its attack, delivered from about 10,000 ft (3048 m), was made with three Mk 82 bombs and the buddy refuelling store! Another patrol boat was sunk by a VS-24 Viking three days later.

Throughout the conflict the S-3 provided tanker services, especially around the carrier (freeing KA-6Ds to escort strike packages). Another role was support of the 'Scud'-hunting missions in western Iraq, the Vikings using their ISAR radar to search for missile launchers along desert highways.

ES-3A Shadow

In the late 1970s Lockheed proposed a signals intelligence (Sigint) version of the Viking known as the TASES (Tactical Aircraft Signal Exploitation System) to replace the elderly Douglas EA-3B Skywarriors serving in small carrier detachments from VQ-1 and VQ-2. Although TASES was rejected at the time, it was later revisited and overhauled to create the ES-3A Shadow.

By 1989 Lockheed had been awarded an order for modification kits for 16 'production' ES-3As, preceded by a ground-test airframe and an aerodynamic prototype. The second YS-3A (BuNo. 157993) was converted for the latter purpose, being used to assess the aerodynamic impact of the numerous fairings and antennas which supported the Shadow's Sigint suite. BuNo. 159401 was the first true ES-3A – with systems installed – and it flew in its new incarnation for the first time on 15 May 1991. BuNo. 159404 was the first of 15 conversions performed at NAS Cecil Field.

The Shadow mission was to collect and analyse emissions across a wide spectrum, but concentrating on radars and communications. The crew consisted of a pilot (EW Aircraft Commander) in the left-hand seat, EW Combat Co-

ordinator in the right-hand seat (which did not have flight controls), and two EW operators or cryptologic tacticians behind. The ES-3 was intended to be incorporated into the BGPHES (Battle Group Passive Horizon Extension System – 'big fees') network, which effectively expanded the carrier group's passive detection capability, but not all aircraft/vessels received the necessary datalink equipment. ES-3As also routinely carried buddy refuelling pods to augment the air wing's other tanker assets.

Below: VS-38's CAG-bird flies in the pattern near Constellation in the Arabian Gulf in late March 2003, during Iraqi Freedom. The squadron undertook a few precision attacks with Maverick missiles against both land and maritime targets.

On 1 May 2003 President George W. Bush flew as co-pilot on 'NAVY 1', an S-3B of VS-35 'Blue Wolves'. After landing aboard USS Abraham Lincoln, *which was returning from a 10-month deployment to the Arabian Gulf, President Bush addressed the nation to announce the end of the 'combat phase' of Iraqi Freedom. Bush became the first incumbent President to trap aboard a carrier.*

Rather than being allocated to VQ-1 and VQ-2, which continued to operate the land-based EP-3E Aries II in the Sigint role, the Shadow was assigned to two new squadrons: VQ-5 'Sea Shadows' at Agana (Guam) to serve the Pacific Fleet's needs, and VQ-6 'Black Ravens' at Cecil Field for Atlantic Fleet duty. Each squadron had eight aircraft and was divided into detachments, which were deployed with two aircraft to each of the active air wings.

VQ-5's Det Alpha was the first unit to get the ES-3A, on 22 May 1993, and it undertook the first deployment when it joined the air wing aboard *Independence*. In 1994 VQ-5 also moved to North Island to join the rest of the Pacific S-3 community, although Det 5 was permanently assigned to Air Wing Five and its forward deployment base at Atsugi in Japan. In the Atlantic Fleet, VQ-6 also undertook its first operational deployment in 1993 with a detachment to USS *America*.

In service the Shadow was heavily utilised. It was heavier than the S-3B and was based on some of the oldest Viking airframes. Employment in the heavy tanking role also further ate into the limited remaining fatigue life. Its continued supportability was further undermined when the Pentagon outlined its Joint Airborne Sigint Architecture (JASA) system, which would bring the Sigint assets of all services into step with each other. Rather than spend the money necessary to keep the ES-3s airworthy and modified to meet JASA requirements, the Navy announced in June 1998 that it would scrap the entire fleet. After a very short career of just six years, the Shadow left the fleet in September 1999. The gap left by its withdrawal was covered by land-based EP-3Es and other Sigint platforms.

Changing roles

In the meantime, the S-3 community had been facing up to new challenges. From Desert Storm onwards the role of the S-3B changed dramatically. In the post-Cold War era there were no submarines to chase, while attentions turned firmly to littoral warfare. As the USW (under-sea warfare) mission waned in importance, so the Viking was re-roled into what the Navy termed sea control (in 1993 the VS squadrons changed their designations to Sea Control Squadrons).

Sea control was a generic term to cover a variety of tasks. Surveillance formed a major part of this, employing the S-3B's ISAR radar to plot and identify shipping, especially in coastal waters. Electronic surveillance was also performed, using the ALR-76 ESM. The Viking increasingly monitored land regions. It also strengthened its anti-surface attack capabilities – against both ships and coastal targets – with the addition of the AGM-65 Maverick and AGM-84H SLAM-ER. CSAR-coverage, chaff-laying, decoy-launching and mine-sowing were also entrusted to the Viking. Inflight

A VS-38 Viking is about to launch from Constellation *on 20 March 2003. As well as its buddy refuelling pod, it carries a single AGM-65 Maverick. The day before, VS-38 had participated in an attack on Saddam Hussein's presidential yacht with this weapon.*

refuelling rose in importance as the number of KA-6D tankers dwindled.

These missions were often flown simultaneously, resulting in numerous 'swing' loadouts. It was not unusual to see S-3s armed with a Maverick, SLAM-ER or Harpoon on one wing and a D-704 or later ARS 31-301 buddy refuelling store on the other. The buddy pod was carried on most missions, the Viking refuelling other aircraft after launch, then continuing with its own tasks, before tanking other aircraft on their return. Additionally, the Viking would also carry chaff and flares, including the ALQ-190 AIRBOC rapid-blooming chaff store.

Maverick capability was first added in 1996 with the conversion of four aircraft to carry the AGM-65F imaging infra-red version of the missile, giving the Viking a capability against land targets, and also against the small patrol craft which are the main targets in littoral warfare. The quartet was first deployed with VS-22 to the Persian Gulf for Southern Watch operations. Further conversions followed the generally successful introduction of the missile. Later, the AGM-65E laser-guided version became available, requiring off-board designation – mainly provided by F/A-18 Hornets.

Development of the Viking in the 1990s centred on a number of 'proof-of-concept' aircraft which introduced new capabilities based on the S-3's mission avionics suite. Outlaw Viking covered the addition of OASIS equipment. OASIS integrated the data from all the Viking's sensors into a single tactical plot, which was then datalinked to the battle group command centre to provide commanders with an enhanced situation display at over-the-horizon ranges. Although OASIS was discontinued, the results were fed into the US Navy's current CEC programme. Beartrap Viking and Orca Viking were two USW enhancement programmes, the first classified and with no hardware changes, and the second covering new submarine detection equipment, including a laser ranger and a surface SAR radar. Additional programmes were the Calypso Viking, a proposal for an anti drug-smuggling upgrade with a variety of sensors, for use in the Caribbean, and the Brown Boy Viking, reportedly used to drop seismic sensors to monitor road traffic in Bosnia under Project Aladdin.

Gray Wolf was the best-known of the 'proof-of-concept' S-3s. The programme added a Norden APG-76 synthetic aperture radar in a wing pod, interfaced with GPS/INS, to give the Viking a 'mini-J-STARS' capability for overland

High over the Pacific Ocean in June 2004, a VS-33 S-3B pilot looks out at a squadron-mate armed with an AGM-84 Harpoon missile. Offering over-the-horizon, all-weather anti-ship capability, the Harpoon (and its SLAM-ER land attack derivative) is an important weapon in the Viking's repertoire. VS-33 was embarked aboard USS Carl Vinson (CVN 70). At the time Vinson and Carrier Air Wing Nine were operating off the coast of southern California, conducting carrier qualifications and training in preparation for their next deployment.

S-3B Viking fleet status, 2004

Unit	Base	Air Wing	Carrier	Notes
VS-21 'Redtails'	NAF Atsugi	CVW-5	*Kitty Hawk*	to deactivate February 2005
VS-22 'Checkmates'	NAS Jacksonville	CVW-3	*Harry S. Truman*	to deactivate January 2009
VS-24 'Scouts'	NAS Jacksonville	CVW-8	*Theodore Roosevelt*	to deactivate January 2007
VS-29 'Dragonfires'	*NAS North Island*	*(CVW-11)*	*(Nimitz)*	*deactivated 30 April 2004*
VS-30 'Diamondcutters'	NAS Jacksonville	CVW-17	*John F. Kennedy*	to deactivate December 2005
VS-31 'Topcats'	NAS Jacksonville	CVW-7	*George Washington*	to deactivate May 2008
VS-32 'Maulers'	NAS Jacksonville	CVW-1	*Enterprise*	to deactivate May 2007
VS-33 'Screwbirds'	NAS North Island	CVW-9	*Carl Vinson*	to deactivate September 2007
VS-35 'Blue Wolves'	NAS North Island	CVW-14	*John Stennis*	to deactivate March 2005
VS-38 'Red Griffins'	*NAS North Island*	*(CVW-2)*	*(Abraham Lincoln)*	*deactivated 30 April 2004*
VS-41 'Shamrocks'	NAS North Island	Fleet Readiness Squadron		to deactivate September 2007

S-3B specification

Wings: span 68 ft 8 in (20.93 m); width folded 29 ft 6 in (8.99 m); area 598 sq ft (55.56 m²)
Fuselage: length 53 ft 4 in (16.26 m), or 67 ft 4 in (20.52 m) with MAD boom extended; height 22 ft 9 in (6.93 m), or 15 ft 3 in (4.65 m) with tail folded
Powerplant: two General Electric TF34-GE-400B turbofans, each rated at 9,275 lb (41.26 kN)
Weights: empty 26,650 lb (12088 kg); maximum take-off 52,540 lb (23832 kg)
Fuel and load: maximum internal fuel 12,863 lb (5835 kg); external fuel 2,025 lb (919 kg); maximum ordnance 7,000 lb (3175 kg) on two underwing hardpoints and in internal bay
Performance: maximum speed 506 mph (814 km/h) at sea level; ferry range 3,454 miles (5558 km); operational radius 1,088 miles (1751 km); endurance 7 hours 30 minutes; maximum rate of climb at sea level 4,200 ft (1280 m) per minute; service ceiling 35,000 ft (10670 m)

A Plane Captain assigned to the 'Fighting Redtails' of Sea Control Squadron Twenty One (VS-21) secures 'his' S-3B, which is loaded with CBU-99 anti-tank cluster bombs, just prior to flight operations from USS Kitty Hawk (CV 63). Although the accent is now on precision attacks, the Viking's accurate navigation suite makes it a useful free-fall bomber to augment the air wing's Hornets.

surveillance. Gray Wolf could scan large areas of land to gain a general plot, and then use Doppler beam sharpening and SAR in 'spotlight' modes for high-resolution radar imaging. A moving target indicator was also included. Gray Wolf proved to be very successful in exercises but development was not pursued.

In 1998 the US Navy finally relieved the S-3 of its USW commitments, the anti-submarine equipment being removed from that time, as was the enlisted sensor operator. The threat posed by submarines had reduced enormously, and could be handled more effectively by a mix of land-based aircraft (P-3 Orion), surface vessels and inner zone USW assets (SH-60/MH-60 Seahawk). The Viking maintained its place on the carrier decks, for a while at least, by being tasked with sea control missions with additional overland surveillance tasks. Most importantly, however, the Viking remained the air wing's only tanker asset, a position it had held since the retirement of the KA-6D Intruder at the end of 1996.

Viking twilight

However, in an era of shrinking budgets, the S-3 community came under ever closer scrutiny to join the F-14 Tomcat as a candidate for retirement. While the Viking still had much to offer – especially its ISAR capability – its benefits were not considered significant enough to warrant the expense of maintaining a separate type, and it was earmarked for retirement in the first decade of the new century.

In April 2004 the 107-aircraft Viking fleet entered the final draw-down phase with the disbandment of the first two Pacific Fleet units (VS-29 and VS-38). S-3B squadrons are being disbanded at roughly the same rate as air wings

gain new F/A-18E/F Super Hornet squadrons. The Super Hornet is taking over the Viking's refuelling role, offering a much faster tanker able to accompany strike packages, albeit at a reduction in fuel offload capability. The Viking's other roles have also largely been assumed by the F/A-18. Details of the Navy's plans for the retirement of the S-3 are given in the accompanying squadron table.

Before the draw-down got under way, the Viking went to war over Afghanistan in 2001, and again as part of the large coalition force which attacked Iraq in March 2003. Operation Enduring Freedom saw the operational debut of a trials programme known as SSU (Sensor Systems Upgrade). This single aircraft (BuNo. 159766) was fitted with advanced communications links and sensors to provide a platform for time-sensitive targeting and surveillance. Visible differences are a circular JTIDS antenna on the aircraft's spine and a Wescam ASX-4 steerable FLIR turret under the port central fuselage. The radar has extra modes and is designated APS-137(V)5. The key ability of the SSU machine is to provide real-time video stream into command centres or stations that could be deployed with ground forces. The aircraft was undergoing evaluation aboard *Enterprise* and *Carl Vinson* when Operation Enduring Freedom was launched.

Each of the carriers involved in Iraqi Freedom in 2003 embarked eight S-3Bs, and for the most part they were used as tankers. On a number of occasions, however, the Viking got to fire in anger. The first instance was on 19 March when an S-3 from VS-38 aboard *Constellation* successfully fired an AGM-65E Maverick against Saddam Hussein's presidential yacht – essentially a small cruise liner. Designation was provided by an F/A-18, which the S-3 also refuelled during the mission.

An S-3B Viking assigned to the 'Maulers' of Sea Control Squadron Three Two (VS-32) launches from the flight deck of USS Enterprise (CVN 65) in June 2004. Enterprise was one of seven aircraft-carriers involved in Summer Pulse 2004. This exercise involved the simultaneous deployment of seven aircraft-carrier strike groups (CSGs), demonstrating the ability of the Navy to provide credible combat power across the globe, in five theatres, with other US, allied and coalition military forces. Summer Pulse was the Navy's first deployment under its new Fleet Response Plan (FRP).

Vikings often flew with either an AGM-65E or SLAM-ER loaded, as well as a pair of Mk 82s in the bomb bay, but the call to action came all too infrequently for the crews. On 25 March VFA-151 Hornets designated a target for an S-3B Maverick shot – the first time the Viking used Maverick for an overland strike.

The single SSU Viking was dispatched to the Gulf, arriving just 13 days after its test programme had been completed, in time to begin operations on 15 April with VS-29 aboard *Nimitz*. The value of the system became rapidly obvious, the secure voice and real-time video feed being in constant demand, especially to reconnoitre along highways ahead of advancing ground forces. The SSU aircraft remained in-theatre after the war.

In the aftermath of Iraqi Freedom an unusual task fell to a Viking. VS-35's CAG-bird landed on board USS *Abraham Lincoln* as it returned to US waters, with President George W. Bush as co-pilot. The aircraft used the callsign NAVY 1, which was also painted on the side of the aircraft. This distinguished S-3 has been given a place in the Naval Aviation Museum at Pensacola, Florida.

New life for the Viking?

By January 2009 the S-3 is scheduled to have been completely retired from US Navy service. When built, the Viking was designed with an airframe life of 13,000 hours and 3,000 catapult launches, and the current average of the fleet is around 9,000 hours. A Lockheed Martin fatigue study, conducted between 2001 and 2003, revealed lower than expected fatigue levels, and the company believes that, with a minor amount of modification, the S-3Bs can be good for around 17,750 hours. This, of course, leaves a large number of aircraft with many thousands of useful hours remaining after they have been retired.

Thus, the Viking has become a candidate for export and other duties. Venezuela was very interested in the S-3, but continuing political unrest has ruled out any purchase for the foreseeable future. In the meantime, in 2004 Bulgaria emerged as a serious sales prospect. It is looking for aircraft to equip a maritime strike/surveillance unit to patrol the Black Sea, and has requested information concerning the supply of surplus S-3s. Another role for which the Viking is being considered is fire-fighting, as a means of fulfilling the US Forest Service's need for modern aerial tankers to replace the elderly prop-driven fleet, which was grounded in 2004.

David Donald

Above: The boxy shape of the Viking will be seen around the US Navy's carrier decks for a few more years yet, but the Viking fleet's planned drawdown began in the spring of 2004. Excellent avionics systems and a good endurance have allowed the S-3 to continue to be a versatile and useful asset, despite the withdrawal of its primary role (USW).

Left: An S-3B Viking assigned to the 'Blue Wolves' of VS-35 prepares to make an arrested landing aboard USS John C. Stennis in March 2004. Stennis and its embarked Air Wing Fourteen were at sea conducting training exercises.

Northrop Grumman C-2 Greyhound

The propellers of a VRC-30 C-2A churn the moist air as it departs from USS Carl Vinson. The Greyhound is receiving the eight-bladed NP2000 propeller that is also being fitted to the Hawkeye.

authorise production of 39 new Greyhounds in 1982. The first new C-2A flew on 4 February 1985, with deliveries to VAW-120 at NAS Norfolk, Virginia, commencing in June 1985. All had been delivered by 1989.

Squadron service

The C-2A entered squadron service with VRC-50 at Naval Air Facility Atsugi, Japan, on 6 December 1966 and was immediately put to work in support of operations in Southeast Asia. Greyhounds were also assigned to fleet logistic support squadrons VR-24 at Naval Air Station Sigonella, Italy, VRC-30 at NAS North Island, California, and VRC-40 at NAS Norfolk, Virginia.

In the post-Cold War drawdown of US Navy forces, the COD fleet was rationalised. The Navy turned away from having forward-deployed COD squadrons supporting aircraft-carriers as they arrived in the theatre in favour of a scheme under which a squadron on each coast provided a detachment for each carrier air wing as it embarked for an operational cruise. Thus, the two overseas squadrons – VRC-50 and VR-24 – were disbanded. The Mediterranean-based VR-24 'Lifting Eagles' closed down in January 1993, while WestPac-based VRC-50 was disestablished at the end of September 1994. Shortly before this disbandment, VRC-50 also lost the US-3A Vikings it had flown in the COD role. Today, the Pacific Fleet Greyhound squadron (VRC-30) maintains a permanent forward-deployed detachment at Atsugi in support of Air Wing Five.

Greyhounds are typically deployed aboard US Navy aircraft-carriers in two-aircraft detachments, accumulating approximately 1,000 flight hours, transporting about 5,000 passengers and delivering about one million pounds of cargo during a typical six-month period. They typi-

The Greyhound was designed to transport personnel and cargo between land bases and deployed aircraft-carriers in the carrier onboard delivery (COD) role. Development of the C-2A began in May 1962 and the prototype flew for the first time on 18 November 1964.

Developed from the airframe of the E-2A, the C-2A retains the Hawkeye's wing but has a larger, deeper fuselage and is equipped with an aft cargo ramp. Although the Hawkeye's empennage is retained, it has been modified with dihedral eliminated from the tailplanes, with the result that the vertical fins are vertically aligned, rather than canted inwards. This was made possible by the lack of the Hawkeye's rotodome and the smoother flow of air over the

Here comes the mail – a VRC-40 C-2A traps aboard USS George Washington (CVN 73) in April 2004, while 'GW' was sailing on Iraqi Freedom duties. The Greyhound is a major morale booster to the ship's complement: not only does it bring in the mail but it also provides transport for compassionate evacuations or medical emergencies.

tail which resulted. Fuel capacity was also increased, and the nosewheel was strengthened to permit operations at higher weights.

Two flying prototype C-2As and a static test airframe were produced using E-2A airframes as a basis, and 17 production examples followed between 1966 and 1967. A second production lot of 12 aircraft was cancelled. The aircraft were powered by two 4,050-shp (3020-kW) Allison T56-A8B turboprop engines. Between 1985 and 1990 39 new C-2As were built. Externally identical to the original aircraft, the new Greyhounds differed in being equipped with modern avionics, improved structure and landing gear, a new auxiliary power unit (APU) and more powerful T56-A-425 turboprops.

Although Naval Air Rework Facility (NARF) North Island carried out a service life extension programme (SLEP) on 12 C-2As between 1979 and 1982, high utilisation rates within the C-2A fleet, combined with the need to replace the ageing C-1A Trader, prompted the Navy to

Left: The Greyhound holds a rare distinction of having been put back into production, and the type will serve in the COD role for many years yet. This VRC-40 aircraft is taking off from USS George Washington.

Below: A wide-angle shot captures a VRC-40 Greyhound leaping from the deck of the Navy's newest carrier – USS Ronald Reagan (CVN 76). In June 2004 Reagan transferred to the Pacific Fleet after the completion of sea trials in the Atlantic.

cally fly ashore when the carrier has reached its operating location, maintaining a shuttle service between ship and shore.

Training for the Greyhound fleet is now handled only by VAW-120 at Chambers Field, Norfolk, which also acts as the Hawkeye FRS. Until Hawkeye/Greyhound training was consolidated at Norfolk in September 1994, VAW-110 'Firebirds' also flew C-2s and E-2s in the FRS role at Miramar.

Assigned to the carrier on-board delivery role, the C-2A is known affectionately as 'COD' and operates as both a passenger and cargo transport, connecting the carrier battle group with support units on land. The aircraft is designed to carry priority cargo such as jet engines. The large aft cargo ramp and powered winch allow straight-in loading and unloading of cargo. A cage system provides a means for restraining loads during carrier launches and arrested landings. The Greyhound is also equipped to accept up to 20 litter patients in medical evacuation missions. Its three-man crew includes a pilot, co-pilot and loadmaster.

In 2002 the C-2 fleet began a service life extension programme, which involves replacement of the wiring looms, installation of ARC-210 radios and the addition of ground proximity and traffic collision avoidance systems, as well as structural modifications to prolong life to 36,000 landings and 15,000 hours. The first 'SLEPed' Greyhound (BuNo. 162169) flew again in early 2004. The C-2 is also receiving the eight-bladed NP2000 propeller, as fitted to the E-2C Hawkeye. They are being fitted at the Naval Air Depot at NAS North Island, California, as the Greyhounds cycle through depot-level maintenance.

Grumman C-2A Greyhound
Wing: span 80 ft 7 in (24.56 m) or 29 ft 4 in (8.94 m) folded; aspect ratio 9.27; area 700 sq ft (65.03 m²)
Fuselage: length 57 ft 7 in (17.32 m); height 16 ft 10.5 in (4.84 m), tailplane span 26 ft 2.45 in (7.99 m)
Powerplant: two Rolls-Royce (Allison) T56-A-425 turboprops, each rated at 4,910 shp (3661 kW)
Weights: basic empty 36,346 lb (16486 kg); normal

take-off 52,540 lb (23832 kg); maximum take-off 54,354 lb (24655 kg)
Fuel and load: fuel 1,824 gal (6905 litres); passengers 28; cargo 10,000 lb (4536 kg)
Performance: maximum speed 345 mph (556 km/h) at 12,000 ft (3657 m); normal range 1,106 miles (1780 km) with a 10,000 lb (4536 kg) load; maximum rate of climb 2,600 ft (796 m) per minute at sea level; service ceiling: 30,000 ft (9144 m)

C-2A Greyhound squadrons

Unit	Base	Notes
VAW-120 'Greyhawks'	NAS Norfolk	Fleet Readiness Squadron
VRC-30 'Providers'	NAS North Island	Pacific Fleet carriers
VRC-30 Det 5	NAF Atsugi	*Kitty Hawk*
VRC-40 'Rawhides'	NAS Norfolk	Atlantic Fleet carriers

Greasing the wheels of war: above a C-2A from VRC-40's Det 5 taxis towards the catapult with its wings still folded aboard Roosevelt during Iraqi Freedom operations in the eastern Mediterranean, while at right mail and supplies are unloaded from another VRC-40 Greyhound on Enterprise during Operation Enduring Freedom.

Sikorsky MH-53E Sea Dragon

Development of an AMCM (airborne mine countermeasures) version of the three-engined Sikorsky S-80 (CH-53E) got under way in 1980. The resulting MH-53E Sea Dragon combined the greater lifting/pulling power of the S-80 with the mine-sweeping gear of the RH-53D, which was then in use in the role. A prototype was produced by modifying a single CH-53E (BuNo. 161395) to YMH-53E standard, in which form it first flew on 23 December 1981. As well as the towing gear for the mine-sweeping sleds, the YMH-53E also featured prominent rear-view mirrors carried on stalks either side of the forward fuselage. In 1983 huge sponsons were added which raised internal fuel capacity from 1,017 to 3,200 US gal (3850 to 12113 litres). These gave the MH-53E the ability to sweep for mines for over four hours when operating 30 minutes from base.

In order to tow mine-sweeping sleds, the MH-53E is fitted with a tow boom rated for a tension of 30,000 lb (13608 kg) and a 450-ft (137-m) steel cable. Extra features of the flight control system are functions which automatically maintain towing tension and hold offset towing lines. The standard flight crew of three is augmented by three to five enlisted crew members whose job it is to deploy and retrieve the mine-clearance equipment. They also man the two 0.5-in (12.7-mm) machine-guns which are used to detonate mines which have been brought to the surface.

A production MH-53E was first flown in June 1986 and deliveries to two operational AMCM squadrons began in April 1988. The two mine-sweeping squadrons, HM-14 and HM-15, are today both administered by the Atlantic Fleet. HM-15 was previously at Alameda, but moved to Corpus Christi to be co-located with Mine Warfare Command. HM-15 was due to join it, but it remains at Chambers Field, Norfolk. The squadrons are unique as they are joint active-duty/Reserve units, the Naval Reserve's mine warfare squadrons HM-18 and HM-19 having been deactivated in the 1990s.

For some time the MH-53Es were deployed aboard the Navy's dedicated mine warfare vessel – USS *Inchon*. This ship was retired in June 2002 without replacement. The MH-53E fleet would deploy aboard other vessels, such as aircraft-carriers and assault ships, if required. The lifting power of the Sea Dragon is also greatly appreciated in the VOD (vertical onboard delivery) role, and the type is occasionally seen operating from aircraft-carriers. HC-4 at Sigonella uses MH-53Es exclusively for VOD tasks in the Mediterranean theatre. These aircraft are surplus to the Navy's mine-sweeping needs.

The Sea Dragon is destined for replacement in the mine-clearing role by the MH-60S Block 2 Knighthawk, which is undergoing tests in 2004. It is due to be fielded in late 2005, leading to the eventual retirement of the MH-53E. The Knighthawk does not have the 'pulling' power of the Sea Dragon, and cannot tow the big sleds. However, improvements in mine-hunting technology have reduced the size of sensor systems.

An MH-53E of HC-4 lands on Theodore Roosevelt *during operations off Afghanistan during Enduring Freedom. Although VOD duties are normally carried out by the MH-60S, the Sea Dragon's extraordinary lifting power is appreciated at times.*

Sikorsky MH-53E Sea Dragon
Rotor system: main rotor diameter 79 ft 0 in (24.08 m); tail rotor diameter 20 ft 0 in (6.10 m); main rotor disc area 4,901.67 sq ft (455.38 m²)
Fuselage and tail: length overall, rotors turning 99 ft 0.5 in (30.19 m), fuselage 73 ft 4 in (22.35 m), and overall with rotor and tail pylon folded 60 ft 6 in (18.44 m); height overall, rotors turning 29 ft 5 in (8.97 m), and to top of rotor head 17 ft 5.5 in (5.32 m)
Powerplant: three General Electric T64-GE-416 each rated at 4,380 shp (3266 kW) for 10 minutes, 4,145 shp (3091 kW) for 30 minutes and 3,696 shp (2756 kW) for continuous running
Weights: empty 36,336 lb (16482 kg); maximum take-off 69,750 lb (31640 kg) with an internal payload or 73,500 lb (33340 kg) with an external payload
Performance: maximum level speed at sea level 196 mph (315 km/h); ferry range 1,290 miles (2075 km) without flight refuelling; operational radius 575 miles (925 km) with 20,000-lb (9072-kg) external payload or 57.5 miles (92.5 km) with 32,000-lb (14515-kg) external payload; service ceiling 18,500 ft (5640 m); hovering ceiling 11,550 ft (3520 m) in ground effect and 9,500 ft (2895 m) out of ground effect

Sikorsky MH-53E operators

Unit	Base	Notes
HC-4 'Black Stallions'	NAS Sigonella	tasked by Fleet Air Mediterranean
HC-4 Det	Palese Macchie AP, Bari	
HM-14 'Vanguard'	NAS Norfolk	Fleet Readiness Squadron
HM-14 Det 1	NSA Bahrain IAP	
HM-15 'Black Hawks'	NAS Corpus Christi	
CSS AOD 'Dragon Masters'	NSWC Panama City	Coastal Systems Station, Naval Surface Warfare Center

Above: Operating from USS Ponce *(LPD 15), an HM-14 MH-53E sweeps for mines in the Khawar Abd Allah river that separates Kuwait from Iraq during Iraqi Freedom in March 2003. It is towing a Mk 105 megnetic sled.*

Left: This HM-14 Sea Dragon lifts off from newly-occupied Umm Qasr during the first days of Iraqi Freedom. It helped to clear the entrance to the harbour.

Boeing/BAE Systems T-45 Goshawk

In November 1981 the US Navy selected a version of the British Aerospace Hawk to fulfil its VTXTS training system requirement, which called for an advanced trainer to replace the TA-4 and T-2. The aircraft forms one element of the T45TS training system, a complete package which also includes academic, simulator and logistics support. McDonnell Douglas (now Boeing) is the prime contractor, with British Aerospace (now BAE Systems) as principal sub-contractor, the two companies building on their partnership during the Harrier programme. An engineering development contract was awarded in 1986, leading to a first flight in April 1988. The programme was originally envisaged to encompass the T-45A version, which is fully carrier-capable for deck landing instruction, and the 'dry' T-45B which was restricted to dummy deck instruction at shore bases. Owing to the practicality of extending the service lives of the TA-4 and T-2, the decision was taken to cancel the T-45B.

Although based on the Hawk Mk 60, the Goshawk has many differences to tailor it for carrier operations and to the needs of the US Navy. The forward fuselage was made deeper to accommodate a strong twin-wheel nose undercarriage, while the main undercarriage was strengthened and lengthened. The fin and tailplanes were enlarged, and side-mounted airbrakes were installed, above which are 'smurfs' (side-mounted unit horizontal root fins) to cure pitch-down related to the new airbrakes. US Navy-standard instrumentation and Martin-Baker Mk 14 NACES ejection seat were installed, and an arrester hook was added. The wing was modified with full-span leading-edge slats. A pylon was provided under each wing, and another on the centreline, for light weapons.

Two pre-production aircraft were built, powered by the Adour 861-49 engine. Production deliveries to the US Navy with the more powerful Adour 871 began in October 1990, with carrier suitability trials first performed on *John F. Kennedy* in December 1991. The original requirement for 302 T-45s was scaled back to 187, the majority of which had been funded by FY01.

In 1998 deliveries of T-45As were completed, the remainder of the batch being built as T-45Cs with a digital 'glass' cockpit. The first of this model had flown in October 1997. The new cockpit makes the Goshawk better suited to training pilots for modern fighters, and the T-45As will be upgraded to the new standard in a programme scheduled to end in 2007.

T-45As were delivered to Training Air Wing 2 (tailcode 'B') at NAS Kingsville, Texas. T-45Cs have been delivered to Training Air Wing 1

This view of a T-45A highlights the new nosewheel arrangement which was adopted for carrier operations. The T-45B (below) does not differ significantly from the outside, but has a more modern cockpit which is better suited to training F/A-18 pilots.

(tailcode 'A') at NAS Meridian, Mississippi. As well as the primary role of advanced training and carrier instruction for US naval aviators.

Since the retirement of the T-2 Buckeye from the advanced training role, all student naval aviators now make their first carrier 'trap' in the T-45. There is no dedicated training carrier, as there used to be, the training wings making use of fleet carriers for carrier qualification campaigns.

Boeing/BAE Systems T-45A Goshawk
Wings: span 30 ft 9.75 in (9.39 m); area 176.9 sq ft (16.69 m²)
Fuselage: length 39 ft 3 in (11.97 m); height 14 ft (4.27 m)
Powerplant: one Rolls-Royce/Turboméca F405-RR-401 (Adour 871) turbofan, rated at 5,845 lb (26.00 kN) thrust
Weights: empty 9,399 lb (4263 kg); maximum take-off 12,758 lb (5787 kg)
Performance: maximum speed 620 mph (997 km/h) at 8,000 ft (2440 m); ferry range 1,152 miles (1854 km); maximum rate of climb at sea level 6,982 ft (2128 m) per minute; service ceiling 42,250 ft (12875 m)

T-45 squadrons

Squadron	Variant	Base	Wing
VT-7 'Strike Eagles'	T-45C	NAS Meridian	Training Air Wing One
VT-9 'Tigers'	T-45C	NAS Meridian	Training Air Wing One
VT-21 'Fighting Red Hawks'	T-45A	NAS Kingsville	Training Air Wing Two
VT-22 'Golden Eagles'	T-45A	NAS Kingsville	Training Air Wing Two

Picture acknowledgments

The publishers would like to thank the following individuals and organisations for their assistance in providing illustrations for this book.

6-7: Rick Llinares. **8:** Rick Llinares, US Navy. **9:** US Navy via Tony Holmes (two). **10:** Gert Kromhout, Rick Llinares, Ted Carlson/Fotodynamics, US Navy via Tony Holmes. **11:** Ted Carlson/Fotodynamics, US Navy via Tony Holmes. **12:** Rick Llinares (two), Ted Carlson/Fotodynamics. **13:** Chuck Lloyd, Rick Llinares. **14:** Geoff Lee (two), Gert Kromhout. **15:** Rick Llinares, Ted Carlson/Fotodynamics. **16:** Ted Carlson/Fotodynamics, Tony Holmes. **17:** Clive Bennett, Frédéric Lert (two). **18:** via Shlomo Aloni, Cees-Jan van der Ende, Tony Holmes. **19:** Rick Llinares, Scott R. McDowell. **20:** Tony Holmes (two). **21:** Rick Llinares, Gert Kromhout. **22:** Tony Holmes (two), Ted Carlson/Fotodynamics. **23:** Bill Crimmins, Rick Llinares, Ted Carlson/Fotodynamics. **24:** US Navy, Alex Harpunov, Frédéric Lert. **25:** Frédéric Lert (two), US Navy. **26:** Gert Kromhout (two). **27:** José M. Ramos (two). **28:** Tony Holmes, US Navy. **29:** US Navy (four). **32:** Ted Carlson/Fotodynamics, Gert Kromhout. **33:** Luigino Caliaro, US Navy via Tony Holmes. **34-35:** US Navy. **36:** José M. Ramos, Frédéric Lert (two), Luigino Caliaro (three). **37:** Rick Llinares (two), Gert Kromhout. **38:** Ted Carlson/Fotodynamics, Jim Winchester, Rick Llinares. **39:** José M. Ramos, Jim Winchester, Rick Llinares. **40:** Luigino Caliaro, Rick Llinares, Ted Carlson/Fotodynamics, Nigel Pittaway. **41:** Rick Llinares (two), Ted Carlson/Fotodynamics (two). **42-43:** Ted Carlson/Fotodynamics. **44:** Ted Carlson/Fotodynamics, Boeing via Terry Panopalis. **45:** Boeing via Terry Panopalis (two). **46:** Tom Kaminski (five), Boeing via Terry Panopalis (two). **47:** Boeing via Terry Panopalis (two), Ted Carlson/Fotodynamics. **48:** Ted Carlson/Fotodynamics, Boeing. **49:** Rick Llinares (three). **50:** Ted Carlson/Fotodynamics (two). **51:** Ted Carlson/Fotodynamics (two), Boeing. **52:** Ted Carlson/Fotodynamics (two). **53:** Boeing, Jonathan Chuck, Eric Katerburg. **54:** Ted Carlson/Fotodynamics, General Electric. **56:** Ted Carlson/Fotodynamics (six), VFA-115 via Tony Holmes (two). **57:** VFA-115 via Tony Holmes (five), Eric Katerburg, Boeing, US Navy. **58:** Eric Katerburg (three). **59:** Boeing (two). **60:** Boeing (two), Ted Carlson/Fotodynamics. **61:** Ted Carlson/Fotodynamics (three). **62:** VFA-115 via Tony Holmes (three). **63:** VFA-115 via Tony Holmes (three), US Navy. **64:** VFA-115 via Tony Holmes (three), US Navy. **65:** US Navy (two), VFA-14 via Tony Holmes. **68:** US Navy (two), VFA-41 via Tony Holmes. **69:** VFA-41 via Tony Holmes, Tony Holmes (two). **70:** Tony Holmes (three). **71:** US Navy (four). **72:** Eric Katerburg (two), via Jim Winchester. **73:** US Navy, Eric Katerburg (two). **74:** Tony Holmes, VFA-2 via Tony Holmes. **75:** Tony Holmes (three), Eric Katerburg, Boeing. **76:** Boeing, US Navy. **77:** Tony Holmes (four). **78:** Boeing, Boeing via Brad Elward. **79:** Paul Bird via Brad Elward (two), Boeing, Ted Carlson/Fotodynamics. **80:** US Navy (two). **81:** US Navy, Joe Cupido. **82:** Joe Papay, Joe Cupido, McDonnell Douglas. **83:** Rick Llinares. **84:** F. Lert (two). **85:** A. Buonomo, Luigino Caliaro. **86:** Ted Carlson/Fotodynamics, Luigino Caliaro. **87:** Frank B. Mormillo, Robbie Shaw. **88:** Gary Bihary, Ted Carlson/Fotodynamics. **89:** Ted Carlson/Fotodynamics, McDonnell Douglas. **90:** Gert Kromhout, Richards, Ted Carlson/Fotodynamics. **91:** Ted Carlson/Fotodynamics. **92:** Joe Cupido. **93:** Randy Jolly. **94:** Warren Thompson (two), Ted Carlson/Fotodynamics. **96:** Yves Debay. **97:** Randy Jolly, Ted Carlson/Fotodynamics. **98:** Randy Jolly, Joe Papay. **99:** Yves Debay. **100:** Joe Papay (three). **101:** Randy Jolly (two). **103:** Ted Carlson/Fotodynamics, McDonnell Douglas (two), Tim Ripley, Jeff Rankin-Lowe, Raffaele Mancini, Hughes. **104:** Frank B. Mormillo. **105:** Randy Jolly, Joe Cupido. **106:** Ted Carlson/Fotodynamics, Douglas R. Tachauer. **107:** Randy Jolly. **108:** Ted Carlson/Fotodynamics (two). **109:** Jose M. Ramos, Luigino Caliaro. **110:** McDonnell Douglas (two). **111:** Randy Jolly (three). **112:** Randy Jolly, Jody Louviere. **113:** Jose M. Ramos, F. Lert. **114:** Raytheon (two), US Navy. **115:** Boeing (two). **116-119:** US Navy. **120:** US Navy (two), Jose M. Ramos (two), Jim Dunn, Ted Carlson/Fotodynamics. **121:** Randy Jolly (two), Rick Llinares, Ted Carlson/Fotodynamics. **122:** Ted Carlson/Fotodynamics, Rick Llinares/Dash 2. **123:** Chuck Lloyd/Dash 2. **124:** Mark Munzel (two), Randy Jolly. **125:** Chuck Lloyd/Dash 2, Randy Jolly. **127:** Randy Jolly, Chuck Lloyd/Dash 2, Ted Carlson/Fotodynamics. **128:** via Robert F. Dorr (two), Ian C. Anderson. **129:** Randy Jolly (two), Ted Carlson/Fotodynamics (four). **130:** David F. Brown. **132:** Rick Llinares/Dash 2, M. Ottagalli & V. Marchetti/G.R.S.A, Tieme Festner. **133:** Luigino Caliaro, Ted Carlson/Fotodynamics. **134:** Tim Ripley, Jeremy Flack/Aviation Photographs International. **135:** Matt Olafsen/Fox 1, Jeremy Flack/Aviation Photographs International, Randy Jolly. **136:** Ted Carlson/Fotodynamics, Luigino Caliaro, Hans Nijhuis. **137:** Randy Jolly, Luigino Caliaro. **138:** US Navy, Northrop Grumman (two). **139:** US Navy (three), US Air Force. **142:** Rick Llinares/Dash 2, Jose M. Ramos. **143:** Grumman, Ted Carlson/Fotodynamics. **144:** Ted Carlson/Fotodynamics (two). **145:** Bruce R. Trombecky, Rick Llinares/Dash 2 (two). **146:** Gary Bihary, Grumman, Ted Carlson/Fotodynamics (two), Jose M. Ramos, Matthew Olafsen. **147:** David Donald (two), Northrop Grumman. **148:** US Navy, Carl L. Richards. **149:** Graham Robson, Malcolm Nason, Andrew H. Cline, Rick Llinares/Dash 2, Luigino Caliaro, Matthew Olafsen. **150:** Ted Carlson/Fotodynamics (two), Northrop Grumman, Graham Robson. **151:** Rick Llinares/Dash 2, Matthew Olafsen. **152:** US Navy (three). **153:** Northrop Grumman (four), David Donald. **156:** US Navy via Tom Kaminski (two). **157:** US Navy via Tom Kaminski (three). **158:** US Navy via Tom Kaminski (two), Mike Anselmo/AIR. **159:** US Navy via Tom Kaminski (three). **160:** US Navy via Tom Kaminski (three). **161:** US Navy (two), Sikorsky via Tom Kaminski, Ray Rivard via Tom Kaminski. **162-163:** US Navy via Tom Kaminski. **164:** Lockheed Martin, US Navy. **165:** US Navy, Lockheed Martin. **166-170:** US Navy. **171:** Lockheed Martin, US Navy. **172-174:** US Navy. **175:** Boeing, BAE Systems.